Chekhov Becomes Chekhov

Chekhov Becomes Chekhov

THE EMERGENCE OF A LITERARY GENIUS:
1886–1887

BOB BLAISDELL

PEGASUS BOOKS

NEW YORK LONDON

CHEKHOV BECOMES CHEKHOV

Pegasus Books, Ltd.
148 West 37th Street, 13th Floor
New York, NY 10018

First Pegasus Books cloth edition December 2022

Interior design by Maria Fernandez

Library of Congress Cataloging-in-Publication Data is available.

ISBN: 978-1-63936-264-6

10 9 8 7 6 5 4 3 2 1

Printed in the United States of America
Distributed by Simon & Schuster
www.pegasusbooks.com

To Paul Richardson

Contents

Introduction

—w—

You should never describe yourself. It would have been
better had you made Pospelov fall in love with some
woman, and incorporated your feelings in her.

—To a fellow writer[1]

If someone offers you coffee, don't go looking for beer
in it. If I present you with the ideas of the Professor,
trust me and don't look for Chekhov's ideas in them,
thank you kindly.

—To his friend and editor Aleksei Suvorin[2]

Anton Chekhov's biography in 1886–1887 is captured almost completely in the
writing that he was doing. Reading the stories, we are as close as we can be to
being in his company.

In 1886, the twenty-six-year-old Moscow doctor published 112 short stories, humor
pieces, and articles. In 1887, he published sixty-four short stories.[3] The young author was,
to his surprise and occasional embarrassment, famous; admired by, among others, Russia's
literary giants Lev Tolstoy and Nikolay Leskov.[4] In these two years, three volumes of his
short stories were published. Meanwhile, three hours a day, six days a week, Dr. Chekhov
treated patients in his office at his family's residence, and also made house calls; he lived
with and supported his parents and younger siblings. In the winter of 1886, he became
engaged and unengaged to be married. He mentored other writers with matter-of-fact
encouragement and brilliant criticism. He carried on lively, frank, funny correspondence
with editors, friends, and his older brothers. Having written, he was exhausted, but in the
midst of writing, whether venting and making jokes in letters or amusing himself and us

with stories, his senses seemed fully alive, consciousness and imagination flowing together. Weary and suffering from various ailments including the tuberculosis he had contracted at twenty-four, he took a long trip south in the spring of 1887 to Taganrog, where he had grown up. He continued writing even on vacation. In his short stories he identified with a variety of characters: doctors, patients, actors, drivers, writers, artists, children, women, men, drunks, religious folk, Muscovites, Petersburgers, exiles, villagers, judges, criminal investigators, cheats, lovers, midwives, business owners, and animals. After a blue and dreary summer of 1887, he wrote a four-act play in the space of two weeks. He concluded these two years of artistic work by composing one of Russia's most famous children's stories, "Kashtanka."

Chekhov's imagination is what brought him to the world's attention and has kept him there. His imagination—and its prodigious flowering during these years—is the focus of this biography; the facts of his life build the frame around the picture of that imagination. In 1888 until to the end of his life, the amount of his writing only slowed to a pace that any other great author would have been proud of, and he eventually curtailed his medical duties. He died in 1904, the most famous writer in Russia other than Tolstoy; posthumously his short stories and plays became in translation the English-speaking world's model of everyday comedy and tragedy.

The stories and humor pieces that he was producing on deadline for St. Petersburg newspapers and magazines required that he keep an eye on topicality (e.g., New Year's, Lent, Easter, spring thaws, summer dachas, return to school, winter snows, Christmas). What I did not expect to discover in researching his life in these years is that when those 178 pieces are read in chronological order and in conjunction with the personal letters to and from him, they become a diary of the psychological and emotional states of this conspicuously reserved man. For example, when he was in the midst of his frustrating and anxious engagement, young couples in his stories are continually making their rancorous way into or out of their relationships. When Dr. Chekhov was overtaxed by his medical duties, the doctor characters explode or implode. Chekhov's talented but drunken older brothers and domineering father became transmuted into characters, but almost always Chekhov converted the circumstances of the people he knew into fictional ones at various removes: the opposite gender, a younger or older age, a different profession, a different place, a different family. His clever brothers would have recognized themselves, though not the circumstances, in many comic and serious stories. His father, born a serf to a "slave-driving" serf-father, was reputedly incapable of recognizing the similarities between himself and the brutal or ridiculous fathers in his son's stories.

Anyone who writes about Chekhov has an easy time of it when quoting his work. Just like that, in a sentence or two, the situation and the people involved are clear to the mind's eye and the body's senses: "In the low-pitched, crooked little hut of Artyom, the forester, two men were sitting under the big dark ikon—Artyom himself, a short and lean peasant with a wrinkled, aged-looking face and a little beard that grew out of his neck, and a well-grown young man in a new crimson shirt and big wading boots, who had been out hunting and come in for the night. They were sitting on a bench at a little three-legged table on which a tallow candle stuck into a bottle was lazily burning" ("A Troublesome Visitor"). Chekhov continually makes us aware of our senses taking in impressions. He gives us and the characters the experience of melding those impressions into coherence. "Chekhov as an artist cannot even be compared with previous Russian writers—with Turgenev, Dostoevsky, or myself," remarked Tolstoy. "Chekhov has his own peculiar manner, like the Impressionists. You look and it is as though the man were indiscriminately dabbing on whatever paints came to his hand, and these brush strokes seem to be quite unrelated to each other. But you move some distance away, you look, and you get on the whole an integrated impression. You have, before you, a bright, irresistible picture of nature."[5] He continually gives us the sensory atmosphere, our awareness of being or imagining ourselves being in an absolutely particular place. While Chekhov is not quotable for witty or profound statements, he is quite quotable for efficiency and depth: in an opening sentence or two, he creates each story's shape and momentum.

To indicate instances of Chekhov's imagination at work and at play, I quote at length from his stories and letters and provide continual biographical commentary. It's possible, perhaps likely, that readers may become annoyed by how often I interrupt his stories with my remarks. Chekhov later wrote to Maxim Gorky, who would soon become the *third* most famous Russian author, that in his stories, "You are like a spectator at a play who expresses his enthusiasm so unrestrainedly that he cannot hear what the actors are saying and does not let others hear it. This lack of restraint is particularly felt in the descriptive passages with which you interrupt your dialogue . . ."[6] Gorky didn't try to justify his "lack of restraint," so for the moment neither will I. Readers should keep in mind, however, that most of the stories I quote from can be read complete, uninterrupted, online for free in thirteen volumes of translations by Constance Garnett and in additional volumes by other competent translators.[7] In Russian, there is an excellent comprehensive site.[8] This biography is not about my special experience along narrow scholarly paths, I hope, but about a route anybody can take with Chekhov.

In the following few pages of the introduction, I provide some background to Chekhov's life before I proceed to trace the day-to-day and week-to-week routines and varieties of experience of this period. Because the stories encapsulate the life of his mind, mood, and imagination, they reveal him more clearly and deeply than can any biography, chronicle,[9] or collection of letters. His psychological portraits of distinct, carefully observed characters are, I show, sometimes incidental portraits of himself; the story-situations are sometimes previews or replays of the domestic, financial, and romantic problems he was trying to clarify. The reserved man who had trained himself to never break down or weep or lash out[10] nevertheless always identified himself, in some detail, with his sensitive, naïve, cynical, eruptive, or fragile characters.

—⁂—

Chekhov and his siblings were well educated, though their father Pavel had been born a serf. Pavel's father had been, unusually for a serf, literate, and became so much of a wheeler-dealer that he earned enough money to buy himself and his family out of serfdom in 1841.[11] When Anton was born, the third of six children, in January of 1860, serfdom in Russia, like slavery in America, was finally on the verge of ending.

Taganrog, a southern Russian port town on the Sea of Azov, is where Chekhov was born and raised. As a boy, Anton and his two older brothers were shown off as singers in the orthodox church by their father. Pavel was artistically minded and outwardly pious but, in regard to his three oldest sons, brutal. He was an ineffective shopkeeper. Mikhail Chekhov, born five years after brother Anton, recalled:

> Our father was [. . .] fond of praying, but the more I think about it now, the more I realize that he enjoyed the ritual of religion more than its sub-stance. He liked church services and listened to them standing reverently throughout. He even organized prayers at home, my siblings and I acting as the choir while he played the role of the priest. But the church served more as his club, a place where he could meet his friends [. . .]
>
> But in everyday life, our Father had as little faith as all the rest of us sinners. He sang, played violin, wore a top hat, and visited friends and family on Easter and Christmas. He loved newspapers. [. . .] He always read newspapers out loud from cover to cover. He liked talking politics and discussing the doings of the town's governor. I never saw him without a starched shirt on. [. . .]
>
> Music was our Father's calling. He would sing or play his violin [. . .] To satisfy this passion, he put together choirs with our family and others and

we would perform at home and in public. He would often forget about the
business that earned him a living [. . .] He was also a gifted artist: one of his
paintings, "John the Evangelist," made it into the Chekhov Museum in Yalta.
[. . .] He liked philosophizing, but while Uncle Mitrofan read only books of
a lofty content, our Father read and reread (always out loud) cheap French
novels. Sometimes, preoccupied with his own thoughts, he would stop in the
middle of a sentence and ask our Mother [Evgenia], "So, Evochka, what was
it that I just read?"[12]

To Pavel Chekhov's credit (which he acknowledged to himself generously), he sought
opportunities for his children's education, and the three oldest boys and then their three
younger siblings all succeeded in their studies.

Alexander, the eldest child, born in 1855, survived Anton, and in a memoir explained
that from Anton's "very early childhood, owing to the beneficent influence of his mother,
he could not look on with indifference when he saw animals being treated cruelly, and
almost cried when he saw a driver beating his dray horse. And when he saw people being
beaten, he used to tremble nervously. . . . But in his father's routine, smacks on the face,
cuffs on the nape of the neck, flogging were of most ordinary occurrence, and he exten-
sively applied those corrective measures both to his own children and to his shop boys.
Everyone trembled before him and were more afraid of him than of fire. Anton's mother
always rebelled against her husband, but always received the invariable answer: 'I myself
was taught like that, and you see I have turned out a man. One beaten man is worth two
unbeaten ones.'"[13]

Alexander described their wearisome and unhappy choir practices and the schoolboy
Anton's duties "at the very small, cheap general store, helping his father. His impressions
of carefree childhood were based on observations made from a distance. He never experienced these happy years, filled with joy and pleasant memories. He did not have time
to do this because he spent most of his free time at his father's general store. Besides, his
father had rules and prohibitions regarding everything. He could not run around because,
as his father told him, 'You will wear out your boots.' He could not jump because 'only
street bums hop around.' He could not play games with other children because 'your peers
will teach you bad habits.'"[14]

I imagine Alexander wincing, remembering his own traumatized childhood, as he
noted: "When [Anton] was older, he would tell his friends and relatives, 'During my
childhood, I did not really have a childhood.'" When fifteen-year-old Alexander and
eleven-year-old Anton went to visit their father's father on the steppe, "Chekhov was

shocked by his Ukrainian grandmother's revelations: privation and thrashings from Egor, in an outpost surrounded by resentful peasants, had broken her. For the first time the boys understood how their father had been formed, and that his childhood had been even worse than theirs."[15] Pavel may have broken the spirit of Alexander, who as an adult was prone to rages and alcoholism, but Anton seems to have had the temperament and composure to withstand his father.

Alexander and Mikhail became writers and editors. Nikolay, the second son, born in 1858, whom Anton thought the most talented of the family, was a painter and illustrator. Unfortunately he, like Anton, contracted tuberculosis in 1884.[16] Unlike Anton, charming Nikolay succumbed to hopelessness. Two of the younger siblings, Ivan (born 1861) and the lone sister, Maria (born 1863), became schoolteachers.[17] The biographer Ronald Hingley assesses Chekhov's younger siblings as "dependable, sympathetic, conventional souls, much respected and beloved by Anton, whom all three idolized. He does not seem to have found them dull. But deadly dull they were by comparison with the two eldest boys Alexander and Nikolay: both so gifted yet so wayward, with their drunken habits, irregular love lives, and financial unreliability. . . . The talent, the high spirits, the verve of the two eldest sons were Anton's, but so too were the resourcefulness and persistence of the three youngest children."[18]

Even as a teenager, Chekhov was so responsible that when his father's store went bankrupt, his parents left the sixteen-year-old Anton behind to finish high school. His presence in town covered for his family's escape from creditors. They fled to Moscow, where the two oldest boys were attending university. Independent Anton tutored for his room and board and eventually was sending any extra money he earned to his family. In 1879, as the recipient of a Taganrog town scholarship, he moved to Moscow to rejoin his family, which he had been able to visit only once since their departure, and began his medical studies. They were living in a rough Moscow neighborhood, but Anton brought with him two student-boarders, whose contributions helped keep the family afloat. Medicine was a respectable but not necessarily lucrative career. He immediately took charge of organizing the family's finances and through his earnings as a writer became its primary breadwinner for the rest of his life. Anton was the boss, and the family needed him to be. Hingley writes that "the other Chekhovs already looked on him as their rescuer, for little could be expected from the older members of their family. Both parents seemed defeated by poverty and disappointment. . . . [Pavel] was abdicating as head of his household, but without leaving any obvious successor."[19]

With each passing year, Anton moved the family to better neighborhoods and healthier housing. Pavel, the bankrupted shopkeeper, was eventually working as a shop boy on the other side of Moscow; by 1886 he spent many of his nights at his son Ivan's government-issued apartment, and only rejoined the family for occasional meals and on days off.

As kind and mild and reserved as Chekhov was with friends and acquaintances and patients, he was sometimes sharp and commanding with his siblings. It's not clear how he spoke to his parents. "Our mother, Evgenia Yakovlevna," remembered Alexander, "was different from our father. She was a soft and quiet woman. She had a poetic nature. By contrast to the father, who seemed very strict, her motherly care and tenderness were amazing. Later, Anton Pavlovich said very truly: 'I have inherited the talent from the father's side, and the soul from the mother's side.'"[20]

Chekhov was protective of his mother, and brother Mikhail recounts instances of her doting on him: "After a few hours of writing, Anton would come to the dining room around eleven and look at the clock meaningfully. Catching this, Mother would immediately stand up from her sewing machine and begin fussing. 'Ah, my-my, Antosha is hungry!' . . . After lunch Anton would usually go to his bedroom, lock himself in, and mull over his plots—if Morpheus did not interrupt him, that is. We would all go back to work from three in the afternoon until seven in the evening."[21]

My favorite of Chekhov's biographers, Ernest Simmons, writes: "The years 1885 to 1889 were among the happiest in Chekhov's relatively short life. By the end of this brief period he had emerged from obscurity to become one of the most appreciated and discussed writers of the day. . . . He had brought his family from indigence to a position of material security and social acceptance. . . . Many publishers were bidding for the products of his pen."[22]

> To have as few failures as possible in fiction writing,
> or in order not to be so sensitive to failures, you must
> write more, around one hundred or two hundred
> stories a year. That is the secret.
>
> —Letter to his brother Alexander[23]

In the midst of those "happy years," March of 1886 was the most productive month of his writing life; he published fifteen short stories, a few of them among his most excellent. As soon as he finished a story, off it went in the overnight mail to St. Petersburg, and within the week it was in print. He was not writing without thinking, he was writing without blocking. There was nothing in the way between his imagination and the paper he was writing upon. For example, "Poison" ("Otrava,"[24] published March 8) is not an especially good or memorable story, and yet it is interesting in the context of what I'm regarding as his creative diary: A father-in-law, instead of paying the groom a dowry, gives him a note for an overdue loan. The anxious groom discovers that the doctor-debtor, one Klyabov, won't pay it, because the interest has fraudulently ballooned.

The palming-off of the bad debt on the son-in-law doesn't seem to reflect very much on Chekhov's immediate circumstances, except that Chekhov was as usual in debt and was himself at the moment a fiancé. The story's most personal vibrations are activated when it comes to poor Dr. Klyabov, who after working all night has been roused from his sleep. These are the aggravations that Dr. Chekhov suffered:

> "God knows what!" Klyabov waved his arm, getting up and making a tearful face. "I thought that you were sick, but you're here with some nonsense . . . This is shameless on your side! I went to lie down at seven today, but you for some Devil knows reason wake me! Decent people respect others' peace . . . I'm even ashamed for you!"[25]

Chekhov wrote to his editor Nikolay Leykin about "Poison":

> Having written and reread the story I sent you yesterday, I scratched my ears, raised my brows and grunted—activities every author does after having written something long and boring . . . I began the story in the morning; the idea wasn't bad and the beginning came out quite okay, but the misfortune was that I came to write with interruptions. After the first page, A. M. Dmitriev's wife came to ask for a medical certificate; after the second I received a telegram from Schechtel: *Sick!* I had to go treat him . . . After the third page—lunch and so on. But writing with interruptions is like an irregular pulse.[26]

And even in the midst of this letter to editor Leykin, he was interrupted: "Someone's pulled at the bell . . ."; after that ellipsis, Dr. Chekhov announced, with relief, "Not for me!"[27] In "Poison," Chekhov re-experienced Dr. Klyabov's frustrations and distractions. Who would interrupt him next?

On this day he was writing or about to write "A Story without an End." In these two years, Chekhov seemingly had stories "without end." This new one, about a would-be suicide, is told by an unnamed first-person narrator, whom Chekhov, putting some space between himself and the storyteller, didn't allow to be a doctor, even though he is remarkably knowledgeable about physiology; the narrator, it turns out, is only a humor writer.

⸺⁓⁓⸺

On my middle-aged way to learning Russian so I could read *Anna Karenina* in the original, I read dozens and dozens of Chekhov's stories, some in heavily annotated editions for us Russian learners. In English I had read all of Constance Garnett's translations of Chekhov, and I either didn't notice or didn't care that she didn't arrange the stories chronologically. She gathered the stories the way a florist might arrange bouquets: loosely, occasionally thematically, occasionally by time-range, size, or quality. When I was reading Russian collections, however, I kept noticing that so many of my favorite stories had been published in 1886 and 1887. I loved Chekhov's later stories too, but there weren't so *many* of them. Had anyone else noticed all those 1886 and 1887 publication dates? . . . Of course others had! In the best book about Chekhov, read by me at least a few times since the early 1980s and "forgotten," there is this emphatic and dead-on declaration: "Eighteen eighty-six and early 1887 brought a whole stream of stories, unprecedented in Russian literature for the originality of their form and subject matter and for their compression and concision."[28] I second that evaluation.

I chose to study the two years where Chekhov took center stage in Russian literature so that I could give myself and you, my reader, the illusion of comprehensiveness. There is no comprehensive biography of Chekhov, though there are many good biographies. Like Garnett's story collections, they too seem to focus on a theme or aspect of his life. Rosamund Bartlett, who seems to me to have the most thoroughly knowledgeable appreciation of Chekhov's life and work, focused her biography, *Chekhov: Scenes from a Life* (2005), on the places where he lived and visited. Donald Rayfield's *Anton Chekhov: A Life* (1997, updated and revised in 2021) is large and long but not focused on his writing. It is informative about the Chekhov family's dynamics and is full of unexpurgated material from Chekhov's and his correspondents' letters that had never even been published in Russian.[29] Michael C. Finke's *Freedom from Violence and Lies: Anton Chekhov's Life and Writings* (2021) is a good but brief biography that fairly balances the life and work. I have read all of Chekhov's 1886–1887 letters in Russian, and there are several collections of his letters in English, which I draw on and quote from.

It's possible to catch Chekhov in the looking-glass in the miracle years of 1886 and 1887 because he had almost no time to look away.

—∿∿—

"My work is like a diary. It's even dated like a diary."
—Pablo Picasso[30]

I wish we really knew how he wrote his stories or even any single tale. In that hour or three wherein Chekhov's hand and imagination inscribed a story, even if we watched his quick right-handed penmanship slide and scritch across his narrow notebook pages, with sometimes not even a cross out, what would we know beyond the appreciation of his speed and focus? Perhaps it would be like viewing the replayed iPad paintings of David Hockney, where in about sixty seconds the screen displays a flurry of the artist's eyes' and finger's decisions: lines, shapes, colors, tones, resizings . . . and voilà, a beautiful tree-lined road. Chekhov's mother Evgenia said, "When he was still an undergraduate, Antosha would sit at the table in the morning, having his tea and suddenly fall to thinking; he would sometimes look straight into one's eyes, but I knew that he saw nothing. Then he would get his notebook out of his pocket and write quickly, quickly. And again he would fall to thinking."[31]

From some such perspective we can at least imagine him at work, and certainly we can see the proof in the pudding. Chekhov's stories are as personal as any great artist's landscapes and portraits. David Hockney is not the trees and he is not the friends he paints. But from Hockney's many works we know a lot more about how he sees and understands the world than we probably know about our own ways of seeing. He and Chekhov help us appreciate what can be appreciated, if only we were focused geniuses. We know from Chekhov's thousands of pages of writing that the challenge of his life was to free himself to feel the entirety of his humanity, which meant in his case a combination of intelligence and wit and a deep well of sympathy for the weak and the vulnerable:

> What aristocratic writers take from nature gratis, the less privileged must
> pay for with their youth. Try and write a story about a young man—the
> son of a serf, a former grocer, choirboy, schoolboy and university student,
> raised on respect for rank, kissing the priests' hands, worshiping the ideas
> of others, and giving thanks for every piece of bread, receiving frequent
> whippings, making the rounds as a tutor without galoshes, brawling,

torturing animals, enjoying dinners at the houses of rich relatives, need-lessly hypocritical before god and man merely to acknowledge his own insignificance—write about how this young man squeezes the slave out of himself drop by drop and how, on waking up one fine morning, he finds that the blood coursing through his veins is no longer the blood of a slave, but that of a real human being.[32]

That fearsome "young man" who squeezed "the slave out of himself drop by drop" was of course Chekhov. This declaration, written to his closest friend and confidant of the time (1889), is the most personal revelation he ever made, but unfortunately he himself never wrote that story, though his memoirist siblings and his conscientious biographers have ever since his death tried to do so. My modest suggestion is that his own stories do tell, in pieces and flashes, that story of himself, the "real human being."

No one has tracked his daily routines beyond what the editors of the invaluable *Letopis'*[33] ("*Chronicle*") of his life have compiled. We have a few contemporary facts about some particular days, but there isn't an appointments calendar or a record of the patients he saw. He was on the other hand very good at keeping track of publications, sending follow-up letters and commissioning various brothers to round up the late payments from forgetful or tight-fisted editors. During my mostly happy days of research, I had the big, great obvious idea of compressing this biography of two years of his life—writer, doctor, financial provider, joker, lover, friend—into a short story, written as if by himself. It would be brilliant, amusing, and concise. We would know Chekhov from the outside through carefully selected observations and from the inside through his buzzing thoughts. . . .

I didn't manage to write that story.

For this biography, Chekhov would have advised me, had he been unable to dissuade me from writing it at all, to *Keep it simple. Sketch the mundane everyday life and activities, but vividly. Admit what you don't know. Be modest. Be brief!* That sounds simple, but as his friend Viktor Bilibin eventually protested when Chekhov cajoled him toward greater artistry in his writing: *I'm not you, Anton Pavlovich!*

Some notes on the text: I use the present tense in describing and discussing Chekhov's creative works; I use the past tense when describing and presenting letters and memoirs. The variations from that rule are either intentional or accidental. I use the transcription from Cyrillic method of, for example, х to *kh* (as in Чехов/Chekhov) and the й and ы to *y* (sorry, but the scholarly transcription of the й to *j* makes me cringe), the ю to *yu*, the я to *ya*. I ignore the ë ("yo") in names (Kiseleva) and use the simple *e*. I ignore the *ye* pronunciation that some Russian *e*'s have and stick to the *e* (for example, not Dostoyevsky but *Dostoevsky*). I accept the soft sign and render it as what looks like an apostrophe (Леонтьев/ *Leont'ev*), except in familiar names like Tatyana or Gogol. I refer to Chekhov as Anton only in discussing or presenting exchanges between him and his siblings: that is, when he was not *Chekhov* but Anton or Antosha. I refer to his brother Aleksandr as Alexander. I have silently corrected British-translated spellings (e.g., colour, mould, theatre) for American spellings. I have silently replaced Garnett's and others' *tch* spelling of the Russian *ch* (ч) as *ch*. That particular spelling is why we still see Tchaikovsky spelled that way, and why some translations of Chekhov before the 1920s render his name as Tchekhov. Because the translations of individual story titles vary so much into English, I indicate the Russian title in transliteration for each. In the appendix, I list in English and Russian all of the titles of the stories and skits in chronological order.

PART ONE

Chekhonte & Chekhov

January 1886

—⁓—

It is not up to me to permit or prohibit you to write. I
referred to the need for learning to punctuate properly
because in a work of art punctuation often plays the
part of musical notation and can't be learned from a
textbook; it requires instinct and experience. Enjoying
writing doesn't mean playing or having a good time.
Experiencing enjoyment from an activity means loving
that activity.

—To a young writer[1]

There was a costume party at the Chekhovs' on New Year's Eve, December 31, 1885.
They lived in Moscow on the north side of the Moscow River, in a merchants'
quarter known as Yakimanka. They had moved into this apartment at the beginning of
December. The apartment was damp, but for the first time Dr. Chekhov "had a room
of his own: a study with an open fireplace where he worked and received his patients.
The flat was on the ground floor, and that turned out to be a serious disadvantage,
for the [second] floor of the house was occupied by a restaurant that was regularly let out for
wakes and wedding parties."[2] This New Year's Eve, the Chekhovs would contribute to
the building's happy noise.

Among the guests was Maria Yanova.[3] She presented a photo album to Chekhov.
Opening the photo album, Chekhov would have read Yanova's inscription: "My humble
gift to Anton Pavlovich Chekhov in memory of saving me from typhus." He had tended
to her and to her mother and sisters when they had typhus in early December. Her
mother and one sister had died, the sister with Chekhov at her bedside. Maria Yanov's
brother Alexander was a painter and had been a classmate of Chekhov's brother Nikolay

at a Moscow art institute. Yanov could not afford a doctor for his mother and sisters and Chekhov had volunteered for the dangerous and tragic job.[4]

He was twenty-five. He was tall, handsome, with dark brown hair; he had a trim beard and moustache, dark eyes, and in photos sometimes had a smart-alecky expression he directed at the camera.[5]

 In 1894, Chekhov with two of his friends, Tatyana Shchepkina-Kupernik and Lidiya Yavorskaya. He must have made them laugh, but he had trained himself not to laugh at his own jokes. He named this photograph *The Temptation of St. Anthony*.

"All were captivated by his appearance and manner," writes one biographer. "With his capacity to make friends, many, upon meeting him for the first time, felt that they had known him for years. As he talked his face grew animated, and he occasionally brushed back his shock of thick hair or toyed lightly with his youthful beard."[6] He had a baritone voice. If he had a Southern Russian accent, or a special rhythm to his phrasing, no one ever remarked on it. "Simplicity dominated his movements and gestures. All were struck by his expressive eyes set in a long, open face with well-defined nose and mouth."

The six-foot-one doctor was also amusing. He wrote funny stories and skits for Moscow and St. Petersburg newspapers and magazines, for which work he used pen names, the most common and popular being Antosha Chekhonte.

—⁓—

It had only been a few weeks before, during his first ever visit to St. Petersburg, that Chekhov discovered that Antosha Chekhonte was a very popular writer. For five years already Chekhov had been writing comic stories and cultural journalism under various pen names and anonymously for Moscow and Petersburg publications. In his most frequent venue, *Fragments* (a title sometimes translated into English as *Splinters* or *Shards*), Antosha Chekhonte was the star attraction. His *St. Petersburg Gazette* short stories, some of which were serious, were attracting the literati. Famous authors in the capital wanted to meet him and when they did, they encouraged him to write more and longer pieces. His host in Petersburg, the *Fragments* editor and publisher Nikolay Leykin, himself a popular humorist whom Chekhov and his brothers read growing up, had wanted to show him off but was anxious not to lose him.

From his two weeks of being recognized and admired in Petersburg, Chekhov understood that there would be new, more prestigious, and better-paying venues where he could publish his writing.

He was tied into a couple of particular formats at *Fragments*: paragraph-long anecdotes and jokes, or one hundred–line stories of about a thousand words. Leykin also had a heavy editing hand and didn't hold himself back from crabbing about Chekhonte's less inspired pieces. Chekhov provided *Fragments* with two or three pieces a week, among them an occasional gossipy Moscow culture column, all the while also conducting his medical practice and, ever since the spring of 1885, writing a story a week for the *Petersburg Gazette*.

Chekhov would joke this year and for the next few years that medicine was his wife and writing was his mistress—and that he had no trouble hopping beds. But really, it was that his mistress and wife had their own close and invigorating relationship. "There is no doubt in my mind that my study of medicine has had a serious impact on my literary activities. It significantly broadened the scope of my observations and enriched me with knowledge whose value for me as a writer only a doctor can appreciate,"[7] he told a former medical school colleague.

As New Year's was an important publishing week, there being an uptick of readers during the holidays, Chekhov wrote six timely pieces for various publications.

The skit "The Maskers" ("Ryazhenye") appeared in the *St. Petersburg Gazette* newspaper on New Year's Day 1886. Many of the pieces Chekhov wrote from 1880 to 1886 I would call by the not necessarily demeaning word "skits," corresponding to the wide range of humor we can find today in *New Yorker* magazine Shouts & Murmurs pieces or in *McSweeney's*. He had probably written "The Maskers" five or six days before. Mail service was dependable and fast between Russia's two biggest cities, about 400 miles apart.

Masking, or mumming—dressing up and acting out a pantomime—is a New Year's tradition in some communities around the world. In "The Maskers," Chekhov describes a parade: one person after another, one dressed as a pig, another a pepper-pot, a female fox, an entrepreneur, a chained dog. A character sketch follows of a dissipated fellow, "a talent," who will soon have mourners and an obituary, and then an account of this "pet goose" of a drunken writer who needs quiet, quiet, quiet! "At home, when he sits alone in his room and creates 'a new piece,' everyone goes on tiptoe. Good lord, if it's not 15 degrees in his room, if beyond the door a dish clinks or a child squeaks, he seizes himself by the hair and with a chesty voice, 'Dammmmmit! . . . There's nothing good to say about a writer's life!' When he writes, he's performing a holy act: he wrinkles his brow, bites his pen, puffs, sniffs, and continually crosses out."[8] Chekhov was probably teasing his oldest brother Alexander, an editor, family-man, and part-time writer, whom Chekhov regularly addressed in letters as "You Goose."

On January 2, Chekhov met with an emissary of the powerful publisher and editor Aleksei Suvorin. The journalist Alexander Kurepin asked Chekhov if he would be willing to write for *New Times*. Kurepin knew that Chekhov had already promised to write two pieces a week for the *Petersburg Gazette* and was on a one-year salary of 600 rubles with *Fragments*. (To give some sense of monetary value, the yearly rent on the four-bedroom, two-story house in Moscow that the Chekhovs would move into in September was 650 rubles.) Kurepin was able to report to Suvorin that Chekhov "eagerly agreed"[9] to write for *New Times*. Most of the twenty-eight stories for *New Times* that he would write over the next two years paid more than 100 rubles each.

Chekhov had sent four pieces on December 28 to Leykin for *Fragments* for the New Year's issue (January 4), the most important of the year for the magazine, as it inspired new subscriptions. Chekhov was dismayed about the first piece, "New Year's Great Martyrs" ("Novogodnie Velikomucheeniki"). He told Leykin: "I wanted to write it shorter and spoiled it."[10] One such martyr, Sinkletev, recounts his drunken New Year's Day wanderings: From Ivan Ivanich's "to the merchant Khrymov's to offer him my hand . . . I went to greet . . . my family . . . They asked me to drink for the holiday . . . And how not drink? You offend if you don't drink . . . Well, I drank about three glasses . . . ate sausage . . . From there, to the Petersburg side to Likhodev . . . A good man . . ."[11]

Ellipses are a distinctive form of Chekhov's punctuation. Usually the ellipsis is *not* a pause for dramatic effect. The dots usually function as a *tick-tick-tick*, a moment of hesitation preceding Chekhov's next stroke of the pen. The ellipses are notable because they indicate that he wrote fast and directly, so fast that these ellipses are like pit stops for an Indianapolis 500 race car driver. His stories of the time and his letters are full of ellipses and in the scholarly edition often consist of two periods rather than three. English-language translators, if they acknowledge them, adjust them to the standard English three periods, as will I. For us, in this book, my *deletions* of material will be an ellipsis in brackets [. . .]. The other ellipses are Chekhov's own.

His other January 4 pieces are "Champagne (Thoughts from a New Year's Hangover)" ("Shampanskoe (Mysli s Novogodnego pokhmel'ya)"), a monologue cursing the apparent beauties and joys of champagne; "Visiting Cards" ("Vizitnye Kartochki"), a list of visitors, among them "Court Counselor Hemorrhoid Dioskorovich Boat-y"[12]; and finally "Letters" ("Pis'ma"), wherein a reader, hounded by the magazine's advertising promotions, writes: "You asked me to recommend your journal to my acquaintances; I did. Pay me my expenses." That is, he took the journal's command literally and went and recommended it to his acquaintances who happened to live far away. The second fictional letter-writer complains about receiving unwanted mail—essentially spam. The third complains that when Russia's Julian calendar catches up to Western Europe's, women will age twelve to thirteen days. (Here is an opportunity to mention that all the dates in *this* book correspond to the laggard Julian calendar, indeed in 1886–1887 twelve days behind our own. Chekhov's January 1 was January 13 in England and the United States.) The fourth letter is an invitation to a home-performed drama night.

The first real short story of the year—one Chekhov would have considered and did consider an actual short story for length and semi-seriousness—was published in the Monday issue of the *Petersburg Gazette* on January 6, "Art" ("Xhudozhestvo"). (Russians then and now usually leave off the *Saint* from Petersburg; they also often, as Chekhov sometimes did, leave off the *burg*. I will use simply Petersburg.) Chekhov describes a villager known as Seryozhka who knows he is a wretch but that also, once a year, through carving and coloring ice on the river, that is, through making art, he has value—the art elevates him: "He obviously enjoys the peculiar position in which he has been placed by the fate that has bestowed on him the rare talent of surprising the whole parish once a year by his art. Poor mild Matvey [his assistant] has to listen to many venomous and contemptuous words from him. Seryozhka sets to work with vexation, with anger. He is lazy. He has hardly described the circle when he is already itching to go up to the village to drink tea, lounge about, and babble."[13]

Once a year, Seryozhka is a prima donna:

> Seryozhka displays himself before the ignorant Matvey in all the greatness of his talent. There is no end to his babble, his fault-finding, his whims and fancies. If Matvey nails two big pieces of wood to make a cross, he is dissatisfied and tells him to do it again. If Matvey stands still, Seryozhka asks him angrily why he does not go; if he moves, Seryozhka shouts to him not to go away but to do his work. He is not satisfied with his tools, with the weather, or with his own talent; nothing pleases him.

Every stage of making art is a challenge—but a true artist is respected and honored:

> He swears, shoves, threatens, and not a soul murmurs! They all smile at him, they sympathize with him, call him Sergey Nikitich; they all feel that his art is not his personal affair but something that concerns them all, the whole people.

One creates, the others help him. Seryozhka in himself is a nonentity, a slug-
gard, a drunkard, and a wastrel, but when he has his red lead or compasses in
his hand he is at once something higher, a servant of God.

One point: Chekhov was an atheist. A second point: he was very knowledgeable about
Russian Orthodox ritual. Third: he respected religion's moral and artistic bases. Fourth
and final point: while teasing his lazy, drunken, talented older brothers with this depiction
of reckless, wayward Seryozhka, he was also describing his own and their own struggles
and sense of fulfillment as artists.

When Chekhov faulted himself in his letters, it was often for laziness and lack of discipline. What this tells us, I think, is not that he was deluded (he wrote and did so much!)
but that he was constantly having to overcome those traits. Though he usually immediately
found the entrance and rhythm he needed for writing, it always took an effort. A couple of
weeks after he had completed medical school back in 1884, he began working that summer
at a district hospital. He wrote in his usual lively way to his then- and future-editor Leykin:

> I am in fine fettle, for I have my medical diploma in my pocket. The coun-
> tryside all around is magnificent. Plenty of room and no holiday-makers.
> Mushrooms, fishing, and the district hospital. The monastery is very romantic.
> Standing in the dim light of the aisle beneath the vaulted roof during an
> evening service, I am thinking of subjects for my stories. I have plenty of
> subjects, but I am absolutely incapable of writing anything. I'm too lazy. . . . I
> am writing this letter—lying down. With a book propped up on my stomach,
> I can just manage to write it. I'm too lazy to sit up. [. . .] My family lives with
> me, cooking, baking, and roasting whatever I can afford to buy for the money
> I earn by my writing. Life isn't too bad. One thing, though, is not so good: I
> am lazy and not earning enough . . . [14]

In "Art," meanwhile, Chekhov admiringly concludes the story of a slothful artist's
dazzling display on the icy river:

> Seryozhka listens to this uproar, sees thousands of eyes fixed upon him, and
> the lazy fellow's soul is filled with a sense of glory and triumph.

I like to think that Chekhov's New Year's wish was to inspire Alexander and Nikolay
to experience Seryozhka's "sense of glory and triumph."

Alexander, Anton's oldest brother and his most frequent correspondent for the next couple of years, had plenty of difficulties. For one, he was working in a customs office in the provinces and had missed the Moscow family's New Year's party. Alexander had a common-law wife, and they had two children; a baby who was about to arrive would be named after Anton. Though Alexander had led the Chekhov brothers into freelance work at humor periodicals, he did not have Anton's tact, steadiness, or self-discipline. He drank too much. He could be oafish, rude, and pathetic. However, Alexander "was the only Chekhov who could match, or even outdo, Anton in wit, intelligence, and mordant irony."[15]

Alexander was a touchstone for Anton about what *not* to do or become. When scolding another young author who simply wasn't putting in the hours, Chekhov used Alexander as an example of premature "impotence" through lack of use:

> If you go on writing so little, you will write yourself out without having written anything. As a warning you can take my brother Alexander, who was very miserly as a writer and who already feels that he has written himself out.[16]

In these two years of breakout success for Anton, there are forty-five letters from Chekhov to Alexander. Most are full of news, teasing, and advice; a few are only a handful of sentences, almost invariably about fees Chekhov needed Alexander to pick up from Petersburg periodicals and send—but he always included a joking brotherly insult. Alexander's replies are lively and equally full of teasing and name-calling.

The first surviving 1886 letter of Chekhov's was written on January 4 to Alexander. Anton wished him a happy New Year and scolded him, in the usual comically outraged tone he used only with his brothers and closest friends, for not having written: "You wretch! Raggedypants! Congenital pen-pusher! Why haven't you written? Have you lost all joy and strength in letter-writing? Do you no longer regard me as a brother? Have you not therefore become a total swine? Write, I tell you, a thousand times write! It doesn't matter what, just write . . . Everything is fine here, except for the fact that Father has been buying more lamps. He is obsessed by lamps."[17]

This is one of the rare mentions between them of their father. He and Alexander preferred not to write about him, and there are only five known letters in his life from Anton to Pavel.[18] On the other hand, Anton regularly emphasized keeping connections open among the siblings and with their mother.

He briefly recounted for Alexander his two-week mid-December trip to Petersburg and his stay there with Leykin: "He did me proud with the meals he fed me but, wretch that he is, almost suffocated me with his lies . . . I got to know the editorial staff of the *Petersburg Gazette*,[19] and they welcomed me like the Shah of Persia. You will probably get some work on that paper, but not before the summer. Leykin is not to be relied upon. He's trying all sorts of ways to stab me in the back at the *Petersburg Gazette*, and he'll do the same with you. Khudekov, the editor of the *Petersburg Gazette*, will be coming to see me in January and I'll have a talk with him then."

Chekhov vented more about Leykin than about any other person, partly because Anton's brothers knew him and could join him in taking their own lazy shots at him. Anton didn't mention in this letter to Alexander, however, that he had just received a letter from Leykin complaining about Alexander's recent work, how only one of the two stories that Alexander had sent was publishable, and even that one consisted, said Leykin, simply of various tellings-off.[20]

Chekhov's letter to Alexander became a critique of his brother's writing:

> For the love of Allah! Do me a favor, boot out your depressed civil servants! Surely you've picked up by now that this subject is long out of date and has become a big yawn? And where in Asia have you been rooting around to unearth the torments the poor little pen-pushers in your stories suffer? For verily I say unto thee: they are actively unpleasant to read!

How many of us writers are lucky enough to have absolutely candid readers who can express their impatience while simultaneously guiding us? Anton complimented, with reservations, one particular piece: "'Spick and Span' is an excellently conceived story, but oh! those wretched officials! If only you had had some benevolent bourgeois instead of your bureaucrat, if you hadn't gone on about his pompous rank-pulling fixation with red tape, your 'Spick and Span' could have been as delicious as those lobsters Yerakita was so fond of guzzling. Also, don't let anyone get their hands on your stories to abridge or rewrite them . . . it's horrible when you can see Leykin's hand in every line . . ."

Alexander often made excuses about his personal behavior, but he seems to have always respected and trusted Anton's criticisms of his writing. Even three years before, Anton had lectured him by letter regarding the distinction between subjective and objective writing. ("You must deny yourself the personal impression that honeymoon happiness produces on all embittered persons. Subjectivity is an awful thing—even for the reason that it betrays the poor writer hand over fist.")[21] Anton went on in this vein in the present: "It may be hard to resist the pressure to prune, but you have an easy remedy to hand: do it yourself, pare it down to its limits, do your own rewriting. The more you prune, the more often your work will get into print . . . But the most important thing is: keep at it unstintingly, don't drop your guard for an instant, rewrite five times, prune constantly."

The message Chekhov offered and would continue to offer to brothers and unknown writers alike was: "Keep at it unstintingly." Make writing look effortless, make writing quick and effective. Keep at it and reread one's own work with the same intensity one gives the best literature. Chekhov could have been a prima donna if he had wanted to, but he was determinedly modest and self-critical. He was so modest that he was amazed, he told Alexander, by his apparent renown: "I have never seen anything like the reception I got from the Petersburgers. Suvorin, Grigorovich, Burenin . . . they all showered me with invitations and sang my praises . . . and I began to have a bad conscience that I had been such a careless and slovenly writer. Believe me, if I had known I was going to be read in that way, I would never just have turned out things to order . . . Remember: People are reading you." Chekhov gave lessons only about what he himself had learned from experience.

Alexander had been excusing his hasty, careless pieces partly because of his job as a customs official, where he felt he had to hide his association to humor magazines. Anton wouldn't grant him that excuse, providing examples of other writers working for government agencies: "There are plenty of people in the Officer Corps, which has the strictest of regulations, who don't conceal the fact that they write. There may sometimes be a need for discretion, but you shouldn't be hiding away yourself [. . .]. Excuse the moralizing, I'm only writing to you like this because it upsets me and makes me angry . . . You're a good writer, you could earn twice as much as you do and yet you're living off wild honey and locusts . . . all because of the crossed wires you have in your noodle . . ."

The twenty-five-year-old moved to wrap up his letter to the twenty-nine-year-old by acknowledging that his situation was different from Alexander's: "I'm still not married, and I have no children. Life is not easy. There'll probably be some money in the summer. Oh, if only!" The pressure to make money was relentless. The biographer David Magarshack believes these "two years were the worst years of financial worry Chekhov had ever experienced."[22]

Chekhov reemphasized his letter's main point: "Please write!" The family wanted to hear from Alexander. "I think of you often, and rejoice when I remember you are alive . . ." But not to get too sappy, he added: "So don't be a fathead, and don't forget your *A. Chekhov*." In a postscript he tossed in the latest family "news": "Nikolay is sitting on his backside. Ivan, as before, is being a real Ivan. Our sister is whirling around in a daze: admirers, symphony concerts, a big apartment . . ."

This most independent man coveted and created family unity.

The next day, January 5, Chekhov sent Leykin four new short pieces, one of which, "The Fiasco" ("Neudacha," January 11), I will quote in its entirety as a good example of the kinds of humor stories he was writing for *Fragments*.[23] He had probably written it in one sitting that day, a Sunday, his medical day off.

> Ilya Sergeich Peplov and his wife Cleopatra Petrovna were standing by the door and ravenously listening in. Behind the door, in the little parlor, was proceeding, evidently, a declaration of love; their daughter Natashenka and the teacher of the district school were declaring themselves.
>
> "He's nibbling!" whispered Peplov, trembling with impatience and rubbing his hands. "Look now, Petrovna, as soon as they're talking about feelings, right then snatch the ikon off the wall and we'll go bless them. . . . We've got it under control. . . . A blessing with a holy ikon is inviolable. . . . He wouldn't get away then, even if he brings a lawsuit."
>
> And behind the door proceeded this very conversation:
>
> "Leave that manner aside," said Shchupkin, lighting a match on his checked pants. "I most definitely didn't write you letters!"
>
> "Oh, sure! As if I don't know your handwriting!" guffawed the girl, artificially squealing and at the same time taking glances at herself in the mirror. "I knew it right away! And what a strange one you are! A writing teacher, but your handwriting's like a chicken's! How can you teach writing if you yourself write so poorly?"
>
> "Hm! . . . That doesn't mean anything, miss. In calligraphy the main thing isn't the handwriting, the main thing is that the students don't forget. You hit one on the head with a ruler, another one on the knees. . . . That's what handwriting is! A simple matter! Nekrasov was a writer, but it's embarrassing to see how he wrote. In his *Collected Works*, his handwriting is shown."
>
> "That's Nekrasov, but you . . . (sighs). It would be a pleasure to marry a writer. He'd constantly be writing verses to remember me by!"

"I could write you verses, if you wanted me to."

"What could you write about?"

"About love . . . about feelings . . . about your eyes . . . You'd read them—you'd go crazy. . . . Tears would pour out! If I were to write you poetical verses, then would you give me your hand to kiss?"

"Big deal! . . . You could kiss it right now!"

Shchupkin hopped up and, widening his eyes, fell upon her plump hand, fragrant with egg-soap.

"Snatch the ikon!" said Peplov all aflutter, pale with agitation, buttoning up, and nudging his wife with his elbow.

"Let's go! Go!"

And not hesitating a second, Peplov burst through the door.

"Children . . ." he muttered, raising his arms and tearfully blinking his eyes. "The Lord blesses you, my children. . . . Live . . . be fruitful . . . multiply . . ."

"And . . . and I bless you . . ." added Mommy, weeping with happiness. "Be happy, dear ones! O, you're depriving me of my only treasure!" she said turning to Shchupkin. "Love my daughter, be kind to her . . ."

Shchupkin's mouth gaped in confusion and fright. The parents' assault had been so sudden and bold that he could not utter a single word.

"Caught, surrounded!" thought he, faint with fear. "Done for, brother! You're not escaping this."

And he humbly bowed his head, as if desiring to say: "Take me, I'm beaten!"

"Ble—I bless . . ." continued Papa and he also began crying. "Natashenka, my daughter . . . stand alongside . . . Petrovna, give me the ikon . . ."

But here the father suddenly stopped crying and his face winced in anger.

"Dummy!" he angrily said to his wife. "You stupid-head! But where's the ikon?"

"Oh, Holy Fathers!"

What happened? The handwriting teacher timidly raised his eyes and saw that he was saved: In confusion Mama had snatched from the wall not the ikon but the portrait of the writer Lazhechnikov. Old Peplov and his wife Cleopatra Petrovna, with the portrait in their hands, stood in bewilderment, not knowing what to do or what to say. The handwriting teacher took advantage of the confusion and ran out.

Chekhov originally titled this skit "Busted!" ("Sorvalos'!"). Eventually, thirteen years later, in his *Collected Works*, he retitled it as "Neudacha" ("The Fiasco"), revising the ending so that he has the teacher skipping out of the room instead of the parents exclaiming "All is lost!" (which resembles a Gogolian curtain line).[24]

He wrote most of the purely farcical pieces with a restraint and focus that had to skedaddle down an expected route or fit a genre's tone: they were apparently impersonal or, as he had described them to Alexander, *objective*. He certainly seems to have sympathized, however, with the cornered Shchupkin, and he himself was about to tumble into a real-life engagement.

—⁓—

He published the suspenseful but comic "A Night in the Cemetery" ("Noch na Kladbishche") on January 8. A first-person narrator tells of a scary night that concluded with his waking up in a monuments storeroom. He announces: "My story begins, as begin in general all the best Russian stories: I was, I confess, drunk . . ." He eventually becomes philosophical: "It can't be forgotten that with the new year the closer it is to death, to wider baldness, more twisted wrinkles, the wife older, more kids, less money . . ."[25]

For January 11 he wrote up a contest announcement for *Fragments* titled "The Contest" ("Konkurs") that isn't quite a joke. But Chekhov's idea, which Leykin allowed him to try out to inspire more reader participation, doesn't seem to have paid off; it received few responses. Another piece, "Tips for Husbands" ("K Svedeniyu Muzhei"), was blocked by censors. One possible reason for the censorship is that the "tips" aren't really for husbands but for the Don Juans attempting to seduce those husbands' wives.[26] One of Leykin's headaches as the editor of a humor magazine was dealing with censors, who were idiosyncratic and inconsistent. The magazine's illustrations, which are surprisingly racy, were as much of a game for Leykin to sneak past censors as the written pieces.[27] By January 12, Chekhov had selected most of the seventy-seven short stories that Leykin would publish that spring in the book *Motley Stories*.

The marriage theme was percolating in Chekhov's life and fiction. He needed to borrow a jacket and vest to serve as the best man at the wedding of an acquaintance, the doctor Pavel Rozanov, on January 12. Rozanov was not from Moscow and didn't have friends or family close by, but Chekhov and his sister Maria (often addressed or referred to as Masha), studying to become a teacher, agreed to represent Rozanov's side.

Chekhov scheduled a "Tatyana Day" dinner with other friends the night of the midday wedding, and he got home only early the next morning. (That his brother Mikhail noted this detail means, I think, that such carousing was unusual.) Tatyana Day was an annual celebration by Moscow University students.[28] Though his older brothers had drinking problems, Chekhov was a moderate drinker and none of his friends ever recounted his acting drunkenly. Two days after the wedding, Chekhov wrote and teased Rozanov that it was now Rozanov's wife's duty to find him a spouse: "If Varvara Ivanovna doesn't find me a bride, I'll definitely shoot myself." When Chekhov expressed despair in letters to friends, he often declared this most self-dramatic act; he was continually threatening to shoot himself. In his fiction, the characters, equally self-dramatic, actually sometimes do it. He further teased Rozanov: "It's time I was ruled with a rod of iron, as you now are . . ."[29] He was in such sorry shape from the Tatyana Day all-nighter, as he told Rozanov, that he realized he needed to get married. "In the choice of bride, let you guide her taste, as ever since January 12 I began believing in your taste."[30]

In "First Debut"[31] ("Pervyi Debyut"), published on January 13, Chekhov describes a young lawyer's awful, humiliating first day on the circuit. He leaves the district court with his driver; the winter weather is so bad, however, that they have to stop for the night at a house that the driver finds. The two lawyers who opposed him in court are already there, and he gets huffy and silent. When the water for tea has been made, they all realize he has sugar, and they have tea, but he, feeling petty and unforgiving, won't share. He lies down by the oven; they think he's asleep and they talk about him in ways that show their understanding of his rookie self-consciousness. He is awake, though, and cries out his hurt to them, and they talk him around—explaining that debuts are always challenging. They help cover him from the cold with their heavy coats and they go to sleep.

Among the many observations we could make about this fine little story, one is to note how well Chekhov understands shame. It had been only a year and half since he himself had debuted as a doctor out in the countryside. Mikhail Chekhov recounts how his debuting brother lost his nerve in the midst of operating on a boy's foreskin. Dr. Rozanov himself took over and to everyone's relief completed the work.[32]

On January 16, Chekhov turned twenty-six.[33] (He and other Christian Russians celebrated name days rather than birthdays; his name day was January 17.) He had eighteen and a half more years to live. Knowing but not admitting to others that he had tuberculosis, he might not have been surprised by that literal deadline. And though money was tight, there just had to be a big party. In his invitation to his friend Mikhail Dyukovskiy, he kidded that "I'm a poor man: my wife's a widow, my children orphans," and thus had a request for Dyukovskiy: to bring a dozen and a half knives and forks, teaspoons, glasses, small plates, and a cast-iron stove.[34]

Chekhov's sister Maria was in a women's higher education program, and one of her classmates and invitees to the party was the twenty-four or twenty-five-year-old Evdokiya (known to the family as "Dunya") Isaakovna Efros. Chekhov had known Efros since at least the spring of 1885.

The longest letter of the month, besides the New Year's letter to Alexander, was on January 18 to Viktor Bilibin, Leykin's sub-editor, and it was long partly because it had to make up for a January 2 letter that Bilibin never received. That letter, Chekhov said, "was so big that there wasn't a driver who would agree to take me with it to the mailbox."[35]

He caught Bilibin up with what he remembered was in it, including a scolding for not having let him pay for their meal together when he was visiting Petersburg in December. He remembered having written Bilibin about the New Year's costume party and the photo album he had been given and "how the fish in my aquarium died from a cigar thrown in their water." He said the party had cost a bundle and that he had poisoned himself with alcohol.

> À propos Christmas has cost me 300 rubles. Don't you think I'm just crazy? Yes, it certainly is a great misfortune to have a family. . . . Thank goodness Christmas is over. If it had gone on for another week I should have had to go begging in the streets. At the moment I haven't a farthing in my pocket.[36]

Note that if he actually spent 300 rubles, that was nearly half a year's rent. But the big moment, shared only with his new friend Bilibin and the details of which were otherwise known only to Dunya Efros herself, was that "Last night, bringing a young lady home, I made her a proposal. I went out of the frying pan and into the fire . . . Bless my marriage."

If Efros took the proposal seriously and told anybody about it, no one accounted for her ever having done so. Maria Chekhova, who outlived her brother by more than fifty years, claimed (probably disingenuously) that she had never heard of the engagement until decades later. As Chekhov devoted three most casual sentences to his engagement in the middle of a long letter to a man actually getting married, the biographer Ronald Hingley suggests that there never was an engagement. I, on the other hand, think that there was an engagement, but that it started out as a joke. That is, at the conclusion of his wild name day party, Chekhov proposed and Efros accepted . . . *as a joke*. And they played along at this together until they didn't know themselves whether it was a joke or not.

There was marriage all around: for friends and for characters in his fiction. Why not try it himself? Even upstairs from his family's apartment there were weddings. He wrote to Leykin the very next day about the wedding party that he was overhearing: "Somebody banging their feet like a horse has just run over my head . . . Must be the best man. The band is thundering . . . For the groom who is going to screw his bride this music may be pleasant, but it will stop me [. . .] getting any sleep."[37]

After more joking around with Bilibin, he got down to business. He wanted Bilibin to send him copies of *Fragments* that had some short stories Chekhov wanted to consider including in his book. He didn't want to cut up his own copies of the magazine, and he included a list of those stories and the issues they had appeared in. He thanked Bilibin for that task and also for his praise of Chekhov's recent stories in the *Petersburg Gazette*. He suggested that he didn't enjoy knowing that literary people were reading him: "Before, when I didn't know that I was being read and judged, I wrote unconcernedly, just as if I were eating bliny; now I write and I'm afraid . . ."

He asked when Bilibin would be in Moscow: "Here's what you're going to do: get married and you and your wife come to me in May at the dacha for a week or two." He told him about the Tatyana Day festivities on the 12th and about the name day party, and that if the holidays were to go on any longer he would be done for, as he was now completely broke: "Pray for me." He then confided that he had been invited to write for *New Times*, but that he didn't want Bilibin to tell Leykin yet, as he didn't know when that assignment would start.

—⁓—

"On the Phone" ("U Telefona," January 19) is a skit in dialogue format about a caller's misconnections trying to reach the Slavyansky Bazaar. A Soviet editor informs us that the first telephones in Petersburg were installed in 1882–1883.[38] There are no accounts I have read of Chekhov using a phone until 1901, when Tolstoy, recuperating from various ailments in Crimea, called Chekhov, who was convalescing in the neighboring town. I would welcome a tsarist secret-police transcript of that call.

Meanwhile, Chekhov was trying to placate Leykin: "As hard as I tried, kind Nikolay Aleksandrovich," Chekhov wrote to Leykin on January 19, "I didn't have time to send you a story by Monday."[39] He now apparently enclosed the short story "The Discovery." "You say I write as if I want to cut things off. Why do you say that?" he asked warily. The only person in these two years that Chekhov deliberately and repeatedly deceived was editor Leykin. Chekhov did in fact "want to cut things off," and had told others so. He was displaying the bad conscience of a boyfriend intending to dump his girlfriend. Despite their long professional and personal relationship, Chekhov didn't tell him about the offer he had received on January 2 to write for *New Times*, though now would have been a fitting time.

In "Children" ("Detvora," January 20) one recognizes Chekhov's awareness of the sophistication of children's feelings and relationships. The situation: While the parents are out and the servants are occupied, young children play lotto; they make their own rules and resolve their own disputes. The story is amusing, but Chekhov is strict with himself about psychology: The children talk and behave like children. It is as if he was giving a writing lesson to his brother Alexander; these children are not projections of parents' love or created with "subjectivity":

> "I did see something yesterday!" says Anya, as though to herself. "Filipp Filippich turned his eyelids inside out somehow and his eyes looked red and dreadful, like an evil spirit's."
>
> "I saw it too," says Grisha. "Eight! And a boy at our school can move his ears. Twenty-seven!"

Illustration from "Children."

Later, one of them hears bells:

> "I believe they are ringing somewhere," says Anya, opening her eyes wide.
> They all leave off playing and gaze open-mouthed at the dark window. The reflection of the lamp glimmers in the darkness.
> "It was your fancy."
> "At night they only ring in the cemetery," says Andrey.
> "And what do they ring there for?"
> "To prevent robbers from breaking into the church. They are afraid of the bells."
> "And what do robbers break into the church for?" asks Sonya.
> "Everyone knows what for: to kill the watchmen."
> A minute passes in silence. They all look at one another, shudder, and go on playing.

The children are not adults; they're also not "subjective" projections of a sentimental adult; they argue and fight and recover from their disputes quickly and thoroughly:

Andrey turns pale, his mouth works, and he gives Alyosha a slap on the head! Alyosha glares angrily, jumps up, and with one knee on the table, slaps Andrey on the cheek! Each gives the other a second blow, and both howl. Sonya, feeling such horrors too much for her, begins crying too, and the dining-room resounds with lamentations on various notes. But do not imagine that that is the end of the game. Before five minutes are over, the children are laughing and talking peaceably again. Their faces are tear-stained, but that does not prevent them from smiling . . .[40]

Chekhov was a keen observer of the behavior of animals, children, sick people, family, friends, and lovers. Those who knew him well noticed how patients, children, and animals relaxed in his presence and could be themselves.

In "The Discovery" ("Otkrytie"), published on January 25, a fifty-two-year-old engineer sees a woman he was in love with decades before; she is no longer beautiful, and his thoughts about time's toll are sour. But watch what happens as he does something Chekhov in these years almost never did, which is sit "behind his desk with nothing to do." From his unhappy thoughts about the transience of beauty, the engineer looks down at the paper on which he has been doodling:

On the sheet of paper upon which he had mechanically dragged his pencil, by crude strokes and a scrawl, a charming womanly head peeped out, the very one he had once upon a time fallen in love with. In general the drawing was shaky, but the languid, severe look, the softness of the features, and the disordered full wave of hair were done to perfection . . .[41]

Amazed by his hidden talent, the engineer draws other things, and out they brightly appear. He remembers the respect his mother gave writers, painters, composers—kissing their hands in reverence. "And in his imagination a life was revealed not resembling millions of other lives. Comparing it with the lives of the usual mortals was absolutely impossible." His own engineering projects? No one will know about them or care! . . . But if he had been a famous artist? When he goes to bed, however, looked after by his lackey, he remembers, under a warm blanket, the poverty of artists and he is happy to be as he is.

Is the engineer an unflattering future projection caricature of Chekhov himself? What if he hadn't had artistic "talent"? Or what if his talent had remained hidden? And maybe, what if he, like the engineer, could avoid marriage? Now that he had been engaged for a few days, perhaps he was imagining himself disentangled. Like children and literary artists, Chekhov squared up to his quandaries through dramatizing them in the lives of his characters.

He also published on January 25 a clever one-page joke story, "The Biggest City" ("Samyi Bol'shoi Gorod"): Every time the touring Englishman journalist wakes up from a long nap, he and the carriage are in the city of Tim. What he hasn't noticed is that his driver is continually climbing out of the carriage to pull it or the horses out of the mud. The journalist reports to his newspaper: "In Russia, the biggest city is neither Moscow nor Petersburg, but Tim."[42]

The most famous of Chekhov's stories this month was the last published in January: "Misery" ("Toska," January 27). A sledge driver in midwinter is mourning the death of his son but no one will listen sympathetically to his story:

> Iona looks at his fare and moves his lips. . . . Apparently he means to say something, but nothing comes but a sniff.
>
> "What?" inquires the officer.
>
> Iona gives a wry smile, and straining his throat, brings out huskily: "My son . . . er . . . my son died this week, sir."
>
> "H'm! What did he die of?"

Iona's misery "is immense, beyond all bounds," but Chekhov also shows us how and why it is awkward for the listeners, even when they make some attempt at pity: "Iona looks to see the effect produced by his words, but he sees nothing." The customers are busy, self-occupied. They don't want to hear or think about this. And Iona sees they can't or won't give him the quiet listening he needs.

> He puts on his coat and goes into the stables where his mare is standing. He thinks about oats, about hay, about the weather. . . . He cannot think about his son when he is alone. . . . To talk about him with someone is possible, but to think of him and picture him is insufferable anguish. . . .
>
> "Are you munching?" Iona asks his mare, seeing her shining eyes. "There, munch away, munch away. . . . Since we have not earned enough for oats, we will eat hay. . . . Yes, . . . I have grown too old to drive. . . . My son ought to be driving, not I. . . . He was a real cabman. . . . He ought to have lived. . . ."

Iona is silent for a while, and then he goes on:

"That's how it is, old girl. . . . Kuzma Ionich is gone. . . . He said goodbye to me. . . . He went and died for no reason . . . . Now, suppose you had a little colt, and you were own mother to that little colt. . . . And all at once that same little colt went and died. . . . You'd be sorry, wouldn't you? . . ."

The little mare munches, listens, and breathes on her master's hands. Iona is carried away and tells her all about it.[43]

The mare is the only creature doing this human thing that all the humans are failing to do. If Chekhov had written only this story, it would still be read and appreciated today. It was translated in his own lifetime into more languages (eight) than any of his others. Years later, when his brother Alexander was grieving over the serious illness of one of his sons, he recalled details of this story and declared that "Misery" had made Chekhov "immortal."[44]

Chekhov included it in the book that he was preparing, the yet untitled *Motley Stories*. He made few corrections from the original publication in the *Petersburg Gazette*, but one of them was deleting a too obvious conclusion: "There is nothing one can do better than listening to a person."[45] Chekhov's medical friends noted that he was an excellent listener and observer. Nodding, chewing oats but otherwise silent. A critic, L. E. Obolenskiy, wrote ecstatically about the story, declaring that Antosha Chekhonte's "loving heart sees a whole life behind it, which he is so able to understand and so love that we begin to love and understand it!"[46]

Before Chekhov had ever deliberately signed a story with his own name, in the single month of January 1886, he wrote two gold-star stories, "Children" and "Misery." The author Antosha Chekhonte was already Anton Chekhov, only not quite yet in name.

———————

It's not clear what records if any Chekhov kept of his patients. As the chronology of his life is revealed in the streamlined *Letopis'*, that almost daily chore is scarcely mentioned, though medicine, he continued to joke, was his "wife." The first mention of medical work in the *Letopis'* of 1886 comes on January 28, when the editors note that Chekhov "treated" his friend Isaac Levitan, for what Chekhov told Leykin was psychosis.[47] Earlier in the month Chekhov had tried to persuade Leykin to give Levitan, on the cusp of artistic fame as a landscape painter, an advance of forty rubles. But Leykin had had enough for the time being of Levitan and Nikolay Chekhov as illustrators. He had a good case against them: they would agree to do pieces for *Fragments* and then forget or put them off and be late, so he turned Chekhov down. Leykin suggested instead that Levitan submit completed drawings, for which he would indeed pay him forty rubles.

Levitan was a year younger than Chekhov, also hugely talented, but unlike Chekhov in that he was conspicuously moody and susceptible to falling in love. He was attractive and had various affairs. This summer or next, he would ask Maria Chekhova to marry him, and Chekhov disapproved of his sister's accepting him.[48] Levitan and Chekhov had a falling out in the early 1890s over a story Chekhov wrote, "The Grasshopper." Levitan thought it too closely resembled details of an affair of Levitan's with one of Chekhov's former girlfriends. But they made up; Chekhov's fallings out with friends never seemed to last. He was characteristically forgiving and regularly forgiven.

—⁓—

Nine days after his last letter to Leykin, Chekhov seemed to be trying to make up to him, but he was also preparing his editor for being left behind. He wondered in his January 28 letter to Leykin, *Why are you mad? Can we take care of matters with the book?* He agreed to all the conditions about the book that Leykin had mentioned in the last letter. But Chekhov wanted to clarify what his own duties would be: "All the editing I leave to your oversight, counting myself impotent in publishing. I take on myself only the choice of stories, the look of the cover and those functions that you find necessary for me on the part of the passing it to Stupin and so on. I consider myself at your command. Know that for all you give the book and time, I count the publication of my book a large kindness on the part of *Fragments* and I award you for this work a would-be Stanislas of the 3rd Rank."[49] (That is, a worthless honorary medal.)

He also had questions and desires about the book. He could send more stories if needed, or take some out if there were too many. He would like his friend Franz Schechtel to draw the cover. He didn't know why, but he thought the book would be a hit. Couldn't there be 2,500 copies instead of 2,000? These were humble enough questions, but Leykin did not take writers' suggestions on publication matters.

And what did Leykin want to call the book, wondered Chekhov: "I've gone over all the botanical, zoological and all the verses and elements, but I didn't find one. I thought up only 'Stories of A. Chekhonte' and 'Trifles.' [. . .] The price of the book and so on, don't ask me. I repeat, I agree with everything . . . However, wouldn't it be possible to send me the latest galley?"

Leykin answered grouchily a couple of days later that he would consider Schechtel's drawing, and this after all resulted in the use of Schechtel's work.

The frontispiece illustration by Franz Schechtel of *Motley Stories*.

Finally, at the end of January, we learn that Dr. Chekhov had in fact been working "every day" and going out to treat N. S. Yanov, another brother of Maria Yanova.[50]

Chekhov would soon explain to his new editor Suvorin the special demands of his schedule:

> I write comparatively little: no more than two or three brief stories a week. I can find the time to work for *New Times*, but I'm glad nonetheless that you didn't make deadlines a condition for my becoming a contributor. Deadlines lead to haste and the feeling of having a weight around your neck. Both of these together make it hard for me to work. For me personally a deadline is inconvenient if only because I'm a physician and practice medicine. I can never guarantee that I won't be torn away from my desk for a whole day on any given day. The risk of my being late and not finishing a story is always there.[51]

On top of his medical duties and weekly deadlines for two publications, he added one more, because his family "needed the money" . . . and because he must have wanted to see where his pen would lead him if it had no constraints on length or topics—or treatment of those topics. Despite his various duties, he would almost never miss a *New Times* deadline.

February 1886

—⁓—

> Yes, I wrote to you once that you must be unconcerned
> when you write pathetic stories. And you did not
> understand me. You may weep and moan over your
> stories, you may suffer with your heroes, but I consider
> one must do this so that the reader does not notice it.
> The more objective, the stronger will be the effect.
>
> —To a young writer[1]

Even when he was blue, there was spirit and tone in his letters. He seems to have felt obliged to be entertaining; this usually meant kidding around. With only a couple of exceptions, his letters are fresh, written at a dash, without drafts. He communicated fast, his mind's eye on his correspondent, musing and joking as if aloud to this particular person.

He had met Bilibin, Leykin's assistant editor, in Petersburg in December 1885, and took to him immediately. In the friendship's early stages, Chekhov was especially confidential. Bilibin was getting married, and Chekhov and Dunya Efros were at least playing with the idea.

On February 1, he wrote to Bilibin about various topics, among them a visit to the poet Iliodor Palmin:

> True, while talking to him, you have to drink a lot, but then you can be certain that during an entire three- or four-hour talk with him you won't hear a single lying word or trite phrase, and that's worth sacrificing your sobriety.[2]

During the next few years, Chekhov did not harp on any particular human failing except one, lying.

He recalled or created a comic turn in his and Palmin's conversation:

> By the way, he and I tried to think up a title for my book. After racking our
> brains for hours, all we could come up with was *Cats and Carps* and *Flowers
> and Dogs*. I was willing to settle for *Buy This Book or You'll Get a Punch in the
> Mouth* or *Are You Being Helped, Sir?*, but after some thought the poet pro-
> nounced them hackneyed and cliché. [. . .] I would prefer what Leykin wants,
> to wit: *A. Chekhonte. Stories and Sketches* and nothing else, even though that
> kind of title is suited only to celebrities [. . .]

It seems to me Chekhov had edged himself along to what he really wanted to discuss
with Bilibin:

> And now a few words about my fiancée and Hymen. [. . .] Thank your fiancée
> for remembering me and tell her that my wedding will most likely—alas and
> alack! The censor has cut out the rest. . . . My one and only is Jewish. If the rich
> young Jewess has enough courage to convert to Orthodoxy with all that this
> entails, fine. If not, that's fine, too. Besides, we've already had a quarrel. We'll
> make up tomorrow, but in a week we'll quarrel again. She breaks pencils and
> the photographs on my desk because of her annoyance at being held back by
> religion. That is the way she is. . . . She has a terrible temper. There is no doubt
> whatsoever that I will divorce her a year or two after the wedding. But . . . *finis.*

Dunya Efros, as Maria's friend and classmate, was a regular visitor to the Chekhovs'
home, and we learn in the next letter that Maria and her young women friends liked to
sit in Chekhov's study by the fire. My theory is that Chekhov was writing the letter while
Efros was in the room with him, and she came over and sat beside him or stood over
his shoulder at his desk. . . . She began reading what he was writing, and she squawked
and pretended to or threatened to break his pencils and tear up his photos. So he wrote:
"She has a terrible temper," and further taunted her about their destined divorce. Efros,
I speculate, had become his immediate audience. Chekhov took his eye off Bilibin to
tease Efros. This was not a confidential message revealing deep feelings to his new friend.

When he had actual life news, he passed it along matter-of-factly to his brother Alexander or Leykin, but as far as can be told from the letters to and from those correspondents,
neither confidant was aware of this engagement. Alexander was never one to hold back,
and his letters contain no querying about Chekhov's relationship with Efros.

"Probably there never was any such engagement," writes the biographer Ronald Hingley, "for Chekhov's letters so abound in flights of whimsy that it may have been a figment of his imagination from the start: a private joke between himself and Bilibin. As for Dunya Efros—whether briefly affianced to Chekhov or not, she later became a Mrs. Konovitser; and remained, with her husband, on friendly terms with the Chekhovs throughout the years."[3]

But what about the issue of her Judaism versus his Russian Orthodoxy? . . . Chekhov did not note Efros being Jewish in the only previous mention in the letters. Now he did. Does that mean it wasn't important on January 19? Was the religious issue only a new complicating narrative detail in their make-believe or semi-serious engagement?

On February 3, Anton scolded Alexander: "Remember, that if you would write stories the way you write letters you would have long been a great tremendous person."[4] Alexander's letters were as lively and engaging as Anton's, and perhaps even more revealing—as Alexander had been to the depths many times. Anton then repeated his message to Alexander of a month before: "I'm still not married." There was no mention of the engagement to Efros, even though she was, possibly at this very moment in his presence: "I have now a separate room, and in the room is a fireplace, close to which Masha and her Efros—Reve-Khave [Efros' Jewish name], Nelli and the baroness, the Yanova girls and so on often sit."

"An Upheaval" ("Perepolokh," February 3) was published in the *Petersburg Gazette*. A young governess, Mashenka, is, as one of the household staff, suspected of having filched her employer's expensive brooch. Her room and things are searched: "For the first time in her life, it was her lot to experience in all its acuteness the feeling that is so familiar to persons in dependent positions, who eat the bread of the rich and powerful, and cannot speak their minds." She is humiliated by the suspicion.

Chekhov could not bear being looked down upon. He could not bear his family being condescended to. Mashenka's suffering and resentment are acute to him. He even imagines the humiliating position of the doctor who lives with the aristocrats:

> "Come, don't let us agitate ourselves," Mamikov, her household doctor, observed in a honeyed voice, just touching [Madame Kushkin's] arm, with a smile as honeyed. "We are nervous enough as it is. Let us forget the brooch! Health is worth more than two thousand rubles!"

Even though she is poor and her parents are depending on her employment, Mashenka doesn't see how she can remain working for such people. The man of the house, a browbeaten wimp, tries to persuade her to stay, even finally confessing that he, needing money but fearing his wife's refusal, stole the brooch. Mashenka's exit is swift and triumphant: "Half an hour later she was on her way." Chekhov practically cheers for the vulnerable young woman's bravery.

"Conversation of a Drunken Man with a Sober Devil" (February 8) is a quick skit for *Fragments* about a drunk who is more poised and confident than the Devil. The narrator makes one uninspired marriage joke: "Even if he is not married, a devil has a pair of horns on his head."[5]

In "An Actor's End" ("Akterskaya Gibel'," February 10), an actor has suffered a stroke (Chekhov describes the symptoms). His lone desire is to return home, far away from where the troupe is performing. His fellow actors visit him on his deathbed to offer remedies or to cheer him up: "Sigaev began comforting Shchiptsov, telling him untruly that his comrades had decided to send him to the Crimea at their expense, and so on, but the sick man did not listen and kept muttering about Vyazma. . . . At last, with a wave of his hand, the comic man began talking about Vyazma himself to comfort the invalid."

In a dozen years Chekhov himself would be advised to go to Crimea for his health.

Sometime on or near February 10, Chekhov mailed Suvorin "The Requiem." How anxious was he about his first submission to *New Times*? One short story would pay more than what Chekhov received monthly from Leykin for a dozen pieces. By the 14th, Suvorin sent Chekhov a telegram with the welcome announcement about his intention to publish it. The discombobulating news, however, was that he wanted Chekhov to use his actual name.[6] While some of Chekhov's medical colleagues did not even know he was a humor writer, now they would know he was a literary writer.

He explained the dilemma to Bilibin in a letter on February 14: "I, having thought it over, prefer the pen name and not without a basis . . . Family and my family arms I gave to medicine, from which I won't leave off until the grave. Sooner or later I'm giving up literature. Secondly, medicine takes itself seriously, while the game of literature ought to have distinctive names . . ."[7] Pen names in Russian literature were common enough, but Chekhov relented and allowed *New Times* to use his real name.

In the meantime, as he told Bilibin, he was busy with doctoring: "Every day I go out into the country for my medical practice. What ravines, what views!"[8] Even so, he had knocked off a quick story: "Having at my disposal only 2½ hours, I spoiled this monologue ["Bliny"] and . . . I sent it not to the devil [that is, to Leykin] but to 'Pet Gaz.' Intentions were good, but the result was most awful." He was rushing so much—from wife (medicine) to mistress (literature)—that he hadn't even eaten, except imaginatively and gorgingly in the story about bliny. Then he brought up Bilibin's marriage: "You're going to Finland! When your honeymoon turns into ice cream in Finland, remember then my invitation and curse yourself for your faintheartedness . . . How much will this trip to your wild Finland cost you? A hundred rubles? And for this money you could very well travel south or, at least, to me in Moscow . . . Overhead, wedding music is playing now . . . Some donkeys are marrying and they stamp their feet like horses . . . They don't let me sleep."

He added, beginning a series of seemingly random thoughts: "About my wedding, nothing yet is known . . ."

On February 15, Chekhov made his debut in *New Times*, an important though right-wing St. Petersburg newspaper that had a Saturday literary section, which is where "The Requiem" appeared.[9]

"The Requiem" ("Panikhida") begins:

> In the village church of Verhny Zaprudy mass was just over. The people had begun moving and were trooping out of church. The only one who did not move was Andrey Andreyich, a shopkeeper and old inhabitant of Verhny Zaprudy. He stood waiting, with his elbows on the railing of the right choir. His fat and shaven face, covered with indentations left by pimples, expressed on this occasion two contradictory feelings: resignation in the face of inevitable destiny, and stupid, unbounded disdain for the smocks and striped kerchiefs passing by him.[10]

Chekhov has conjured up a face that is fascinating to imagine, even though it's not attractive. Would the shopkeeper's plumpness lead us to assume he's doing well? He shaves; he keeps up appearances. With the pimple-dents, we know he had an unattractive face in the past. Chekhov has described such a particular human face that we understand the "two contradictory feelings" he's expressing: 1) his resignation at what promises to become a funeral, and 2) his being distracted by others' fashion choices at church. He himself is duded up:

> As it was Sunday, he was dressed like a dandy. He wore a long cloth overcoat with yellow bone buttons, blue trousers not thrust into his boots, and sturdy galoshes—the huge clumsy galoshes only seen on the feet of practical and prudent persons of firm religious convictions.

The shopkeeper is dignified, conscious of his physical and moral stature, but Chekhov's assessment of Andrey being "practical and prudent" and pious means that we are ridiculing Andrey's self-assessment:

> His torpid eyes, sunk in fat, were fixed upon the ikon stand. He saw the long familiar figures of the saints, the verger Matvey puffing out his cheeks and blowing out the candles, the darkened candle stands, the threadbare carpet, the sacristan Lopuhov running impulsively from the altar and carrying the holy bread to the churchwarden. . . . All these things he had seen for years, and seen over and over again like the five fingers of his hand. . . . There was only one thing, however, that was somewhat strange and unusual. Father Grigory, still in his vestments, was standing at the north door, twitching his thick eyebrows angrily.

Not only is Andrey Andreyich familiar with the church ceremonies, but so is Chekhov, obviously. Chekhov only presents as strange what the character would have thought strange. This is not about local color, though we get that, too.

> "Who is it he is winking at? God bless him!" thought the shopkeeper. "And he is beckoning with his finger! And he stamped his foot! What next! What's the matter, Holy Queen and Mother! Whom does he mean it for?"
>
> Andrey Andreyich looked around and saw the church completely deserted. There were some ten people standing at the door, but they had their backs to the altar.
>
> "Do come when you are called! Why do you stand like a graven image?" he heard Father Grigory's angry voice. "I am calling you."

This is not what he or we expected—the familiar priest angry at him.

The shopkeeper looked at Father Grigory's red and wrathful face, and only then realized that the twitching eyebrows and beckoning finger might refer to him. He started, left the railing, and hesitatingly walked toward the altar, tramping with his heavy galoshes.

Andrey is not so dignified that he cannot be intimidated by Father Grigory, and the priest has the confidence to beckon him and expect obedience:

"Andrey Andreyich, was it you asked for prayers for the rest of Mariya's soul?" asked the priest, his eyes angrily transfixing the shopkeeper's fat, perspiring face.

"Yes, Father."

"Then it was you wrote this? You?" And Father Grigory angrily thrust before his eyes the little note.

And on this little note, handed in by Andrey Andreyich before mass, was written in big, as it were staggering, letters:

"For the rest of the soul of the servant of God, the harlot Mariya."

"Yes, certainly I wrote it . . ." answered the shopkeeper.

"How dared you write it?" whispered the priest, and in his husky whisper there was a note of wrath and alarm.

The shopkeeper looked at him in blank amazement; he was perplexed, and he, too, was alarmed. Father Grigory had never in his life spoken in such a tone to a leading resident of Verhny Zaprudy.

Doesn't this perplexity on Andrey's part make the story even more compelling? It's like the surprise one feels in a dream: *Me? You're calling me over? Me? How could you be calling me? I didn't do anything!*

Both were silent for a minute, staring into each other's face. The shopkeeper's amazement was so great that his fat face spread in all directions like spilt dough.

Chekhov already gave us Andrey's great distinctive face, and now we get to enjoy it again.

"How dared you?" repeated the priest.

"Wha . . . what?" asked Andrey Andreyich in bewilderment.

"You don't understand?" whispered Father Grigory, stepping back in astonishment and clasping his hands. "What have you got on your shoulders, a head or some other object? You send a note up to the altar, and write a word in it which it would be unseemly even to utter in the street! Why are you rolling your eyes? Surely you know the meaning of the word?"

"Are you referring to the word harlot?" muttered the shopkeeper, flushing crimson and blinking. "But you know, the Lord in His mercy . . . forgave this very thing, . . . forgave a harlot. . . . He has prepared a place for her, and indeed from the life of the holy saint, Mariya of Egypt, one may see in what sense the word is used—excuse me . . ."

The shopkeeper wanted to bring forward some other argument in his justification, but took fright and wiped his lips with his sleeve.

Andrey's fright is not the resistance or anger that we might have been expecting. He doesn't understand why Father Grigory is so mad!

"So that's what you make of it!" cried Father Grigory, clasping his hands. "But you see God has forgiven her—do you understand? He has forgiven, but you judge her, you slander her, call her by an unseemly name, and whom! Your own deceased daughter! Not only in Holy Scripture, but even in worldly literature you won't read of such a sin! I tell you again, Andrey, you mustn't be over-subtle! No, no, you mustn't be over-subtle, brother! If God has given you an inquiring mind, and if you cannot direct it, better not go into things. . . . Don't go into things, and hold your peace!"

The phrase *"Don't be subtle"* is odd. The Russian has it as a colloquial "Don't philosophize."

"But you know, she, . . . excuse my mentioning it, was an actress!" articulated Andrey Andreyich, overwhelmed.

"An actress! But whatever she was, you ought to forget it all now she is dead, instead of writing it on the note."

"Just so, . . ." the shopkeeper assented.

"You ought to do penance," boomed the deacon from the depths of the altar, looking contemptuously at Andrey Andreyich's embarrassed face, "that would teach you to leave off being so clever! Your daughter was a well-known actress. There were even notices of her death in the newspapers. . . . Philosopher!"

"To be sure, . . . certainly," muttered the shopkeeper, "the word is not a seemly one; but I did not say it to judge her, Father Grigory, I only meant to speak spiritually, . . . that it might be clearer to you for whom you were praying. They write in the memorial notes the various callings, such as the infant John, the drowned woman Pelagea, the warrior Yegor, the murdered Pavel, and so on. . . . I meant to do the same."

"It was foolish, Andrey! God will forgive you, but beware another time. Above all, don't be subtle, but think like other people. Make ten bows and go your way."

"I obey," said the shopkeeper, relieved that the lecture was over, and allowing his face to resume its expression of importance and dignity. "Ten bows? Very good, I understand. But now, Father, allow me to ask you a favor. . . . Seeing that I am, anyway, her father, . . . you know yourself, whatever she was, she was still my daughter, so I was, . . . excuse me, meaning to ask you to sing the requiem today. And allow me to ask you, Father Deacon!"

"Well, that's good," said Father Grigory, taking off his vestments. "That I commend. I can approve of that! Well, go your way. We will come out immediately."

Andrey Andreyich walked with dignity from the altar, and with a solemn, requiem-like expression on his red face took his stand in the middle of the church. The verger Matvey set before him a little table with the memorial food upon it, and a little later the requiem service began.

There was perfect stillness in the church. Nothing could be heard but the metallic click of the censer and slow singing. . . . Near Andrey Andreyich stood the verger Matvey, the midwife Makaryevna, and her one-armed son Mitka.

Who makes those little distinctive characterizations as succinctly as Chekhov? He puts us in the small world where we all know "the infant John, the drowned woman Pelagea" and this Mitka, Makaryevna's "one-armed son."

There was no one else. The sacristan sang badly in an unpleasant, hollow bass, but the tune and the words were so mournful that the shopkeeper little by little lost the expression of dignity and was plunged in sadness.

What Chekhov does next is maybe the only conventional turn he makes in the whole story. Touched by his feelings, Andrey "remembers" Mariya's story and their life together.

Chekhov usually conveys background information less conventionally. Or maybe this is just in the nature of narrative or maybe simply what does actually happen in real life at funerals. In reflection, in mourning, we review our history with that person:

> He thought of his Mashutka, . . . he remembered she had been born when he was still a lackey in the service of the owner of Verhny Zaprudy. In his busy life as a lackey he had not noticed how his girl had grown up. That long period during which she was being shaped into a graceful creature, with a little flaxen head and dreamy eyes as big as kopeck-pieces passed unnoticed by him. She had been brought up like all the children of favorite lackeys, in ease and comfort in the company of the young ladies. The gentry, to fill up their idle time, had taught her to read, to write, to dance; he had had no hand in her bringing up. Only from time to time casually meeting her at the gate or on the landing of the stairs, he would remember that she was his daughter, and would, so far as he had leisure for it, begin teaching her the prayers and the scripture. Oh, even then he had the reputation of an authority on the church rules and the holy scriptures!

Andrey, so much like Chekhov's shopkeeping, churchgoing, blunt-speaking father Pavel, is a stickler for rules and distinctions and likes formality.

> Forbidding and stolid as her father's face was, yet the girl listened readily. She repeated the prayers after him yawning, but on the other hand, when he, hesitating and trying to express himself elaborately, began telling her stories, she was all attention. Esau's pottage, the punishment of Sodom, and the troubles of the boy Joseph made her turn pale and open her blue eyes wide.

A point for Andrey. He was a storyteller to his girl. And good at it.

> Afterward when he gave up being a lackey, and with the money he had saved opened a shop in the village, Mashutka had gone away to Moscow with his master's family. . . .
>
> Three years before her death she had come to see her father. He had scarcely recognized her. She was a graceful young woman with the manners of a young lady, and dressed like one. She talked cleverly, as though from a book, smoked, and slept till midday. When Andrey Andreyich asked her what she was doing,

she had announced, looking him boldly straight in the face: "I am an actress." Such frankness struck the former flunky as the acme of cynicism. Mashutka had begun boasting of her successes and her stage life; but seeing that her father only turned crimson and threw up his hands, she ceased.

She knew her father well enough to realize the cause of his dismay.

And they spent a fortnight together without speaking or looking at one another till the day she went away. Before she went away she asked her father to come for a walk on the bank of the river. Painful as it was for him to walk in the light of day, in the sight of all honest people, with a daughter who was an actress, he yielded to her request.

Is it out of place to mention that in fifteen years, Chekhov would marry an actress?

"What a lovely place you live in!" she said enthusiastically. "What ravines and marshes! Good heavens, how lovely my native place is!"

And she had burst into tears.

"The place is simply taking up room . . ." Andrey Andreyich had thought, looking blankly at the ravines, not understanding his daughter's enthusiasm. "There is no more profit from them than milk from a billy-goat."

And she had cried and cried, drawing her breath greedily with her whole chest, as though she felt she had not a long time left to breathe.

Though we judge him as having behaved harshly to her, Andrey has no shame recalling this past. He has complete confidence in his judgment of her; but still, she was his daughter. That's as far as his sentimentality goes—and as far, really, as Chekhov lets ours go.

Andrey Andreyich shook his head like a horse that has been bitten, and to stifle painful memories began rapidly crossing himself. . . .

"Be mindful, O Lord," he muttered, "of Thy departed servant, the harlot Mariya, and forgive her sins, voluntary or involuntary. . . ."

The unseemly word dropped from his lips again, but he did not notice it: what is firmly imbedded in the consciousness cannot be driven out by Father Grigory's exhortations or even knocked out by a nail. Makaryevna sighed and whispered something, drawing in a deep breath, while one-armed Mitka was brooding over something. . . .

"Where there is no sickness, nor grief, nor sighing," droned the sacristan, covering his right cheek with his hand.

Bluish smoke coiled up from the censer and bathed in the broad, slanting patch of sunshine which cut across the gloomy, lifeless emptiness of the church. And it seemed as though the soul of the dead woman were soaring into the sunlight together with the smoke. The coils of smoke like a child's curls eddied around and around, floating upward to the window and, as it were, holding aloof from the woes and tribulations of which that poor soul was full.

This is the place in biographies and literary studies where we read of the various critical reactions to the story, but I think that besides noting that Suvorin clipped off a sentence at the end (there's no trace of that excised sentence), there is nothing to note now except that only Chekhov could have written a story about an oafish yet grieving father that is both touching and funny.

—⁓—

He published three comic Lenten pieces in the second half of February that deal with bliny, the Russian pancakes that are traditional pre-Lenten fare. In "A Foolish Frenchman" ("Glupyi Frantsuz," February 15) a French circus clown in a restaurant on the eve of Lent doesn't understand the Russian custom of gorging on bliny.[11] In "Bliny" (February 19): only women, according to the blathering narrator, can cook them correctly. In "On Mortality: A Carnival Tale" ("O Brennosti," February 22), a man delightedly relishes his plate of bliny but is stricken by a stroke just as he opens his mouth.[12] In these and in other stories about food, Chekhov shows he knew as well as Gogol did how to whet one's appetite.

On February 16, Chekhov had business correspondence with Leykin about the impending book; there were rather a lot of errors in the galley, though Chekhov thought the font and page size were good. Chekhov also had excuses to make about his not having been able to finish a piece for Leykin this past week—there were too many interruptions. He explained that he had woken up early, but now he was going to bed late, as it was almost 2:00 A.M. Besides that, "The practice is picking up a bit," and such medical work would make it harder for him to keep to Leykin's deadlines.

He resisted pointing out that Suvorin would give him whatever time and as much room as he needed.

We know a lot about Chekhov's friendships because we have so many of his letters. His friends and acquaintances saved them. His female friends loved, adored, and, when necessary, forgave him—and saved his letters. In his letters he was a clowning extrovert. We have a short note of his from February 17 to his friend Mikhail Dyukovskiy: "I'm writing you so that you'll have one more autograph of a great writer . . . In 10–20 years you'll be able to sell this letter for 500–1,000 rubles. I envy you." In fact, we know M. M. Dyukovskiy today because he saved this letter. Chekhov mentioned the grand pay he now expected from *New Times*, but asked all the same if his friend could lend him twenty-five rubles.

On the 17th Leykin sent his congratulations to Chekhov for "The Requiem" and added that Suvorin had told him three weeks before that Chekhov would be writing for *New Times*. Those excuses about his medical practice demanding more of his time were, Leykin knew, just excuses. Chekhov had enough time to write for *New Times* but not for *Fragments*! It was hard to keep literary scuttlebutt from Leykin.

Though Chekhov's relationship with Suvorin is the one that takes up more space in biographies and is ultimately more important, in these two years Chekhov's relationship with Leykin was vastly more involving and revealing of his everyday life. Through his excuses to Leykin about why he hadn't been able to write for *Fragments*, we learn all sorts of details that Chekhov didn't normally complain about—but that normal people would have. He rarely shared, except with Leykin, the legitimate excuses about how busy he was with medicine and writing, how hectic and distracting his crowded apartment was, how sick he often felt.

On February 20, he offered Leykin two weeks' worth of reasons for not having any new pieces for *Fragments*: "I cheated you, but you will forgive . . . I'm so tired, crazy and nuts the last couple of weeks that my head's going in circles . . . In my apartment there is a never-ending crowd, uproar, music . . . My office is cold . . . there are patients . . . and so on."[13]

Mostly, usually, he would explain to friends and demonstrate to his family that he very much enjoyed the bustle of home life. He described his medical practice in such a way that he revealed his satisfaction with it; it was rewarding, fulfilling. He was enjoying the challenge of writing under the obligation of artistic creation. He did not, however, let himself complain to Leykin about the pressure he felt writing for *New Times*; he was in the midst of writing "The Witch" for Suvorin, but he didn't share that information.

The writing of weekly skits no longer replenished him as an artist, and Leykin's "demands" dogged him into completing work, but it exhausted him: "The unfinished story will be finished and sent off on time. [. . .] Writing more than I now write, I don't have enough time, or the push or energy, even if you knife me. [. . .] It's time for spring to start. I have such sleeplessness—the devil knows why—that swimming and fresh air are a pressing need."

Chekhov wouldn't get the swimming and perhaps not even the fresh air until May, when he and the family would pack up and leave Moscow for the summer.

Chekhov's correspondence with Suvorin began for good on February 18 when Suvorin wrote Chekhov about the ending that he, Suvorin, had clipped from "The Requiem" and why Chekhov really shouldn't use a pen name. We know these details of Suvorin's letter because Chekhov would reply to those points. We don't have Suvorin's letters because he had them retrieved from Maria Chekhova's possession when Chekhov died in 1904.

Suvorin's motive for retrieving and destroying his letters was his fear that the letters seemed to compromise his reputation as an unblinking right-winger; corresponding with Chekhov, he was much more reasonable than anyone suspected from his newspaper's adamantly pro-autocratic government views. Fortunately, in exchange for his letters, he gave Maria all 337 of Chekhov's letters to him.[14] Chekhov eventually had a sharp falling-out with Suvorin as a result of *New Times*' anti-Semitism and political propaganda, but that number of letters over the period of 1886 to 1903 works out, nonetheless, to about two letters a month.

Suvorin, born in 1834, was twenty-six years older than twenty-six-year-old Chekhov. What did they have in common, anyway, besides that they were both intelligent and independent and grandsons of serfs?[15] Suvorin had built a popular newspaper, and through his support for the tsar he had obtained a monopoly on train-station book kiosks. He was at heart a literary man and did not ever require Chekhov to toe the party line. Chekhov was a forward, liberal, and modern thinker, but as he would declare to Suvorin, he didn't want to belong to *any* party or have to heed anybody's latest political views. That Suvorin's *New Times* was politically right-wing was only problematical when it was.[16]

Pleased by Suvorin's encouragement and attention, Chekhov replied on February 21. For the first time in this year's correspondence Chekhov was shy, formal, deferential, accommodating. That is, he was not quite himself:

> I received your letter. Thanks for the flattering comments on my work, and for the speedy printing of my story. You can judge how refreshing and even inspiring to my authorship is the kind attention of an experienced and talented man like you.

> I share your opinion regarding the omission of the last words of my story, and I thank you for the helpful advice. I have been writing all of six years, but you are the first to take the trouble to advise and guide me.[17]

If editor Leykin had read this letter, his head would have spun around: "*Advice*, Anton Pavlovich? *Guidance*? . . . This means you never read my letters!"

> The pen name A. Chekhonte probably sounds odd and recherche. But it was thought up at the dawn of my misty youth, and I've grown accustomed to it. That's why I don't notice how odd it is.[18]

He apologized for his new submission, "The Witch": "This time I send a story that is exactly double longer than the last and . . . I'm afraid it's doubly worse . . ."[19] That sounds over-humble, but in the disparagement of his story he was completely characteristic; he never praised what he had written. He was aware of each piece's defects. And yet, as far as we can tell from Chekhov's letters, Suvorin never expressed any dissatisfaction or discontent with Chekhov's submissions in these years. Suvorin only wanted *more*. Leykin, a very attentive and critical editor, unrestrainedly and casually disparaged particular pieces. Chekhov's younger brothers and Leykin's right-hand man Bilibin, too, perhaps having grown accustomed to Chekhov's sharp assessments of their work and of his own, matter-of-factly expressed their disappointment with stories by Chekhov that they deemed subpar.

Meanwhile, "Anyuta" (the same, "Anyuta") was published February 22. Leykin had had to deal with the censor's objections to the undisguised sexual exploitation of the good, trusting, vulnerable title character, a young, impoverished medical student's lover and human anatomy dummy:

> "These ribs are like the keys of a piano," he said. "One must familiarize oneself with them somehow, if one is not to get muddled over them. One must study them in the skeleton and the living body. . . . I say, Anyuta, let me pick them out."
>
> Anyuta put down her sewing, took off her blouse, and straightened herself up. Klochkov sat down facing her, frowned, and began counting her ribs.[20]

Anyuta does not know she is special. We observe her exploitation by the medical student and his friends; an artist comes by to get her to pose for him. She is a type, a body, someone intended, they feel, for their use. Chekhov feels for her, brings to light her distinctiveness, her pride, her helplessness: "In the six or seven years of her wanderings from one furnished room to another, she had known five students like Klochkov. Now they had all finished their studies, had gone out into the world, and, of course, like respectable people, had long ago forgotten her."[21] As a former medical student himself, as the brother of and friend of artists, Chekhov was familiar with and ashamed of such behavior and of all such "respectable people."

To not be left in the dust, Leykin wrote Chekhov with a plan: he advised him to certainly keep writing for *New Times*, but to submit rarely to the *Petersburg Gazette*, "because you say you're not in the position to write more than you're writing."[22] He goaded Chekhov to ask the *Gazette*'s editor Sergey Khudekov for more money—he would give it, Leykin assured him—but, in the meantime, he reminded Chekhov, write the story that you started for *Fragments* and were supposed to send by Saturday. Leykin, perhaps to make up for the lack of satisfactory pieces, said he himself would start writing two stories. Chekhov's friend, the architect Schechtel, who had designed the frontispiece for Chekhov's book of stories, wrote a note warning Chekhov that, after his (Schechtel's) conversation with the book's printer, Roman Golike, Chekhov was right not to trust Leykin. What Leykin was trying to do, Schechtel did not make clear.

On February 25, Chekhov received a gift from Leykin: a small sculpture of a dog. Was this the Trojan Horse through which Leykin would overcome Chekhov? Leykin and Chekhov loved dogs, and eventually Leykin would send Chekhov the offspring of his own adored dogs. Chekhov was moving on to a bigger literary world and Leykin was jealous and hurt.

March 1886

Doctors have disgusting days and hours; God forbid anyone experiencing them. It is true that ignoramuses and sneaks are not a rarity among doctors any more than among writers, engineers, people generally, but those disgusting hours and days of which I am speaking fall only to doctors, and because of that, in fairness, much should be forgiven them.

—Letter to Suvorin[1]

Though Chekhov's first letter of March is dated February 28, he wrote it to Bilibin the night of the 28th *after* midnight; he wandered through various topics:

Leykin, when he writes me a letter, has the need to put on the heading not only the year and date, but even the hour of the night that he, sacrificing sleep, writes to his lazy employee. I will imitate him: it's now 2 in the morning . . . Appreciate that! [. . .] I'm busy up to my neck! [. . .]

I write and I doctor. In Moscow typhus spreads rampantly. I'm especially afraid of this typhus. It seems to me that once I got sick from this awfulness, I wouldn't get well, and there are occasions for infection at each step . . . Why aren't I a lawyer instead of a healer? Tonight I went to a girl sick with croup, and every day I go to a Jewish schoolgirl who I am treating for the disease of Nana—small pox. [. . .]

For the themes, merci . . . Oh, how I need themes! I have written about everything [. . .] Going on 5–6 years, I won't be in the position to write a story a year. [. . .][2]

It does sometimes seem that he wrote about "everything," and yet from the contents of his letters we'll see that he let a few of his own experiences go untold, among them suffering from hemorrhoids, performing surgery, conducting gynecological exams, having sexual intercourse, and using certain kinds of rough words. Of course, the mores of his times would not have allowed stories presenting those subjects to be published. Finally, he landed on the subject he only confided to Bilibin:

> However, all that's boring. . . . Let's talk about marriage.
> I'm still not married. With my fiancée, I broke off completely. That is, she broke off with me. But I still didn't even buy a revolver and I don't write journals. Everything in the world is perverse, circular, rough and relative.

This paragraph seems significant, and yet after that glum conclusion, he changed the subject to his book and again to Leykin, and finally to Bilibin's own health. This was an especially diary-like, rambling letter by Chekhov—written after a long day of medical work before going to bed. Was he actually broken up by the breakup? He assured Bilibin he wasn't. Was he putting a fiction to rest? That is, *we pretended we were engaged, and now we're not pretending anymore, and we're certainly not marrying. We were kind of making it all up anyway.*

I'm inclined to think that Chekhov guiltily backed away from Efros, forcing her to do the breaking up.

Why did Chekhov only talk about his engagement to Bilibin? There are no surviving letters from Chekhov to Efros. There are only two surviving letters from her to him, which we will encounter when he does.

———— ⁓ ————

The first two of fifteen stories that Chekhov published in March were about disingenuous young men. "The Big Wig" ("Persona," March 1) describes the daydreams of an eighteen- or nineteen-year-old answering, like hundreds of others, a want ad for a big-wig scribe:

> "I don't know how to compose, Mama," Misha sighed. "I confess I've already sat behind the writing desk five times, and not a line of mine has come. I want to write smartly, but it comes out simple, like you're writing to Auntie in Kremenchug."[3]

Chekhov himself would have preferred reading such "simple" writing to whatever writing Misha might think of as "smart."

> Misha sat behind the table, laid out before him a sheet of paper and set to thinking. After a long while staring at the ceiling, he took the pen and swinging his arm, as all do who venerate their own writing, began, "Your highness! I was born in 1867 in the town of K. to my father Kyrill Nikanoro-vich Naballashnikov and my mother Natalia Ivanovna. My father worked in a sugar factory of the merchant Podgoyskov in the office and received 600 rubles a year. Then he quit and for a long time lived without a place. Then . . ."

Misha, who shares his nickname and perhaps his swinging writing arm with Chekhov's youngest brother (who was born in 1865), did not want to mention his drunken father's death, but he does because for the sake of his poor mother he is more or less begging for a job.

> Misha wrote up a whole page. He wrote sincerely, but pointlessly, without any plan or chronological order, repeating and entangling himself.

He's sincere and any reader would want to give the innocent, earnest, and devoted boy a job. After two weeks of painful anticipation of a reply, he ventures to the Big Wig himself, who scolds him for bothering him, as he already has his scribe.

"Ivan Matveyich" ("Ivan Matveich," March 3), is the next winning, charming, under-prepared young man. Was Chekhov remembering his own earnestness and naïvete, or mostly appreciating those qualities now in his brother Ivan, a year and a half younger than Anton, who indeed had obtained a secretary job himself? Chekhov's youngest brother Mikhail remembered that a friend "once told Anton . . . a story about our brother Ivan needing money so badly that he walked to the other end of the city to do dictation for the writer P. D. Boborykin, on which Anton later drew for his story 'Ivan Matveich.'"[4]

But fifteen stories in a month! Unlike the two young men in these two stories—and in his family—Chekhov was the dreamer who realized his potential and made the most of it.

Ivan Matveyich is less disciplined than Chekhov was. He is eighteen and not unusually is late for duty with "a fairly well-known man of learning." His tardiness this afternoon exasperates the man of learning (otherwise unnamed) to no end: "feeling a craving to vent his wrath and impatience upon someone, the man of learning goes to the door leading to his wife's room and knocks." He announces that is going to fire Ivan finally. The tonic, as his wife knows, is Ivan's presence.

Chekhov enjoys describing Ivan, "with a face oval as an egg and no moustache, wearing a shabby, mangy overcoat and no galoshes." Look at a photo of Chekhov at nineteen:

Chekhov, graduation day in Taganrog, June 1879.

We understand why the employer is charmed: "Seeing the man of learning, [Ivan] smiles with that broad, prolonged, somewhat foolish smile which is seen only on the faces of children or very good-natured people." Ivan Matveyich is irresistible. Chekhov has superimposed for us a childish face on that of a very good-natured young man.

The man of learning corrals him to take dictation. Ivan is sloppy, and the man of learning scolds him for it. They pause for tea and cookies and Ivan happily and greedily partakes. He's hungry. He's a boy! He talks about growing up in the South, in the Don region, not far, actually, from Taganrog, where Chekhov grew up, and how he caught tarantulas, as coincidentally Chekhov also used to do. The man of learning, though crankily impatient, is delighted by Ivan's disingenuous stories. He sees potential in the young man and encourages his further education. They haven't done, after all, very much work by the time Ivan has used up his hours:

> Ivan Matveyich lays down his pen, gets up from the table and sits in another chair. Five minutes pass in silence, and he begins to feel it is time for him to go, that he is in the way; but in the man of learning's study it is so snug and light and warm, and the impression of the nice rusks and sweet tea is still so fresh that there is a pang at his heart at the mere thought of home. At home there is poverty, hunger, cold, his grumbling father, scoldings, and here it is so quiet and unruffled, and interest even is taken in his tarantulas and birds.

Both parties are grateful for the other:

> Almost every evening he sits in this study and always feels something extraor-
> dinarily soft, attracting him, as it were akin, in the voice and the glance of

the man of learning. There are moments when he even fancies that the man of learning is becoming attached to him, used to him, and that if he scolds him for being late, it's simply because he misses his chatter about tarantulas and how they catch goldfinches on the Don.

Chekhov has revealed through the fictional character Ivan Matveyich his brother Ivan's and his own attractiveness to other people—and the attraction of all three of them to culture and leisure. If we're similar to the man of learning, it's because we are fascinated by good-natured hopeful young people. Ivan is attracted to the professor's refined life and in this we see something of the world's attraction to Chekhov: his unpretentiousness, well-meaningness, and his ability to awaken our consciousness of pleasures.

—⁓—

On March 5, Chekhov had to pay the debts that his brothers Alexander and Nikolay had racked up to the merchant Semenov.[5] He wrote to Leykin a few days later: "I have nearly forgotten to tell you a pleasant piece of news. I had to appear in court to answer to a summons and was ordered to pay fifty rubles. If you have ever had to pay someone else's debts, you will appreciate what a revolution these absurd and unexpected 50 rubles have made in my small financial world."[6] What does this say about Alexander and Nikolay? They were talented, young, capable, yet out of fecklessness were willing to cheat a merchant and put their own family in financial jeopardy. Chekhov, as the moral center of the family, tried to rein them in.

While tuberculosis seemed to spur Chekhov into greater action, Nikolay's "reaction to having been given this death sentence," writes Rosamund Bartlett, "was to give up."[7] Yet, even before they both contracted tuberculosis in 1884, Chekhov was frustrated by Nikolay's laziness and drinking. When Chekhov was working on his medical degree and writing weekly pieces for humor magazines, he remarked in a February 1883 letter to Alexander:

> Nikolay is loafing about, as you know very well; a fine, strong Russian talent is being wasted. Another year or two and our artist is finished. He will be lost in the crowd of pub-crawlers. You know his present work. What does he do now? He does everything that is cheap and vulgar, and yet in our drawing room we have a remarkable picture of his which he does not want to finish.

The Russian Theater has asked him to illustrate Dostoevsky. He promised to do so, but he won't keep his promise, and yet these illustrations would have made his reputation and provided him with a piece of bread. . . .[8]

In the youngest Chekhov brother Mikhail's assessment, Nikolay was "highly gifted: talented on both the violin and piano, a serious painter, and an original caricaturist."[9] Ernest Simmons, in his biography, sees Nikolay as Chekhov's closest brother:

[. . .] their mutual recognition of the artist's soul in each drew Nikolay and Anton very close together during these first few years in Moscow. Both loved laughter, music, and nature. Together they bargained with editors, wandered the Moscow streets for material, sat in cheap taverns, and visited the friends they had in common. More important—they worked together, Nikolay illustrating Anton's tales. . . . But [Nikolay] was completely undependable, and no urging of Anton would persuade him to fulfill a commission on time or accept one that he was not in the mood to undertake. He would prefer to talk with his brother about his love affairs—he had already acquired a mistress—and his naïve notion that any girl he cared for ought to be willing to sacrifice her hopes of marriage and a family for the sake of his art. Or he would disappear for several days on a prolonged drunk, returning home finally, late at night, to vomit all over the house; and, fully clothed, he would fall on the divan and pull a covering over his head, his feet sticking out grotesquely in filthy socks filled with holes.[10]

A book of Chekhov's that Nikolay illustrated when Chekhov was twenty-two, *The Prank* (*Shalosht'*), was finished but never published. Nikolay's illustrations are comic and racy, in the fashion of the humor magazines of the time.

Illustrations by Nikolay Chekhov from *The Prank* and other stories.

Then there are the photos from 1882 of the two young creative artists pretending to consider their work:

The brothers Anton and Nikolay consider one of Nikolay's illustrations
for Anton's *The Prank* (1882).

On some date in March, apparently after his payment of his brothers' debt, Chekhov wrote to Nikolay. It is the sole surviving letter to Nikolay from these two years, and it is famous enough to be included in most selections of his letters and to be quoted at length in the biographies. Nikolay otherwise appears in the communications between Anton and Alexander and the rest of the family as the worrisome brother: *What's Nikolay doing? Where is he? He was here. He just left. He might be coming next week.* Now it was time for a reckoning.

My little Zabelin,

I've been told that you have taken offense at gibes Schechtel and I have been making.

Franz Schechtel, the architect and artist, had been a classmate of Nikolay's at art school and became a good friend to Anton. But who told Nikolay about the gibes and who told Anton about Nikolay's having been offended?

The faculty of taking offense is the property of noble souls alone, but even so, if it is all right to laugh at Ivanenko, me, Mishka and Nelly, then why is it wrong to laugh at you? It's unfair. . . . However, if you're not joking and really do feel you've been offended, I hasten to apologize.

People only laugh at what's funny or what they don't understand. . . . Take your choice. The latter of course is more flattering, but—alas!—to me, for one, you're no riddle. It's not hard to understand someone with whom you've shared the delights of Tatar caps, Voutsina, Latin and, finally, life in Moscow. And besides, your life is psychologically so uncomplicated that even a non-seminarian could understand it. Out of respect for you let me be frank. You're angry, offended . . . but it's not because of my gibes or of that good-natured chatterbox Dolgov. The fact of the matter is that you're a decent person and you realize that you're living a lie. And, whenever a person feels guilty, he always looks outside himself for vindication: the drunk blames his troubles [on his grief], Putyata blames the censors, the man who bolts from Yakimanka Street [where the Chekhovs were living] with lecherous intent blames the cold in the living room or gibes, and so on. If I were to abandon the family to the whims of fate, I would try to find myself an excuse in Mother's character or my blood spitting or the like.

What's that? Evgenia Chekhova was sacred territory. What excuse would there be in their mother's character? Chekhov never ever said. But he wouldn't let Nikolay blame their mother; she was Anton's mother, too! And he couldn't let Nikolay have the tuberculosis excuse, as he himself had it. Those were ready-made excuses, "lies," and if Anton cut Nikolay off from those, his brother was going to have to turn back and look at himself. Doing so would reveal to him where the remedy was.

[. . .] You're no riddle to me, and it is also true that you can be wildly ridicu-lous. You're nothing but an ordinary mortal, and we mortals are enigmatic only when we're stupid, and we're ridiculous forty-eight weeks a year. Isn't that so?[11]

How does one effectively argue with a sibling, talk him out of self-pity and back to decency? I don't know of a better example than Chekhov's:

You have often complained to me that people "don't understand you"! Goethe and Newton did not complain of that. . . . Only Christ complained of it, but He was speaking of His doctrine and not of Himself. . . . People understand you perfectly well. And if you do not understand yourself, it is not their fault.

Chekhov was trying to shake Nikolay from his position of self-pity and egotism. He compared him to great men, with whom Nikolay would not have dreamed of comparing himself, and he aligned him with Jesus and then radically distinguished them.

Chekhov was not writing for an audience. He was writing to one absolutely particular person in the world, someone he knew better than he knew anyone else:

> I assure you as a brother and as a friend I understand you and feel for you with all my heart. I know your good qualities as I know my five fingers; I value and deeply respect them. If you like, to prove that I understand you, I can enumerate those qualities. I think you are kind to the point of softness, magnanimous, unselfish, ready to share your last farthing; you have no envy nor hatred; you are simple-hearted, you pity men and beasts; you are trustful, without spite or guile, and do not remember evil. . . .

We'll pause here with Chekhov's latest ellipsis. He needed Nikolay to respect himself, to appreciate himself. He needed Nikolay to trust that he saw him clearly, that he saw the best in him. His approach was through generosity, sympathy, forgiveness. And then he sprang on us (eavesdroppers!) and on Nikolay the responsibility Nikolay bore:

> You have a gift from above such as other people have not: you have talent. This talent places you above millions of men, for on earth only one out of two millions is an artist. Your talent sets you apart: if you were a toad or a tarantula, even then, people would respect you, for to talent all things are forgiven.

Nice touch with the toad and the Taganrog tarantula! Nikolay had something precious that needed to continue to be cultivated. Did Anton at this point foresee that his own talent in literature was the gift *he* would cultivate? As acts of generosity to his fellow humans, medicine fit the bill. Dr. John Coope observes that Chekhov "sometimes treats his medical work as self-evidently valuable whilst his literature was done out of self-indulgence, or justified by bringing him in an income."[12] But Chekhov's medical talent was not one in two million. And so far, Chekhov's literary talent has shown itself as rare as perhaps one in two billion.

> You have only one failing, and the falseness of your position, and your unhappiness and your catarrh of the bowels are all due to it. That is your utter lack

of culture. Forgive me, please, but *veritas magis amicitiae* [truth is a better friend]. . . . You see, life has its conditions. In order to feel comfortable among educated people, to be at home and happy with them, one must be cultured to a certain extent. Talent has brought you into such a circle, you belong to it, but . . . you are drawn away from it, and you vacillate between cultured people and the lodgers *vis-a-vis*. It's the bourgeois side of you coming out, the side raised on birch thrashings beside the wine cellar and handouts, and it's hard to overcome, terribly hard.[13]

That is, it was their father's side, those "birch thrashings," that had developed Nikolay's worst tendencies. Did Anton hate their father so much he preferred not naming him? In writing intimately to his brother, who suffered the abuse alongside him, he could refer to the events about which they and Alexander would wince. Chekhov was working like mad to ensure that such shame didn't return.

But how is one to be a decent person? Chekhov, whom I love as a literary artist for seeming not to give us lessons, for describing irreducible situations from which there does not seem to be a solution, had, like a doctor rather than a writer, a remedy for Nikolay:

Cultured people must, in my opinion, satisfy the following conditions:
1. They respect human personality, and therefore they are always kind, gentle, polite, and ready to give in to others.

This is what Anton had striven to attain and maintain—and his brother could not call him out on this because he and his family and friends knew it was true of him. What recent specific incidents did Anton have in mind in regard to Nikolay?

They do not make a row because of a hammer or a lost piece of India-rubber; if they live with anyone they do not regard it as a favor and, going away, they do not say "nobody can live with you."

So we know that Nikolay did *all that*. What he couldn't do was what Anton and the rest of the family could do:

They forgive noise and cold and dried-up meat and witticisms and the presence of strangers in their homes.

Like bystanders in a restaurant or on a train (only less innocent as we have sidled right next to them on purpose), we know more than we have a right to know about the conditions in the Chekhov household. We know Nikolay had lost his temper over trifles; we know he had blamed his family rather than himself for the atmosphere in the apartment; we know what Anton himself had had to bear and forgive.

> 2. They have sympathy not for beggars and cats alone. Their heart aches for what the eye does not see.[14] If for instance, Pyotr knows that his father and mother are turning gray and losing sleep over seeing their Pyotr so rarely (and seeing him drunk when he does turn up), then he rushes home to them and sends his vodka to the devil. They do not sleep nights the better to help the Polevayevs, help pay their brothers' tuition, and keep their mother decently dressed.

These were Anton's challenges. Why did he write so much in these years? To keep the family afloat and sailing toward calmer seas. And we know that Nikolay, meanwhile, didn't even let his anxious mother know of his whereabouts, and we know that when he did show up, he might be drunk. What could Nikolay do? Just what Anton had been doing.

> 3. They respect the property of others, and therefore pay their debts.

Having had to pay off Nikolay's debts to the merchant, he had the perfect right to press his bootheel on Nikolay's toes.

> 4. They are sincere, and dread lying like fire. They don't lie even in small things. A lie is insulting to the listener and puts him in a lower position in the eyes of the speaker. They do not pose, they behave in the street as they do at home, they do not show off before their humbler comrades. They are not given to babbling and forcing their uninvited confidences on others. Out of respect for other people's ears they more often keep silent than talk.

Was Chekhov less merciful here to his brother than he tried to be to his dissolute characters? Perhaps, but this is a family intervention and a matter more personal than art. Anton conveyed understanding of Nikolay's character not in artistic fashion but through expressions of care. There were specific things Nikolay could do better.

Anton was not telling Nikolay "Be like me" or "Follow my lead." He was asserting, rather, that in the interests of independence and dignity such behavior needed to be set in stone. He believed, for now, that it was possible for Nikolay to come back to his better self. He was writing to an equal—a wavering equal who had the capacity to right himself.

> 5. They do not disparage themselves to rouse compassion. They do not play on the strings of other people's hearts so that they may sigh and make much of them. They do not say "I am misunderstood," or "I have become second-rate," because all this is striving after cheap effect, is vulgar, stale, false. . . .

Don't be pathetic, Nikolay! So much of Chekhov's character, like his art, shows restraint. It pained him to see Alexander and Nikolay letting go.

> 6. They have no shallow vanity. They do not care for such false diamonds as knowing celebrities, shaking hands with the drunken P., ecstasy over the first person they happen to meet at the Salon de Varietes, being renowned in the taverns. . . . If they do a pennyworth, they do not strut about as though they had done a hundred rubles' worth, and do not brag of having the entry where others are not admitted. . . . The truly talented always keep in obscurity among the crowd, as far as possible from advertisement. . . . Even Krylov has said that an empty barrel echoes more loudly than a full one.

Chekhov was himself having to be leery of the thrill of getting to know (and be known by) celebrities. To his family, he did indeed exult about meeting the famous writers in Petersburg, but he did not otherwise namedrop. I would guess he believed that it was good for the family to realize that he was becoming known and that his being in the public eye was another reason they should all behave.

> 7. If they have a talent they respect it. They sacrifice to it rest, women, wine, vanity. . . . They are proud of their talent[15] and so they do not go out carousing with trade-school employees or Skvortsov's guests, realizing that their calling lies in exerting an uplifting influence on them, not in living with them. Besides, they are fastidious.

By now, if I were Nikolay reading this letter, my head would be hanging. Maybe I would also become defensive: "What's wrong with Skvortsov's guests?!" I think Anton knew Nikolay would review this letter more than once, and that even if he read it and felt hurt, Nikolay was intelligent and sensitive, and he would get it, as Anton's plan of action was clear, and the points were specific. Nikolay had "talent," that rare valuable gift that "cultured people" must respect and honor in themselves.

8. They develop the aesthetic feeling in themselves. They cannot go to sleep in their clothes, see cracks full of bugs on the walls, breathe bad air, walk on a floor that has been spat upon, cook their meals over an oil stove. They seek as far as possible to restrain and ennoble the sexual instinct. . . .[16] to endure her logic and never stray from her. What's the point of it all? People with good breeding[17] are not as coarse as that. What they want in a woman is not a bed-fellow or horse sweat, [Soviet edition deletion] not the kind of intelligence that expresses itself in the ability to stage a fake pregnancy and tirelessly reel off lies. They want especially, if they are artists, freshness, elegance, humanity, the capacity for motherhood, not a [Soviet edition deletion]. They do not swill vodka at all hours of the day and night, do not sniff at cupboards, for they are not pigs and know they are not. They drink only when they are free, on occasion. . . . For they want *mens sana in corpore sano.*

I imagine that Nikolay, who has been dead now for more than a hundred and thirty years, squirms every time someone reads this letter.

And so on. This is what cultured people are like. In order to be cultured and not to stand below the level of your surroundings it is not enough to have read "The Pickwick Papers" and learnt a monologue from "Faust." It is not enough to hail a cab and drive off to Yakimanka Street if all you're going to do is bolt out again a week later.

Chekhov identified one of Nikolay's patterns: Return home, be at loose ends, and then flee.

What is needed is constant work, day and night, constant reading, study, will. . . . Every hour is precious for it. . . . Come to us, smash the vodka bottle, lie down and read. . . . Turgenev, if you like, whom you have not read. . . . You must drop your [Soviet edition deletion] vanity, you are not a

child . . . you will soon be thirty. It is time! I expect you. . . . We all expect
you. . . .

Yours,

A. Chekhov

Now what? This is an important letter because it *worked*?

No, it didn't work. Nikolay stayed away, except, as far as the record shows, for a visit
to Babkino for a spell this summer and next summer. Nikolay did not produce much
more with his rare artistic talent.

Is it possible that Chekhov's letter to Nikolay closed a door between them? Had it been
too much? Was it simply too late?

This is the last surviving letter Chekhov ever wrote to Nikolay.

Nikolay died in 1889, at thirty-one.

Chekhov's second story for Suvorin and *New Times*, "The Witch," takes an exciting turn.
On the night of a snowstorm, the sexton Savely believes that his restless, sexually frustrated
wife is somehow luring men to their remote cabin.

The wife tells her jealous husband: "'When father was alive and living here, all sorts of
people used to come to him to be cured of the ague: from the village, and the hamlets, and
the Armenian settlement. They came almost every day, and no one called them devils. But
if anyone once a year comes in bad weather to warm himself, you wonder at it, you silly, and
take all sorts of notions into your head at once.'" The sexton has the self-torturing assured-
ness of all jealous people, but he tops off that characteristic with a bent for superstition:

> "It's not for nothing the postman is lost! Blast my eyes if the postman isn't
> looking for you! Oh, the devil is a good hand at his work; he is a fine one to
> help! He will turn him around and around and bring him here. I know, I see!
> You can't conceal it, you devil's bauble, you heathen wanton! As soon as the
> storm began I knew what you were up to."
>
> "Here's a fool!" smiled his wife. "Why, do you suppose, you thick-head,
> that I make the storm?"

She calls him out on his suspicions. If she had such power, we know and she knows,
Savely would be toast.

". . . Whether it's your doing or not, I only know that when your blood's
on fire there's sure to be bad weather, and when there's bad weather there's
bound to be some crazy fellow turning up here. It happens so every time! So
it must be you!"

And of course Savely is ridiculous: *there's no such thing as witches!* And yet, once we see
her in the presence of the postman, we can't help wondering:

> The postman began undoing the knot in his hood. The sexton's wife gazed
> into his eyes, and seemed trying to look right into his soul.
> "You ought to have a cup of tea . . ." she said.

The weary postman is hooked:

> And the postman, not yet quite awake, not yet quite able to shake off the intoxi-
> cating sleep of youth and fatigue, was suddenly overwhelmed by a desire for the
> sake of which mail-bags, postal trains . . . and all things in the world, are forgotten.
> He glanced at the door in a frightened way, as though he wanted to escape or hide
> himself, seized Raissa around the waist, and was just bending over the lamp to
> put out the light, when he heard the tramp of boots in the outer room, and the
> driver appeared in the doorway. Savely peeped in over his shoulder. The postman
> dropped his hands quickly and stood still as though irresolute.

Okay, I admit the postman might also believe Raissa is a witch. And Chekhov, in this
month of March, wonders here, as he will in next week's "Agafya," what is it, how is it
that we can be "overwhelmed by a desire for the sake of which [. . .] all things in the world
are forgotten"? What does it mean that there are desires bigger than all our conscious
and deliberate choices?

He wrote to Leykin on March 8 to compliment the proofreader who had reviewed the
first galley of *Motley Stories*: "I didn't find a single mistake on all of the five sheets.
You're right when you called her ideal. If of course she wouldn't be insulted and if
you advise me so, on the publication of the book I will give her something."[18] He also
caught up Leykin on his brothers; namely, that Alexander "is crawling with debt and

wants to get out of Novorossiysk. . . . The Devil knows how he arranges his life! He doesn't drink, smoke, attend balls, but he can't live in the provinces at 120–150 rubles a month, while I with a big family for the last 2–3 years live in Moscow at 100–120 rubles. Apparently, he lives disgustingly, eats crap!" Leykin would question Chekhov's own financial management. It might seem to some of us that the twenty-six-year-old was managing pretty well.

Meanwhile, Chekhov told Leykin, "Today I went to Nikolay and brought him back home. He only just received the money from *The Whole World Illustrated*, to which he gave Aksakov's funeral. He lives of course not just as he might. To my question if he desired to work for *Fragments*, he answered: 'Of course! Tomorrow I'm sending them a drawing!'" Chekhov added, in case Leykin wasn't skeptical enough already, that the "tomorrow" might mean weeks or months. Though Maria Chekhova as an editor twenty years later of her brother's letters didn't suggest an early or any particular March date of Chekhov's long letter to Nikolay, the mentions of Alexander's debts and Chekhov's retrieval of Nikolay on March 7 from some sort of dissipated setting indicate that the letter had been sent and received, and that Chekhov was now following up and bringing Nikolay back under the family's wing.

On Chekhov's medical day off, Sunday, he would be writing Leykin a new piece (probably "My Conversation with the Postmaster"), "if nothing bothers me."

By the time Chekhov wrote Leykin on March 4 about the distractions he had had while writing "Poison" ("Otrava," published March 8), he was writing or about to write "A Story without an End" ("Rasskaz bez Kontsa," March 10), in which an unnamed narrator tells of being awakened in the middle of the night to go check on the lodger of an old landlady next door. Confused, annoyed, he goes to investigate and finds a coffin with a body in it and discovers in the dark a man who has shot himself but is still alive. The impoverished and grieving husband Vassilyev is a suicide in all but achievement, as the bullet has passed through his ribs and out his back. The narrator, though not a doctor, neatly analyzes the wound and helps patch up Vassilyev and listens to him. (The narrator would have gone for a doctor, but the wounded man doesn't want him to leave.)

The crummy living situation suggests to the narrator what has led to this double tragedy:

> I sat silent, looking about the room into which fate had brought me so unex-
> pectedly. What poverty! This man who was the possessor of a handsome,
> effeminate face and a luxuriant well-tended beard, had surroundings which a
> humble working man would not have envied. A sofa with its American-leather

torn and peeling, a humble greasy-looking chair, a table covered with a little
bit of paper, and a wretched oleograph on the wall, that was all I saw. Damp,
gloomy, and gray.[19]

Vassilyev is irritated when the narrator recognizes him from a party in which Vassilyev
was an actor "in some private theatricals":

"I don't understand your curiosity," he muttered. "You'll be asking me next
what it was drove me to commit suicide!"

Before a minute had passed, he turned around toward me again, opened
his eyes and said in a tearful voice:

"Excuse me for taking such a tone, but you'll admit I'm right! To ask a
convict how he got into prison, or a suicide why he shot himself is not generous . . . and indelicate. To think of gratifying idle curiosity at the expense
of another man's nerves!"

"There is no need to excite yourself. . . . It never occurred to me to question
you about your motives."

"You would have asked. . . . It's what people always do. Though it would
be no use to ask. If I told you, you would not believe or understand. . . .
I must own I don't understand it myself. . . . There are phrases used in
the police reports and newspapers such as: 'unrequited love,' and 'hopeless
poverty,' but the reasons are not known. . . . They are not known to me,
nor to you, nor to your newspaper offices, where they have the impudence
to write 'The diary of a suicide.' God alone understands the state of a
man's soul when he takes his own life; but men know nothing about it."

This complaint or observation is Chekhov's as much as it is Vassilyev's. We outsiders
assign motives and reasons to others' actions—and yet even the person who has taken
the action doesn't know why they did it. Although Chekhov himself could have spoken
Vassilyev's next words, the narrator is skeptical; he says that Vassilyev "went on in the
tone of some great professor":

"Man will never understand the psychological subtleties of suicide! How can
one speak of reasons? Today the reason makes one snatch up a revolver, while
tomorrow the same reason seems not worth a rotten egg. It all depends most
likely on the particular condition of the individual at the given moment. . . .

Take me for instance. Half an hour ago, I had a passionate desire for death, now when the candle is lighted, and you are sitting by me, I don't even think of the hour of death. Explain that change if you can! Am I better off, or has my wife risen from the dead? Is it the influence of the light on me, or the presence of an outsider?"

"The light certainly has an influence . . ." I muttered for the sake of saying something. "The influence of light on the organism. . . ."

"The influence of light. . . . We admit it! But you know men do shoot themselves by candle-light! And it would be ignominious indeed for the heroes of your novels if such a trifling thing as a candle were to change the course of the drama so abruptly. All this nonsense can be explained perhaps, but not by us. It's useless to ask questions or give explanations of what one does not understand. . . ."

Besides that the narrator is an author (of humor pieces, in fact), he does not closely resemble Chekhov—except perhaps at this next moment, when he says, abruptly and to my and Vassilyev's surprise:

"Forgive me," I said, "but . . . judging by the expression of your face, it seems to me that at this moment you . . . are posing."

"Yes," Vassilyev said, startled. "It's very possible! I am naturally vain and fatuous. Well, explain it, if you believe in your power of reading faces! Half an hour ago I shot myself, and just now I am posing. . . . Explain that if you can."

But why does Chekhov then let the nearly hysterical, possibly "posing" Vassilyev make what are actually Chekhov's own philosophical musings? He won't let us or his narrator "explain that." We can't; this is one of Chekhov's assertions about human psychology, and is not a point of argument. At his most sincere and earnest, he puts his own words into the mouth of an *actor*, who may or may not be posing. This is for Chekhov's sake—not to disguise his beliefs, but to test them, to try them out in a situ[20]ation of someone experiencing the feelings.[21]

About the word "posing." The verb in Russian is *risovat'*—to draw, to paint, and, figuratively, to portray. As I understand it, Chekhov is talking about the self-dramatizing impulse: *I feel so bad I want to kill myself. Let me prove that feeling to the world—and do it!* His good friend, the painter Isaac Levitan, was something of a poser himself, continually threatening suicide.[22]

This story's inspiration was not of the immediate moment, but from an incident in early January 1886 involving an acquaintance of Chekhov's, Pyotr Kicheev, an editor at *The Alarm Clock*, who shot himself, but the bullet was a dud, and a few days later Kicheev was making jokes.[23] (Perhaps Kicheev recognized that event in this story and resented it; in any case, in late 1887 he reviewed and panned Chekhov's *Ivanov*, a play that features a "successful" suicide.)

Vassilyev anticipates his wife's funeral the next day. From his musings, it is not after all clear to me if Vassilyev is actually an actor or just an educated person who quotes *Hamlet* and happened to be included in General Lukhachev's "theatricals."

> "Ah. . . . Do you remember how I pranced about like a needle, like an enthusiastic ass at those private theatricals when I was courting Zina? It was stupid, but it was good, it was fun. . . . The very memory of it brings back a whiff of spring. . . . And now! What a cruel change of scene! There is a subject for you! Only don't you go in for writing 'the diary of a suicide.' That's vulgar and conventional. You make something humorous of it."
>
> "Again you are . . . posing," I said. "There's nothing humorous in your position."
>
> "Nothing laughable? You say nothing laughable?" Vassilyev sat up, and tears glistened in his eyes. An expression of bitter distress came into his pale face. His chin quivered.
>
> "You laugh at the deceit of cheating clerks and faithless wives," he said [as Chekhov indeed did laugh], "but no clerk, no faithless wife has cheated as my fate has cheated me! I have been deceived as no bank depositor, no duped husband has ever been deceived! Only realize what an absurd fool I have been made! Last year before your eyes I did not know what to do with myself for happiness. And now before your eyes. . . ."
>
> Vassilyev's head sank on the pillow and he laughed.
>
> "Nothing more absurd and stupid than such a change could possibly be imagined. Chapter one: spring, love, honeymoon . . . honey, in fact; chapter two: looking for a job, the pawnshop, pallor, the chemist's shop, and . . . tomorrow's splashing through the mud to the graveyard."

The narrator leaves Vassilyev to get medication from the chemist's, and returns to find Vassilyev having torn his bandages off and unconscious. In the morning, after the funeral service, the narrator accompanies Vassilyev to and from the cemetery.

The story without an ending has a break in time: "Only one year has passed since that night." The narrator is now hosting a lively gathering that includes Vassilyev and two young women. He interrupts Vassilyev to show him the story so far—the story is everything up to what we have just read:

> Always condescending about my authorship, he stifles a sigh, the sigh of a lazy reader, sits down in an armchair and begins upon it.
> "Hang it all, what horrors," he mutters with a smile.

I imagine Chekhov in his study having handed over a manuscript to an impatient friend or brother and watching its effects.

> But the further he gets into the reading, the graver his face becomes. At last, under the stress of painful memories, he turns terribly pale, he gets up and goes on reading as he stands. When he has finished he begins pacing from corner to corner.

Chekhov is famous for the open-endedness of his stories—that they reflect the title of this story and have no end. The narrator, like Chekhov, doesn't know how or if stories of actual human beings end, if not by death.

> "How does it end?" I ask him.
> "How does it end? H'm. . . ."
> He looks at the room, at me, at himself. . . . He sees his new fashionable suit, hears the ladies laughing and . . . sinking on a chair, begins laughing as he laughed on that night.
> "Wasn't I right when I told you it was all absurd? My God! I have had burdens to bear that would have broken an elephant's back; the devil knows what I have suffered—no one could have suffered more, I think, and where are the traces? It's astonishing. One would have thought the imprint made on a man by his agonies would have been everlasting, never to be effaced or eradicated. And yet that imprint wears out as easily as a pair of cheap boots. There is nothing left, not a scrap. It's as though I hadn't been suffering then, but had been dancing a mazurka. Everything in the world is transitory, and that transitoriness is absurd! A wide field for humorists! Tack on a humorous end, my friend!"

The would-be suicide asks how can there be no evidence remaining of that long terrible night? So many suicides . . . and this one, interrupted and botched, shows him
or us what? Suicide is folly? Pointless? That all such shows of dramatic grief ought
to be discounted? He is not saying he's lucky—but that the grief dissipates, as if
mocking us. *That* is the disappointment. We can end our lives on a sincere, sane
impulse, and yet if we accidentally survive, we find life quite satisfactory enough to
keep participating in it.

Chekhov doesn't think that any of these questions and reflections are funny and neither
does the humor-writer narrator, who, like Chekhov, recognizes the limitations of a comic
or tragic denouement.

And yet the narrator wants an ending, something to settle down upon, to conclude
once and for all, to give him and his readers peace of mind:

> "How will it end?" I ask myself aloud.
>
> Vassilyev, whistling and straightening his tie, walks off into the drawing
> room, and I look after him, and feel vexed. For some reason I regret his past
> sufferings, I regret all that I felt myself on that man's account on that terrible
> night. It is as though I had lost something. . . .

Chekhov won't comfort us with an answer that isn't there. He has described what has
come to be recognized as Chekhovian—a story without an end. Feelings have been roused;
reflections on fate have been stirred. Are such experiences a waste?

There is, perhaps, a latter-day reflection that shows that Chekhov believed that the
unsettled ending is probably, because it doesn't lie, the closest we can come to truth. In
May 1888, Chekhov wrote to Suvorin, who by then was his most serious friend and correspondent concerning literary and philosophical topics:

> It seems to me that the writer of fiction should not try to solve such questions
> as those of God, pessimism, etc. His business is but to describe those who have
> been speaking or thinking about God and pessimism, how, and under what
> circumstances. The artist should be, not the judge of his characters and their
> conversations, but only an unbiased witness. . . . My business is merely to be
> talented, i.e., to be able to distinguish between important and unimportant
> statements, to be able to illuminate the characters and speak their language. . . .
> The time has come for writers, especially those who are artists, to admit that
> in this world one cannot make anything out, just as Socrates once admitted

it, just as Voltaire admitted it. The mob think they know and understand everything; the more stupid they are, the wider, I think, do they conceive their horizon to be. And if an artist in whom the crowd has faith decides to declare that he understands nothing of what he sees—this in itself constitutes a considerable clarity in the realm of thought, and a great step forward.[24]

Though Chekhov and others would see this period of his life as being under Tolstoy's influence, he was asserting something in direct opposition to the ambitions of Tolstoy and Dostoevsky: They were problem-solvers. They thought they could make out the world. Chekhov believed in many things, but he did not believe in his powers to comprehend human life. See it and describe it, like a doctor, like a psychologist, like a generous man, that he could do—but he was no prophet or visionary.

—◇—

The knot that I can't untie, but that I keep worrying over, is Chekhov's relationship with Dunya Efros. He wrote in his usual jokey tone to Bilibin on March 11, and it seems to me he was creating his own comically unhappy and ill-matched "marriage" in contrast to Bilibin's real one:

> I've split from my fiancée to the farthest measure. Yesterday we saw each other, I spoke about devilish things (the devilish things we have in Moscow are modern furniture), I complained to her about being broke, but she told me that her brother-Jew drew a three-ruble note so perfectly that the illusion was complete: the cleaning woman picked it up and put it in her pocket. That's all. I'm not going to write to you anything more about her.
>
> Maybe you're right saying that it's too early for me to marry . . . I'm light-minded, despite that I'm only a year younger than you . . . I still at times dream of grammar school: an unlearned lesson and a fear that the teacher is going to call me out . . . Perhaps I'm a youth. [. . .][25]

And here, readers, we can squirm together, as Chekhov, commenting on Bilibin's weakness as a humor writer, described a particular kind of lovemaking:

> Your one fault—your softness [. . .]. If you're not afraid of the comparison, you as an essayist are similar to a lover to whom the woman says: "You do it

tenderly . . . I need it rougher!" (À propos: a woman is just like a chicken—she loves to be beaten at the very moment.) You do it particularly tenderly . . ."[26]

Well? Can we suppose that Chekhov and a lover had gone at it in a rough manner? We can wish Chekhov was as enlightened as we are in 2022 and that he would watch his language and behavior, but . . . ! And here I also imagine Bilibin, who had been offended by the sexual suggestiveness of "The Witch," blushing. "A Little Joke" would be published the next day. The sexuality in that story and the reference here suggest that lately, at least, Chekhov was thinking a lot about sex. That is, when he was not terrified of a doctor's everyday danger: "In Moscow," he told Bilibin, "typhus (spotted) is raging, taking off in a very short time six of my fellow graduates. I'm afraid! I'm not afraid of anything, but I'm afraid of this typhus . . . It's as if there is something mysterious about it."

<center>~~~</center>

On March 12, "A Little Joke" ("Shutochka") was published in *The Cricket* in Moscow under the pen name "A Person without Means." Was Chekhov purposefully hiding this story from his friends? Did he think the censors would nab it in Petersburg if he submitted it to Leykin for *Fragments*? He had published one story in *The Cricket* in January, and the next would be in September. It wasn't his usual landing spot, but this was 1886, and he was firing off stories so quickly he later completely forgot some of them. This one he remembered and would substantially revise for the *Collected Works*.

"A Little Joke" is often anthologized in Russian and English; it is about a young couple sledding. I read it in Russian a few times before I started to imagine that there was more to Chekhov's little joke than the narrator's mischievous trick.

By medical, psychological, and literary reflex, Chekhov describes the physiological changes his characters go through. He's being "objective." What if one stands outside of the moral and subjective judgments and observes instead how people under stress or excitement breathe, move, and express themselves?

I'm going to quote from my own translation, rather than Constance Garnett's perfectly good one, because my realizations about the story came in the midst of translating it from Russian. Chekhov starts some stories with a weather report, as if he needs to take one step into the setting: "A clear winter noontime . . ." and there he is, almost instantaneously, in its midst, able to look, hear, and smell around. He has made himself aware of his immediate surroundings. Grounded like so, he could then fly off for five or ten pages. At the end of this flight he has made a Story.

A clear winter noontime. . . .[27] A strong frost, it cracks, and Nadenka, who holds me by the arm, has silver frost covering the curls on her temples and the down on her upper lip. We stand atop a high hill. The sun is shining on the sloping surface as if on a mirror that extends from our feet to the ground below. A small sled, upholstered in bright red cloth, is beside us.

"Let's go down, Nadezhda Petrovna!" I beg her. "Just once! I assure you that we'll be safe and sound."

A young man tries to persuade a young woman that they try something she fears is dangerous: "Just once!" But how can we tell he's a young man? Is it his casualness, which is more apparent in the Russian? And how can we tell she's a young woman? It's a combination of her nickname, "Nadenka" for Nadezhda ("Hope"), her naïvete, and the "down on her upper lip" that the unnamed narrator notices that suggests she's young:

But Nadenka is frightened. All that space from her little boots to the end of the icy hill seems terrifying to her, an immeasurably deep abyss. When I only suggest just sitting in the sled, her breath freezes and halts as she glances down; but what will happen if she risks flying into the abyss! She will die, she'll go out of her mind.

"I beg you!" I say. "You don't need to be frightened. Just understand, this is faintheartedness, cowardice!"

This is sledding down a hill, that's all. Why is she so scared? And, as I reflect remembering what it was like to be a young man myself in the company of an attractive young woman, why is it so important to him that she take a ride with him? How big a thrill could sledding be to him, and if it's such a big thrill, why doesn't he, with a swagger, go himself, alone?

Nadenka finally gives in, and I see by her face she is setting out risking her life. I seat her shaking in the sled, pale, and I wrap my arm around her and together we descend into the abyss.

It's just a sled-ride, isn't it? Another word for abyss, *bezdna* in Russian, is "neverendingness."

The sled flies like a bullet. The tearing air beats in our faces, roars, whistles in our ears, rips painfully, nips from spite, wants to tear our heads off our shoulders. From the wind pressure it's an effort to breathe. It seems the devil

himself has seized us in his paws and with a roar is dragging us into Hell. The
surrounding objects slide into one long extended streak. . . . Here, here, one
more moment and it seems—we'll be destroyed!

"I love you, Nadya!" I say in an undertone.

The sled begins running quieter and quieter, the roar of the wind and the
buzzing of the sled-runners is less terrifying, our breath comes back to life,
and we finally get down. Nadenka is neither living nor dead. She's pale, barely
breathing. . . . I help her get up.

Quite an experience for young Nadenka! But there, not yet identified as such by
Chekhov or the narrator, is the "little joke," the narrator's unconscious or perhaps cal-
culated teasing declaration of love in the midst of their sensory overload. Did he mean
it? Does he know?

"I'm not going another time for anything," she says, looking at me with wide,
terror-filled eyes. "Not for anything in the world! I nearly died!"

To this the narrator says . . . nothing! He doesn't apologize, he doesn't argue with her
about her exaggeration of the danger. He doesn't tell her that he knows from experience
that she'll likely want to try it again.

In a little while, she comes back to herself and is already questioningly looking
me in the eyes: had I said those four words or had she only heard them in
the din of the whirlwind? I stand beside her, I smoke and carefully examine
my glove.

How infuriating he is. He won't confess, he won't disabuse her. He can pretend he
didn't say what he said or maybe he wants her to decide what she should do about that
declaration. The joke for now is that the burden is on Nadenka:

She takes me by my arm, and we wander by the hill for a long while. The riddle
is obviously not giving her peace. Had the words been said or not? Yes, or no?
Yes, or no? This is a question of self-love, honor, life, happiness; the question
is very important, the most important in the world. Nadenka impatiently,
sadly, with a pronounced expression, peeks at my face, answers randomly,
waits, whether I will speak.

The only passage that seems better in the original 1886 version of the story is this [the underlined phrases are identical between the versions]:

> This is a question of self-love, honor . . . you cannot joke about this!! Nadenka continually looks me in the face, answers inattentively, impatiently presses her lips . . . Her face flickers with happiness, now twitches under a rueful cloud . . . Soon I notice a struggle in her, a wobbly feminine spirit . . . She stops, she apparently wants to say something, ask about something, but is completely unable to gather the strength . . . [28]

Back to the final version:

> Oh, what play on this sweet face, what play![29] I see her wrestling with herself, she needs to say something, ask about something, but she can't find the words, she's awkward, terrified, the joy confuses her. . . .

"Joy"? What joy? Where has that come from? The terror has receded and exposes the undisguised thrill. We have seen this in children, their apprehension becoming appreciation. But Nadenka is a young lady.

> "You know what?" she says, not looking at me.
> "What?" I ask.
> "Let's go one more time . . . let's ride."

Every time I read this story now I cannot help thinking that Chekhov was playing another kind of joke on us. The humor magazines of his time were full of sexual innuendos in their illustrations and skits. I will suggest now that the narrator has introduced the hesitant Nadenka not to sledding but to lovemaking. Chekhov continually made fun of the romantic fiction that abounded; he knew that 19th century authors and readers weren't always conscious of the sexual connotations of naïvely presented activities. He, however, was quite conscious. The ice has been broken:

> We go up the staircase on the hill. I seat the pale, shaking Nadenka in the sled, and again we fly into the terrifying abyss, again the wind roars and the runners buzz, and again, at the sled's fastest and noisiest rush, I say in an undertone:
> "I love you, Nadenka!"

The narrator is taking a risk in his teasing. It is the spice he's adding to his own experience, and he knows there is attraction he is creating in her through his indistinct but "most important" declaration.

> When the sled stops, Nadenka takes a sharp glance at the hill down which we have only just sledded, then looks a long time in my face, listens to my voice, cool and passionless, and everything, everything, even her muff and hood, everything in her bearing—expresses the most extreme confusion. And on her face is written:
>
> "What's all this? Who pronounced those words? Did he, or was I only hearing things?"
>
> This unknown bothers her, draws out her impatience. The poor girl doesn't answer my questions, frowns, is ready to cry.

She is overwhelmed, she is unsure of the ground on which she stands with him, her partner.

> "Shouldn't we go home?" I ask.
>
> "But I . . . I like this sledding," she says, blushing. "Couldn't we go down one more time?"

Not that I want to argue, but to the readers skeptical about the sexual connotations, I will only ask: Why does she blush? It's just *sledding*. But maybe *you* argue, impatient with me, an old man, that she's timid because she hasn't confirmed to herself that he said, "I love you." And I will answer that I don't understand why her timidity would make her blush. Trying to confirm his words is not embarrassing. Admitting that she wants more of whatever you prefer to call that activity, however, is very familiar to some of us and can cause blushing.

> She likes this sledding, but meanwhile, seated in the sled as the other times, she is pale, and sighing with fear, shakes.
>
> We go down the third time, and I see how she looks at me in the face, observes my lips. But I place the handkerchief to my lips, cough, and, when we reach the middle of the hill, I successfully utter:
>
> "I love you, Nadya!"
>
> And the riddle remains a riddle! Nadenka goes silent, thinks about something. . . .

Here we pause in one of Chekhov's own ellipsis-pauses. The puzzle, the trick, the story's explicit joke, is about the declaration, not about the thrill of this new exhausting and satisfying physical activity. The narrator's cruelty is what makes her unhappy. The sexual or physically exciting activity, though fearful, attracts her. The words of love would, it seems, deplete some of her shame in desiring more of the activity.

> I lead her home from the skating rink, she tries to go quietly, begins slowing
> her feet and keeps waiting for whether I will say those words to her. And I
> see how her soul suffers as she makes an effort on herself in order not to say:
>
> "It can't be that the wind said those things! And I don't want that the
> wind said it!"

Chekhov was never accused of cruelty, except perhaps this coming fall by Efros herself. As an adult he pitied and sympathized with all creatures, great and small. But his narrator, as Chekhov saw later and thus modified the story, is indeed cruel—for this "little joke."

> The morning of the next day I receive a note: "If you go sledding today,
> come for me. N." And after that I begin going to the skating rink every
> day, and each time, flying down on the sled, I recite in an undertone these
> very words:
>
> "I love you, Nadya!"
>
> Soon Nadenka is accustomed to this phrase, like to wine or morphine.
> She cannot live without it. Truly, flying down the hill was terrifying before,
> but now already the fears and danger give a special enchantment to the
> words of love, words that as before set up a riddle and tortured her soul.
> She suspects the same two: the wind and me. . . . Whichever of the two
> confesses the love to her, she doesn't know, but to her it is all, apparently,
> one and the same; from whichever vessel she drinks—it is all the same
> from which to get drunk.

She wants the activity, and she wants the words. She gets them both. But she is like the scientist Chekhov himself was, and she has to keep testing to discover the source of "the words of love."

An unaccounted amount of time passes after the "every day." Chekhov begins the next paragraph:

For some reason at midday I make my way alone to the rink; mixing in
with the crowd, I see Nadenka, searching with her eyes for me as she goes
up to the hill. . . . Then she slowly ascends the steps. . . . It's terrifying to
go alone, oh, how terrifying! She is as pale as snow, she shakes, she goes as
if to an execution, but she goes, goes without looking around, decisively.
She, apparently, decided finally to test it out: Will those splendid, sweet
words be heard when I'm not there? I see when she, pale, with her mouth
open from terror, sits in the sled, closes her eyes and, bidding the earth
goodbye forever, moving off. . . . "Zhhhh!" . . . the runners buzz. Whether
or not Nadenka hears the words. I don't know. . . . I only see how she gets
up out of the sled incapacitated, weak. And it's apparent by her face that
she herself doesn't know whether she heard something or not. Her fears
while she was sledding down drove off her ability to hear, distinguish
sounds, to understand. . . .

And up there I encounter a problem that all interpreters of literature face: If one activity
is *really* actually another, does that hold true in all instances, or in just the ones I want to
focus on? If sledding is sex, how is the narrator witnessing this, her solo ride? I don't have
a good answer for that, and maybe Chekhov has had a joke on me.

When Chekhov was writing the story, he had just remarked on March 4 to Leykin
that "We're having absolutely springy weather. How passionately I want to take up spring
themes."

The winter story becomes a spring story:

But now begins the spring-like month of March. . . . The sun becomes warmer.
Our ice hill darkens, loses its shine and melts finally. We stop sledding. Poor
Nadenka will never again hear those words, nobody ever pronounces them,
just so the wind isn't heard, and I begin packing up for Petersburg—for a long
time, most probably forever.

What? Chekhov has told us nothing of the casual narrator's life or plans. He is about
to set out for Petersburg, but where has he been? Where are we?

Somehow, two days before my departure, I am sitting at sunset in the little
garden beside the yard where Nadenka lives; this garden is separated by a high
fence with nails. . . . It's far too cold, there is still snow atop the manure, the

trees seem dead, but it already smells of spring, and the crows, getting ready for their sleep, loudly caw. I go up to the fence and look a long time through a crack.

Aha! The literary device that goes back at least to the ancient Greeks, the crack in the wall or fence:

> I see how Nadenka goes out on the little porch and extends her sad, miserable gaze at the sky. . . . The spring wind blows straight into her pale, dejected face. . . . It reminds her of that wind that roared at us then on the hill, when she heard those four words, and her face becomes sad, sad and a tear crawls down her cheeks. . . . And the poor girl extends both her arms as if asking this wind to bring her those words once more. And I, having awaited the wind, say in an undertone:
>
> "I love you, Nadya!"
>
> Oh, my God, what's going on with Nadenka! She screeches, smiles across her whole face, and extends her arms in greeting to the wind, joyful, happy, so beautiful.

So there we get something of the narrator's pleasure in and justification for the joking declaration: It has made her so happy. And maybe she's especially happy now that she knows it's Nature, not he, making the declaration. Life loves her, Nature loves her.

And his trick has gone full circle, with no harm done! Right?

They have had their fun, their excitement. Sex (or sledding) has been only an enlivening experience.

And I go off to pack.

But what has he been doing there? Why has he been in Nadenka's company? Is he a doctor doing district work? He has met her because she lives next door? Is there some unaccounted-for long-term friendship between families?

> This was a long time ago. Now Nadenka is already married; they married her off, she herself married—it's all the same, a secretary of trustees of the gentry, and now she already has three children. That we went sledding together at some time and how the wind brought to her the words "I love you, Nadenka," is not

forgotten; for her now this is the most happy, most touching and beautiful memory in her life.

But now for me, when I've become old, I still don't understand why I said those words, what was I joking for. . . .

So ends the version of the story as radically revised by Chekhov in 1899.

I believe both versions of the story reveal Chekhov's guilt, his sympathy, his half-heartedness about his various affairs. According to the 1899 narrator, his and Nadenka's relationship, whatever its precise physical nature, was harmless, in fact all to the good, because she has since then married and had kids. In 1886, the story ends with the narrator's revelation that he is in fact Nadenka's husband, that all the teasing and joking led to lawful matrimony. Even if the sledding was to various degrees a metaphor for sex, the story does not resound; it's a light piece, unengaged with and distanced by Chekhov. In revising it, he heightened the sexual suggestiveness and made the piece less of a joke, though the joke was also his having been able to slip the innuendos past various censors; in the original, the narrator doesn't understand what his joking declaration meant about his actual feelings, and that the joke is finally on him.

Perhaps Chekhov's proposal to Efros had been a joke on himself as much as on her. In any case, she got over their confusing engagement sooner than he, as he was still spinning over it thirteen years later.

In "Agafya" (just so, "Agafya," March 15), the protagonist is Savka, the handsome lazy village bum who attracts the local women, among them Agafya.

He could read and write, and very rarely drank, but as a workman this strong and healthy young man was not worth a farthing. A sluggish, overpowering sloth was mingled with the strength in his muscles, which were strong as cords. . . . His old mother begged alms at people's windows and he himself lived like a bird of the air; he did not know in the morning what he would eat at midday. It was not that he was lacking in will, or energy, or feeling for his mother; it was simply that he felt no inclination for work and did not recognize the advantage of it. . . . His favorite attitude was one of concentrated immobility.

This is one of Chekhov's model stories: graceful, quiet, inhabited by interesting, sympathetic, accidentally reckless people. This is the third of three first-person stories in a row, and in this one, a most Chekhov-like narrator sits back and watches and tries not to interfere in the action and in fact fails in his attempt to prevent any drama. Savka, who has even more women than he wants, as they cause him trouble with the village authorities, prefers on this evening the company of the learned unnamed narrator.

> Our hooks with live bait on them had long been in the river, and we had nothing left to do but to abandon ourselves to repose, which Savka, who was never exhausted and always rested, loved so much.

And how much Chekhov enjoyed lazily fishing on the river, and how rarely he could do so in these years!

> Knowing how fond Savka was of listening, I told him all I had learned about the landrail from sportsman's books. From the landrail I passed imperceptibly to the migration of the birds. Savka listened attentively, looking at me without blinking, and smiling all the while with pleasure. [. . .]
>
> "It's interesting," said Savka. "Whatever one talks about it is always interesting. Take a bird now, or a man . . . or take this little stone; there's something to learn about all of them . . . Ah, sir, if I had known you were coming I wouldn't have told a woman to come here this evening . . . She asked to come today."

Savka, in his relations with women, is similar to Chekhov's brother Nikolay and somewhere on a continuum with Chekhov:

> With all his soft-heartedness and good-nature, Savka despised women. He behaved carelessly, condescendingly with them, and even stooped to scornful laughter of their feelings for himself. God knows, perhaps this careless, contemptuous manner was one of the causes of his irresistible attraction for the village Dulcineas. He was handsome and well-built; in his eyes there was always a soft friendliness, even when he was looking at the women he so despised, but the fascination was not to be explained by merely external qualities.

I'm not sure what Chekhov means by "merely external qualities." That is, Savka's good looks? Chekhov himself was certainly good-looking.

Apart from his happy exterior and original manner, one must suppose that the touching position of Savka as an acknowledged failure and an unhappy exile from his own hut to the kitchen gardens also had an influence upon the women.

On the other hand, no one ever looked at Chekhov as "an acknowledged failure." The narrator finds Savka fascinating and is amused that women have a pitying attraction for him. Anxious Agafya, having sneaked over to see Savka while her husband is at work on the train, sees her time dwindling while Savka chases a leery bird. She stays the night despite her husband's return home, and in the morning, the narrator, pitying her, watches her fearful reencounter:

> In the village, near the furthest hut, Yakov was standing in the road, gazing fixedly at his returning wife. He stood without stirring, and was as motionless as a post. What was he thinking as he looked at her? What words was he preparing to greet her with? Agafya stood still a little while, looked around once more as though expecting help from us, and went on. I have never seen anyone, drunk or sober, move as she did. Agafya seemed to be shriveled up by her husband's eyes. At one time she moved in zigzags, then she moved her feet up and down without going forward, bending her knees and stretching out her hands, then she staggered back. When she had gone another hundred paces she looked around once more and sat down.
>
> "You ought at least to hide behind a bush . . ." I said to Savka. "If the husband sees you . . ."
>
> "He knows, anyway, who it is Agafya has come from . . . The women don't go to the kitchen garden at night for cabbages—we all know that."

On the same Saturday "Agafya" was published, so was "My Conversation with the Postmaster" in Leykin's *Fragments*. Chekhov paid close attention to postage and rates, occasionally advising friends, family, and editors about the most sensible practices. In this piece, the unnamed narrator engages with his acquaintance, the postmaster, about the wastefulness and inefficiencies of the postal service. The postmaster would prefer not to think about those problems: "If you get into everything [. . .] and think about the why and wherefore, minds will jostle apart."[30] Chekhov's narrator shows concern for mothers having to wait in long postal-service lines and being frustrated by the number of forms. The Chekhov family was continually sending money across Russia. Chekhov seems, however, never to have lost a story-manuscript in the mail. Letters, though? Yes.

Next up was another story Chekhov would exclude from his *Collected Works*, though it is uncharacteristically eventful and exciting, "The Wolf" ("Volk," March 17, titled "Hydrophobia," another term for rabies, in the only translation I have found in English). A rabid wolf gets his teeth into the protagonist, who fears the worst. He has a nightmarish vision: "The moon was reflected in the animal's eyes; there was nothing like anger in them; they were tearful and looked human."[31] Despite a doctor's reassurances that chances are the wolf's poison washed out with the bloody wound or was trapped in the clothing that was bitten through, the protagonist becomes obsessed by the potential symptoms and goes to see various village healers.

There were many fearful diseases that doctors and patients could encounter in the late 19th century; the biggest fear that Chekhov, already infected with tuberculosis, ever regularly expressed was about catching typhus. But the very next story, published five days later (March 22), a comic tale for *Fragments*, "To Paris!" also focuses on the dangers of rabies. Two academics are bitten by a stray dog that "perhaps" has rabies. The town's administrators order them to go to Paris to see the French scientist Louis Pasteur, just in case. But barely starting on the way there, at a station stop in Kursk, they get drunk and spend all their money and never get "to Paris." Had Chekhov treated a case of rabies earlier this month or been reading some medical literature about it?

Early in March, Chekhov was detecting signs of spring in Moscow and wrote his own "In Spring" ("Vesnoy," March 24) for the *Petersburg Gazette* about a self-conscious writer out in the sticks. The protagonist becomes bitter and resentful because he feels mocked by the townspeople for not being a great or famous writer:

> "Ah, Mr. Writer! . . . Hello there!"
> If Makar Denisych were merely a clerk or junior manager, no one would dare speak to him in such a condescending, casual tone, but he is a "writer," giftlessness, mediocrity!

Poor fellow! mocks the narrator: "Authorial vanity is painful, it is an infection of the soul; whoever suffers from it no longer hears the singing of the birds, nor sees the shining of the sun, nor sees the spring . . ."

> It is obvious enough, even without this letter from
> Grigorovich, that Antosha Chekhonte would have
> become Anton Chekhov. But the "awakening" effect
> of the letter is understandable. The year 1886 marks
> a dividing point in Chekhov's career.
>
> —Sophie Laffitte[32]

We have come to the letter that supposedly spurred Chekhov to fulfill his genius.

Dmitry Vasil'evich Grigorovich, born in 1822, was regarded by this time, perhaps nostalgically, in the same literary circle as Tolstoy and the late Dostoevsky and Turgenev. He had shared an apartment with Dostoevsky when they were young and had published two novels himself in the 1850s that brought him renown and regard. As a friend of Suvorin, he had met Chekhov in Petersburg in December of 1885, but in his famous advice letter it is odd that he didn't mention that. Chekhov had remembered and noted that encounter and had, probably for one of the last times in his life, been in awe at the people he was meeting because of his writing. Chekhov did not like to bow and scrape, and yet there was something in his relationship to Grigorovich that would bring him to at least bow.

Grigorovich appreciated himself at the end of his life and career as "the man who discovered Chekhov." On March 25, 1886, Grigorovich had the experience that everybody has when we read a distinctive writer for the first time: *Who is this person? How did I not know of him already? He is extraordinary. . . . I have made a discovery!* And some of us might, from high to low or low to high, let that person know that *we have discovered them.* We are staking our claim, in case anyone comes asking afterward, "When did you, Brilliant Bob, announce to the world Annie's genius?"

> Dear Sir, Anton Pavlovich:
>
> About a year ago I read by chance a story of yours in *Petersburg Gazette*; I do not recall its title. I remember only that I was struck by its qualities of outstanding originality and chiefly its remarkable accuracy and truthfulness in its descriptions of people and nature.
>
> Since then I have read everything that bore the signature of Chekhonte, although I was inwardly vexed at a man who held so poor an opinion of himself as to consider the use of a pseudonym necessary.[33]

Grigorovich's biographer observes that "The tone of the letter is very much de haut en bas."[34] The praise is as condescending as it is lavish:

While reading you, I continually advised Suvorin and Burenin to follow my example. They listened to me and now, like me, they do not doubt that you have real talent—a talent which places you in the front rank among writers in the new generation.

By the time Grigorovich wrote this, Suvorin had already, since the beginning of January, signed Chekhov on to write for *New Times*. So Grigorovich was shouldering aside the man who more obviously decided that Chekhov should have carte blanche and had actually given it to him.

I am not a journalist nor a publisher. I can be useful to you only as one of your readers. If I speak of your talent, I speak out of conviction. I am almost sixty-five [he had just turned sixty-four], but I still feel so much love for literature and follow its success with so much ardor and rejoice when I find in it something living and gifted, that I cannot refrain—as you see—from holding out both hands to you.

Grigorovich sounds like another one of Chekhov's comic windbags.

But this is by no means all. Here is what I wish to add. By virtue of the varied attributes of your undoubted talent—the precise truth of your internal analysis, your mastery of description (the snowstorm, the night, the background in "Agafya" etc.[35]), the plasticity of your feelings which in a few lines projects a complete picture (the clouds above the setting sun "like ashes over dying coals," etc.)—I am convinced that you are destined to create some admirable and truly artistic works. And you will be guilty of a great moral sin if you do not live up to these hopes. All that is needed is esteem for the talent which so rarely falls to one's lot. Cease to write hurriedly.

I am trying to imagine Chekhov's face as he read and reread this paragraph. Is it expressing "two contradictory feelings" as Andrey Andreyich's did in "The Requiem"? Chekhov smiles as it is dawning on him that famous people are reading him and talking about him. But there is also a grimace at being prematurely reproached. Though Chekhov would scold his brother Alexander using some of Grigorovich's very ideas about responsibility to one's talent, Chekhov would write to his brother as an equal and not as a prince to a pauper. And Chekhov, at this time a speedy genius, would later, when he was slower, refute Grigorovich about speed; that is, Chekhov would assert that speedy writing is a good thing, all things being equal: "Potapenko is an extraordinary man. He can write 16 pages a day without a single correction. Once he earned 1,100 rubles in five days. In my opinion, writing at a terrific speed is not, as Grigorovich thinks, a blemish but a special gift."[36]

Grigorovich goes on:

> I do not know what your financial situation is. If it is poor, it would be better for you to go hungry, as we did in our day, and save your impressions for a mature, finished work, written not in one sitting, but during the happy hours of inspiration.

Hmph! Two things: (1) Grigorovich had some idea of Chekhov's financial situation and knew the young man needed the money; (2) Grigorovich remembered himself as one of those "inspired" artists who in the midst of maturing their masterpieces dined on air and rocks. If Grigorovich had included a check for a thousand rubles, we could forgive him for his presumption.

It gets worse:

> One such work will be valued a hundred times higher than a hundred fine stories scattered among the newspapers at various times. In one leap you will reach the goal and will gain the notice of cultivated people and then all the reading public.

One thing I have learned in my research for this book is that Chekhov, that is, *Antosha Chekhonte*, appearing weekly in *Fragments* and the *Petersburg Gazette*, already had an immense "reading public." Was that public "cultivated"? No. But among his readers was Tolstoy himself, who appreciated Chekhov's comic sensibility as one of the rarest of artistic gifts. Grigorovich sniffed:

> Why is it that you often have motifs with pornographical nuances at the basis of your tales? Truthfulness and realism not only do not exclude refinement but even gain from it.

Was Grigorovich scandalized by "The Witch"? Was he offended by Agafya's passion for the big lunk Savka? Though a notorious womanizer, Grigorovich was, as regards literature, a prude. Some of the heat and power of Chekhov's arguments about art and its acceptable subjects (that is, there is nothing unclean in nature) are going to redound in January 1887 on the head of one of his proteges, Maria Kiseleva, rather than back on Grigorovich's noggin, where they would have bounced off anyway.

> You have such a powerful sense of form and a feeling for the plastic, that you have no special need, for example, to speak about dirty feet with turned-in toenails or a clerk's navel. These details add exactly nothing to the artistic beauty of a description and only spoil the impression among readers of taste. Have the generosity to forgive such observations, for I resolved to make them only because I sincerely believe in your talent and with all my soul desire its fullest development.

How Chekhov must have cringed at the phrase "readers of taste"! And yet . . . Grigorovich was in the high-end literary game, and his words were flattering and his practical advice as to publishing was, Chekhov decided, worth heeding:

> Several days ago I was told that you are publishing a book of tales. If it is to appear under the pseudonym of CHE-KHON-TE, I beg you earnestly to telegraph the publishers to print it under your real name. After your recent stories in *New Times* and the success of "The Huntsman" [1885], the book will also have great success. It would be agreeable to have some assurance that you are not angry over my remarks, but that you accept them in the spirit that I write—not as an authority but out of the simplicity of an old heart.

If Chekhov forgave Grigorovich his presumption, why can't I? Chekhov was young, modest, generous, and respectful. Maybe Grigorovich was right about some things. The old man had ridden in a lot of rodeos. Grigorovich was trying to be nice and was. The biographer Donald Rayfield has a theory: "Wary of his own father for twenty years, Anton responded with trusting affection to the father figures of Russian literature. Great writers—Leskov, Grigorovich and, later, Tolstoy—and self-made patriarchs like Suvorin aroused filial devotion in Anton."[37]

Chekhov, humble and cowed, but not at all *filial*, replied on March 28:

> Your letter, my kind, fervently beloved bringer of good tidings, struck me like a flash of lightning. I almost burst into tears, I was overwhelmed, and now I feel it has left a deep trace in my soul! May God show the same tender kindness to

you in your age as you have shown me in my youth! I can find neither words
nor deeds to thank you. You know with what eyes ordinary people look at
the elect such as you, and so you can judge what your letter means for my
self-esteem. It is better than any diploma, and for a writer who is just beginning it is payment both for the present and the future. I am almost dazed. I
have no power to judge whether I deserve this high reward. I only repeat that
it has overwhelmed me.[38]

He never wrote another letter as humble and deferential as this one. He would defer
to Suvorin for the first year or so of their working relationship, but he would not bow this
far. Notice, if possible, that there is scarcely a piece of correspondence that Chekhov ever
wrote that does not contain a joke. There are no jokes in this long, humble, grateful letter.
In the next paragraph Chekhov even sniffed back pretentiously and did dirt on his friends
and relatives who *did* know that Chekhov as an author was the real deal. The photostatic
reproduction of the first page of this letter shows it is handwritten neatly, well-spaced,
with no cross-outs—suggesting that Chekhov recopied it from a draft:[39]

If I have a gift which one ought to respect, I confess before the pure candor
of your heart that hitherto I have not respected it. I felt that I had a gift, but
I had got into the habit of thinking that it was insignificant. Purely external
causes are sufficient to make one unjust to oneself, suspicious, and morbidly
sensitive. And as I realize now I have always had plenty of such causes. All my
friends and relatives have always taken a condescending tone to my writing,
and never ceased urging me in a friendly way not to give up real work for the
sake of scribbling. I have hundreds of friends in Moscow, and among them a
dozen or two writers, but I cannot recall a single one who reads me or considers
me an artist. In Moscow there is a so-called Literary Circle: talented people
and mediocrities of all ages and colors gather once a week in a private room of
a restaurant and exercise their tongues. If I went there and read them a single
passage of your letter, they would laugh in my face. In the course of the five
years that I have been knocking about from one newspaper office to another
I have had time to assimilate the general view of my literary insignificance. I
soon got used to looking down upon my work, and so it has gone from bad
to worse. That is the first reason. The second is that I am a doctor, and am
up to my ears in medical work, so that the proverb about trying to catch two
hares has given to no one more sleepless nights than me.

But . . . but . . . but! Upon reflection, for the rest of his life, Chekhov concluded again and again in his letters and conversations that the medical duties did not block him in his literary endeavors and only made him a better writer.

> I am writing all this to you in order to excuse this grievous sin a little before you. Hitherto my attitude to my literary work has been frivolous, heedless, casual. I don't remember a *single* story over which I have spent more than twenty-four hours, and "The Huntsman," which you liked, I wrote in the bathing-shed! I wrote my stories as reporters write their notes about fires, mechanically, half-unconsciously, taking no thought of the reader or myself. . . . I wrote and did all I could not to waste upon the story the scenes and images dear to me which—God knows why—I have treasured and kept carefully hidden.

Don't we already see those "carefully hidden" "scenes and images" in Chekhov's nature passages? I think so. And he had experienced as all fruitful artists do that the more images he created, the more images he discovered.

> The first impulse to self-criticism was given me by a very kind and, to the best of my belief, sincere letter from Suvorin. I began to think of writing something decent, but I still had no faith in my being any good as a writer. And then, unexpected and undreamed of, came your letter. Forgive the comparison: it had on me the effect of a Governor's order to clear out of the town within twenty-four hours—i.e., I suddenly felt an imperative need to hurry, to make haste and get out of where I have stuck. . . .

Chekhov was certainly documenting that Suvorin was there first, and also, I admit, validating Grigorovich's claim that he guided Chekhov to the path of "literature":

> I agree with you in everything. When I saw "The Witch" in print I felt myself the cynicism of the points to which you call my attention. They would not have been there had I written this story in three or four days instead of in one.

And yet, given a dozen years and various publications of the story, Chekhov scarcely modified "The Witch" a hair.

I shall put an end to working against time, but cannot do so just yet.[40] . . . It
is impossible to get out of the rut I have gotten into. I have nothing against
going hungry, as I have done in the past, but it is not a question of myself.

I sincerely hope that Grigorovich woke up at that phrase—that young Dr. Chekhov was
supporting not just himself but others. (I think of "A Nightmare," the story Chekhov
published the very next day and so must have finished that very week, before receiving
Grigorovich's letter, about the contempt and disgust a government official feels for the
nearly starving priest who at tea bewilderingly squirrels away the offered cookies.)
Meanwhile, Chekhov humbly went on:

> . . . I give to literature my spare time, two or three hours a day and a bit of
> the night, that is, time which is of no use except for short things. In the
> summer, when I have more time and have fewer expenses, I will start on
> some serious work.
>
> I cannot put my real name on the book because it is too late: the design
> for the cover [of *Motley Tales*] is ready and the book printed. Many of my
> Petersburg friends advised me, even before you did, not to spoil the book by
> a pseudonym, but I did not listen to them, probably out of vanity. I dislike
> my book very much. It's a hotch-potch, a disorderly medley of the poor stuff I
> wrote as a student, plucked by the censor and by the editors of comic papers.
> I am sure that many people will be disappointed when they read it. Had I
> known that I had readers and that you were watching me, I would not have
> published this book.

Chekhov was insincere here. After *Motley Stories* came out this spring, he would himself note to his uncle the many tales that he especially valued,[41] and finally, in 1899, he
would include most of them in his rather selective *Collected Works*. On the other hand,
Grigorovich's advice did lead him to ask Leykin on March 31 to add his real name to his
pseudonym on the title page. And so it was.

> I rest all my hopes on the future. I am only twenty-six. Perhaps I shall succeed
> in doing something, though time flies fast.
>
> Forgive my long letter and do not blame a man because, for the first time
> in his life, he has made bold to treat himself to the pleasure of writing to
> Grigorovich.

Those and the following were the kinds of phrases that Chekhov was trying to purge from his everyday speech and thought:

> Send me your photograph, if possible.[42] I am so overwhelmed with your kindness that I feel as though I should like to write a whole ream to you. God grant you health and happiness, and believe in the sincerity of your deeply respectful and grateful
> A. Chekhov.

On March 29 Chekhov published three pieces: "A Lot of Paper," a series of serious reports, each with a "happy news" ending, similar to network TV news stories today; "The Rook," a dialogue between an "I" and a bird, who moralizes in a manner that Chekhov usually shunned: "I've lived 376 years and I never once saw rooks fight among themselves and kill each other, but you don't remember a year in which there wasn't a war";[43] and the excellent "A Nightmare" (referred to, above, in Chekhov's reply to Grigorovich), about a young, privileged government official who is sent to a town in the provinces, where he is disgusted by a young, desperate, slovenly priest:

> By now Kunin almost hated Father Yakov. The man, his pitiful, grotesque figure in the long crumpled robe, his womanish face, his manner of officiating, his way of life and his formal restrained respectfulness, wounded the tiny relic of religious feeling which was stored away in a warm corner of Kunin's heart together with his nurse's other fairy tales. The coldness and lack of attention with which Father Yakov had met Kunin's warm and sincere interest in what was the priest's own work was hard for the former's vanity to endure. . . .[44]

The government official recommends that Father Yakov be fired, and only then he finds out the selfless priest's desperate financial circumstances.

Chekhov knew the faults of shoddy workers, but he was a very conscientious defender of those engaged in social work; if they were teachers, doctors, and priests working for the government or church, they were most usually poorly paid. Though I pointed out in "The Rook" Chekhov's customary reluctance to speak out directly on social issues, in "A Nightmare," Chekhov's narrator is so disheartened by the incomprehending official's lack of imagination concerning the overburdened priest that he ends the story with a blunt point: "So had begun and had ended a sincere effort to be of public service on the part of a well-intentioned but unreflecting and over-comfortable person."[45]

Finally, to close out his extraordinary month of fiction, Chekhov wrote "On the River" ("Na Reke"), subtitled "Spring Pictures" (March 31), an essay-like story about people on a bridge watching the river-ice break apart while adventurous peasants are floating down on a raft. Their tricky navigation of the river is blocked by a footbridge that a factory owner has laid across it for his workers. Frustrated, the peasants have to take apart the raft and walk it around.

Though Chekhov had been looking forward to spring, writes Dr. John Coope, he "connected the melting of the river with his renewed bleeding."[46] This was one of the times of the year where Chekhov's tuberculosis especially manifested itself.

PART TWO

"Hymns of Praise"

C hekhov's world had changed forever. He was being recognized and celebrated as an emerging literary star in a most literary Russia. His work was continually being evaluated. In the glare of attention, he could have granted himself allowances and abandoned his commitments to *Fragments* and the *Petersburg Gazette*. He could have closed the door to his medical practice. Easing up, however, would have left his financially dependent family floundering. Who would support them? He had to keep going with his overwhelming schedule and, if possible, increase his output. He accepted that he would have to work in haste, but he would demand of himself an increased artistic rigor.

He saw this year and next as an opportunity to write full speed ahead, trusting himself to "avoid subjectivity" and tell simple stories of complex people. When he was suffering from tubercular symptoms, his pace slowed, but he labored on. One immediate result this spring was the most extraordinary evocation in literature of the art of writing, more particularly of composing "hymns of praise," in the short story "Easter Eve."

April 1886

—⁓—

Don't invent sufferings you have not experienced, and
don't paint pictures you have not seen . . .
                              —Letter to his brother Alexander[1]

On April 2, Grigorovich answered Chekhov's letter, the "sincerity" of which had gratified the old man. "You're doing excellently that you flee from and don't waste images and pictures that are especially dear to you. . . . think up a good plan (an architectural structure of the story is the important thing)—and in summer start with God to work. If your personal talent is not in line with a novella or novel, write short stories, but work them over into refinement. With only 'A Sportsman's Sketches' Turgenev would have made himself a great name!"[2]

On April 4, Chekhov wrote Bilibin: "You write that my last two stories in the *Pete Gaz* are weak . . ." These would have been "On the River" and "Spring." He took Bilibin's critiques, as he took everyone's, in stride, even outdoing them in their criticism. Chekhov said the next ones would be even weaker. He explained, "I wore myself out." But then he turned to anti-Semitism, using it and reproaching its use. "As for the good women about whom you asked, I hasten to maintain that there are so many of them in Moscow. Just now my sister had a whole bouquet, and I melted like a Jew before gold . . . By the way: in the last 'Fragments of Petersburg Life' [a gossipy culture section, the Moscow installments of which Chekhov usually wrote] there were three swipes you took at Jews. Why's that?"[3]

Considering that Chekhov occasionally used loaded words and stereotypes about Jews and in fact had just done so in this letter, this scolding is surprising, and Bilibin could have asked in return: *What about you?* Chekhov then returned to one of his special topics with Bilibin and asked about the date of Bilibin's wedding and told him that "During St. Thomas week [the week beginning the Sunday after Easter] I will be a best man for two: a doctor and an artist."

But Chekhov was not well. With springtime he was coughing up blood. "Chekhov suffered from ill health most of his adult life," writes Dr. Richard Carter, "and the year he graduated from medical school [1884] he experienced the first of many episodes of hemoptysis, a harbinger of an early death. For several years he suffered recurrent bouts of fever, productive cough, and chest pain that kept him awake many nights. In retrospect, this was most likely from tuberculous bronchiectasis. . . . However, Chekhov often complained about less serious ailments such as hemorrhoids, diarrhea, constipation, heart palpitations, muscular twitching, migraine headaches, and phlebitis. He was nonchalant and minimized the nature of his more serious lung disease . . ."[4]

He usually had symptoms twice a year. When friends queried him, he soberly or jokingly fended them off: "I am not going to have any treatment. I shall drink mineral waters and quinine, but I shall not allow myself to be examined," he wrote to a concerned Suvorin in 1891.[5] Lest we non-medical people feel too bewildered by Chekhov's long denial of his own tuberculosis, Dr. John Coope explains:

> Only someone with little experience of sick doctors would be surprised to find such an attitude in someone whose chosen pursuit is the treatment of illness. There is a great, almost impassable gulf between being in professional charge of illness and being a patient. In part this is due to knowing the limits as well as the advantages of treatment, but perhaps even more to an unwillingness to relinquish control over the management of one's everyday life to others.[6]

He only admitted to having tuberculosis in 1897. Suvorin visited him in the hospital that spring:

> "To calm patients," [Chekhov] said, "we say when they have a cough it is gastric and when they have a hemorrhage it is a burst vein. But gastric coughs do not exist and coughed up blood definitely comes from the lungs. Blood is coming from my right lung as it did in the case of my brother, and another of my tuberculosis relatives. The doctors try and tell me, as a doctor, that it is a gastric hemorrhage. I listen to them but don't take any notice. I know I have tuberculosis."[7]

~m~

April was much slower for Chekhov as far as literary production went; he published only six stories, one of them the soon-to-be very popular story called "Grisha" ("Grisha," April 5), about a two-year-eight-month-old toddler who goes out for a walk with his nursemaid. Grisha takes in a lot of sights, and fortunately for the nursemaid can't communicate them all to his mother: "When he reached home, Grisha explained to mamma, the walls, and his crib where he had been and what he had seen. He told it less with his tongue than with his hands and his face; he showed how the sun had shone, how the horses had trotted, how the terrible oven had gaped at him, and how the cook had drunk."[8] Chekhov credited Bilibin with the idea for this story.

By April 6, it was time to scold Alexander about the debts that Nikolay and he had rung up. Anton had apparently heard from Alexander about it, but he had a multi-pointed argument ready. By Point 3, Anton was mocking Alexander's trying to weasel out of payments:

> You say: "They burn, cut, trample and suck." That is, they demand payment of debts? My dear fellow, but one must pay debts! One must at whatever cost, even to little Armenians, even at the price of starving. If university men and writers see suffering in paying debts, what about the rest? I wonder. But the whole point is in the principle. . . . Anyhow, why contract debts? Forgive me this silly question, but I vow this is not a sermon. One could, surely, do without debts. I judge by myself; I have on my shoulders a family which is much bigger than yours, and provisions in Moscow are ten times dearer than in your place. For your house you pay as much as I do for the piano. I dress no better than you. . . . The whole trouble is in expenses and purchases you have no right to make and with which you should long since have dispensed: Nestle's flour, a superfluous servant, and so on. When husband and wife have no money they do not keep a servant—that is a practical rule. [. . .] The magistrate has sentenced me to pay 105 rubles, the debt which you and Nikolay made at Semenov's shop. [. . .] During the summer holidays I'll squeeze myself somehow. I and the family will spend fifty rubles a month, and there will be no debts. [. . .]
>
> (5) Why do you write so little? How disgusting! [. . .] All the stories you sent me for Leykin smell strongly of idleness. [. . .] Respect yourself, for the love of Christ; don't give your hands liberty when your brain is lazy!

Write no more than two stories a week, shorten them, polish them. Work should be work. Don't invent sufferings you have not experienced, and don't paint pictures you have not seen—for a lie in a story is much more boring than a lie in conversation. . . .

Remember every minute that your pen and your talent you will need in the future more than you do now, so don't profane them . . .[9]

He echoed Grigorovich's warning to him, translated into brotherly scolding:

[. . .] Literature has been no labor to you, but most surely it is labor. Were you a decent man, were you to sit at a story (of 150 or 200 lines) for five or seven days, what a result there would be! You would not recognize yourself in your lines, just as you don't recognize yourself in the mirror. . . . Consider, you are not piled up with pressing work, and therefore you can work on one little thing for several evenings. Is it profitable? Count. With great minuteness you could write five or seven stories a month, which would make about a hundred rubles; and now, though you write a great deal, you don't make fifty. [. . .]

Leykin is out of fashion now. I have taken his place. In Petersburg I am now in great fashion, and I do wish you were not straggling behind. [. . .]

[. . .] Do remember, now: work on your stories. I can judge by experience. Write. Write to Mother. [. . .]

He encouraged Alexander to hold onto his job until the fall, and then he would use his connections to help him get editorial work in Petersburg.

Chekhov also wrote Leykin on April 6, but about *Motley Stories*, over which they were still negotiating the final contents and the number of copies to be printed. Chekhov admitted to Leykin that he was in poor health:

Spitting of blood and weakness. I am not writing anything. . . . If I don't sit down to write tomorrow, you must forgive me—I shall not send you a story for the Easter number. I ought to go to the South but I have no money.

[. . .] I am afraid to submit myself to be sounded by my colleagues. I am inclined to think it is not so much my lungs as my throat that is at fault. . . . I have no fever.

Leykin replied with annoyance about Chekhov not allowing "A Nightmare" and his *New Times* stories to be included in the collection.

In "Love" ("Lyubov'," April 7), the narrator has a writing experience that makes me wonder how often Chekhov enjoyed such a feeling himself: "I wanted endlessly to prolong the process of this writing, when one sits in the stillness of one's study and communes with one's own daydreams while the spring night looks in at one's window."[10] Coughing blood, Chekhov was not feeling such leisurely pleasure just now.

On April 11, Chekhov wrote his uncle Mitrofan, who was more of a father figure than Chekhov's own father, Mitrofan's brother. Letters to Mitrofan, down in Taganrog, were always newsy and informative, with Chekhov knowing that Mitrofan would share the news with relatives this Easter season:

> Forgive me that it's been so long I haven't written you. You yourself write a lot, and so you understand a person who writes from sunrise to sunset: there's no time! When there's a free minute, you try to give over to reading or something else. Yes, speaking sincerely, I don't understand writing to dear, close people which you write by obligation, but not in a moment of a good mood, when you're not afraid of sincerity or the reason of the letter.[11]

He recalled Mitrofan's visit the past winter and caught him up on family news and health (though not about his own), including that he had just treated his maternal aunt and his brother Ivan: "Having a doctor in the house—a big comfort!"[12]

> My writing is a full-time activity, undertaken with order. I'm already working on the big Petersburg newspaper—in *New Times*, where they pay me 12 kopecks a line. Last night I received from this newspaper for 3 not-big stories, appearing in three issues, 232 rubles. A miracle! I simply with my own eyes don't believe it. But the little *Petersburg Gazette* gives me 100 rubles a month for 4 stories.

In letters to his uncle, he often gave the kinds of financial details that would satisfy the curiosity of a fond, proud relative and businessperson:

> Mama is very happy that Ivan has got a job in a state school in Moscow, where he will be his own boss. He has a government apartment with five rooms. Servants, firewood, and lighting are also all paid for by the state

. . . Papa is delighted that Ivan has bought himself a peaked cap with a
cockade, and has ordered a professional morning frock-coat with bright
buttons.

Nikolay is working very hard now, but has trouble with his eyes. [. . .]

What a pity you can't also be with us for Easter! We'll have plenty to
break the fast with. We would sing together, as we will on our return from
the midnight service.

The bells have just rung at the Cathedral of Christ the Savior.[13]

Maybe it's not a *lie* to suggest to one's uncle that one's immediate family is doing
great, just great!

———

For publication in *New Times* on the eve of Easter, April 13, Chekhov wrote "Easter
Eve."

Mikhail Chekhov remembered their childhood in Taganrog: "We were not allowed
to miss a single Saturday-night vigil or Sunday liturgy, which explains why Anton
exhibited such a thorough knowledge of church services in his story 'Easter Eve' and
others."[14]

Despite the physical abuse with which their father enforced their church and choral
attendance and participation, Chekhov loved Easter and church bells. He respected
respectable priests and monks. He knew the Bible, he appreciated unselfishness. He shed
trappings that did not seem to him to have a moral or practical basis, and he wouldn't lie
and pretend to believe what he didn't believe, but he was a model of someone ever striving
toward moral behavior.

Chekhov wrote so many great stories that it's easy for even some of us fervent admirers
to have overlooked or never even read dozens of gems. "Easter Eve" is one that I had
completely forgotten until I started reading for this biography.

It begins:

I was standing on the bank of the River Goltva, waiting for the ferry-boat
from the other side.

Is the "I" of Chekhov's first-person narrated stories ever himself? . . . The story
will point toward the idea that the narrator's experience is only important to the

extent that it is a reliable source of observation and judgment about the meaning of someone else's experience. Chekhov insisted that the subjects of the stories were not himself and tried to make sure in circumstantial details that they were not, and yet he, like this narrator, was a good traveler and evoked the pleasures and weariness of travel as well as anyone. The narrator describes the flooded stream and the night sky:

> The world was lighted by the stars, which were scattered thickly all over the sky. I don't remember ever seeing so many stars. Literally one could not have put a finger in between them.

So simple! We are indeed in the narrator's shoes looking up at the sky and lifting our hand and pointing our index finger. How does a writer present perspective? Chekhov does it this way, sometimes. He engages the reader's *physical* imagination. And such an imagination also shifts to look before him.

> The sky was reflected in the water; the stars were bathing in its dark depths and trembling with the quivering eddies.

The narrator remains nameless throughout the story, because, as Chekhov might say, *the narrator knows who he is.* He now realizes he has company on the riverbank, and he asks the unnamed peasant about the ferry. The peasant says the ferry is due, but he himself is not waiting for it. The peasant is there to watch the light and fireworks across the way at the monastery. The peasant calls out through the darkness to the ferryman, the monk Ieronim.

The first peal of the bell is heard, followed by a celebratory cannon shot. How Chekhov savored the bells of Easter! He tomcatted for them every year. Donald Rayfield writes: "During his adult life, right up until his death, Chekhov would rarely spend an Easter night in bed; instead he would wander the streets, listening to the church bells."[15]

> Before the vibrations of the first peal of the bell had time to die away in the air a second sounded, after it at once a third, and the darkness was filled with an unbroken quivering clamor.

For a while, there is no sign or sight of Ieronim, and the narrator is impatient.

[. . .] but behold at last, staring into the dark distance, I saw the outline
of something very much like a gibbet. It was the long-expected ferry. It
moved toward us with such deliberation that if it had not been that its
lines grew gradually more definite, one might have supposed that it was
standing still or moving to the other bank.

How have I never noticed before how active Chekhov makes our imagination? He
creates our perspective so efficiently: those lines growing "gradually more definite." The
ferry arrives and Ieronim, unlike a bus driver, apologizes:

"Why have you been so long?" I asked jumping upon the ferry.
"Forgive me, for Christ's sake," Ieronim answered gently. [. . .]

Chekhov has immediately inclined us in Ieronim's favor, though we are taking in
the story from the narrator's perspective. Chekhov has us rely on the narrator's observations to reveal not the narrator's inner life but that of the person he is observing.
And off the narrator and Ieronim go, floating slowly toward the monastery.
The core of the story, we'll discover, happens *now*, not at the destination that they can
see lit up by barrels of burning tar, but here during the seemingly casual conversation
between Ieronim and the narrator. A firework shoots off.

"How beautiful!" I said.
"Beautiful beyond words!" sighed Ieronim. "Such a night, sir! Another time
one would pay no attention to the fireworks, but today one rejoices in every
vanity. Where do you come from?"
I told him where I came from.

Chekhov is suggesting where the narrator comes from doesn't matter and/or the narrator knows, so why state it? The idle conversation leads to what the narrator thinks at
first is an idle question:

"To be sure . . . a joyful day today. . . ." Ieronim went on in a weak sighing
tenor like the voice of a convalescent. "The sky is rejoicing and the earth
and what is under the earth. All the creatures are keeping holiday. Only tell
me kind sir, why, even in the time of great rejoicing, a man cannot forget
his sorrows?"

Reading that question in the midst of being steeped in Chekhov's life, I conclude: This is one of Chekhov's own recurring questions, but it doesn't, at first, interest the narrator.

> I fancied that this unexpected question was to draw me into one of those endless religious conversations which bored and idle monks are so fond of. I was not disposed to talk much, and so I only asked:
>
> "What sorrows have you, father?"
>
> "As a rule only the same as all men, kind sir, but today a special sorrow has happened in the monastery: at mass, during the reading of the Bible, the monk and deacon Nikolay died."
>
> "Well, it's God's will!" I said, falling into the monastic tone. "We must all die. To my mind, you ought to rejoice indeed. . . . They say if anyone dies at Easter he goes straight to the kingdom of heaven."
>
> "That's true."

The "idle" chat, we see, is the narrator's, not humble Ieronim's. The narrator replies without feeling, or rather trying to undermine feeling. But Ieronim is in one of those moods or states where the heart is open and the tongue is free:

> [. . .] "The Holy Scripture points clearly to the vanity of sorrow and so does reflection," said Ieronim, breaking the silence, "but why does the heart grieve and refuse to listen to reason? Why does one want to weep bitterly?"

The narrator does not try to answer. Ieronim's sincerity has humbled him.

> Ieronim shrugged his shoulders, turned to me and said quickly:
>
> "If I died, or anyone else, it would not be worth notice perhaps; but, you see, Nikolay is dead! No one else but Nikolay! Indeed, it's hard to believe that he is no more! I stand here on my ferry-boat and every minute I keep fancying that he will lift up his voice from the bank. He always used to come to the bank and call to me that I might not be afraid on the ferry. He used to get up from his bed at night on purpose for that. He was a kind soul. My God! how kindly and gracious! Many a mother is not so good to her child as Nikolay was to me! Lord, save his soul!"

The narrator's silence—having been moved to silence, to humility, in the presence of actual, sincere grief—is ours too, with tears perhaps as well.

> Ieronim took hold of the rope, but turned to me again at once.
>
> "And such a lofty intelligence, your honor," he said in a vibrating voice. "Such a sweet and harmonious tongue! Just as they will sing immediately at early matins: 'Oh lovely! Oh sweet is Thy Voice!' Besides all other human qualities, he had, too, an extraordinary gift!"
>
> "What gift?" I asked.

There we are—as is the narrator—quietly entranced by this wonderful man and interested in all he can tell us.

> The monk scrutinized me, and as though he had convinced himself that he could trust me with a secret, he laughed good-humoredly.
>
> "He had a gift for writing hymns of praise," he said. "It was a marvel, sir; you couldn't call it anything else! You would be amazed if I tell you about it. Our Father Archimandrite comes from Moscow, the Father Sub-Prior studied at the Kazan academy, we have wise monks and elders, but, would you believe it, no one could write them; while Nikolay, a simple monk, a deacon, had not studied anywhere, and had not even any outer appearance of it, but he wrote them! A marvel! A real marvel!" Ieronim clasped his hands and, completely forgetting the rope, went on eagerly:
>
> "The Father Sub-Prior has great difficulty in composing sermons; when he wrote the history of the monastery he worried all the brotherhood and drove a dozen times to town, while Nikolay wrote canticles! Hymns of praise! That's a very different thing from a sermon or a history!"
>
> "Is it difficult to write them?" I asked.
>
> "There's great difficulty!" Ieronim wagged his head. "You can do nothing by wisdom and holiness if God has not given you the gift. The monks who don't understand argue that you only need to know the life of the saint for whom you are writing the hymn, and to make it harmonize with the other hymns of praise. But that's a mistake, sir. Of course, anyone who writes canticles must know the life of the saint to perfection, to the least trivial detail. To be sure, one must make them harmonize with the other canticles and know where to begin and what to write about. [. . .] but the lives of the saints and conformity

with the others is not what matters; what matters is the beauty and sweetness of it. Everything must be harmonious, brief, and complete. There must be in every line softness, graciousness, and tenderness; not one word should be harsh or rough or unsuitable. It must be written so that the worshipper may rejoice at heart and weep, while his mind is stirred and he is thrown into a tremor. [. . .]"

I keep stopping in the midst of this paragraph with the realization that the very best biography that I could write of Chekhov would be such a canticle. I would know the life of St. Anton "to perfection, to the least trivial detail" (including all the unsaintly jokes and his sexual follies). In sum: "conformity with the others is not what matters; what matters is the beauty and sweetness of it. Everything must be harmonious, brief, and complete."

But my second thought and realization is this: that these qualities of canticles describe Chekhov's own principles of writing. The qualities of Monk Nikolay's writings are Chekhov's. (Chekhov later told Suvorin: "I know how to speak briefly on important subjects. It is odd but I have contracted a sort of mania for brevity. Everything I read, whether written by myself or someone else, seems to me to be too long."[16]) Is it a coincidence that the great canticle-artist shares Chekhov's talented but wayward brother's name? Chekhov saw the good in his sin-laden brother, but the good is actually what we, from our distance, perceive in Chekhov himself:

"To think that a man should find words like those! Such a power is a gift from God! For brevity he packs many thoughts into one phrase, and how smooth and complete it all is! [. . .] 'Light-radiating!' There is no such word in conversation or in books, but you see he invented it, he found it in his mind! Apart from the smoothness and grandeur of language, sir, every line must be beautified in every way, there must be flowers and lightning and wind and sun and all the objects of the visible world. And every exclamation ought to be put so as to be smooth and easy for the ear. 'Rejoice, thou flower of heavenly growth!' comes in the hymn to Nikolay the Wonder-worker. It's not simply 'heavenly flower,' but 'flower of heavenly growth.' It's smoother so and sweet to the ear. That was just as Nikolay wrote it! Exactly like that! I can't tell you how he used to write!"

The narrator is moved, but for now he thinks his destination is what's important:

"Well, in that case it is a pity he is dead," I said; "but let us get on, father, or we shall be late."

The narrator asks if the hymns have been published, and Ieronim explains that no one at the monastery was interested. Ieronim was Nikolay's primary audience:

> "What did he write them for?"
>
> "Chiefly for his own comfort. Of all the brotherhood, I was the only one who read his hymns. I used to go to him in secret, that no one else might know of it, and he was glad that I took an interest in them. He would embrace me, stroke my head, speak to me in caressing words as to a little child. He would shut his cell, make me sit down beside him, and begin to read. . . ."
>
> Ieronim left the rope and came up to me.
>
> "We were dear friends in a way," he whispered, looking at me with shining eyes. "Where he went I would go. If I were not there he would miss me. And he cared more for me than for anyone, and all because I used to weep over his hymns. It makes me sad to remember. Now I feel just like an orphan or a widow. You know, in our monastery they are all good people, kind and pious, but . . . there is no one with softness and refinement, they are just like peasants. They all speak loudly, and tramp heavily when they walk; they are noisy, they clear their throats, but Nikolay always talked softly, caressingly, and if he noticed that anyone was asleep or praying he would slip by like a fly or a gnat. His face was tender, compassionate. . . ."

Father Nikolay's qualities are Chekhov's—but Chekhov would not have wanted us to conclude that. Still, we know Chekhov did indeed respect and admire refinement of behavior, and unlike his older brothers he could resist stomping around and bothering others.

Ieronim asks the narrator to be sure to appreciate the Easter hymn, as tonight he has to continue running the ferry. None of the other monks are coming to relieve him. The narrator reaches the muddy shore and surveys the festivities outside and inside the monastery.

He goes and listens to the choir, yet in the midst of the crowd, he has sympathetic pangs for Ieronim:

> I looked at the faces; they all had a lively expression of triumph, but not one was listening to what was being sung and taking it in, and not one was "holding his breath." Why was not Ieronim released? I could fancy Ieronim

standing meekly somewhere by the wall, bending forward and hungrily drinking in the beauty of the holy phrase. All this that glided by the ears of the people standing by me he would have eagerly drunk in with his delicately sensitive soul, and would have been spell-bound to ecstasy, to holding his breath, and there would not have been a man happier than he in all the church. Now he was plying to and fro over the dark river and grieving for his dead friend and brother.

The narrator attempts to find where "dead Nikolay, the unknown canticle writer," is lying. He is unable to do so and decides, after all, it's better he hasn't.

God knows, perhaps if I had seen him I should have lost the picture my imagination paints for me now. I imagine the lovable poetical figure solitary and not understood, who went out at nights to call to Ieronim over the water, and filled his hymns with flowers, stars, and sunbeams, as a pale timid man with soft mild melancholy features. His eyes must have shone, not only with intelligence, but with kindly tenderness and that hardly restrained childlike enthusiasm which I could hear in Ieronim's voice when he quoted to me passages from the hymns.

In the early light of dawn, the narrator and a merchant's wife and a peasant ride back across the river with Ieronim. The narrator couldn't find the deceased Nikolay, but he can now see Ieronim:

He was a tall narrow-shouldered man of five-and-thirty, with large rounded features, with half-closed listless-looking eyes and an unkempt wedge-shaped beard. He had an extraordinarily sad and exhausted look.

They don't chat much this time.

We floated across, disturbing on the way the lazily rising mist. Everyone was silent. Ieronim worked mechanically with one hand. He slowly passed his mild lustreless eyes over us; then his glance rested on the rosy face of a young merchant's wife with black eyebrows, who was standing on the ferry beside me silently shrinking from the mist that wrapped her about. He did not take his eyes off her face all the way.

There was little that was masculine in that prolonged gaze. It seemed to me
that Ieronim was looking in the woman's face for the soft and tender features
of his dead friend.

The end. Again and again, Chekhov's dearest characters realize their connections to
and dependence on others.

———

From Moscow on the actual Easter Eve, Chekhov wrote to Leykin: "The day has gone
merrily. Last night I went to the Kremlin to listen to the bells, walking by the churches; I
returned home at 2, drank and sang with two opera basses, whom I found in the Kremlin
and fetched home to talk . . . One of the basses excellently imitated an archdeacon. I
listened to Grand Vespers in the Church of Christ the Savior and so on."[17]

Then he fended off Leykin's criticism of his spending: "You ask me what I am doing
with my money. I don't lead a dissipated life, I don't walk about dressed like a dandy.
I have no debts, and I don't even have to keep my mistresses (*Fragments* and love I get
gratis), but nevertheless I have only 40 rubles left from the 312 I received from you and
Suvorin before Easter, out of which I shall have to pay 20 tomorrow. Goodness only knows
where my money goes."[18]

Chekhov and Leykin did not see eye to eye on the physical well-being that one needed
for writing. In a letter that has been lost, but of which we know something of the contents
through Leykin's reply on April 13, Chekhov had reproached Leykin for reproaching him,
Chekhov, for being lazy. "I reproached you for laziness," wrote Leykin, "not concerning
work; you write a lot; but concerning writing letters. Of course you lazily write letters. And
I can't believe that it's possible to get sick from such work as ours. I write more than you;
for sixteen years I have been writing every day without taking a breath, but if I get sick, I
get sick not from work but from colds, from overeating [. . .] You say further on, 'By god,
someday I'll have to describe you.' Write it. I'll be glad. I'll even put it in *Fragments*."[19]
It's not clear how or if Chekhov ever characterized Leykin in a story.

A week later, he and Leykin were squabbling over the contents of *Motley Stories*. "As
for 'A Nightmare,'" declared Chekhov, "I again stand on it not suiting the book. The
stories are so motley, but if side by side with 'Swedish Match' you present 'A Nightmare,'
you'll get a motley from which you'll sicken. No, my pigeon, spit on 'A Nightmare!'"[20]
Perhaps as a concession, Chekhov told Leykin he was intending to write something
for *Fragments*.

In most Chekhov biographies, Leykin comes off as the crooked editor and publisher that all of us writers have in mind as blocking or exploiting our genius. But however much Chekhov defamed and mocked him, however much we naturally side with our hero and hold in contempt anyone or anything hampering his literary development, Leykin is my favorite supporting character.

Nineteen years older than Chekhov, Leykin was of peasant stock. As a provincial boy he was apprenticed to a shop owner in St. Petersburg, where he was also enrolled in a school. "He had written, by his own account, more than 20,000 short stories and sketches, and called himself 'a man of letters' with great pride," writes Mikhail Chekhov.[21] According to Michael Henry Heim and Simon Karlinsky, Leykin's humorous writings, which the Chekhov brothers had grown up reading, were primarily about Russian merchants and their domestic lives, but the fiction's "wide popularity with less-literate readers rapidly dwindled at the beginning of the 20th century."[22]

Leykin had been a literary father to the three eldest Chekhov boys. Mikhail Chekhov, who did not work for him, described him: "He was short, broad-shouldered, lame in one leg, and eccentric."[23] Because he was unattractive and had a bad leg, Chekhov and Alexander would refer to him as "Quasimodo."

Nikolay Leykin.

Earlier in their relationship, Chekhov could and did explain the difficulties he had crafting comic stories to size. Though a proud professional, Chekhov always had an artist's sense of proportion, and he sought space and the allowance for his own discretion about topics. Even at the age of twenty-three, Chekhov had stood up for himself to Leykin:

I must confess that an imposed limit "from here to there" does cause me a great deal of trouble. It is not always easy to accept such a limitation. For instance, you do not want any stories of over a hundred lines, and you may have a good reason for it. Now, I get a subject for a story and sit down to write it, but the thought of one hundred and no more interferes with my writing from the very start. I condense as much as I can and keep cutting it down, sometimes (as my literary sense warns me) to the detriment of my subject and, (above all) to the story's form. Having strained and compressed it, I begin to count the lines, and having counted 100, 120, 140 (I never wrote more than that for *Fragments*) I begin to get frightened and I don't send it. Very often I have to rewrite the ending of the story in a hurry and send you something I should not ordinarily have liked to send you. As soon as I get over the fourth page of small note-paper I begin to be assailed by doubts. . . . I should therefore like to ask you to increase the length of my stories to 120 lines. I am sure I shall not avail myself of this concession too frequently, but the knowledge that I have been granted it will save me a lot of worry.

Leykin replied: "While I rely on you not to misuse it, I willingly give you my blessing on 120, 140, and even 150 lines, only please send me something without fail for every issue of the magazine."[24]

The biographer David Magarshack well narrates the pair's evolving and yet fraying relationship. By October 1885, Magarshack explains, Chekhov "had already made up his mind to cut adrift from Leykin":

The only thing that stopped him was his fear of insecurity: he could always get an advance from Leykin and he was sure of his monthly check. [. . .] Leykin, too, realized that unless he found a market for Chekhov's longer stories, Chekhov would sooner or later find one himself and quite possibly give up writing for *Fragments*. He therefore had a talk to Sergey Khudekov, the owner and editor of the *Petersburg Gazette*, to which he was a regular contributor himself, and arranged with him to publish a weekly story by Chekhov. "I have had an offer from Khudekov for you. Would you be willing to write each Monday a story for the *Petersburg Gazette*? But having agreed to write every Monday, you must not let the paper down and must send your story punctually every Saturday. You will paid seven kopecks a line." Chekhov

[. . .] was overjoyed at the offer. [. . .] "I shall be glad to write for the *Petersburg Gazette*, and I promise to be as punctual as possible."[25]

The biographer Ronald Hingley adds that "however much Chekhov might from time to time rail against Khudekov and his [*Petersburg Gazette*], the plain fact is that they freed him from a double tyranny exercised by Leykin: the compulsion to be funny."[26]

Freedom! Chekhov's opportunity to stretch himself led to greater artistic development. After five years, writing for *Fragments* had become a chore. In 1885 he kept up with his new deadlines for the *Petersburg Gazette* but occasionally played hooky from *Fragments*. Leykin took this badly: "I was very angry indeed about your failure to send me your stories regularly. Two of your stories have been published in the *Petersburg Gazette* and I was half minded to stop their publication and I was sorry I ever recommended you there. I am still sorry I did it, because I am sure that now you will be even less punctual with your contributions because of the *Petersburg Gazette*. I must always have one of your stories in reserve—remember that. It's the only way I can make sure that you won't leave me in the lurch, especially in the summer months when it is so confoundedly difficult to get contributors to send in their stories in time."[27]

If we could only see their testy but close relationship the way Chekhov would have in a short story. In such a story, for all of Leykin's orneriness, despite his bad leg, despite his suspicions that Chekhov was shirking his magazine in deference to the others, he would become a sympathetic if comic character. Leykin naturally wanted the professional and most excellent Chekhov to keep writing for him.

Biographer Magarshack, impatient to get Leykin off the stage, writes, inaccurately, that Chekhov "summed up his final opinion of Leykin in a letter to Suvorin in November 1888: 'Leykin is a good-natured and harmless man, but a bourgeois to the marrow of his bones. If he goes to see someone or says something, there is always something at the back of his mind. . . . A fox is always in fear for his life, and so is he. A subtle diplomatist! . . . In his letters to me he always warns me, frightens me, advises me, reveals all sorts of secrets to me. Poor limping martyr! He could have lived happily for the rest of his life, but some evil genius doesn't let him.'"[28] Chekhov didn't have a "final opinion" of Leykin. Summing up and disposing of a friend wasn't his style as a writer or a man. They continued to correspond and meet until 1900. Leykin died in 1906.

⚬⚬⚬

In "Ladies" ("Damy," April 19), a school district director tries to be generous to a teacher who has lost his voice; he cannot, however, defeat the "ladies," who push for a particular handsome but vapid young man to take the suitable job the director has found for, and more or less promised to, the disabled teacher. The story's setup and resolution seem to have been based on a joke or an offhand word about the influence of "ladies" on government appointments. Their patronage can overwhelm even a conscientious official.

In "Strong Impressions" ("Sil'nye Oshchushcheniya," April 21), members of a jury who are having to spend the night together "decided that before going to sleep, each one of them should ransack among his memories and tell something that had happened to him. Man's life is brief, but yet there is no man who cannot boast that there have been terrible moments in his past." This is not as common a setup for a story in Chekhov's work as for his French contemporary Guy de Maupassant's, but proceeding this way enabled Chekhov to provide a casual first-person speaking voice courtesy of "a foppishly dressed, fat little man." The little man's memory returns to what perhaps was Chekhov's present, or at least the present of those of Chekhov's friends who were marrying left and right: "I was not more than twenty-two or twenty-three when I fell head over ears in love with my present wife and made her an offer. Now I could with pleasure thrash myself for my early marriage, but at the time, I don't know what would have become of me if Natasha had refused me. My love was absolutely the real thing, just as it is described in novels—frantic, passionate, and so on."[29] He recalls a philosophical argument with a lawyer friend at the time of his engagement about the persuasiveness of a "talented" speaker:

> "As I listen to an orator I may perhaps grow sentimental and weep, but my fun-
> damental conviction, based for the most part on unmistakable evidence and
> fact, is not changed in the least. My lawyer maintained that I was young
> and foolish and that I was talking childish nonsense. In his opinion, for one
> thing, an obvious fact becomes still more obvious through light being thrown
> upon it by conscientious, well-informed people; for another, talent is an ele-
> mental force, a hurricane capable of turning even stones to dust, let alone such
> trifles as the convictions of artisans and merchants of the second guild. [. . .]
> One simple mortal by the power of the word turns thousands of convinced
> savages to Christianity [. . .] All history consists of similar examples, and in life
> they are met with at every turn; and so it is bound to be, or the intelligent and
> talented man would have no superiority over the stupid and incompetent. [. . .]
> "'Take you, for example,' said the lawyer. 'You are convinced at this
> moment that your fiancée is an angel and that there is not a man in the whole

town happier than you. But I tell you: ten or twenty minutes would be enough for me to make you sit down to this table and write to your fiancée, breaking off your engagement. [. . .]'"

And it was! The "little man" did write that letter.

He reflects: "What my friend said was not new, it was what everyone has known for ages, and the whole venom lay not in what he said, but in the damnable form he put it in." The storyteller mailed the fateful letter; the lawyer, having won the argument, immediately counter-argued for the future happiness of his friend's marriage. When the storyteller then broke down in despair over what he had just done, the lawyer explained that he himself had misaddressed the envelope on purpose so that it would be lost.

It's a clever story about, among other things, storytelling, persuasion, the fragility and ephemeral nature of romantic love, about fallibility. And what about *Chekhov's* broken engagement? Would he rue its dissolution? How the devil was he to know what the right thing to do was? About marrying Efros there were persuasive arguments for (love, settling down, dowry) and against (feisty antagonism, "cultural" differences).

Meanwhile, here the jury members are, deciding the fate of a murderer, based on arguments of talented lawyers. When the last member of the jury asks the others to think now at midnight about the thoughts of the murderer whose fate they are weighing, they don't like realizing how vulnerable they are to the strong impressions the trial lawyers have left on them.

―――

On April 24, Chekhov set out for Petersburg to see Leykin about *Motley Stories*; he arrived the next morning. Rosamund Bartlett notes that "The fact that Chekhov wrote so few letters during his St. Petersburg visits says a lot about the frenetic social life he led there; it also means we actually know comparatively little about what he actually got up to."[30] But on his first day of two weeks there this spring, Chekhov, "within 5 hours after arrival," filled in a lot of details in a giddy account to his brother Mikhail:

Coming and staying in the furnished rooms of the merchant Oleynichikov (the corner of Nevsky and Pushkin), I washed up, put on my new coat, new pants, and sharp shoes and traveled for 15 kopecks on the Troitsky Alley to the editorial office of *Fragments*. There the office manager greeted me as her fiancé of the future, and she began to pour out her soul, calling Leykin a burdened person and I his favorite employee . . . From the editorial office to the printer Golike was no distance. But I didn't find Golike so I went over to Bilibin's. His fiancée opened the door to me with a lesson in her hands (she, Misha, is in two departments!), and was very glad to see me. I shuffled my new shoes and asked: "How is your health?" But later . . . Having drunk at I. Grek's a glass of tea that was strong as tar, I went with him to stroll along the Neva, i.e., not with the tea, not with the tar, but with Bilibin. On the Neva we went in a boat, which made an impression on me. Off the boat we took ourselves to Dominico's, where for 60 kopecks we ate pie, drank a glass and a cup of coffee . . . But that's not all! You'll be amazed!

From Dominico's I went to the *Petersburg Gazette*.

From *Pet Gaz* I went to *New Times*, where I met with Suvorin. He received me very graciously and even gave me his hand. [. . .]

From Suv I went to the office [. . .]. The office manager Leont'eva, paying out the money to me, was quite not-bad. I gave her, Misha, my hand and tomorrow I will go to her to change my address . . . From the office I went to the office of Volkov and sent you a hundred (100) rubles [. . .]. From Volkov I went along Nevsky to my place on Pushkin and lay down to sleep . . . O wonders and miracles! In five hours I did so much! Who would have predicted that from an outhouse would come such a genius?

This "such a genius" line was a Chekhov family standard, originating when Anton had arrived in Moscow to rejoin his family at nineteen. Donald Rayfield recounts it this way: "Aleksandr had brought home Fiodor as a kitten who had been abandoned in a freezing latrine. Anton was much comforted when Fiodor stretched out on his lap and to this cat he first addressed an expression he applied to himself and his brothers: 'Who would have thought that such genius would come out of an earth closet?'"[31] After this, mock praise of one's own or another's cleverness would prompt this remark by the Chekhov brothers.[32] Fedor Timofeich's name and personality would characterize the subsequently famous cat in Christmas 1887's story "Kashtanka." In closing, Chekhov appended a greeting to "Dunechka [Dunya Efros], Sirusichka [?] and the other laxative weaknesses."[33] Not flattering to Efros, but a mention all the same. In Petersburg, free of medical duties and immediate responsibilities to the family, Chekhov could socialize and be primarily a writer, but Efros was in his thoughts.

As Bartlett points out, though, the socializing also freed him, for the most part, from letter-writing. In the next two weeks he wrote only three letters, two of them notes, including one to his sister, in which he sent greetings again to Efros ("with the long nose") and announcing, "I got married." The editors of the Soviet edition note that this fib was followed by an excision from the letter.[34]

"About Women" ("O Zhenshchinakh,"[35] April 26) satirizes men's arrogance and condescension. The only good thing about women, the buffoon essayist-narrator declares, is that they give birth to men.

May 1886

———

Day and night I'm obsessed by one recurring thought:
I must write, I must write, I must write. . . . The
moment I finish a tale, I must, for some reason, write
another one, then a third, and after the third, a fourth
one . . . I'm writing nonstop, like a traveler switching
horses midway, and I can't do otherwise.

—Trigorin, *The Seagull*[1]

May started with Chekhov still in Petersburg. He would be on the move throughout the month, and perhaps coincidentally the ten stories that he would publish in May are not especially grounded or vital, except for the last one, "The Boredom of Life."

Moving chronologically through Chekhov's year, reading his letters and translating portions of them, I notice patterns. He writes frequently to this person or that, but then there is a new friend I have not been familiar with, or there appears the beginning of a relationship I have known about, or there is an unusual tone. I notice that in busy May there are not very many letters and only a couple that now seem of significance. Because he was good at keeping up his correspondence, was there an anxiety he felt as he rushed about and the communications from friends were being forwarded after him? . . . He expressed longing to get away from his Moscow medical duties and regain his bearings at Babkino, where, although he would have office hours every day to treat the local peasants, he could also wander in the woods hunting mushrooms or sit on the riverbank fishing.

On May 3 he and Bilibin took a steamer from Petersburg to Leykin's estate on the left tributary of the Neva.[2] It seems to have been a day trip. By May 6, *Motley Stories* was in print and at least available to Chekhov; he signed one for the printer Golike and gave another to Leykin.[3] He wrote to his sister the same day, teasing her and Dunya Efros again about his having gotten married.

―――

In "A Gentleman Friend" ("Znakomyi Muzhchina," May 3), a kept woman who is down on her luck tries to entice a Jewish dentist, but she loses her nerve—and a tooth. She is undaunted and by that night finds a new man. Also published in *Fragments* on May 3, "A Fairy Tale: Dedicated to the Idiot Who Brags about His Contributions to the Newspaper" ("Skazka: Posvyashchaetsya Balbesu, Khvastayushchemu svoim Sotrudnichestvom v Gazetakh") is a skit in which a fly boasts that he writes for the newspapers. The other bugs challenge him to prove it. He shows them a newspaper and all its fly-speck punctuation.

Perhaps thinking of his friend Bilibin's honeymoon in Finland, Chekhov wrote "A Happy Man" ("Chastlivchik," May 5), which is about a groom on his honeymoon who gets out of the train at a station-stop to have a smoke. Back on board, the cheerful groom boasts to fellow passengers about his happiness. They soon help him realize that at the station he must have accidentally got on this train, which is going the opposite direction to the one he was on. Chekhov could not, it seems, figure out which way to go about his own marriage.

He worked especially diligently on his stories for Suvorin. "The Privy Councillor" ("Taynyy Sovetnik," May 6), however, is one of his least ambitious or impressive *New Times* stories. The adolescent narrator's uncle, the privy councillor, is a big shot short on cash, and comes to his sister's to summer while he works remotely. The uncle has Chekhov's ability to focus on the paperwork in front of him:

> For days together he sat in his own room working, in spite of the flies and the heat. His extraordinary capacity for sitting as though glued to his table produced upon us the effect of an inexplicable conjuring trick. To us idlers, knowing nothing of systematic work, his industry seemed simply miraculous. Getting up at nine, he sat down to his table, and did not leave it till dinner-time; after dinner he set to work again, and went on till late at night. Whenever I peeped through the keyhole I invariably saw the same thing: my uncle sitting at the table working.

And what the narrator as a boy witnesses is what Chekhov's family saw of him. He was systematic. He showed them how to get a lot of work done. But it is doubtful whether

Chekhov was as carefree as the merry privy councillor; also, while Chekhov appreciated fine scents, he was no dandy:

> The work consisted in his writing with one hand while he turned over the leaves of a book with the other, and, strange to say, he kept moving all over—swinging his leg as though it were a pendulum, whistling, and nodding his head in time. He had an extremely careless and frivolous expression all the while, as though he were not working, but playing at noughts and crosses. I always saw him wearing a smart short jacket and a jauntily tied cravat, and he always smelt, even through the keyhole, of delicate feminine perfumery. He only left his room for dinner, but he ate little.[4]

The uncle (nameless in the story) uses his little bit of idle time to flirt with the bailiff's wife, with whom the young narrator's tutor is also in love. The narrator's mother, tired of the disruptions at her well-ordered estate, finally gives the uncle money to go away and summer at his usual place abroad.

—⁓—

Chekhov took the May 8 train from Petersburg to Moscow and arrived the next day. The family apartment had been given up and they were staying at Babkino until they found a new place in the fall. He stayed the night on the Arbat at his brother Ivan's school-issued apartment.

He wrote Alexander on the 10th about Petersburg:

> The time I spent there was great. I couldn't have gotten closer to Suvorin and Grigorovich. There are so many details that I can't pass them along in a letter, and so I'll tell them to you when we meet.[5]

He had commenced an intimacy already, not quite a friendship, with Suvorin and Grigorovich. What details did Anton relate to Alexander as they sat together later this summer at Babkino? In the next paragraph, he critiqued Alexander's latest story:

> "The City of the Future" will become an artistic production only by the following conditions: 1) the absence of prolix wordy politico-socialistic-economic features; 2) continuous objectivity; 3) correctness in describing people and

objects; 4) special brevity; 5) boldness and originality; fleeing from stereo-types; 6) heart.

In letters, Chekhov often resorted to list-making, which makes me wonder if it was a habit he had developed as a student or from writing prescriptions for patients.

> In my opinion, a true description of nature must be very brief and pos-sess the character of relevance. Commonplaces such as "the sinking sun, bathing in the waves of the darkening sea, sheds a light of purple gold," and so forth, or "the swallows, flying over the surface of the sea, twittered merrily"—such commonplaces must be excluded. In descriptions of nature one ought to seize upon the little particulars, grouping them in such a way that when you close your eyes after reading you see a picture. For example, you will get the effect of a moonlit night if you write that a glow like a light from a star flashed from the broken bottle on the milldam, and the round, black shadow of a dog or wolf appeared, etc. Nature becomes animated if you are not squeamish about employing comparisons about its phenomena with human activities, etc.[6]

He was thinking of the nature-descriptions in his own recent stories, particularly "The Wolf," as he wrote that.

> Details are also the thing in the sphere of psychology. God preserve us from generalizations. Best of all, avoid depicting the hero's state of mind; you ought to try to make it clear from the hero's actions. It is not necessary to portray many active figures. The center of gravity should be two persons—he and she.

He was making plain to himself, to Alexander, and to us the sharp focus and method he had been using in his fiction. And we and Alexander nod and agree, *Oh, sure, it's not complicated . . . if you are a super-focused self-disciplined genius!*

A short piece for *Fragments* came out on May 10, "A Literary Table of Ranks" ("Liter-aturnaya Tabel' o Rangakh"), atop of which list are Tolstoy and Goncharov. The purpose of the skit, however, according to the Soviet editors, was to name and *exclude* S. Okreyts, the reactionary editor of *Luch* (The Ray), who Chekhov had been making the butt of jokes for a few years, including nicknaming him Judophobe Judophobovich.[7] While Chekhov himself made Jewish jokes, he did not suffer writers who were seriously anti-Semitic.

On May 11 or 12 he went to join his family, including wayward Nikolay, in Babkino,[8] where the family had rented a furnished cottage for the first time the previous summer from an artistic and aristocratic family, the Kiselevs. Chekhov could unwind and the extended family and a wide range of friends could gather as time and opportunity allowed. Chekhov had described his first impressions of their situation to Leykin the year before:

> The country house is situated on the steep bank of a river. It is a very pictur-
> esque spot. Below is the river, famed for its fish; on the other side of the river
> is a huge forest; and there are woods on this side of it. Near the cottage are
> hot-houses, flowerbeds, etc. I love to be in the country at the beginning of
> May. It is so jolly to watch the buds opening on the trees and to listen to the
> first songs of the nightingales. There are no houses near the estate, and we
> shall be completely alone. Kiselev and his wife, Begichev, the former opera
> tenor Vladislavlev, Markevich's ghost, and my family—that is all. The month
> of May is excellent for fishing, especially crucian carp and tench, that is, pond
> fish, and there are ponds on the estate.[9]

Babkino

He would spend happy hours in the woods and on the river and at the ponds. In May of 1885, he further described the estate's attractions to his brother Mikhail:

> At last I have taken off my heavy waders, my hands no longer smell of fish,
> and I can sit down to write to you. It is six o'clock in the morning now. Our
> people are asleep. It is extraordinarily quiet all around. Only from time to
> time is the silence broken by the twittering of the birds and by the scratching
> of the mouse behind the wallpaper. I am writing these lines sitting before the
> large square window of my room. From time to time I glance through it. An

extraordinary enchanting and lovely landscape stretches before my eyes: the little stream, the distant woods, a corner of the Kiselev house. . . .

—⁓—

The most sentimental story Chekhov ever wrote might be "A Day in the Country" ("Den' za Gorodom," May 19), about an old man educating children about nature: "there is no secret in Nature which baffles him. He knows everything. Thus, for example, he knows the names of all the wild flowers, animals, and stones. He knows what herbs cure diseases, he has no difficulty in telling the age of a horse or a cow. Looking at the sunset, at the moon, or the birds, he can tell what sort of weather it will be next day. And indeed, it is not only Terenty who is so wise. Silanty Silich, the innkeeper, the market-gardener, the shepherd, and all the villagers, generally speaking, know as much as he does. These people have learned not from books, but in the fields, in the wood, on the river bank. Their teachers have been the birds themselves, when they sang to them, the sun when it left a glow of crimson behind it at setting, the very trees, and wild herbs." Though the depictions of the folk seem too good to be true, Terenty does remark, rather beautifully: "'The nightingale is a singing-bird, without sin. He has had a voice given him in his throat, to praise God and gladden the heart of man. It's a sin to disturb him.'"

Chekhov excluded "A Day in the Country" from his *Collected Works* as well as the next four he wrote, an unusual streak of what he later judged to be unworthy stories. And while I wonder occasionally at his exclusions, I will save my disagreement with him only over the last one of the month.

"In a Pension" ("V Pansione," May 24) is about a teacher who, wanting a raise, butters up his woman boss while denying the beauty of a beautiful seventeen-year-old student, about whom the boss says: "You won't find a better nose in all of Russia." The only nose Chekhov regularly remarked upon was Dunya Efros's. He may have seen her in Moscow, as he was there on May 20 before returning on May 24 to Babkino and his family.

Reviews of *Motley Stories* were appearing.

After Leykin wrote and asked him to "push himself" and send him some pieces, he replied on May 24 with excuses so weak that he seemed to hope Leykin would become disgusted and fire him.

I'm guilty before you: I'm working poorly for *Fragments*. Now I'm working poorly for everywhere. What happened with me, I don't know. Probably the prophet with the praises turned my head . . . But if you believe in the evil eye,

I can in justification say "Jinxed!" Mostly these trips to Peter always act on me badly. I get off track and for a long time can't get the intoxication from my head . . . I will be lazy *until June 1*, and then I give you my word to work.[10]

But, right now, this week, he had been writing the excellent "The Boredom of Life." He was also, he explained in his next letter to Leykin on May 27, seeing patients:

> The post bell's ringing . . . Someone's gone . . . I run out to see . . . A guest has come, but I continue writing. [. . .]
>
> I have a lot of sick patients. Rickety children and old ones with rashes. There's a 75-year-old woman with erysipelas on her hand; I'm afraid I'll have dealings with erysipelas of the tissue. There will be abscesses, but cutting into an old woman is frightful . . .

In response to the May 24 letter, Leykin suggested that Chekhov think up or "steal" themes for Nikolay to illustrate.

"At a Summer Villa" ("Na Dache," May 25) is one of his humor stories where he seems to have worked out the plot before writing it. When Chekhov was writing his best or most seriously-minded stories, they seem to have formed in front of his mind and pen as he wrote. "At a Summer Villa" is clever enough that there is an amusing short film of it in Russian.[11] The wife wants to clean up the dacha, their summer cabin, but her lazy husband and studious younger brother are in the way, so she sends each a love note from a mysterious young woman who wants to meet them the next afternoon. The husband and brother show up at the same spot and are angry with each other for being in the way. At dinner that evening, the wife/sister laughs and tells the grumpy pair, who have been stood up, what she did to trick them.

In "Nothing to Do: A Dacha Story" ("Ot Nechego Delat'," May 26), Chekhov imagines married life with a lazy, wanton woman. Nikolay, a lawyer, catches his children's tutor Vanya, a nineteen-year-old engineering student, kissing his wife. Vanya runs off in fright and the husband mocks his thirty-three-year-old wife," 'You should not turn a boy's head, old dear. You shouldn't, you know. He is a nice, kind boy.'"[12] Nikolay finds Vanya and teases him that Vanya will now have to provide for his wife and pay child support. If Vanya refuses, they will have to duel. Having tormented him, Nikolay returns home to scold his wife again for idly seducing Vanya. Nikolay goes for a stroll, the sights and sounds of which Chekhov, happily ensconced at Babkino, would not have had to invent, only describe: "When evening came and twilight shrouded the earth, the lawyer went for another walk. It was a glorious evening. The trees were sleeping and looked as though no storm could wake them from their young springtime slumber. The drowsy stars looked down on the earth. Frogs croaked and an owl screeched somewhere behind the garden. The short, jerky whistles of a nightingale's song could be heard from afar."[13]

Nikolay encounters Vanya again. Vanya, feeling guilty, accepts the terms for dueling. Nikolay immediately laughs it off, tells Vanya that his wife is not worth it, and he and the young man take a friendly walk.

On May 31, he published his second story of the month in *New Times*, "The Boredom of Life" ("Skuka Zhizni"). Before doing the research on this book, I had never read it, and because Constance Garnett had not translated it, or as far as I knew neither had anyone else, I read it in Russian. With each new paragraph, I felt I was making a major literary find for the English-reading world. I would translate it! It's a fateful, moving and great novel in only 4,000 words (about ten pages of this book you're reading).

Now is an appropriate time to talk about *translating* versus *reading*.

What's Chekhov like in Russian?

I described it once as Chekhov being just a little funnier. You can hear Chekhov's smile. You can hear his particular voice, the tuning as clear as a bell.

But if your Russian isn't completely fluent, or you're not a compulsive reader, maybe reading him in translation doesn't matter, or it's a trade-off. For me, reading Chekhov in English, I get speed at the expense of revelation. I read more freshly in Russian, because it's hard. I continually have to dig out words and phrases, and the images develop slowly but deeply. Unfortunately, in Russian I also step into an occasional hole and get distracted by my stumbling. *There's a key word I'm missing! Do I stop or do I wait until I see that word again? But maybe the story turns on that particular word?* After I finished one pass through of a translation of "The Boredom of Life," which I might compare to one feed-through of a color-spray printer (there! the blue is down, next comes magenta, then yellow), I discovered a preexisting translation, disguisedly entitled "Taedium Vitae"; April FitzLyon and Kyril Zinovieff's translation is better than what I was doing, and so I'll quote from it rather than from my motley one.

In "The Boredom of Life" (I'll keep my title), Anna Mikhailovna Lebedeva, an estate-owner, has given up on life because her teenaged daughter has died. "As soon as someone consciously begins to question the point of existence—in no matter what way—and feels an acute need to look beyond the grave, then neither sacrifices nor fasting, nor knocking about from place to place will satisfy him. But, fortunately for Anna Mikhailovna, just as she arrived at Zhenino, fate brought her face to face with an occurrence which made her forget about old age and the nearness of death for a long time."[14]

Her cook burns himself with boiling water and she treats him. She realizes she is good at nursing and always has been, and she dedicates herself to treating the local peasants. She had affairs when her daughter was little ("doctors had been numbered among her lovers, and she had learned a bit from them"), and her husband left her.

Chekhov is fascinated by her, an untrained but devoted healer: "The greater the suffering of the patient and the dirtier and more disgusting his ailment, the sweeter her work seemed to her." But he is also leery of her messianism:

> She adored her patients. Sentiment suggested that they were her saviors, but reason made her want to see them not as individual personalities, not as peasants, but as something abstract—the people!

Through a revived correspondence with her husband, she reconciles with him. He is a general stationed somewhere in the south, and he retires and comes to her at the Zhenino estate. He is bored with life and full of aches and pains. He notices that she has given up meat. He is curious but skeptical about her treating the peasants, as she is not a doctor, and he hates what he judges to be the peasants' ingratitude. He knows he's cranky and hates himself for it. He and Anna won't or can't talk about their daughter.

> It was only in the evenings, when darkness filled the rooms and a cricket chirped despondently behind the stove, that this awkwardness disappeared. They sat side by side in silence, and on those occasions it was just as if their souls were whispering about the thing that neither of them could bring themselves to say aloud.

Insufferably irritable with the household servants and the peasants, the husband revives in the spring and becomes outwardly religious; he has a mass said for his daughter, and he attends church regularly. Dr. Chekhov diagnoses him for us: "It was a paroxysm of elderly grief, but the old man imagined that a reaction, a radical change was taking place in him." Indeed, his religious fervor disappears and he goes in instead for his more characteristic carping at the peasants who are still coming for his wife's treatment. They become so offended that they begin staying away.

Anna complains at him for this and he explains, crankily but from Chekhov's point of view as a medical professional rightly, that they're better off seeing real doctors: "'In my opinion, you'll do much more good to a sick man if you shove him off roughly to see a doctor than if you treat him yourself.'"

The unhappy old man repeatedly gives clear voice to Chekhov's own opinions:

> "Alexander of Macedon was a great man, but there's no need to go and make a song and dance about it, and it's the same with the Russian people—it's a great people, but it doesn't follow that you can't tell it the truth to its face. You can't make a lap-dog of the people. These [peasants] are human-beings just like you and me, with the same shortcomings, and therefore you shouldn't worship them, nor coddle them, but you should teach them, reform them . . . inspire them . . ."

When Anna suggests that they themselves can learn "how to work" from the peasants, he blows up. Hasn't *he* worked hard and endured so much as a soldier and general?

> "Perhaps you'll tell me, I can learn how to suffer from that people of yours? Of course, it isn't as if I ever suffered! I lost my own daughter . . . the only thing that still tied me to life in this damned old age! And I haven't suffered!"
> At this sudden memory of their daughter the old people all at once began to weep and to wipe their eyes with their table-napkins.

They cry and talk about their daughter and begin sharing Anna's bed. He is still grumbly, but they relax and she completely halts seeing patients. He tempts his vegetarian wife with some delicious fish, and she succumbs, and for the next few months they laze around, doing little but planning elaborate dishes: "The old people gave themselves up to gustatory sensations." He can't read for long stretches, as he never did so. He putters, she sags. One day in early fall, he has eaten too much, feels heartburn and hopelessness and asks Anna if she still has her medicines. He goes to the cabinet and helps himself, and comes back to bed and never wakes up. She does not investigate his death (not wanting to know, it seems, if he had only taken the wrong drug). The story ends with Anna's resolution to join a monastery.

Chekhov not only didn't choose to put "The Boredom of Life" in his *Collected Works*, but noted on it to *not* put it in.[15] I believe that there's a story behind this story, but what? Chekhov wrote it after arriving at Babkino this summer. The setting of the story, Zhenino, part-rhymes with Babkino, so I am going to make the undaring suggestion that Chekhov had Babkino in mind.[16] My pet theory, which means there is no evidence for or against it, is that there were details in it that even in 1899 were too close to some living person's experiences. Perhaps the old couple were based on friends or relatives of the Babkino estate owners, Chekhov's friends the Kiselevs.

June 1886

—◈—

What I have come to like best in the whole of
Russian literature is the childlike Russian quality
of Pushkin and Chekhov, their modest reticence in
such high-sounding matters as the ultimate purpose
of mankind or their own salvation. It isn't that they
didn't think about these things, and to good effect, but
to talk about such things seemed to them pretentious,
presumptuous.

—Boris Pasternak, *Doctor Zhivago*[1]

Leykin pinched pennies, and the Chekhovs did not, though Anton continually strove
to keep the family finances in the black. In a letter at the beginning of June, Leykin
wondered: "You write: *No money.* Lordy! Where do you put your money? It seems I live
on even less than you do."[2]

Chekhov taunted Leykin a few days later, in a postscript to his brother Nikolay's letter:
"You ask where I spend my money? On women!!!!"[3] This, Leykin knew, was not so.

There is a copy of *Motley Stories* dated and dedicated to Chekhov's father Pavel on June 2,
1886: "To the deeply respected Pavel Egorovich from the loving and faithful author." We
know from Pavel's children's letters and memoirs that Pavel read newspapers and "French
novels" and Nikolay Leskov's short stories.[4] There is no record of Pavel's response to his
son's writings.

Meanwhile, Bilibin was forwarding reviews of the book to Chekhov, who did not
pretend *not* to read them, but, having read them, he disdained them. A few years later he
would remark in a letter to a fellow writer:

And as regards the word "art," I fear it as merchants' wives fear a Sodom rain of brimstone. When people talk to me of the artistic and the anti-artistic, of that which is theatric and non-theatric, of tendency, realism, etc., I become confused, consent irresolutely, and answer with platitudinous half-truths that are not worth a penny. I divide all literary works into two classes: those that I like and those that I do not like. I have no other criterion, and if you were to ask me why I like Shakespeare and dislike Zlatovratsky, I should be unable to answer. Perhaps in time, when I become wiser, I shall acquire a criterion, but meanwhile, all this talk about "artistry" only tires me and seems to me only the continuation of the same scholastic discourses with which people wearied themselves in the Middle Ages.[5]

Chekhov really disliked high-faluting art discussion.

—⁓—

His first story in June, "Romance with Double-Bass" ("Roman s Kontrabasom," June 7), is a farce unlike his usual comic stories. It's a professionally polished comedy, with all the pluses and minuses of that. A minus for me is that there seem to be no incidentally personal details of the moment. A musician and a woman separately have their clothes stolen while swimming. She hides in his music case, which is discovered by the double-bassist's fellow musicians, who heft it with them to her engagement party, where, upon the case's opening, she is literally completely exposed. Meanwhile, the bass player Pitsikatoff "put on his top-hat, swung the double-bass onto his back and padded off toward the bushes. Naked, with his musical instrument slung over his shoulders, he resembled some ancient mythological demigod." As in a fairy tale, he remains forever naked under a bridge. The clever plot makes me wonder if Chekhov was fed the idea from a friend or a brother and wrote it up. The short British 1974 movie of the story, starring John Cleese, is fully in the story's spirit.

In the same issue of *Fragments*, he had the skit "List of People Having the Right to Travel Free on the Russian Railroad." Chekhov did not have this "right," but his friend Schechtel did, and on June 8 he followed up his late May letter to Schechtel to encourage him again to hop on a train and come up to Babkino. The letter is the best kind of invitation to a friend—insistent yet funny. He lists all the reasons why Schechtel should come: fishing, swimming, the grass, the air, the birds; and of course painting (their mutual friend the landscape master Levitan was already there painting and so was Nikolay Chekhov). He himself was dashing off numerous skits and stories, but he told Schechtel he felt "lazy."

On June 15 Dunya Efros wrote the first of two surviving letters from her to Chekhov. "Dear Anton Pavlovich. You, perhaps, are amazed at my letter, but I am unable to find another way to find out everything that is going on with you, how you're doing. I sent three letters to your sister and not one reply. What this signifies I decidedly don't know. Couldn't you get her to write me, or maybe, not be too lazy to write me yourself . . ."[6]

Chekhov replied, lazy or not, but what he said is unknown, except as what can be guessed from her reply on June 27.

———

He didn't write a story for *New Times* this month, but he indeed came through for Leykin, as promised. His other stories were for the *Petersburg Gazette*. In "Fears" ("Strakhi," June 16) the narrator relates three instances in his life where he had been scared out of his wits:

> "It's stupid!" I said to myself. "That phenomenon is only terrible because I don't understand it; everything we don't understand is mysterious."[7]

The narrator eventually concludes that "cowardice was stronger than common sense."

Chekhov on the other hand wasn't too cowardly to write to Dunya Efros at this time, though his letter has disappeared. He went to Moscow at some point and returned by June 23.

The biographer Magarshack concludes that Babkino "had a most beneficial effect on Chekhov's health, chiefly owing to the regular life he led there. He usually got up at seven o'clock and immediately sat down at his improvised desk (the bottom part of a big sewing machine from which the treadle had been removed) and wrote his stories, raising his eyes from time to time to have a look at the magnificent view through the large, square window, as though drawing inspiration from it. His room was sparsely furnished: a small bed covered with a striped blanket, a tall wardrobe at the bottom of the bed by the window, a bedside table with a candle in a cheap candlestick, a washbasin, and on the wall above the head of the bed a pair of chemist's scales in which he weighed out the medicines for the patients who flocked to him from all over the countryside. [. . .] His surgery hours were from ten to one o'clock. At one o'clock he usually had lunch and then went for a walk in the woods. After tea he sat down to his writing again. In the afternoon he would fish or have a game of croquet, which would sometimes go on till after nightfall, when they would stick lighted candles near the [wickets]. At eight o'clock he had dinner, after which they all went to spend the evenings with the Kiselevs. . . . Vladislavlev would sing the latest songs . . . (Chekhov's favorite piece of music was Chopin's Nocturne in G major and during his last years in Yalta he would often ask a visiting pianist to play it to him.)"[8]

Mikhail Chekhov's drawing of Chekhov's room at Babkino; Mikhail Chekhov's copy of Levitan's sketch of the prospect by the main Kiselev house.

A simple story without consequential events, and seemingly set near Babkino, is "The Chemist's Wife" ("Aptekarsha," June 21). One early morning after a party, an officer and a military doctor temporarily stationed in the area idly think about how to go about seducing the drugstore owner's wife. They have the usual or typical male arrogance about their right to do so, and as bachelors the usual or typical contempt for husbands:

> "The pharmacist is asleep. And his wife is asleep, too. She is a pretty woman, Obtyosov."
>
> "I saw her. I liked her very much. . . . Tell me, doctor, can she possibly love that jawbone of an ass? Can she?"
>
> "No, most likely she does not love him," sighed the doctor, speaking as though he were sorry for the chemist. "The little woman is asleep behind the window, Obtyosov, what? Tossing with the heat, her little mouth half open . . . and one little foot hanging out of bed. I bet that fool the chemist doesn't realise what a lucky fellow he is. . . . No doubt he sees no difference between a woman and a bottle of carbolic!"[9]

She, for her part, is listless, unsatisfied, and happens to be awake next to her snoozing husband and seems to have overheard them. When they ring, she throws on a dress and slippers and hustles to the shop door.

They don't have much of a plan besides chatting her up. They ask for throat lozenges, then soda powder, then seltzer, all to maintain her company. The doctor knows enough to ask for an alcoholic chemical mixture, and she fetches it for them to add to their seltzer:

> "What a flirt you are, though!" the doctor laughed softly, looking slyly at her from under his brows. "Your eyes seem to be firing shot: piff-paff! I congratulate you: you've conquered! We are vanquished!"
>
> The chemist's wife looked at their ruddy faces, listened to their chatter, and soon she, too, grew quite lively. Oh, she felt so gay! She entered into the conversation, she laughed, flirted, and even, after repeated requests from the customers, drank two ounces of wine.

They linger and kiss her hand farewell. She scolds them, but she is excited: "She ran quickly into the bedroom and sat down in the same place. She saw the doctor and the officer, on coming out of the shop, walk lazily away a distance of twenty paces; then they stopped and began whispering together. What about? Her heart throbbed, there was a pulsing in her temples, and why she did not know. . . . Her heart beat violently as though those two whispering outside were deciding her fate."

By the time the officer works up his nerve and returns to ring at the shop, the bell awakens the chemist, who gets up, irritated with his wife for not answering it. He serves the dismayed officer, and returns to the bedroom:

> "How unhappy I am!" said the chemist's wife, looking angrily at her husband, who was undressing quickly to get into bed again. "Oh, how unhappy I am!" she repeated, suddenly melting into bitter tears. "And nobody knows, nobody knows. . . ."

We know!

These young, attractive, lonely, bored women populate Chekhov's fictional world. The chemist's wife might be, in that world, a cousin of "The Witch," stuck in the boonies (probably in the neighborhood of Babkino) with a dull, unappreciative husband.

"Not Wanted" ("Lishnie Lyudi," June 23), on the other hand, is about an unappreciated husband, a lawyer who takes the train two or three times a week to the dacha community where his wife and son are spending the summer. We learn from his fellow traveler at the station that the trips there and back to the city are "all petty expenditure not worth considering, but, mind you, in the course of the summer it will run up to some two hundred rubles. Of course, to be in the lap of Nature is worth any money—I don't dispute it . . . idyllic and all the rest of it; but of course, with the salary an official gets, as you know yourself, every farthing has to be considered."[10] Chekhov was never free from worry about money, even in "idyllic" Babkino. The lawyer is grouchy from all the inconveniences of the journey. As the title of the story indicates, his wife, occupied with friends putting on amateur plays and musical performances, doesn't actually need him, and he himself is impatient with his son, who needs looking after.

"A Serious Step" ("Ser'eznyi Shag," June 28) is about a father who is irritated with his wife's permissiveness in regard to their daughter, who is being courted and who, in the course of the story, seems to have been proposed to:

> "This is a serious step," Aleksei Borisich thinks to himself. "One can't just decide willy-nilly . . . one has to seriously . . . from all sides . . ."[11]

While awaiting his daughter's explanation of her situation, he continues to grumble to himself: "One has to look at it . . . from all sides, to chat, discuss . . . the holy sacrament of marriage, one can't just approach it with frivolity." But his wife and daughter don't ever get around to discussing the engagement with him. They are happy and after all so is he.

It seems that every time Chekhov contemplated marriage this year, he found reasons not to proceed. But why not go ahead and take that "serious step"? Dunya Efros, however, seems to have had enough for now of his waffling.

Chekhov was writing few letters this month, probably because friends and family were with him, including Alexander and Nikolay, in whose interest he wrote to Leykin on June 24:

> I'm lazy as before. The Devil knows where the energy goes . . . There's almost no money, the weather is more often bad than good, and the soul is foul, and a day doesn't come without mental troubles. I continually find foul news and surprises so that I'm even afraid of receiving letters. [. . .]
>
> [Alexander] was blind, but now he is [. . .] able to see. Nikolay is finishing a charming drawing, which he's sending tomorrow. The drawing's excellent. A talented person, but . . . vous comprenez, a bad workman.
>
> [. . .] In June I'm not coming: family obligations . . . As for July I can't say anything positive. I'm not fishing for now. There are a lot of mushrooms, though their growth is hindered by the outrageously cold nights.[12]

Chekhov, after following up on the prescription he had given Leykin's wife in April, warned Leykin off prescribing the peasants an irritating treatment made from roots: "Why do so if there's castor oil?" It seems that like Anna in "The Boredom of Life," Leykin had taken to treating the local peasants. Castor oil, anyway, couldn't do any harm.

On June 27, Efros again wrote to Chekhov: "I offer you, Anton Pavlovich, sincere thanks for your letter and that you so quickly wrote me back . . . I'm completely in agreement with you that you're happier there than here [she was at a dacha community]. You have Mashenka or Yaden'ka, on whom you make various experiments and whose stupidity makes everyone laugh at her. You put on various extravaganzas for fun, and there's nothing like that here. . . . I was thinking about a rich fiancée for you, Anton Pavlovich, even before receiving your letter. There's the daughter of a Moscow merchant here, not bad, quite tubby (your taste) and quite stupid (also an advantage). She yearns to escape the guardianship of her mother, of whom she's terribly ashamed. Once she even drank a bucket and a half of vinegar to make herself pale and scare her mother. She told us that herself. It seems to me that you'll like her—there's a lot of money."[13]

Efros was hurt and trying to sting him back.

But they weren't through.

Meanwhile, there was Maria Kiseleva, probably thirteen years Chekhov's senior.[14] She was the aristocratic daughter of a playwright, Begichev, who was the director of the Imperial Theaters, and she was the wife of the owner of Babkino, Aleksei Kiselev. As a mother of two, she was an aspiring children's book author; Chekhov, as editor and volunteer agent, would help her publish some of her stories.

The Chekhovs came from a long line of serfs, while the Kiselevs were aristocrats. Both families, however, were theatrical and musical and for three summers they seem to have for the most part enjoyed each other's company. All were cultured and educated, and to Kiseleva's credit, she sought out the genius Chekhov's free literary guidance. Kiseleva's letters to him reveal her as a prim, proud, educated, cultured person. Chekhov was patient with her and encouraged her and they became close enough friends that they could have serious arguments about literature.

July 1886

—◊—

"If your friend truly wants to write, he should write
and let nothing get into his way. He should submit to
newspapers and magazines without caring whether
they accept them or not. One good short story a year
will not make him a writer, any more than hammering
one nail into a piece of wood each year will make him
a carpenter."

—In conversation[1]

C hekhov was in Babkino for most of the month, with two short trips away. By the end
of June, it seems, he had refocused and found all his literary senses engaged again.

"The Chorus Girl" ("Khoristka," July 5) is about a wife harassing the chorus girl that
her husband has been seeing. The wife, with an angry and pitiful sob story, shakes the
young woman down for *all* of her gifted jewelry, even though the husband has only treated
her to a few trinkets.

"I ask you for the things! Give me the things! I am crying. . . . I am humiliating
myself. . . . If you like I will go down on my knees! If you wish it!"

Pasha shrieked with horror and waved her hands. She felt that this pale,
beautiful lady who expressed herself so grandly, as though she were on the
stage, really might go down on her knees to her, simply from pride, from
grandeur, to exalt herself and humiliate the chorus girl.[2]

The cowardly husband, hiding behind Pasha's bedroom door, is impressed by his wife's
having bullied the young woman. When his wife has left, he tells off Pasha:

> "My God! She, a lady, so proud, so pure. . . . She was ready to go down on
> her knees to . . . to this wench! And I've brought her to this! I've allowed it!"
>
> He clutched his head in his hands and moaned.

Chekhov fiddled with many phrasings in this story after its original publication in *Fragments*. It remains however a bitter comedy hinging on the hypocrisy of the wrathful, contemptuous wife, who blames the chorus girl more than her husband, and the self-pitying husband, who also after all blames the chorus girl. With each new insult our sympathy sharpens for Pasha.[3]

Leykin wrote Chekhov on July 5 explaining how sales of Chekhov's book were going. As if resigned, Leykin sighed: "But how soon can books with the title 'Motley Stories' pay off? [. . .] I make glib titles for my books—and they pay off in 7–8 months. If your book pays off in a year, praise God. Accept that besides that, in summer no books come out."[4]

Whatever routine Chekhov had reinstituted for his writing, it was broken up when on July 7 he was asked by a judicial investigator to fill in for his colleague Dr. S. P. Uspensky, who had helped train him, and perform an autopsy several miles away. He set out the next day.[5]

Chekhov supplied Leykin with the humor piece "A Glossary of Terms for Young Ladies" ("Slovotolkovatel' dlya Barishen'") for the July 12 issue, the same day that the first-rate "The Schoolmaster" ("Uchitel'") came out in *New Times*. Sysoev the schoolmaster is dying; everyone sees it. He denies his condition to himself and others.

> Just before the factory manager's house, where the festivity was to take place,
> he had a little mishap. He was taken with a violent fit of coughing. . . . He was
> so shaken by it that the cap flew off his head and the stick dropped out of his
> hand; and when the school inspector and the teachers, hearing his cough, ran
> out of the house, he was sitting on the bottom step, bathed in perspiration.[6]

There is an end-of-school-year banquet with speeches, and Sysoev can't help himself from acting obnoxiously. Only one beleaguered colleague openly states the connection between Sysoev's illness and behavior:

> "He won't leave off," Lyapunov went on, snorting angrily. "He takes advantage
> of his position as an invalid and worries us all to death. Well, sir, I am not
> going to consider your being ill."

"Let my illness alone!" cried Sysoev, angrily. "What is it to do with you? They all keep repeating it at me: illness! illness! illness! . . . As though I need your sympathy! Besides, where have you picked up the notion that I am ill? I was ill before the examinations, that's true, but now I have completely recovered, there is nothing left of it but weakness."

And as the banquet continues, everyone, as if in a dream, ignores his horrible behavior; their failure to note his angry complaining in itself confuses him and dimly, frighteningly awakens in him the awareness that he is in fact about to die. His sense of taste is off; food is unpleasant. He gives a surly, embittered speech:

He several times referred to certain enemies of his, tried to drop hints, repeated himself, coughed, and flourished his fingers unbecomingly. At last he was exhausted and in a perspiration, and he began talking jerkily, in a low voice as though to himself, and finished his speech not quite coherently: "And so I propose the health of Bruni, that is Adolf Andreyich, who is here, among us . . . generally speaking . . . you understand . . ."

When he finished everyone gave a faint sigh, as though someone had sprinkled cold water and cleared the air. Bruni alone apparently had no unpleasant feeling. Beaming and rolling his sentimental eyes, the German shook Sysoev's hand with feeling and was again as friendly as a dog.

Chekhov himself had to lie about or disguise his own tuberculosis, though friends regularly noticed his symptoms and coughing fits.

After the German owner of the factory-school lauds Sysoev to the skies, the praises from all come raining down:

And all present at the dinner began as one man talking of Sysoev's extraordinary talent. And as though a dam had been burst, there followed a flood of sincere, enthusiastic words such as men do not utter when they are restrained by prudent and cautious sobriety. Sysoev's speech and his intolerable temper and the horrid, spiteful expression on his face were all forgotten. Everyone talked freely, even the shy and silent new teachers, poverty-stricken, downtrodden youths who never spoke to the inspector without addressing him as "your honor." It was clear that in his own circle Sysoev was a person of consequence.

Having been accustomed to success and praise for the fourteen years that he had been schoolmaster, he listened with indifference to the noisy enthusiasm of his admirers.

This indifference cracks, however, when the factory boss concludes the round of praises:

"In response to your words I ought to tell you that . . . Fyodor Lukich's family will be provided for and that a sum of money was placed in the bank a month ago for that object."

Sysoev looked enquiringly at the German, at his colleagues, as though unable to understand why his family should be provided for and not he himself. And at once on all the faces, in all the motionless eyes bent upon him, he read not the sympathy, not the commiseration which he could not endure, but something else, something soft, tender, but at the same time intensely sinister, like a terrible truth, something which in one instant turned him cold all over and filled his soul with unutterable despair. With a pale, distorted face he suddenly jumped up and clutched at his head. For a quarter of a minute he stood like that, stared with horror at a fixed point before him as though he saw the swiftly coming death of which Bruni was speaking, then sat down and burst into tears.

Chekhov himself shuddered to think of a roomful of pitying well-wishers with "motionless eyes bent upon him."

No one ever saw Chekhov weep, but they would have seen him mortified while being lauded at the premiere of *The Cherry Orchard*, just six months before his death in 1904: "Chekhov found himself compelled to take the stage and remain standing at length, weak and coughing, to be celebrated. He was presented with such gifts as an antique laurel wreath, [. . .] adorned with portraits of actors and students"; he had to listen to speeches of gratitude from the theater group that "owed so much to Chekhov's 'talent,' 'tender heart,' and 'pure soul' that Chekhov should consider it his own. Endless bombast arrived in telegrams from all over Russia. Chekhov, who had mocked such sententiousness all his writing life, could only submit to being its object."[7]

When Sysoev gets home, he tries to restore his faith in his recovery. Meanwhile, "the district doctor was sitting in the next room and telling his wife in a whisper that a man ought not to have been allowed to go out to dinner who had not in all probability more than a week to live."

Chekhov later touched up this story, even more than he had "The Chorus Girl"; he excised paragraphs and an entire scene after Sysoev's breakdown at the banquet, wherein Lyapunov catches up with him and profusely apologizes.

Commentator after commentator point out how little revising Chekhov did after publication. This occurrence of editing was unusual, and yet in each of these July stories that he later edited, he did not change the tone or feeling, as he had in "A Little Joke."

"A Troublesome Visitor" ("Bespokoinyi Gost'") came out in the middle of July, when Chekhov had happy and untroublesome visitors at Babkino. He was even trying to get Leykin to come for a stay. The nightmarish story's troublesome visitor, on the other hand, is a hunter who has stopped in bad weather at a forester's hut. The forester is skittish and declares: "I am not afraid of wolves or bears, or wild beasts of any sort, but I am afraid of man. You can save yourself from beasts with a gun or some other weapon, but you have no means of saving yourself from a wicked man."[8] As they sit in uneasy company with each other, they hear a cry for help, but the forester refuses to investigate.

> The hunter and the forester fell to listening with their eyes fixed on the window. Through the noise of the forest they could hear sounds such as the strained ear can always distinguish in every storm, so that it was difficult to make out whether people were calling for help or whether the wind was wailing in the chimney. But the wind tore at the roof, tapped at the paper on the window, and brought a distinct shout of "Help!"

The hunter can't persuade the forester to go out with him to look, so he goes himself. Minutes later he returns, having encountered a woman who had run into difficulties with her cart. The hunter is now doubly contemptuous of his host and at the same time becomes suspicious and menacing:

> "You must have money to be afraid of people! A man who is poor is not likely to be afraid. . . ."
>
> "For those words you will answer before God," Artyom said hoarsely from the stove. "I have no money."
>
> "I dare say! Scoundrels always have money. . . . Why are you afraid of people, then? So you must have! I'd like to take and rob you for spite, to teach you a lesson! . . ."

Disgusted with the timid forester, the threatening hunter leaves the hut, and the forester bolts the door. The story ends here, but Dostoevsky (to bring in an expert on nightmares) would have kept it going toward a violent or dramatic resolution.

Chekhov published only two more pieces this month, both of them quite moralistic. "A Rare Bird" (July 19) is a twenty-line tale, published under the Latin title "Rara Avis," wherein a crime novelist asks a detective to show him various types of criminals, which the detective finds easy, but when the novelist wants to see a few good "ideal and honest" folks for contrast, the detective is stumped.

"Other People's Misfortune" ("Chuzhaya Beda," July 28) is an unusually simple tale: a rich conservative expresses his contempt for a down-on-their-luck traditional family, whose estate he and his wife are buying:

> "Of course I'm sorry for them, but it's their own fault. Who forced them to mortgage their estate? Why have they neglected it so? We really oughtn't to feel sorry for them. . . . He's probably a drunkard and a gambler—did you see his mug?—and she is a woman of fashion and a spendthrift. I know these characters!"
>
> "How do you know them, Styopa?"
>
> "I know! . . ."[9]

Not only are we cheap with financial charity, suggests Chekhov, we're cheap with our moral charity. Sympathetic understanding is a moral exercise, and morally flabby Styopa doesn't do that kind of exercise.

On July 20, Dr. Chekhov traveled to Moscow to get a toothache treated and at the end of the month went to Zvenigorod to cover duties for his colleague, Dr. Uspensky. He spent a few days there, but was back in Babkino by the 28th, whence he wrote the actress Elizaveta Sakharova a warm letter. She was getting married and had asked Chekhov to be her "best man." He couldn't help his family friend with that request, but he passed along some news about having just seen her aunt in Zvenigorod and shared a pleasant recollection of when she had hung out with him and Levitan, who was at Babkino now: "His talent grows not by the day but by the hour. Nikolay works little. My sister lives and is well. Misha [Mikhail Chekhov] is in love and philosophizes, and so on and so forth . . ."

On July 30, he wrote defensively, apologetically, evasively to Leykin: "Thank you for the letter, kind Nikolay Aleksandrovich! Thank you that it's not curses, as I expected. . . ." He had had a bad few days, sick for one thing, the toothache for another, and his cursed hemorrhoids:

I wanted to write lying down, but this trick doesn't suit me, and even more that together with the bumps the general situation was revolting. Five days ago I went Zvenigorod to substitute for a short time for my colleague, the district doctor, where I was busy up to my neck and sick. That's all . . . Now: why didn't I write you that there wouldn't be stories? The reason why I didn't write is that with each hour I didn't lose the hope of sitting down and writing a story . . . There was not a telegraph office in Voskresensk. . . .

I'm still sick. My soul's mood is disgusting, and there's no money (in July I didn't work anywhere), and domestic circumstances are not joyful . . . The weather is crummy.[10]

He had invited Leykin to come to Babkino, but Leykin, feeling slighted, didn't come because he said he didn't have the proper directions. Chekhov gave him directions now and reminded Leykin that even though he hadn't received the request for those directions about how to get to Babkino, it would have been very easy and he could've asked anybody once he got to Voskresensk.

August 1886

—᷋᷋᷍—

> You complain that my heroes are gloomy,—alas!
> that's not my fault. This happens apart from my will,
> and when I write it does not seem to me that I am
> writing gloomily; in any case, as I work I am always
> in excellent spirits. It has been observed that gloomy,
> melancholy people always write cheerfully, while those
> who enjoy life put their depression into their writings.
> —To a fellow writer[1]

August was a light month again for writing letters—there were, it seems, three, though only one has survived—but he wrote half a dozen stories, including one of his greatest love stories.

All of the stories except the last touch on or focus on marriage. As far as anyone knows, he saw nothing of Dunya Efros this month, but she was, evidently, on his mind. In August's first story, retitled from "Ty i Vy" ("You [informal] and You [formal]," August 4) to "Women Make Trouble" by Avrahm Yarmolinsky in *The Unknown Chekhov*, a foolish peasant gives rambling testimony about a hooligan who drank and hit everyone in the vicinity, including the hooligan's wife. The peasant, confirming for us that he is a blockhead, blames the innocent wife.

Chekhov leaves no doubt that husbands are, as a category, beasts. "The Husband" ("Muzh," August 9) is about the self-justifying cruelty of a jealous husband who hates seeing his wife enjoy dancing with some visiting regimental soldiers. It's not that Shalikov's wife hasn't been swept off her feet; she has! But so have all the other provincial women:

> The ladies felt as though they were on wings. Intoxicated by the dancing, the
> music, and the clank of spurs, they threw themselves heart and soul

into making the acquaintance of their new partners, and quite forgot their old civilian friends. Their fathers and husbands, forced temporarily into the background, crowded around the meagre refreshment table in the entrance hall. All these government cashiers, secretaries, clerks, and superintendents—stale, sickly looking, clumsy figures—were perfectly well aware of their inferiority. They did not even enter the ball-room, but contented themselves with watching their wives and daughters in the distance dancing with the accomplished and graceful officers.[2]

And *this* husband, instead of resigning himself to the husbands' and fathers' inevitable position, becomes riled: "It was not jealousy he was feeling. He was ill-humored—first, because the room was taken up with dancing and there was nowhere he could play a game of cards; secondly, because he could not endure the sound of wind instruments; and, thirdly, because he fancied the officers treated the civilians somewhat too casually and disdainfully. But what above everything revolted him and moved him to indignation was the expression of happiness on his wife's face."

That last phrase puts me in mind of stories by D. H. Lawrence, who would one day mock Chekhov as "a willy wet-leg,"[3] but who also so well describes aspects of marital spite of the sort that Chekhov depicts in this story. The husband despises his wife:

> Not only her face but her whole figure was expressive of beatitude . . . . The tax-collector could endure it no longer; he felt a desire to jeer at that beatitude, to make Anna Pavlovna feel that she had forgotten herself, that life was by no means so delightful as she fancied now in her excitement . . . .
>
> "You wait; I'll teach you to smile so blissfully," he muttered. "You are not a boarding-school miss, you are not a girl. An old fright ought to realise she is a fright!"

When that mazurka ends, Shalikov steps in with the order that his wife go home with him:

> Seeing her husband standing before her, Anna Pavlovna started as though recalling the fact that she had a husband; then she flushed all over: she felt ashamed that she had such a sickly looking, ill-humored, ordinary husband.

When she balks, Shalikov swears he will make a scene if she doesn't cooperate. Chekhov's keen reading of Shalikov's selfish, resentful impulses shows he hates Shalikov even more than Shalikov's wife does:

> The tax-collector walked behind his wife, and watching her downcast, sorrowful, humiliated little figure, he recalled the look of beatitude which had so irritated him at the club, and the consciousness that the beatitude was gone filled his soul with triumph. He was pleased and satisfied, and at the same time he felt the lack of something; he would have liked to go back to the club and make every one feel dreary and miserable, so that all might know how stale and worthless life is when you walk along the streets in the dark and hear the slush of the mud under your feet, and when you know that you will wake up next morning with nothing to look forward to but vodka and cards. Oh, how awful it is!

The superb next story, "A Misfortune" ("Neschast'e," August 16), which Chekhov wrote for *New Times*, has perhaps made wives and girlfriends blush for themselves and caused lovelorn men, me for instance, to groan with recognition. There are love stories and there are love stories. There are no serious love stories that end happily in Chekhov.

Chekhov's understanding of fidelity and sexuality were completely different from Tolstoy's. Chekhov understood sexuality without typical contemporary prejudices. He knew physiology and accepted the sexual drive as part of our human nature. He was not wanton himself and lived long enough with his illness to see his own sexual drive diminish.

He understood restraint and advised his recklessly horny brother Nikolay to restrain himself sexually. He thought, in fact, that artists needed to conserve their amorousness.

Even so, Chekhov was a very attractive man and quite susceptible to attractive, educated, lively women. He had girlfriends, affairs, flirtations. He was a tough read for his female friends, and women went after him and taunted and teased him, but only at the end, nearing forty, like his hero Gurov in "The Lady with the Dog," did he fall head over heels in love.

"A Misfortune" is nearly as sublime, just as unresolved, as that late wonderful much more famous story.

So is love a misfortune? Is it a misfortune that we fall in love with someone who is already in a relationship? Is it a misfortune that even though we are in a relationship, we are still vulnerable to falling in love with someone else? Why are we so vulnerable?

Those are not necessarily Chekhov's questions.

There are, however, other questions in this story that he and his characters seem to pose:

1) Why should love make us ashamed of ourselves?
2) Why does love make us lie to ourselves?
3) If the love has been declared and accepted, why wait?

"A Misfortune" is not a new *Anna Karenina* but a variation upon it; Chekhov later joked to Suvorin: "To make a fortune, to escape the abyss of petty worries and fears, I have only one choice, an immoral one, to marry into wealth or to say that I wrote *Anna Karenina*."[4]

A married woman and mother is played up to by "a friend."

She pretends she does not like or accept her friend's attention.

It's obvious, on the other hand, that no matter what she says, she enjoys, luxuriates in, and cultivates his attention.

The "she" in "A Misfortune," Sofya Petrovna Lubyantsev, as a cultured twenty-five-year-old in 1886, would have read *Anna Karenina* as a teenager. She would have known, too, that such affairs happen, and that they are full of risks. However, she has an image of herself that she means to maintain: She's "proper." That means she would not participate in such a love affair.

Unlike *Anna Karenina*, we readers are seeing the situation as a comedy. Sofya and Ilyin don't think their situation is funny, but we do. We know that they will have an affair at least. They do not know this.

The story takes place in a dacha community outside St. Petersburg or Moscow. It begins:

> Sofya Petrovna, the wife of Lubyantsev the notary, a handsome young woman of five-and-twenty, was walking slowly along a track that had been cleared in the wood, with Ilyin, a lawyer who was spending the summer in the neighborhood. It was five o'clock in the evening. Feathery-white masses of cloud stood overhead; patches of bright blue sky peeped out between them. The clouds stood motionless, as though they had caught in the tops of the tall old pine-trees. It was still and sultry.
>
>   Farther on, the track was crossed by a low railway embankment on which a sentinel with a gun was for some reason pacing up and down. Just beyond the embankment there was a large white church with six domes and a rusty roof.[5]

Why *these* place-details? Chekhov is so efficient at introducing characters and placing them in a particular environment at a particular time. He paints the picture the characters feel themselves in. We are observers within the scene and the attention or point of view is one that is right beside Sofya or perhaps her own. She may well see herself the way we do: young, attractive, conscious of a potentially awkward situation that she overconfidently believes herself capable of remedying.

> "I did not expect to meet you here," said Sofya Petrovna, looking at the ground and prodding at the last year's leaves with the tip of her parasol, "and now I am glad we have met. I want to speak to you seriously and once for all. I beg you, Ivan Mikhalovich, if you really love and respect me, please make an end of this pursuit of me! You follow me about like a shadow, you are continually looking at me not in a nice way, wooing me,[6] writing me strange letters, and . . . and I don't know where it's all going to end! Why, what can come of it?"
>
> Ilyin said nothing. Sofya Petrovna walked on a few steps and continued:
>
> "And this complete transformation in you all came about in the course of two or three weeks, after five years' friendship. I don't know you, Ivan Mikhalovich!"

(And all at once, in the midst of revising this book, I realize that Sofya Petrovna is the embodiment of Maria Kiseleva. Their motherly, wifely condescension and propriety line up neatly. Chekhov, I believe, imagined the prim thirty-nine-year-old Kiseleva in an awkward position she may have faced a dozen years before.) Sofya is telling Ilyin a story that he knows better than she. She has thought this through and has been marveling at it to herself. She truly does not understand his transformation. She also doesn't understand, as we outsiders do, that she is most certainly taking pleasure in the experience.

Though the story is primarily from her point of view, we learn to analyze her words (and her hesitations, indicated by Chekhov's ellipses) and her behavior from how Ilyin responds to them.

> Sofya Petrovna stole a glance at her companion. Screwing up his eyes, he was looking intently at the fluffy clouds. His face looked angry, ill-humored, and preoccupied, like that of a man in pain forced to listen to nonsense.
>
> "I wonder you don't see it yourself," Madame Lubyantsev went on, shrugging her shoulders. "You ought to realize that it's not a very nice part you are

playing. I am married; I love and respect my husband. . . . I have a daughter. . . .
Can you think all that means nothing? Besides, as an old friend you know my
attitude to family life and my views as to the sanctity of marriage."

Ilyin cleared his throat angrily and heaved a sigh.

"Sanctity of marriage . . ." he muttered. "Oh, Lord!"

Ilyin is no Don Juan (and neither was Chekhov). She too is reading his behavior and,
because he's no Don Juan, there is no explanation for it. Why now? He's known her for
years. It doesn't make sense. She declares:

"Yes, yes. . . . I love my husband, I respect him; and in any case I value the
peace of my home. I would rather let myself be killed than be a cause of unhappiness to Andrey and his daughter. . . . And I beg you, Ivan Mikhalovich, for
God's sake, leave me in peace! Let us be as good, true friends as we used to
be, and give up these sighs and groans, which really don't suit you. It's settled
and over! Not a word more about it. Let us talk of something else."

We recognize her behavior; we know she is saying the right things, the things she
should say as a decent woman of her time. She is trying to be understanding and sympathetic. These things happen, and it's just too bad for him. She thinks of herself as
generous and kind.

Sofya Petrovna again stole a glance at Ilyin's face. Ilyin was looking up; he was
pale, and was angrily biting his quivering lips. She could not understand why
he was angry and why he was indignant, but his pallor touched her.

She is experienced enough to know that he in fact wants to seduce her, but his behavior
is not conforming, it seems, to suaveness. He is a wreck. She is seeing and Chekhov is
showing us what love looks like. It's not happy or blissful. It's misery. What a misfortune!

"Don't be angry; let us be friends," she said affectionately. "Agreed? Here's
my hand."

Ilyin took her plump little hand in both of his, squeezed it, and slowly
raised it to his lips.

"I am not a schoolboy," he muttered. "I am not in the least tempted by
friendship with the woman I love."

"Enough, enough! It's settled and done with. We have reached the seat; let us sit down."

Sofya Petrovna's soul was filled with a sweet sense of relief: the most difficult and delicate thing had been said, the painful question was settled and done with. Now she could breathe freely and look Ilyin straight in the face.

Why won't he behave himself and come to reason? How can he not allow for right and wrong as the overriding principle? But she, to her own satisfaction, and to the world's approval (anyone could have watched this scene and excused her of vacillation or from any wrongdoing), has relaxed, and Chekhov swings his sensory camera out away from her; he has something of his own to note:

She looked at him, and the egoistic feeling of the superiority of the woman over the man who loves her, agreeably flattered her. It pleased her to see this huge, strong man, with his manly, angry face and his big black beard—clever, cultivated, and, people said, talented—sit down obediently beside her and bow his head dejectedly. For two or three minutes they sat without speaking.

This woman is not Dunya Efros or a chorus girl or the bored wife of a druggist or a witch. She is educated and, she thinks, worldly. All those other women, however, would see right through her. Will Sofya look back at this moment in embarrassment or joy? Both? She will eventually analyze her feelings the way that Chekhov has.

"Nothing is settled or done with," began Ilyin. "You repeat copy-book maxims to me. 'I love and respect my husband . . . the sanctity of marriage. . . .' I know all that without your help, and I could tell you more, too. I tell you truthfully and honestly that I consider the way I am behaving as criminal and immoral. What more can one say than that? But what's the good of saying what everybody knows? Instead of feeding nightingales with paltry words, you had much better tell me what I am to do."

"I've told you already—go away."

"As you know perfectly well, I have gone away five times, and every time I turned back on the way. I can show you my through tickets—I've kept them all. I have not will enough to run away from you! I am struggling. I am struggling horribly; but what the devil am I good for if I have no backbone, if I am weak, cowardly! I can't struggle with Nature! Do you understand? I cannot!

I run away from here, and she holds on to me and pulls me back. Contemptible, loathsome weakness!"

Ilyin flushed crimson, got up, and walked up and down by the seat.

Things have gone way past where Sofya is comfortable. And she, as a decent woman, realizes she is now in new territory. She did not foresee this part. She has had control, but she does not have it now.

"I feel as cross as a dog," he muttered, clenching his fists. "I hate and despise myself! My God! like some depraved schoolboy, I am wooing another man's wife, writing idiotic letters, degrading myself . . . ugh!"

Ilyin clutched at his head, groaned, and sat down. "And then your insincerity!" he went on bitterly. "If you do dislike my disgusting behavior, why have you come here? What drew you here? In my letters I only ask you for a direct, definite answer—yes or no; but instead of a direct answer, you contrive every day these 'chance' meetings with me and regale me with copy-book maxims!"

How can someone in love say angry, accusatory things to the person they're in love with—and yet be persuasive? Love is forcing realizations on Ilyin. He is broken. But he is broken by love, and the broken pieces can almost instantly reglue themselves.

Madame Lubyantsev was frightened and flushed. She suddenly felt the awkwardness which a decent woman feels when she is accidentally discovered undressed.

"You seem to suspect I am playing with you," she muttered. "I have always given you a direct answer, and . . . only today I've begged you . . ."

"Ough! as though one begged in such cases! If you were to say straight out 'Get away,' I should have been gone long ago; but you've never said that. You've never once given me a direct answer. Strange indecision! Yes, indeed; either you are playing with me, or else . . ."

Or else what? Or else she's in fact in love with him?

Ilyin leaned his head on his fists without finishing. Sofya Petrovna began going over in her own mind the way she had behaved from beginning to end. She remembered that not only in her actions, but even in her secret thoughts, she had always been opposed to Ilyin's wooing; but yet she felt there was a grain of truth in the lawyer's words. But not knowing exactly what the truth was, she could not find answers to make to Ilyin's complaint, however hard she thought. It was awkward to be silent, and, shrugging her shoulders, she said:

"So I am to blame, it appears."

"I don't blame you for your insincerity," sighed Ilyin. "I did not mean that when I spoke of it. . . . Your insincerity is natural and in the order of things. If people agreed together and suddenly became sincere, everything would go to the devil."

And Chekhov had certainly run himself into this wall: What if people *didn't* lie? . . . If we didn't flinch and deceive others and ourselves, would there be chaos?

Sofya Petrovna was in no mood for philosophical reflections, but she was glad of a chance to change the conversation, and asked:

"But why?"

"Because only savage women and animals are sincere. Once civilization has introduced a demand for such comforts as, for instance, feminine virtue, sincerity is out of place. . . ."

She is where she really never could have imagined. Ilyin's suffering has brought him to an experiential wisdom that she has not achieved. Until now, to her this has all been a happily interesting adventure. And it's still interesting, but she wants to get this situation back under control.

Ilyin jabbed his stick angrily into the sand. Madame Lubyantsev listened to him and liked his conversation, though a great deal of it she did not understand. What gratified her most was that she, an ordinary woman, was talked to by a talented man on "intellectual" subjects; it afforded her great pleasure, too, to watch the working of his mobile, young face, which was still pale and angry. She failed to understand a great deal that he said, but what was clear to her in his words was the attractive boldness with which the modern man without hesitation or doubt decides great questions and draws conclusive deductions.

She suddenly realized that she was admiring him, and was alarmed.

The verb *admire* here is "lyubuetsya." Its root is *lyub-*, love. She's looking at him with too much attention. She has never seen anything like it.

> "Forgive me, but I don't understand," she said hurriedly. "What makes you talk of insincerity? I repeat my request again: be my good, true friend; let me alone! I beg you most earnestly!"

She's offended by his calling out her "insincerity," because as far as she can remember, she has been sincere. But Ilyin is deeply connected to his feelings. Socially his feelings are wrong. He is tormented. He already knows that this relationship is a piece of bad luck.

And now perhaps we can accept the appropriateness of the story's title. We are in the realm of Greek myths rather than *Anna Karenina*. Sofya is overwhelmed by a force that she hasn't expected.

> "Very good; I'll try again," sighed Ilyin. "Glad to do my best. . . . Only I doubt whether anything will come of my efforts. Either I shall put a bullet through my brains or take to drink in an idiotic way. I shall come to a bad end! There's a limit to everything—to struggles with Nature, too. Tell me, how can one struggle against madness? If you drink wine, how are you to struggle against intoxication? What am I to do if your image has grown into my soul, and day and night stands persistently before my eyes, like that pine there at this moment? Come, tell me, what hard and difficult thing can I do to get free from this abominable, miserable condition, in which all my thoughts, desires, and dreams are no longer my own, but belong to some demon who has taken possession of me? I love you, love you so much that I am completely thrown out of gear; I've given up my work and all who are dear to me; I've forgotten my God! I've never been in love like this in my life."

While she has tried to remain in social mode, he has crashed ashore and has the words to describe what he is actually feeling. And it is fascinating to her and terrible! And we and Chekhov are happy, amused. Ilyin couldn't have expressed himself better—though it fits no model of proper pronouncement of feelings.

> Sofya Petrovna, who had not expected such a turn to their conversation, drew away from Ilyin and looked into his face in dismay. Tears came into his

eyes, his lips were quivering, and there was an imploring, hungry expression in his face.

"I love you!" he muttered, bringing his eyes near her big, frightened eyes. "You are so beautiful! I am in agony now, but I swear I would sit here all my life, suffering and looking in your eyes. But . . . be silent, I implore you!"

Sofya Petrovna, feeling utterly disconcerted, tried to think as quickly as possible of something to say to stop him. "I'll go away," she decided, but before she had time to make a movement to get up, Ilyin was on his knees before her. . . . He was clasping her knees, gazing into her face and speaking passionately, hotly, eloquently. In her terror and confusion she did not hear his words; for some reason now, at this dangerous moment, while her knees were being agreeably squeezed and felt as though they were in a warm bath, she was trying, with a sort of angry spite, to interpret her own sensations. She was angry that instead of brimming over with protesting virtue, she was entirely overwhelmed with weakness, apathy, and emptiness, like a drunken man utterly reckless; only at the bottom of her soul a remote bit of herself was malignantly taunting her: "Why don't you go? Is this as it should be? Yes?"

Oh, how can we not sympathize with her? And how can we not admire Chekhov describing her sensations—*her knees in a warm bath!* Only a doctor could get away with that. Tolstoy brings us readers close to Anna Karenina in so many ways—but not quite to that spot.

Seeking for some explanation, she could not understand how it was she did not pull away the hand to which Ilyin was clinging like a leech, and why, like Ilyin, she hastily glanced to right and to left to see whether anyone was looking. The clouds and the pines stood motionless, looking at them severely, like old ushers seeing mischief, but bribed not to tell the school authorities. The sentry stood like a post on the embankment and seemed to be looking at the seat.

"Let him look," thought Sofya Petrovna.

"But . . . but listen," she said at last, with despair in her voice. "What can come of this? What will be the end of this?"

"I don't know, I don't know," he whispered, waving off the disagreeable questions.

He has finally persuaded her of his feelings, and she has had to admit to herself that she has feelings, *those* feelings.

They heard the hoarse, discordant whistle of the train. This cold, irrelevant sound from the everyday world of prose made Sofya Petrovna rouse herself.

"I can't stay . . . it's time I was at home," she said, getting up quickly. "The train is coming in . . . Andrey is coming by it! He will want his dinner."

The train tooted for Agafya in March, and it toots here in August for Sofya.

Sofya Petrovna turned toward the embankment with a burning face. The engine slowly crawled by, then came the carriages. It was not the local train, as she had supposed, but a goods train. The trucks filed by against the background of the white church in a long string like the days of a man's life, and it seemed as though it would never end.

Chekhov has taken one step, maybe two, outside of the story with that simile. I don't believe Sofya or Ilyin are thinking about timelessness or the end of time. Chekhov is reminding us, though not them, because they would not or could not listen, that this is the most excruciating and probably exciting moment of their lives, and it, too, will end. Their love affair, which is their whole world at this moment, will disappear eventually, as will everything else. Chekhov may be the oldest twenty-six-year-old who ever lived.

How the rest of the story goes, you'll have to read and see.

. . . But now that I've shown my hand that I believe Chekhov mischievously embodied his family's hostess and his friend Maria Kiseleva in Sofya, I have to admit that there is no hint of any affair between her and Chekhov. Even Donald Rayfield, a biographer who in Michael C. Finke's opinion sees liaisons everywhere, does not detect anything between them.[7] But as we will see in letters between Chekhov and Kiseleva, there was repeated contentious discussion between them about the propriety of depicting sexuality in literature.

If you're a teacher or editor, how dismayed should you be by your students' or relatives' grammatical or mechanical carelessness in writing? How offended are you or ought you to be about the faulty punctuation of a friend, parent, or spouse?

Chekhov, writes Ronald Hingley, "had been taught to read and write by his mother, whose own spelling and punctuation were rudimentary."[8] Chekhov did not mock his mother to others. Apparently among family he could tease her. His brother Mikhail remembers that "she never used punctuation and would start her letters with lines like:

'Antosha on the shelf in the pantry,' and Anton would poke gentle fun at her, replying, 'After a long search, no Antosha was found on the pantry shelf.'"⁹

In "A Pink Stocking" ("Rozovyi Chulok") published the same day as "A Misfortune" (August 16), a piggish husband, bored with the steady rain, idly glances at a letter that his wife has been writing and is mortified by the lack of punctuation and absence of thought:

> "Well, this is beyond anything!" he mutters, as he finishes reading the letter and flings the sheets on the table, "It's positively incredible!"
>
> "What's the matter?" asks Lidochka, flustered.
>
> "What's the matter! You've covered six pages, wasted a good two hours scribbling, and there's nothing in it at all! If there were one tiny idea! One reads on and on, and one's brain is as muddled as though one were deciphering the Chinese wriggles on tea chests! Ough!"
>
> "Yes, that's true, Vanya, . . ." says Lidochka, reddening. "I wrote it carelessly. . . ."
>
> "Queer sort of carelessness! In a careless letter there is some meaning and style—there is sense in it—while yours . . . excuse me, but I don't know what to call it! It's absolute twaddle! There are words and sentences, but not the slightest sense in them. Your whole letter is exactly like the conversation of two boys: 'We had pancakes today! And we had a soldier come to see us!' You say the same thing over and over again! You drag it out, repeat yourself. . . . The wretched ideas dance about like devils: There's no making out where anything begins, where anything ends. . . . How can you write like that?"
>
> "If I had been writing carefully," Lidochka says in self-defense, "then there would not have been mistakes. . . ."
>
> "Oh, I'm not talking about mistakes! The awful grammatical howlers! There's not a line that's not a personal insult to grammar! No stops nor commas—and the spelling . . . brrr! 'Earth' has an *a* in it!! And the writing! It's desperate! I'm not joking, Lida. . . . I'm surprised and appalled at your letter. . . . You mustn't be angry, darling, but, really, I had no idea you were such a duffer at grammar. . . . And yet you belong to a cultivated, well-educated circle: you are the wife of a University man, and the daughter of a general! Tell me, did you ever go to school?"

There will be no moral to this comic story, except that it reminds me of how jerky we teachers can be with our students . . . and with family!

"You know, Lidochka, it really is awful!" says Somov, suddenly halting in front of her and looking into her face with horror. "You are a mother . . . do you understand? A mother! How can you teach your children if you know nothing yourself? You have a good brain, but what's the use of it if you have never mastered the very rudiments of knowledge? There—never mind about knowledge . . . the children will get that at school, but, you know, you are very shaky on the moral side too! You sometimes use such language that it makes my ears tingle!"

Somov shrugs his shoulders again, wraps himself in the folds of his dressing-gown and continues his pacing. . . . He feels vexed and injured, and at the same time sorry for Lidochka, who does not protest, but merely blinks. . . . Both feel oppressed and miserable. . . . Absorbed in their woes, they do not notice how time is passing and the dinner hour is approaching.

The condescending Somov, having had his fill of carping, repents and decides he would rather his wife be as she is (she "who never pokes her nose into anything, does not understand so much, and never obtrudes her criticism") than an educated woman. Perhaps only here do we detect the couple's similarity to Chekhov's parents. Pavel was a fussy scold, and Evgenia was less educated than he.

Chekhov's lone surviving letter of the month was to Leykin, who had poked his nose into this very story. And just as in the story, there was terrible weather at Babkino: "rain, rain, rain . . . wind, cold and dark clouds."[10]

Chekhov had, as usual, to apologize for his lack of contributions to *Fragments*:

I didn't send a story for the last issue as, sincerely and honestly speaking, I didn't have topics. I thought and thought and thought up nothing, and I didn't want to send nonsense and it's boring. So I got the word of Agafopod [Alexander], who was staying with us, that he was required to send you a story and communicate to you that I wouldn't be sending anything to this issue.

He told Leykin about the family's new rental in Moscow on Sadovaya and its price, 650 rubles a year. "If my sister's to be believed, it's good." He asked Leykin to loan him seventy rubles so he could pay for the two months' rent—and as usual Leykin immediately came through.

He concluded by kidding Leykin about how his editing resulted in an unintended tiny benefit for him, the writer:

You lengthened the end of "A Pink Stocking." I am not opposed to receiving the extra 8 kopecks for the extra line, but in my opinion, "the man" didn't go well at the end . . . The conversation goes only about the women . . . However, it's all the same . . .

Chekhov kept trying to imagine marital situations. In "Martyrs" ("Stradal'tsy," August 18), the wife is a hypochondriac who loves imagining herself dying:

> Lizochka draws a mental picture of her own death, how her mother, her husband, her cousin Varya with her husband, her relations, the admirers of her "talent" press around her death bed, as she whispers her last farewell. All are weeping. Then when she is dead they dress her, interestingly pale and dark-haired, in a pink dress (it suits her) and lay her in a very expensive coffin on gold legs, full of flowers. There is a smell of incense, the candles splutter. Her husband never leaves the coffin, while the admirers of her talent cannot take their eyes off her, and say: "As though living! She is lovely in her coffin!" The whole town is talking of the life cut short so prematurely. But now they are carrying her to the church. The bearers are Ivan Petrovich, Adolf Ivanich, Varya's husband, Nikolay Semyonich, and the black-eyed student who had taught her to drink lemon squash with brandy. It's only a pity there's no music playing. After the burial service comes the leave-taking. The church is full of sobs, they bring the lid with tassels, and . . . Lizochka is shut off from the light of day for ever, there is the sound of hammering nails. Knock, knock, knock.
>
> Lizochka shudders and opens her eyes.[11]

Chekhov lets readers recognize that she is perfectly fine, at most suffering an upset stomach. The doting husband, however, is sincerely anxious. Patiently having been taken care of for two days and two nights, she awakens, ready for rehearsals, as good and prima donnish as ever, and he is finally able to return to work. Because this is a slight and comic story, it will be no surprise to readers that when he gets to the office, he discovers that he is sick; his boss sends him home.

Sometime in the midst of or just after writing "Martyrs," Chekhov wrote to Bilibin, his chosen expert and confidant concerning marriage, for advice. All that is known of this letter is Bilibin's reply at the end of the month.

I keep expecting more of Bilibin. I expect him to have been more appreciative of the amazing quality of the stories Chekhov was cooking up. Instead, there was the shrugging acknowledgment of them or, occasionally, as now, criticism—here of "A Misfortune": "My wife asked me to ask you if you weren't describing yourself in the perspective of Ilyin. [. . .] She also says that it's impossible to write belles-lettres from a 'medical point of view.'" Bilibin felt that the story's husband was "a caricature," and that the protagonists "did not arouse sympathy." Bilibin did not like the story's "one-sided direction." He cursed to the Devil all that "poetic side of love." As for Chekhov's request for advice about marriage, he seemed to discourage it: a married man, wrote Bilibin, accommodates the wife; an unmarried man accommodates literature.[12] (The accommodating Bilibin would leave his wife for another woman a few years later.)

During the last week of August, Leykin wrote Chekhov to complain that Chekhov must not have read the lousy stories that Alexander had sent for the magazine: "It's not possible to replace your presence in *Fragments* with them."[13]

Chekhov seems to have submitted the story "Talent" at this time. Bilibin would inform Chekhov that it was too long to run in *Fragments'* final August issue. And though it wasn't published until September 6, it has relevance now concerning Chekhov's contemplations about marriage. The protagonist, a young, lazy, dissipated painter, is leaving the dacha he has been renting all summer from a widow. Only he hasn't paid her for some time, and the widow's daughter, who worships him, regrets his departure. As if echoing Bilibin's self-serving wisdom, Yegor tells her:

> "I cannot marry."
>
> "Why not?" Katya asked softly.
>
> "Because for a painter, and in fact any man who lives for art, marriage is out of the question. An artist must be free."
>
> "But in what way should I hinder you, Yegor Savvich?"
>
> "I am not speaking of myself, I am speaking in general. . . . Famous authors and painters have never married."[14]

Yegor and his artist friends believe in their pending fame, and so infatuated Katya does, too.

> His fancy pictured how he would become great. He could not imagine his future works but he could see distinctly how the papers would talk of him, how the shops would sell his photographs, with what envy his friends would

look after him. He tried to picture himself in a magnificent drawing room surrounded by pretty and adoring women; but the picture was misty, vague, as he had never in his life seen a drawing room. The pretty and adoring women were not a success either, for, except Katya, he knew no adoring woman, not even one respectable girl. People who know nothing about life usually picture life from books, but Yegor Savvich knew no books, either. He had tried to read Gogol, but had fallen asleep on the second page.

If Chekhov was mocking anybody besides himself and his friend Isaac Levitan, who would indeed experience fame, he was mocking his "talented" brother Nikolay:

> To listen to them it would seem they had the future, fame, money, in their hands. And it never occurred to either of them that time was passing, that every day life was nearing its close, that they had lived at other people's expense a great deal and nothing yet was accomplished; that they were all bound by the inexorable law by which of a hundred promising beginners only two or three rise to any position and all the others draw blanks in the lottery, perish playing the part of flesh for the cannon. . . . They were gay and happy, and looked the future boldly in the face!

Besides marriage, it seems that fame and celebrity were on Chekhov's mind. Some little time preceding Chekhov's exchange of correspondence with Bilibin, Chekhov, the most famous young literary star in Russia, wrote "The First-Class Passenger" ("Passazhir 1-go Klassa," August 23). On the train, two men strike up a post-dinner conversation. One begins:

> ". . . The question that is occupying my mind at the moment, sir, is exactly what is to be understood by the word *fame* or *celebrity*. What do you think? Pushkin called fame a bright patch on a ragged garment; we all understand it as Pushkin does—that is, more or less subjectively—but no one has yet given a clear, logical definition of the word. . . . I would give a good deal for such a definition!"

He goes on:

> "[. . .] I must tell you, sir, that when I was younger I strove after celebrity with every fiber of my being. To be popular was my craze, so to speak. For the sake

of it I studied, worked, sat up at night, neglected my meals. And I fancy, as far as I can judge without partiality, I had all the natural gifts for attaining it. To begin with, I am an engineer by profession. In the course of my life I have built in Russia some two dozen magnificent bridges, I have laid aqueducts for three towns; I have worked in Russia, in England, in Belgium. . . . Secondly, I am the author of several special treatises in my own line. [. . .] I will not fatigue your attention by enumerating my works and my merits, I will only say that I have done far more than some celebrities. And yet here I am in my old age, I am getting ready for my coffin, so to say, and I am as celebrated as that black dog yonder running on the embankment."

The engineer recounts that he thought he had been about to achieve fame many years before when he had finished a bridge in a provincial town, but at the opening day ceremonies, he was outshone by his untalented actress girlfriend. The story ends with the listener asking the engineer if he has heard of *him*—just as famous in his way—and the engineer hasn't. They laugh.

Chekhov thought his own recent fame was undeserved. To his amazement, it would only get bigger and bigger.

PART THREE

At Home with Family and Fame

Leaving Babkino in early September and returning to Moscow was like returning to school after a summer vacation. Their previous apartment had been too noisy[1] and so Chekhov's sister Maria had found the family a house to rent on the then quiet Kudrinskaya-Sadovaya Street. Chekhov's father Pavel, contributing to the family welfare, had tried to deliver the first two months' rent (some of the money arriving as a loan from Leykin), but there was an obstacle set up by the landlord that delayed the family's entry until the furniture arrived.

Drawing by Mikhail Chekhov of the house at the time.

Chekhov probably saw the new lodgings for the first time on September 7. He would note that the neatly stacked red house "looks like a chest of drawers."[2] Fortunately, this Sadovaya "Garden Ring" house remains standing on a busy, noisy boulevard across the street from the Moscow Zoo. We visitors can enter the present-day house-museum on the ground floor and walk through Chekhov's study and bedroom. Bookcases line the study's walls. He saw patients there and wrote. When and where Chekhov did his reading is hard to tell, because nobody describes him reading and Chekhov's recorded remarks on his prodigious reading are scarce.[3] We know he pored over his medical books and kept up with and would help support medical journals. He seems to have read every literary author of consequence and read enough to be familiar with those who weren't of consequence, and he only occasionally made fun of young men, usually men like Nikolay and his younger brothers, who hadn't read the classics. We also know he had stamina and in later years could read, for example, *Resurrection*, an 1899 novel by Tolstoy, in one sitting. "On the foundation of the volumes he had inherited from his dead friend Popudoglo," writes the biographer Ernest Simmons, "he had begun to build a substantial library. He haunted the secondhand bookshops and his purchases were extremely varied—mostly Russian belles-lettres, but also some foreign works, sets of magazines, and quantities of travel books, memoirs, collections of letters, and reference works. For the most part it was a working library, and the well-thumbed appearance of some of the volumes testified to their frequent use by Chekhov in his writing."[4]

The ground floor also had the kitchen and bedrooms for the cook and a maid (these aren't part of the museum tour). The Chekhovs were scraping by, regularly out of money, but they were middle-class now and had servants.

The spiral staircase leading to the second floor, where his sister and parents had bedrooms, is still visible in the museum, but I seem to remember climbing enclosed stairs to the second-floor exhibits. In Chekhov's time, a wolf-skin, a gift to the family from someone, as the Chekhovs do not seem to have been wolf-hunters, hung halfway up the spiral stairs. There was a "dining room, the drawing room and a spare room with a lantern. The drawing room had a piano, an aquarium and a large unfinished painting by Nikolay of a sempstress asleep over her work at daybreak."[5]

His younger brother Mikhail remembered: "Anton coughed particularly violently during the period that we lived on Kudrinskaya-Sadovaya from the fall of 1886 to the spring of 1890. [. . .] My responsibility before bed was to light the lamp in Anton's bedroom because he often woke up and did not like to be in the dark. Only a thin partition separated our rooms, and we used to talk through it whenever we were unable to sleep in the middle of the night. It was through that wall that I was able to hear how bad his cough was."[6]

I appreciate Mikhail reminding us about his brother's health. Chekhov was so active and efficient and had an extraordinary capacity for work, but this was despite the tuberculosis that continually weakened him. I wonder, though, if Mikhail did not overestimate his brother's pleasure in the constant social activities:

Anton could not be alone during that period, and as I mentioned before, our house was always filled with young people playing the piano, joking, and laughing upstairs. He would write at his desk downstairs, energized by the noise. He always shared our fun and thrived on the excitement.[7]

There is some evidence in Chekhov's letters this coming year that a little more peace and quiet would have been appreciated.

September 1886

—◁—

> . . . though they hadn't met, OF COURSE Chekhov
> wrote under his influence, was responding to Tolstoy
> in everything he wrote. I mean, to be a writer in the
> late 1880s meant, no exaggeration: "This is a response
> to Tolstoy."
>
> —Michael A. Denner, editor,
> *Tolstoy Studies Journal*[1]

The eight short stories Chekhov published this September are not, for the most part, among his best, except for one terribly grim tale published September 8, "The Dependents." I puzzled over its Russian title: *Nakhlebniki*. There in the middle of it, apparently its root, is *khleb*, bread. "Dependents" seems a neutral word, but the agitated and painful story feels not at all neutral. The best definition for *nakhlebniki* I found that reflects the story is "Freeloaders."

Chekhov adored animals and agonized when he witnessed cruelty. He understood harsh words as originating in frustration and despair. Some of Chekhov's friends and relatives deemed some of his stories from these years as verging on Tolstoyan, which none of them ever suggested was a compliment. I would deem this story Tolstoyan, but only descriptively, not negatively, and as a way to distinguish the master from his literary pupil.

An impoverished old man of seventy awakens and says his prayers and sweeps up and sets the samovar to boil. It becomes ready:

> "Oh, you've started humming!" grumbled Zotov. "Hum away then, and bad
> luck to you!"

At that point the old man appropriately recalled that, in the preceding night, he had dreamed of a stove, and to dream of a stove is a sign of sorrow.

Dreams and omens were the only things left that could rouse him to reflection; and on this occasion he plunged with a special zest into the considerations of the questions: What the samovar was humming for? and what sorrow was foretold by the stove? The dream seemed to come true from the first. Zotov rinsed out his teapot and was about to make his tea, when he found there was not one teaspoonful left in the box.[2]

Zotov is a homeowner, an artisan, not (he grumbles to himself) a peasant for whom such an impoverished existence might be more acceptable.

He curses his affectionate, scrawny dog Lyska, and surveys his other (indeed) dependent, the bony unnamed horse as she emerges from her decrepit shed. Zotov is a master of sarcasm:

"Plague take you," Zotov went on. "Shall I ever see the last of you, you jail-bird Pharaohs! . . . I wager you want your breakfast!" he jeered, twisting his angry face into a contemptuous smile. "By all means, this minute! A priceless steed like you must have your fill of the best oats! Pray begin! This minute! And I have something to give to the magnificent, valuable dog! If a precious dog like you does not care for bread, you can have meat."

Chekhov tells us nothing to explain Zotov's tone. We wait dumbly, as curious as Zotov's animals. And now the outburst comes that clarifies almost everything:

"I am not obliged to feed you, you loafers! I am not some millionaire for you to eat me out of house and home! I have nothing to eat myself, you cursed carcasses, the cholera take you! I get no pleasure or profit out of you; nothing but trouble and ruin. Why don't you give up the ghost? Are you such personages that even death won't take you? You can live, damn you! but I don't want to feed you! I have had enough of you! I don't want to!"

To our surprise and their perplexity, he orders them out of his yard. They don't go far:

When he had driven out his dependents he felt calmer, and began sweeping the yard. From time to time he peeped out into the street: the horse and the dog were standing like posts by the fence, looking dejectedly toward the gate.

> "Try how you can do without me," muttered the old man, feeling as though
> a weight of anger were being lifted from his heart. "Let somebody else look
> after you now! I am stingy and ill-tempered. . . . It's nasty living with me, so
> you try living with other people. . . . Yes. . . ."

But why should his anger dissipate? What are we learning about psychology here?
The freeloaders have accused him of being difficult! Of depriving them!

Here is where I, raised on the milk of Tolstoy's psychology, see a distinction between
Tolstoy and Chekhov. Tolstoy would have gone softer on the protagonist; Zotov would
not have been so harsh. But I think Chekhov takes us into a realm of psychology that
Tolstoy perhaps could not. Tolstoy's own supernatural sympathy toward animals would
have bent his resolve. Chekhov, however, maintains Zotov's backbone and allows the
animals to remain confused.

Zotov curses them again but allows their return to his yard before he goes off to visit
a friend in his friend's "little general shop," the sort of shop Chekhov's father had run.
They talk about the weather and share his friend's tea. But the awkwardness of asking
for loans! . . . How well Chekhov knew this. Within a week of publishing this story and
having moved into his new Moscow digs, he would have to pawn his gold watch to pay
off a debt. Keeping his dependents, the Chekhov family, financially stable was a constant
in these years.

But what else could Chekhov do? Who else could support his family?

> "I have a favor to ask of you, Mark Ivanich," he began, after the sixth glass,
> drumming on the counter with his fingers. "If you would just be so kind as
> to give me a gallon of oats again today. . . ."
>
> From behind the big tea-chest behind which Mark Ivanich was sitting
> came the sound of a deep sigh.
>
> "Do be so good," Zotov went on; "never mind tea—don't give it me today,
> but let me have some oats. . . . I am ashamed to ask you, I have wearied you
> with my poverty, but the horse is hungry."

Let's all of us give a cheer for the continually mocked Leykin. Whenever Chekhov was
as desperate as poor Zotov, Leykin advanced him rubles.

> "I can give it you," sighed the friend—"why not? But why the devil do you
> keep those carcasses?—tfoo!—Tell me that, please. It would be all right if it

were a useful horse, but—tfoo!—one is ashamed to look at it. . . . And the dog's nothing but a skeleton! Why the devil do you keep them?"

"What am I to do with them?"

"You know. Take them to Ignat the slaughterer—that is all there is to do. They ought to have been there long ago. It's the proper place for them."

"To be sure, that is so! . . . I dare say! . . ."

"You live like a beggar and keep animals," the friend went on. "I don't grudge the oats. . . . God bless you. But as to the future, brother . . . I can't afford to give regularly every day! There is no end to your poverty! One gives and gives, and one doesn't know when there will be an end to it all."

Chekhov would eventually see "an end" to *his* family's tight finances. They weren't *this* poor. We don't want our favorite artists to be desperate for money and have to crank out stories or paintings to pay the rent, but so it happens. Chekhov's older brothers had set out on their independent lives only to have to retreat again and again to their family, which was led in spirit and money-making by Chekhov.

Mark Ivanich points out that Zotov, if he's going to persist living himself, is going to have to move somewhere. Zotov has a distant almost-relative who is bound to inherit his property and he says he can go to her. They decide he should leave that very day:

"I'll go at once! When I get there, I shall say: Take my house, but keep me and treat me with respect. It's your duty! If you don't care to, then there is neither my house, nor my blessing for you! Goodbye, Ivanich!"

And, the gate of his yard unfastened, he sets out, his belongings in hand, determined to walk the "eight or nine miles" to her.

He had not gone a mile into the country when he heard steps behind him. He looked around and angrily clasped his hands. The horse and Lyska, with their heads drooping and their tails between their legs, were quietly walking after him.

"Go back!" he waved to them.

They stopped, looked at one another, looked at him. He went on, they followed him. Then he stopped and began ruminating. It was impossible to go to his great-niece Glasha, whom he hardly knew, with these creatures; he did not want to go back and shut them up, and, indeed, he could not shut them up, because the gate was no use.

"To die of hunger in the shed," thought Zotov. "Hadn't I really better take them to Ignat?"

If you have a weak spot for animals, do not read the concluding paragraphs of "The Dependents."

If Chekhov's master Tolstoy had written the story, the end would not be as devastating and tearful or maybe as sublime.

The other stories he published this month?

The most significant and least trivial is "A Trivial Incident" ("Pustoy Sluchay," September 20), in which Chekhov again wrestles with the conflicting feelings about getting married. The male narrator is out hunting with an impoverished hereditary "prince," of which sort of princes there were many, especially in Russian literature.

A watchman tells them they are forbidden to shoot in this particular forest. He mentions the woman landowner's name. The prince, surprised, excuses himself to the narrator:

> "I used to know her at one time, but . . . it's rather awkward for me to go to her. Besides, I am in shabby clothes. . . . You go, you don't know her. . . . It's more suitable for you to go."

The prince had been, possibly, according to the gossip that the narrator has heard, engaged or nearly so to her.

The narrator is fascinated by this humble and humbled man: "Apparently he was in that mood of irritation and sadness when women weep quietly for no reason, and men feel a craving to complain of themselves, of life, of God. . . ."

Though deeply in debt (as Chekhov feared becoming), the prince held onto his last shred of honesty:

> "I tell you frankly I have had the chance once in my life of getting rich if I had told a lie, a lie to myself and one woman . . . and one other person whom I know would have forgiven me for lying; I should have put into my pocket a million. But I could not. I hadn't the pluck!"

The narrator goes to this very woman's house to ask for her permission to hunt, which she refuses, despite the narrator's dropping the prince's name. She even remarks, reflecting Chekhov's own thinking about hunting at the time: "'And, besides, what pleasure is there in shooting birds? What's it for? Are they in your way?'"

The narrator, as is common in Chekhov's stories, is for the most part inconspicuous, an observer rather than a protagonist. When he notices that she is distracted by the sight of the prince outside talking to her groundskeeper, he reflects on Chekhov's favorite grievance of these years:

> I looked at her and at the prince who could not tell a lie once in his life, and I
> felt angry and bitter against truth and falsehood, which play such an elemental
> part in the personal happiness of men.

Why do our social lives depend on lies?

On second thought she sends after the narrator to grant them permission.

On second thought Chekhov seems to have resolved, as straitened as his finances were, to give marriage with Dunya Efros a pass.

A piece that I did not number among his "stories" is a micro-play published later the same week as he published "A Trivial Incident"; it's titled "Drama" ("Drama," September 25):

> DRAMATIS PERSONAE
> Pappy, having 11 unmarried daughters.
> Young Man.
> Coat-tails.
>
> Young man *(waving his hand and saying: "I don't care! Two deaths won't happen,
> but one will!" and goes into the study to Pappy)*. Ivan Ivanych! Let me ask for
> the hand of your youngest daughter Varvara!
> Pappy *(lowering his eyes and acting coy)*. I'm very pleased, but . . . she's still so
> young . . . so inexperienced . . . As to that . . . you want to deprive me of . . .
> my peace . . . *(tears increase)* the support of my old age.
> Young man *(quickly)*. In that case . . . I don't dare insist . . . *(Bows and wants to
> leave.)*
> Pappy *(reaching out and grabbing him by the coat-tails)*. Stop! I'm glad! Happy!
> My benefactor!

> Coat-tails. *(mournfully)* Trrrr . . . [3]

No one from the Efros family tried to catch Chekhov by the coat-tails.

———

Chekhov did not go for impressive or enticing titles. He preferred the undersell. The last story of the month was "A Trifle from Life" ("Zhiteyskaya Meloch'," September 29) and is truly not a major work. (You're forgiven if you mix up its title with "A Trivial Incident," published all of nine days before.) I will summarize it only to give evidence of Chekhov's continued dismay about lying.

A self-satisfied bachelor, an *Anna Karenina*–style Vronsky-lite, is having an affair with a woman who has an eight-year-old. While the bachelor awaits the return of the woman, he chats with the boy, who tells him about his life in the house, about secretly seeing his father, who loves him; the bachelor-lover, having sworn to the boy complete confidence in that secret, instead rats him out. Chekhov describes the trusting boy's reaction: "Alyosha sat down in the corner and told [his sister] Sonia with horror how he had been deceived. He was trembling, stammering, and crying. It was the first time in his life that he had been brought into such coarse contact with lying; till then he had not known that there are in the world, besides sweet pears, pies, and expensive watches, a great many things for which the language of children has no expression."[4]

———

Chekhov continually veered from annoyance to guilt in his relationship with Leykin. He had moved on in his literary career, though Leykin made him feel he still owed contributions to *Fragments*. Besides Leykin, though, there don't seem to have been other friends from whom he could expect loans. As long as Chekhov needed emergency short-term loans, he would have to contribute pieces.

His September 20 letter to Leykin was newsy, friendly, and a little anxious. Chekhov liked the family's new place after the commotion of setting it up. On the other hand, now he was out of money; he had pawned his watch and gold coins: "What a terribly stupid situation!" he exclaimed. He pointedly didn't ask Leykin for another loan. He wrote that he was mostly sitting at home, recovering from having treated cholera patients, and occasionally going to watch plays at the theater, where he had free tickets. Making an effort to be chatty, he asked after Leykin's getaway house and family and pets, and he told Leykin he was awaiting a letter from him.[5]

He may have been surprised by Leykin's pertinent next letter on September 27: "Why are you always sick? [. . .] Doctor, heal thyself."[6] Leykin would not have twitted his writer had he known he had tuberculosis.

Chekhov answered on September 30, complaining about nonpayment from the *Petersburg Gazette*, and asking for Leykin's intervention both for the payments and for a pay raise: "Put in a good word about the raise, and you'll agree that it's insulting in old age to write for 7 kopecks!" Whether it was Leykin's persuasive word or not, Chekhov's rate per line at the *Gazette* went up to 10 kopecks a line, and Leykin agreed to give him another 15 rubles per month from *Fragments*.[7] He was famous indeed but barely managing the family's rent and expenses. "Nikolay yesterday and for the past few days was seriously and dangerously ill," he wrote. "An unexpected amount of bleeding vomit appeared, which just barely stopped. He's thin in the manner of typhus . . . It's terrible how much trouble I've experienced these days, and there's still no money . . ." He imagined or feared that he would give up writing to go work as a government doctor: "It's probable all the music will end, I spitting, waving my hand, and running away to the district for service." As for his own illnesses, about which Leykin had teased him: "My health is better. It's necessary to radically change my life, but it's not easy. I have 3 sins on my conscience that give me no peace: 1) I smoke, 2) I sometimes drink and 3) I don't know languages."

On this date, he had just finished or was just about to finish one of his most extraordinary stories about family life, "Difficult People."

⁓

Late this September, Chekhov continued his literary mentorship of Maria Kiseleva, but now through long letters. As always with women he corresponded with, Chekhov was both teasing and direct.[8]

On September 21, he wrote to Kiseleva about his "dreary" writer's life: "In order to have the right to be by myself in my room, and not with guests, I hurried off to sit over my writing."[9] He mocked his fame: "It is not much fun to be a great writer. To begin with, it's a dreary life. Work from morning till night and not much to show for it. Money is as scarce as cats' tears."[10] He said, explaining his financial woes, that he wasn't getting paid for some of his literary contributions until October.

> I don't know how it is with Zola and Shchedrin, but in my flat it is cold and
> smoky. . . . They give me cigarettes, as before, on holidays only. Impossible
> cigarettes! Hard, damp, sausage-like. Before I begin to smoke I light the

lamp, dry the cigarette over it, and only then I begin on it; the lamp smokes, the cigarette splutters and turns brown, I burn my fingers . . . it is enough to make one shoot oneself!

Unlike for most of his other correspondents, who were not trying to train themselves to be writers, he explained the range of work he was doing: "I'm writing a play for Korsh (hm!), a story for *Russian Thought*, stories for *N Times, Peterb Gaz, Fragments, Alarm Clock* and other organs. I write a lot and for a long time, but I rush like a madman: I start one thing without finishing another . . . I still haven't allowed my doctor's sign to be put up, but I still have to treat them! Brrr . . . I'm afraid of typhus!"[11]

He wasn't advertising for more patients; he had enough unpaid medical work as it was.

I am more or less ill, and am gradually turning into a dried dragon-fly. [. . .]

I go about as festive as though it were my birthday, but to judge from the critical glances of the lady cashier at *The Alarm Clock*, I am not dressed in the height of fashion, and my clothes are not brand-new. I go in buses, not in cabs.

But being a writer has its good points. In the first place, my book, I hear, is going rather well; secondly, in October I shall have money; thirdly, I am beginning to reap laurels: at the refreshment bars people point at me with their fingers, they pay me little attentions and treat me to sandwiches. Korsh caught me in his theater and straight away presented me with a free pass. [. . .] My medical colleagues sigh when they meet me, begin to talk of literature and assure me that they are sick of medicine. And so on. . . .[12]

[. . .] To your question given to my sister: Did I marry? I answer no, I'm proud of that. I'm superior to marriage![13]

He was laughing and joking it off, all those weeks of real indecision about marrying Efros. He went on, friendly, personal, lively:

Now about our mutual acquaintances . . . Mom and Dad are alive and well. Alexander lives in Moscow. Kokosha [Nikolay] is there where he was before Babkino. Ivan prospers at the school. Ma-Pa [Chekhov's nickname for his sister, Maria Pavlovna] sees the long-nosed Efros [. . .]

His sister did indeed see Efros, but how and when he and Efros saw each other this fall is unknown, except for one particular nasty occasion that we'll get to at the end of

October. He added more random news about acquaintances and, watching his hand, his pen, and his sheet of paper, observed: "The end of the letter is approaching." Having concluded with greetings to Kiseleva's family and a glance toward next year at Babkino, we find the letter, still under his hand, not yet over:

> Scarcely had I finished this letter than the bell rang and . . . I saw the genius Levitan. Zhul cap, French outfit, elegant look . . . He went two times to *Aida*, once to *Rusalka*, ordered frames, almost sold some pictures . . . He says that it's misery, misery and misery . . .
>
> "God knows what I would give to spend only 2 days at Babkino!" he cries, probably forgetting how he was moaning in the last days there.

Chekhov felt free in his correspondence with Kiseleva, and though at least a dozen years younger than she, he moved into the role she had asked of him, to help her develop as a writer. By the early 1890s, there was "a whole horde of young literary hopefuls who constantly sent Chekhov their efforts for advice and approval."[14] For the next year Kiseleva and then a pair of young male humor writers would be his unofficial students. Kiseleva, though, could sometimes seem like one of those students who thinks she is smarter than her teacher.

On September 29, Chekhov wrote his first literary advice letter to her.[15] He tried to tread lightly, praising one of her stories: "I can say, in general and roughly speaking, that from a literary point of view it is stylishly written, lively, and succinct."[16] But as he prepared at his desk for a serious discussion of her story, he found himself drawn in to make a list of what was wrong and what she needed to do:

> Of course, there is no need to assure you that I'm very glad to be your literary-agent, retailer, and guide. This duty flatters my vanity and fulfilling it will be as easy as carrying a pail for you when you return from fishing. If you have to know my conditions, take these:
>
> 1) Write as much as possible! Write, write, write . . . until your fingers are broken. (The main thing in life—penmanship!) Write more, having in view not so much the intelligent development of the big parts as much as the details, so that at first a fair half of your skits, due to your being unaccustomed to the "small press," will be rejected. As for receiving rejections, I am not going to deceive you, be hypocritical or lie—I give you my word. But don't let the rejections bother you. Even if half will receive

rejections, then the work will be more profitable than the Bohemian's in *Children's Recreation*. But as for self-esteem . . . I don't know about you, but I've been used to it a long time.

2) Write on various themes, funny and tearful, good and bad. Do stories, sketches, jokes, witticisms, puns, and so on and so forth.

3) Adaptations from foreign work—the thing is fully legal, but only in the case if your sins against the 8th Commandment don't poke you in your eyes . . . (For "Galoshes" you're going to Hell after the 22nd of January!) Flee from popular subjects. As stupid as our editors are, exposing their ignorance of Parisian literature, especially Maupassant's, is not easy work.

4) Write in one sitting, with full belief in your pen. Honestly, I'm not speaking hypocritically: eight-tenths of the writers of the "small press" in comparison with you are shoemakers and losers.

5) Brevity is recognized in the small press as the first virtue. The best measure would be to work on stationery (the same as that which I'm writing on). As soon as you get 8–10 pages, like so—stop! And the stationery is easier to send . . . Those are all my conditions.

He told her he was treating Nikolay—"He's seriously sick (stomach bleeds, tormenting him to the Devil)"—and his thoughts were straying toward an ultimate conclusion:

> When I'm being serious, it seems to me that people expressing revulsion from death are not being logical. As much as I understand the order of things, life is made up only of terrors, squabbling, and stupidities, all mixed up and in alternation . . . [17]

Even as we remind ourselves of his and Nikolay's tuberculosis, this was a big dose of advice and news for his friend Kiseleva. She would not have assumed the Chekhov brothers had tuberculosis, but she and his other friends would have seen evidence of it.

As for Chekhov's literary advice, what she had wanted (what most of us writers want, usually) was apparently only admiration.[18] The return letter came from her husband Aleksei rather than from her. Kiselev told Chekhov he agreed with Chekhov's suggestions and that his wife would try to follow his guidance.

October 1886

...in short stories it is better to say not enough than to say too much, because—because—I don't know why! At all events, remember that your failings are considered flaws only by myself (altogether unimportant flaws), and I am very often mistaken. Perhaps you are right and not I.... It happens that I have been mistaken quite often, and I have held other opinions than those I have just expressed. On occasion my criticism has proved worthless.

—To a fellow writer[1]

Chekhov began the month still under the stress of insufficient funds. But his first story of October let loose feelings and insights never before so painfully dramatized by him about family life; and then his last story of the month closed down with a slam any possibility of marriage with Dunya Efros.

"Difficult People" ("Tyajhelye Lyudi"), published October 7, is most definitely not about Chekhov's family—or so he seemed to want to assert. If he had imagined we would or could suspect it was a depiction of his own family, he wouldn't have written it or published it. Despite superficial discrepancies between the fictional family and Chekhov's, it is obvious he knew difficult families from the inside out.

"Difficult" is the right word, but the word in Russian, *tyazhelye*, has the connotation of weight, heaviness. "Burdensome People" might be more accurate, but "Difficult" is good enough.

Chekhov right away distinguishes the father from his own father, as if to insist to family and friends, "This is NOT our family." The father is a landowner, seemingly from the steppe near Taganrog, and he is not, as Pavel Chekhov was, a bankrupted Taganrog merchant.

There are only two children who figure in the story, and the oldest is the daughter. There are three younger children, but they have no role to play except as a cowering chorus of witnesses.

In small contrast, in Chekhov's family there were *six* children, the lone girl being the second youngest.

In the story, the son Pyotr expects money from his father to support him at the university, because he knows his father can afford it; he knows his father very well, however, and how difficult he is going to be about the money anyway.

Chekhov figured out early on, as a teenager, that if he wanted money, he had to go earn his own. He knew never to rely on Pavel.

The memoir about Anton by Mikhail Chekhov, the fifth son and last child, is very good and interesting, but he is discreet about family troubles.

The characters in Chekhov's stories usually do not have siblings, or the stories don't mention them. Chekhov continually simplified his stories' situations and sharply limited the number of characters. "You've got to start right off with the merchant's daughter and then concentrate entirely on her," Chekhov would later write to a budding writer who had sent him her stories. "Throw out Verochka, throw out the Greek girls, throw them all out except the doctor and the merchant's offspring."[2] We hardly notice the younger siblings in "Difficult People."

As "Difficult People" opens, the father is not in a good mood. Yevgraf Ivanovich Shiryaev has a "small farm" of 300 acres, which sounds like a lot, but all farmers are vulnerable to Nature's caprices:

> "What weather!" he said. "It's not weather, but a curse laid upon us. It's raining again!"[3]

No one answers him, and he does not seem to expect anyone to do so.

> He grumbled on, while his family sat waiting at table for him to have finished washing his hands before beginning dinner. Fedosya Semyonovna, his wife, his son Pyotr, a student, his eldest daughter Varvara, and three small boys, had been sitting waiting a long time. The boys—Kolka, Vanka, and Arhipka—grubby, snub-nosed little fellows with chubby faces and tousled hair that wanted cutting, moved their chairs impatiently, while their elders

sat without stirring, and apparently did not care whether they ate their dinner
or waited. . . .

Nothing begins until Father is ready. He enjoys his power, the way a priest, professor,
or tsar might enjoy his power to keep his subjects waiting:

> As though trying their patience, Shiryaev deliberately dried his hands, delib-
> erately said his prayer, and sat down to the table without hurrying himself.
> Cabbage-soup was served immediately. The sound of carpenters' axes (Shiryaev
> was having a new barn built) and the laughter of Fomka, their laborer, teasing
> the turkey, floated in from the courtyard.

They're not poor. Shiryaev complains about the weather, but he has the confidence of
someone who sees that he has made a success of his life. (We cannot see Pavel Chekhov
sharing such a feeling, though Pavel's greatest success was being the father of Anton, who
was writing this story; Anton could have been his pride and joy, though we don't know
that Pavel ever did puff with pride over him. Rather, several years later Pavel puffed with
pride over who he himself was: "I am the father of famous children. I must in no way be
embarrassed or humble myself before anyone.")[4]

Chekhov introduces us to the protagonist, Pyotr. He is "round-shouldered" and wears
glasses. Perhaps the round shoulders suggest he is not a farmer or likely to become one.
(Chekhov's closest brother Nikolay wore glasses and was slight of build compared to
Anton.)

Pyotr and his mother have resolved on taking action about something: he "kept
exchanging glances with his mother as he ate his dinner." Pyotr loses heart, re-resolves,
and at the end of dinner "cleared his throat resolutely" and said:

> "I ought to go tonight by the evening train. I ought to have gone before; I
> have missed a fortnight as it is. The lectures begin on the first of September."

As a student he has stayed at home longer than he meant to or expected to. What's the
big deal? Why has he had to work up his courage to make this announcement?

> "Well, go," Shiryaev assented; "why are you lingering on here? Pack up and
> go, and good luck to you."
>   A minute passed in silence.

We know now that Shiryaev is not thinking sentimentally about this. He has already cut himself off from his son. His son has his life, he has his. He either pretends not to understand what the announcement means and what his son needs, or it doesn't occur to him.

> "He must have money for the journey, Yevgraf Ivanovich," the mother observed in a low voice.
>
> "Money? To be sure, you can't go without money. Take it at once, since you need it. You could have had it long ago!"

So *they're* at fault already, Shiryaev asserts, for not having asked for it. Why hadn't they just asked? Why are they making a big deal of it?

But we know something is up. We feel the tension. Nothing is easy with Shiryaev. Son and mother have prepped for this conversation. Shiryaev has not prepared. He can act on a whim, like a king on his throne. He is ready to listen and grant, or not grant, requests.

> The student heaved a faint sigh and looked with relief at his mother. Deliberately Shiryaev took a pocket-book out of his coat-pocket and put on his spectacles.
>
> "How much do you want?" he asked.
>
> "The fare to Moscow is eleven rubles forty-two kopecks. . . ."
>
> "Ah, money, money!" sighed the father. (He always sighed when he saw money, even when he was receiving it.) "Here are twelve rubles for you. You will have change out of that which will be of use to you on the journey."
>
> "Thank you."
>
> After waiting a little, the student said:
>
> "I did not get lessons quite at first last year. I don't know how it will be this year; most likely it will take me a little time to find work. I ought to ask you for fifteen rubles for my lodging and dinner."
>
> Shiryaev thought a little and heaved a sigh.

Shiryaev is thinking or simply going into his natural mode as a farmer and businessman. He does not appreciate how difficult his son finds it to talk to him about this.

> "You will have to make ten do," he said. "Here, take it."

The student thanked him. He ought to have asked him for something more, for clothes, for lecture fees, for books, but after an intent look at his father he decided not to pester him further.

How little we still know of Chekhov's mother. But maybe we know something of Evgenia Chekhova from the narrator's statement: "The mother, lacking in diplomacy and prudence, like all mothers, could not restrain herself [. . .]" Chekhov was not interested in the "courage" of soldiers; here he shows us instead the reckless courage of mothers. She says:

"You ought to give him another six rubles, Yevgraf Ivanovich, for a pair of boots. Why, just see, how can he go to Moscow in such wrecks?"

"Let him take my old ones; they are still quite good."

"He must have trousers, anyway; he is a disgrace to look at."

It's wonderful to Shiryaev that he immediately has a solution to the boot problem. But encountering his wife's persistence, he realizes that they have conspired and are going to push for more than he has been willing to grant.

And immediately after that a storm-signal showed itself, at the sight of which all the family trembled.

In Russian, the "storm-signal" reads as "storm-*petrel*," a storm bird—identified by sailors immediately preceding a storm.

This means that the family is used to this. Maybe all families recognize such indications. Shiryaev's family has learned to cover their heads—everyone except, somehow, Shiryaev's wife!

Shiryaev's short, fat neck turned suddenly red as a beetroot. The color mounted slowly to his ears, from his ears to his temples, and by degrees suffused his whole face. Yevgraf Ivanovich shifted in his chair and unbuttoned his shirt-collar to save himself from choking. He was evidently struggling with the feeling that was mastering him. A deathlike silence followed. The children held their breath.

Fedosya Semyonovna, as though she did not grasp what was happening to her husband, went on:

> "He is not a little boy now, you know; he is ashamed to go about without clothes."

He knows he is getting the full truth from his wife, the whole story, that his son, this round-shouldered, bespectacled boy bound for a student's life in Moscow, feels short-changed by his carefully generous father!

> Shiryaev suddenly jumped up, and with all his might flung down his fat pocket-book in the middle of the table, so that a hunk of bread flew off a plate. A revolting expression of anger, resentment, avarice—all mixed together—flamed on his face.
>
> "Take everything!" he shouted in an unnatural voice; "plunder me! Take it all! Strangle me!"

Here is where Chekhov has most definitely become personal, though the adjective "revolting" is the only judgment he (or his narrator) has so far made. We see into the core of the father's feelings.

> He jumped up from the table, clutched at his head, and ran staggering about the room.
>
> "Strip me to the last thread!" he shouted in a shrill voice. "Squeeze out the last drop! Rob me! Wring my neck!"

We can read Chekhov and not notice ourselves exposed on the page. (And by whom am *I* exposed? By the fuming Shiryaev, unfortunately.) And how is Chekhov himself exposed? Through the pain! He saw this sort of family encounter and knew its damage to everyone in the household.

There is also sympathy somewhere in this story for Shiryaev. It is not in this scene here. We with the children avert our eyes. We wait him out.

But Pyotr, for the first time in his life, cannot let it go:

> The student flushed and dropped his eyes. He could not go on eating. Fedosya Semyonovna, who had not after twenty-five years grown used to her husband's difficult character, shrank into herself and muttered something in self-defense. An expression of amazement and dull terror came into her wasted and birdlike face, which at all times looked dull and scared. The little boys and the elder

daughter Varvara, a girl in her teens, with a pale ugly face, laid down their spoons and sat mute.

Poor Varvara! How will she ever escape this house?

Shiryaev, growing more and more ferocious, uttering words each more terrible than the one before, dashed up to the table and began shaking the notes out of his pocket-book.

Shiryaev only makes a bad situation worse.

"Take them!" he muttered, shaking all over. "You've eaten and drunk your fill, so here's money for you too! I need nothing! Order yourself new boots and uniforms!"

The student turned pale and got up.

"Listen, papa," he began, gasping for breath. "I . . . I beg you to end this, for . . ."

"Hold your tongue!" the father shouted at him, and so loudly that the spectacles fell off his nose; "hold your tongue!"

"I used . . . I used to be able to put up with such scenes, but . . . but now I have got out of the way of it. Do you understand? I have got out of the way of it!"

"Hold your tongue!" cried the father, and he stamped with his feet. "You must listen to what I say! I shall say what I like, and you hold your tongue. At your age I was earning my living, while you . . . Do you know what you cost me, you scoundrel? I'll turn you out! Wastrel!"

How many teenaged children could dodge a parent's accusation of financial dependence? . . . Well, *Chekhov*, for one.

There were lines that Chekhov could not bear seeing crossed. Papa has crossed the line and created agony all around. In this family dynamic, the explosions occur in an enclosed space that doesn't seem to allow for escape or end.

"Yevgraf Ivanovich," muttered Fedosya Semyonovna, moving her fingers nervously; "you know he . . . you know Petya . . . !"

"Hold your tongue!" Shiryaev shouted out to her, and tears actually came into his eyes from anger. "It is you who have spoilt them—you!

It's all your fault! He has no respect for us, does not say his prayers, and earns nothing! I am only one against the ten of you! I'll turn you out of the house!"

The daughter Varvara gazed fixedly at her mother with her mouth open, moved her vacant-looking eyes to the window, turned pale, and, uttering a loud shriek, fell back in her chair. The father, with a curse and a wave of the hand, ran out into the yard.

This was how domestic scenes usually ended at the Shiryaevs'.

There are patterns in the family, and this is one of them: Father blows up and stalks out. It's a bad but predictable outcome. Bad as that is, however, it can become worse, because Pyotr is his father's son:

But on this occasion, unfortunately, Pyotr the student was carried away by overmastering anger. He was just as hasty and ill-tempered as his father and his grandfather the priest, who used to beat his parishioners about the head with a stick. Pale and clenching his fists, he went up to his mother and shouted in the very highest tenor note his voice could reach:

"These reproaches are loathsome! sickening to me! I want nothing from you! Nothing! I would rather die of hunger than eat another mouthful at your expense! Take your nasty money back! Take it!"

The mother huddled against the wall and waved her hands, as though it were not her son, but some phantom before her. "What have I done?" she wailed. "What?"

What the hell! The fighters blame the peacemaker. Every Adam must have his Eve to take the blame.

If Pyotr is the hero of the story, we're stuck with him. But Chekhov's stories don't usually have conventional heroes or villains. Good people are prickly, bad people are charming, weak people are resilient, strong people are brittle.

Pyotr has no plan except to start walking out onto the steppe from the house. This is the first time we know the geography of the farm. The primary location has been a very particular "at home." Pyotr's escape is into the countryside. The fields are wet from the rain. As he walks through the familiar landscape, he imagines, as it occurs to all of us idiots who have ever stormed out of our houses, that he could just keep walking away forever:

Pyotr thought it would not be a bad thing to walk to Moscow on foot; to walk just as he was, with holes in his boots, without a cap, and without a farthing of money. When he had gone eighty miles his father, frightened and aghast, would overtake him, would begin begging him to turn back or take the money, but he would not even look at him, but would go on and on. . . . Bare forests would be followed by desolate fields, fields by forests again; soon the earth would be white with the first snow, and the streams would be coated with ice. . . . Somewhere near Kursk or near Serpuhovo, exhausted and dying of hunger, he would sink down and die. His corpse would be found, and there would be a paragraph in all the papers saying that a student called Shiryaev had died of hunger. . . .

Though he notices details of the road and landscape, Pyotr's mind is occupied with fantasies of dying on the journey north, of his father's guilty conscience, of adventures with pilgrims, robbers, a beautiful rich young woman falling in love with him. Nearly to the train station, from where, apparently, he has been hoping to leave (but he has no money), he is shaken into the immediate moment:

"Look out!" He heard behind him a loud voice.

An old lady of his acquaintance, a landowner of the neighborhood, drove past him in a light, elegant landau. He bowed to her, and smiled all over his face. And at once he caught himself in that smile, which was so out of keeping with his gloomy mood.

Chekhov seems to suggest that young Pyotr is able at this fragile moment to put together a series of thoughts that, I think, probably only Tolstoy or Chekhov himself could have been capable of:

Where did it come from if his whole heart was full of vexation and misery? And he thought nature itself had given man this capacity for lying, that even in difficult moments of spiritual strain he might be able to hide the secrets of his nest as the fox and the wild duck do.

That is (and this was not the narrator so much as Chekhov, who had been thinking about this situation for at least ten years): "*Every family has its joys and its horrors, but however great they may be, it's hard for an outsider's eye to see them; they are a secret.*"

Next summer, in a letter to his cousin Georgy, Chekhov would write:

> In addition, besides to your own family, don't read my letters to anyone; private correspondence is a family secret with which nobody has any business.[5]

In such a personal story as this, Chekhov scarcely managed to disguise the secrets of his family.

While Pyotr has been superseded by the author in the previous moments, Pyotr is, I believe, capable of this next series of thoughts. It's the immediate circumstances that rouse his thoughts. He has this neighbor-woman in mind, and he knows her situation. She has led him into these thoughts:

> The father of the old lady who had just driven by, for instance, had for some offense lain for half his lifetime under the ban of the wrath of Tsar Nicholas I; her husband had been a gambler; of her four sons, not one had turned out well. One could imagine how many terrible scenes there must have been in her life, how many tears must have been shed. And yet the old lady seemed happy and satisfied, and she had answered his smile by smiling, too. The student thought of his comrades, who did not like talking about their families; he thought of his mother, who almost always lied when she had to speak of her husband and children. . . .

And those really have been Pyotr's thoughts, because they're the thoughts that eventually prompt him to turn back. He doesn't turn on his heel; he has too much pride for that. He walks until he knows he has to return. And he is braver now. He has survived the confrontation with his father and is able to steel himself a bit.

There is no description of Chekhov ever battling his father. Having seen his explosive brothers confront his father, he probably found a quieter, more effective way of getting around Pavel.

> As he walked back he made up his mind at all costs to talk to his father, to explain to him, once and for all, that it was dreadful and oppressive to live with him.
>
> He found perfect stillness in the house. His sister Varvara was lying behind a screen with a headache, moaning faintly. His mother, with a look of amazement and guilt upon her face, was sitting beside her on a box, mending Arhipka's trousers. Yevgraf Ivanovich was pacing from one window to another, scowling at the weather. From his walk, from the way he cleared

his throat, and even from the back of his head, it was evident he felt himself
to blame.

"I suppose you have changed your mind about going today?" he asked.

It's there, just there, that Chekhov creates a flash of sympathetic understanding of
the father.

> The student felt sorry for him, but immediately suppressing that feeling,
> he said:
>
> "Listen . . . I must speak to you seriously. . . yes, seriously. I have always
> respected you, and . . . and have never brought myself to speak to you in such
> a tone, but your behavior . . . your last action . . ."
>
> The father looked out of the window and did not speak. The student, as though
> considering his words, rubbed his forehead and went on in great excitement:
>
> "Not a dinner or tea passes without your making an uproar. Your bread
> sticks in our throat. . . nothing is more bitter, more humiliating, than
> bread that sticks in one's throat. . . . Though you are my father, no one,
> neither God nor nature, has given you the right to insult and humiliate us
> so horribly, to vent your ill-humor on the weak. You have worn my mother
> out and made a slave of her, my sister is hopelessly crushed, while I . . ."
>
> "It's not your business to teach me," said his father.

Pyotr has again become Chekhov or Chekhov has become Pyotr:

> "Yes, it is my business! You can quarrel with me as much as you like, but leave
> my mother in peace! I will not allow you to torment my mother!" the student
> went on, with flashing eyes. "You are spoiled because no one has yet dared
> to oppose you. They tremble and are mute toward you, but now that is over!
> Coarse, ill-bred man! You are coarse . . . do you understand? You are coarse,
> ill-humored, unfeeling. And the peasants can't endure you!"

But Chekhov would not have said "the peasants" to his father, as it wouldn't make
sense. Perhaps "servants" would do, as in their present-day Moscow middle-class household, they had a cook and a maid.

We see that the conscience-ridden father has determined to accept some words of
reproach—but not this many:

The student had by now lost his thread, and was not so much speaking as firing off detached words. Yevgraf Ivanovich listened in silence, as though stunned; but suddenly his neck turned crimson, the color crept up his face, and he made a movement.

"Hold your tongue!" he shouted.

"That's right!" the son persisted; "you don't like to hear the truth! Excellent! Very good! begin shouting! Excellent!"

Chekhov would not have mocked his father, probably.

"Hold your tongue, I tell you!" roared Yevgraf Ivanovich.

Fedosya Semyonovna appeared in the doorway, very pale, with an astonished face; she tried to say something, but she could not, and could only move her fingers.

"It's all your fault!" Shiryaev shouted at her. "You have brought him up like this!"

"I don't want to go on living in this house!" shouted the student, crying, and looking angrily at his mother. "I don't want to live with you!"

Varvara uttered a shriek behind the screen and broke into loud sobs. With a wave of his hand, Shiryaev ran out of the house.

Again the father has stalked off!

The student went to his own room and quietly lay down. He lay till midnight without moving or opening his eyes. He felt neither anger nor shame, but a vague ache in his soul. He neither blamed his father nor pitied his mother, nor was he tormented by stings of conscience; he realized that every one in the house was feeling the same ache, and God only knew which was most to blame, which was suffering most. . . .

Aren't all *unhappy* families perhaps alike? Is Chekhov standing Tolstoy's already famous epigraph from *Anna Karenina* on its head?

The misery that envelops a family in expectation of, during, and after such disputes, isn't it always like so? "Despotism and lies so disfigured our childhood that it makes me sick and horrified to think of it," Chekhov wrote his brother Alexander more than two years after writing this story. "Remember the disgust and horror we felt every time father made a scene at dinner because there was too much salt in the soup or called mother a fool."[6]

Chekhov knew the characters' agony. Meanwhile, the "sick and horrified" student Pyotr groans and bears it:

> At midnight he woke the laborer, and told him to have the horse ready at five o'clock in the morning for him to drive to the station; he undressed and got into bed, but could not get to sleep. He heard how his father, still awake, paced slowly from window to window, sighing, till early morning. No one was asleep; they spoke rarely, and only in whispers. Twice his mother came to him behind the screen. Always with the same look of vacant wonder, she slowly made the cross over him, shaking nervously.

And here is Chekhov too—in his quiet sympathy for the mother, for his own mother or for all mothers married to tyrants. How much *she* has had to endure. Chekhov never justified his father, though in his teens he and his brothers and cousins learned to appreciate through meeting Pavel's and Mitrofan's father just how horrible their father's and uncle's lives must have been, and how moderate they as fathers were in comparison. Chekhov witnessed and experienced his own generation's huge leap of improved behavior, of restraint, of education.

"Difficult People" concludes, as nearly all of Chekhov's stories do, with life, damaged or wounded as it is, going on:

> At five o'clock in the morning he said goodbye to them all affectionately, and even shed tears. As he passed his father's room, he glanced in at the door. Yevgraf Ivanovich, who had not taken off his clothes or gone to bed, was standing by the window, drumming on the panes.
>
> "Goodbye; I am going," said his son.
>
> "Goodbye . . . the money is on the round table . . ." his father answered, without turning around.
>
> A cold, hateful rain was falling as the laborer drove him to the station. The sunflowers were drooping their heads still lower, and the grass seemed darker than ever.

Is it possible that Chekhov stood outside these characters, invented them from whole cloth, and didn't know them from within?

"Difficult People" contains more power than any of his famous plays that involve family dramas. In this story, he caught lightning—and thunder—in a bottle. And yet, looking at the original version of this story, I was surprised to see how very much he cut out. There are clipped phrasings throughout; he neatly trimmed several descriptions. He cut the length by more than two pages, the bulk of that coming in three passages. The only significant change, however, resulting in "a softening," as K. S. Overina puts it,[7] occurs after Pyotr's return to the house. In the midst of Pyotr and his father's ferocious screaming, the mother, unseen by either, rushes between them and is "accidentally" struck by her husband's fist between her neck and shoulder. She collapses to a chair and father and son turn away and retreat to opposite corners.[8]

Chekhov deleted this because . . . he never explained such decisions. I suspect that it was because Shiryaev would not have been forgivable. And who could have forgiven Pavel had anyone described such a scene in the Chekhov house?

Chekhov wrote several stories this month, and a few of them are substantial and worth noting. Two of them, not otherwise worth noting, "Oh, My Teeth" ("Akh, Zuby!," October 9) and "Whining: A Letter from Far Away" ("Nyt'e: Pis'mo Izdaleka," October 12), focus on toothaches, which had afflicted Chekhov in July and for which he had had to leave Babkino for treatment in Moscow.

When Chekhov sat at his desk in his book-lined study in Moscow and leaned over the paper to compose a new piece, he did not hunt for distant or special topics. We can hope that the toothache, anyway, was a memory and not a continuation from the summer. But the second tale about toothache made me wonder if it wasn't Chekhov's substitution for tuberculosis. He did not let himself "whine" about his tuberculosis, and for another eleven years denied to everyone that he even had it. The whining letter-writer narrator is in Siberia, where he is serving time for forgery (committed by his mistress). He writes, as Chekhov would, "I swear to you I'm healthy. That is to say, I'm not consumptive and I don't cough [. . .] The thought that there's nowhere and nohow I would be cured [of the toothache] further increased my torment."[9] And in real life, there was nowhere and nohow Chekhov could be cured of tuberculosis. He didn't mention his toothache again in the letters.

He had been making multiple trips this summer and fall, including on October 4, to a court to testify in a case concerning a peasant, and this may have inspired the setting of the Victor Hugo–like tale "In the Court" ("V Sude," October 11), which is about a trial of a peasant who has murdered his wife. The peasant is thoroughly bewildered in this dulling, dispassionate, legal atmosphere: "What he met here was not at all what he could have expected. The charge of murder hung over him, and yet here he met with neither threatening faces nor indignant looks nor loud phrases about retribution nor sympathy for his extraordinary fate; not one of those who were judging him looked at him with interest or for long. . . . The dingy windows and walls, the voice of the secretary, the attitude of the prosecutor were all saturated with official indifference and produced an atmosphere of frigidity, as though the murderer were simply an official property, or as though he were not being judged by living men, but by some unseen machine, set going, goodness knows how or by whom. . . ." A doctor, perhaps in the same role Chekhov had served, indifferently testifies. "The last to be examined was the district doctor who had made a postmortem on the old woman. He told the court all that he remembered of his report at the postmortem and all that he had succeeded in thinking of on his way to the court that morning."[10] The doctor is no clever hero. He is as flattened and dulled as the rest of those involved in the proceedings. His testimony does not clarify the details of the murder.

Chekhov rarely wrote neat stories with surprise endings, but this is one. The awkward soldier who has brought the peasant into the courtroom turns out to be the peasant's son.

After a few other short pieces came another marriage story, "The Proposal: A Story for Young Ladies" ("Predlozhenie: Rasskaz dlya Devits," October 23), a one-page skit about a business and marriage proposal in one: The son of a factory owner assures Princess Vera, "We will sell a million poods[11] of fat a year! Let's build a fat-rendering factory on our adjoining estates and go halfsies!"[12]

Why couldn't Chekhov make his living as a doctor? He loved saying he was lazy; to make a ruble as a doctor in mid-1880s Moscow, he would have had to hustle and seek out more patients than he already had. He would have had to charge his friends and his friends' acquaintances for his services. In "A Peculiar Man" ("Neobiknovenniy," October 25), we meet the kind of client who could have driven Chekhov out of his medical career. This peculiar Kiryakov wants to find the cheapest midwife in town. Quibbling and fussing, he wears down Maria Petrovna until she agrees to his price. Later, having completed her midwifery, she remarks:

> "Well now, thank God, there is one human being more in the world!"
>
> "Yes, that's agreeable," said Kiryakov, preserving the wooden expression of his face, "though indeed, on the other hand, to have more children you must have more money. The baby is not born fed and clothed."

A guilty expression comes into the mother's face, as though she had brought a creature into the world without permission or through idle caprice. Kiryakov gets up with a sigh and walks with solid dignity out of the room.

"What a man, bless him!" says the midwife to the mother. "He's so stern and does not smile."

The mother tells her that *he* is always like that. . . . He is honest, fair, prudent, sensibly economical, but all that to such an exceptional degree that simple mortals feel suffocated by it. His relations have parted from him, the servants will not stay more than a month; they have no friends; his wife and children are always on tenterhooks from terror over every step they take. He does not shout at them nor beat them, his virtues are far more numerous than his defects, but when he goes out of the house they all feel better, and more at ease. Why it is so the woman herself cannot say.[13]

The put-upon exhausted midwife, having rendered her services to the wife, is so glad to be done with the peculiar man that when she realizes she has left without getting paid, she decides not to go back.

On October 7 Chekhov wrote Leykin to ask him to read Maria Kiseleva's story; it was short and, granted, "a bit sentimental," but if Leykin liked it, he could get away with paying her only six kopecks a line. She, as a budding writer, would save Leykin expenses. That was clever of Chekhov, but Leykin wrote back to say he thought her tale was indeed "sentimental" and "unhumorous"[14] and rejected it. Chekhov did, however, help get it published in *The Alarm Clock*. Chekhov also wanted to complain to Leykin about not having received his fees from the *Petersburg Gazette*. "I don't know how I lived through September and how now I can expect to live in expectation of the pay?"[15] He wouldn't write for them again until they paid him.

Leykin didn't mind the *Gazette*'s financial sloppiness, however, if it meant Chekhov would write more regularly for *Fragments*. In his reply, Leykin advised Chekhov to avoid the *Gazette*; he could and should increase his contributions to *Fragments* and *New Times*. Leykin wasn't satisfied with the writers or writing that Chekhov was trying to foist on him as replacements. Leykin remarked about Alexander: "Telling stories aloud he's much better, sharper, more literary than when he writes; when for others it's usually the opposite."[16]

Chekhov felt desperate about money and so wrote desperately and jokingly to Schechtel on the 19th, including even a drawing of himself hanging by a hook. "If you are not touched by this artistic representation of my fate, you don't have a heart, Franz Osipovich! As a matter of fact, the firm 'Doctor A. P. Chekhov and Co.' is now living through a financial crisis . . . If you don't give me by the 1st 25–50 rubles in loan, you are a pitiless crocodile . . ."[17] Chekhov's requests for loans were usually heeded; he knew his recipients, and he was scrupulous about repaying.

He wrote Leykin again on October 23 and in entertaining, scattershot fashion told him about his visit to a mutual friend, the hard-drinking poet Palmin, and about his continued financial woes: "My health is better, but my pocket still has consumption." By the next week, Khudekov, the editor and publisher of the *Gazette*, offered to pay Chekhov two kopecks more per line in 1887. Chekhov, never much of a negotiator, accepted.

Chekhov's literary mentorship of Kiseleva, however, paid quick dividends. He wrote her on October 29 and jumped right in on the fate of the short stories she had sent him:

> 1) "Galoshes" lies on my table and will be put into circulation only after the New Year, in a shortened, corrected way. It's necessary to flush from it the French smell, otherwise it will come out like an adaptation, and that is no good and unfitting, as a novice it's always better to begin with the original. If your first story is "too busy,"[18] all the following ones will be seen with prejudice.
>
> 2) The story about the madwoman, titled by me "Who's Happier" is a very sweet, warm, and gracious story. Even the dog Leykin, not knowing anybody besides Turgenev and me, found that this story is "not-bad and literary." (Not wanting to be the sole judge, I brought it for advice to Leykin and other old literary dogs.) The most successful place for me—*Peterb Gazette*, but alas! Because of the fee I broke off from that periodical (I'm demanding a raise). In *Fragments* it's impossible to place, as it's not humorous. The only thing remaining—wait for it in *The Alarm Clock*, where in its feuilleton-pages they publish "serious" studies (for example, my "Oysters"), which I did. So, your story will be published in *The Alarm Clock*. Thanks to the idiotic manner of journals to mix up signed things, belonging to "names," that is, firms (Zlato-vratsky, Nefedov, Chekhov and such representatives of the fall of contemporary literature), your story will be placed not in the near future. But for you this is indifferent, as the money can be had before publication.
>
> [. . .] We need to talk over many things. So, I have to justify some correc-tions in your stories . . . For example in "Who's Happiest?" the beginning is

pretty bad . . . It's a dramatic story, but you begin with "shooting himself" in a humorous tone. Then the "hysterical laughter" is a much too old effect . . . The simpler the movements the more plausible and sincere, and therefore better . . . In "Galoshes" there are many mistakes of the kind as "House No. 49." In Moscow there is no numbering of addresses . . . Turning to the last story, by memory by the way, that Lentovsky is completely out of place. He is very much not as popular in Moscow as Aleksei Sergeevich, who for some reason loves him.

He concluded with terrific encouragement: "judging by this first experiment, it's possible to guarantee that within 1–2 years you will be in a strong position."[19]

This was the age of literary translation; Russians could read the latest French and English novels in the literary journals and foreign translated short stories in newspapers and magazines. Chekhov's comic August story "The First-Class Passenger" was translated into Czech on October 27.[20] *Moravska Orlice* probably did not pay him for it.

Meanwhile, Chekhov's financial worries had led him into writing the most problematic and longest of all his stories this year, "Mire." Chekhov was mired indeed in anxiety: Where was his money to support the family going to come from? Could he actually obtain it through marriage? He resolved the marriage problem, unfortunately, the way, perhaps, a fourteen-year-old boy would, by blaming and ridiculing an innocent person who had just been minding her own business.

I have given up trying *not* to squirm over "Mire"; it is squirm-worthy. It seems, however, to have made two of Chekhov's keenest advocates, the translators and professors Michael Henry Heim and Simon Karlinsky, whose collection of his letters is the single-best presentation of Chekhov's biography, turn the argument upside down. They counter that those who condemn the story don't understand it:

> . . . "Mire," to this day [is] one of Chekhov's least understood works. Because the story featured a Jewish seductress and because it appeared in *New Times*, the prominent anti-government journalist Vukol Lavrov proclaimed it reactionary and racist. [. . .] But a closer reading of this story within the context of Chekhov's writing of 1886–88 shows that it was one of several works written during that period which examined, possibly under the impact of his broken engagement to Dunya Efros, the reactions of sensitive Russian Jews to the discrimination and repression with which they had to live. [. . .] The wealthy and educated Susannah in "Mire," unlike Sarah and Solomon [in *Ivanov* and

The Steppe], does not have to contend with overt and crude anti-Semitism. But she constantly expects it just the same and her resentment finds its expression in a series of sexual conquests of young Russian noblemen; her promiscuity is the only way she has of asserting her own worth and of defying the hostility of the neighboring Russian gentry. Ironically, the two brothers [they are *cousins*] who are involved with her in the course of the story are not at all anti-Jewish, but they are nevertheless victimized by Susannah's neurotic response to her predicament, which Chekhov depicted with remarkable understanding.[21]

Well, I love Chekhov, too. But when do we finally admit to the errors of even the people we revere? In public, Chekhov defended Jews and called out, for example his friend and editor Bilibin's anti-Semitic newspaper column remarks. So many of Chekhov's friends and literary and medical colleagues were Jews. No one who knew him ever accused him of being anti-Semitic. As far as we can tell from his actions in the world he never *acted* prejudicially against Jews. But publishing "Mire" was in itself an act, and the other stories with anti-Semitic statements in the author's voice are also acts, and hence I squirm.

As Chekhov would have wanted, let's face the problem straight on. And, in an impossible act of imagination, let's try to read it as Dunya Efros could have, if she was looking for similarities and differences. She was not, as Susanna[22] is, a rich daughter of a recently deceased distillery owner. Dunya was twenty-five; Susanna is twenty-seven. Dunya did not live in a grand house in the country. Dunya was a student in Moscow at the same women's program at the university as Maria Chekhova. Her father was alive and a lawyer. Dunya did not steal IOUs from sexually susceptible estate owners or their relatives and silence them by seducing them. Dunya was well-educated and probably would have noticed that Susanna has much less in common with her than with Circe of *The Odyssey*, who welcomes Odysseus and his men on their journey homeward and turns all of them except Odysseus into dull-witted animals.

On the other hand, Susanna is and Dunya was Jewish and Chekhov's attraction to Dunya confused him, just as the protagonist of "Mire," Sokolsky, is attracted as if against his will to Susanna:

> Nothing could be seen behind the woollen shawl in which she was muffled but a pale, long, pointed, somewhat aquiline nose, and one large dark eye. Her ample dressing-gown concealed her figure, but judging from her beautiful hand, from her voice, her nose, and her eye, she might be twenty-six or twenty-eight.[23]

Only in stages, because Susanna is a con artist, does she further reveal herself, both physically and mentally. She bewitches Sokolsky with various misdirections. Before he can do so, she condemns Jews, women, and marriage. He doesn't understand his increasing attraction to her:

"You are a woman yourself, and such a woman-hater!"

"A woman . . ." smiled Susanna. "It's not my fault that God has cast me into this mold, is it? I'm no more to blame for it than you are for having moustaches. The violin is not responsible for the choice of its case. I am very fond of myself, but when any one reminds me that I am a woman, I begin to hate myself. Well, you can go away, and I'll dress. Wait for me in the drawing-room."

The lieutenant went out, and the first thing he did was to draw a deep breath, to get rid of the heavy scent of jasmine, which had begun to irritate his throat and to make him feel giddy.

"What a strange woman!" he thought, looking about him. "She talks fluently, but . . . far too much, and too freely. She must be neurotic."

That's as far as Sokolsky can go in his analysis of her; he's no Chekhov, but in this story, Chekhov doesn't quite seem himself, either. In a panic of confusion or guilt, heterosexual men of all ages label attractive women as crazy or "neurotic." Chekhov has confusing or confused motives: one is to describe a literary type, a newfangled Circe, another is falling under the spell of Dunya Efros. Our author's misogynistic and anti-Semitic vision results in Susanna:

There was scarcely anything in the room definitely Jewish, except, perhaps, a big picture of the meeting of Jacob and Esau. The lieutenant looked around about him, and, shrugging his shoulders, thought of his strange, new acquaintance, of her free-and-easy manners, and her way of talking. But then the door opened, and in the doorway appeared the lady herself, in a long black dress, so slim and tightly laced that her figure looked as though it had been turned in a lathe. Now the lieutenant saw not only the nose and eyes, but also a thin white face, a head black and as curly as lamb's-wool. She did not attract him, though she did not strike him as ugly. He had a prejudice against un-Russian faces in general, and he considered, too, that the lady's white face, the whiteness of which for some reason suggested the cloying scent of jasmine, did not go well with her little black curls and thick eyebrows; that her nose and ears were astoundingly white, as though they belonged to a corpse, or had been molded out of transparent wax. When she smiled she showed pale gums as well as her teeth, and he did not like that either.

But the joke is on Sokolsky. He will lose to her all the money that she owes him and he will borrow more money and lose that, too. In this, we are not getting to the mystery of Chekhov's finances. But we are seeing Chekhov's final insult to Dunya: her looks. He never let her forget that he found her "Jewish" features distinctive and unattractive. This is the only contemporary photograph of Efros that has come to light: [24]

Dunya Efros.

Chekhov describes the guilty, dirty secret of Sokolsky and his equally bewitched cousin Kryukov:

> Both of them felt, somehow, ashamed to speak of the incident aloud. Yet they remembered it and thought of it with pleasure, as of a curious farce, which life had unexpectedly and casually played upon them, and which it would be pleasant to recall in old age.

On the day "Mire" was published, Dunya Efros paid Chekhov a call. To conclude his letter of October 29 to Maria Kiseleva, he confessed, "Mother and auntie are praying for me to marry a merchant's daughter [that is, *not* Efros]. There was Efros just now. I angered her, telling her that a young Hebrew was not worth a groat; she was insulted and left." [25]

Chekhov, one of the most decent literary figures I have ever come to know through books, behaved in this instance like a cad.

Did he have to insult her in person so that she would hate him for good, before she even read "Mire," so that she could thank her lucky stars they didn't end up together when she *did* read it? Or had she read it and, hurting, come over, and he felt himself obliged to show her he was indeed a beast and she was better off without him?

In Chekhov's life and writings of these two years, there are confounding Jewish problems. The biographer Rayfield persuades me with his conclusion: "Dunya's Jewishness was certainly instrumental in bringing her and Anton together and in sundering them. Like many southern Russians, Anton liked and admired Jews. Always a defender of Jews, he asked Bilibin why he used the word 'yid' three times in one letter? Yet he himself used the word 'yid' both neutrally and pejoratively and, like many southern Russians, Anton felt Jews to be a race apart [. . .] 'Jew' and 'non-Jew' were categories in which he classified every new acquaintance, even though his utterances and his behavior make him, by the standards of the times, a judophile."[26]

Characters throughout the fiction wrestle with forgiveness, and I hope we can all conclude our wrestling matches with him over his unfortunate expressions of anti-Semitism. Dunya Efros, the offended one herself, forgave him.

The two most informative works concerning the issue of anti-Semitism in Chekhov's life and work are *Chekhov i Evrei* (Chekhov and the Jews) by Mark Ural'sky and "From Susanna to Sarra: Chekhov in 1886–1887" by Helena Tolstoy. In 1887 Efros married Efim Konovitser, one of Chekhov's Jewish classmates and friends from Taganrog. Chekhov and Konovitser and Dunya continued being friends.

During World War I, Konovitser died, and after the Russian Revolution, Efros and her two children moved to Paris. In 1943, when she was eighty-two, she was arrested by the Nazis and taken to Treblinka and murdered in the Holocaust. Her son Nikolay survived and eventually visited the USSR in 1956 to hand over some Chekhov-related material. Nikolay Konovitser said that in his childhood he often saw Chekhov, who spoke to him about, among other things, writing: "You can write, so write!" When young Konovitser asked him what to write, Chekhov said, "Whatever you want, but especially what you see, and when you're big, you'll become a writer, but write every day."[27]

—⁂—

After his embarrassing encounter with Efros on October 29, 1886, Chekhov went to the theater to watch a play. When he got home, the family was celebrating his parents' thirty-second wedding anniversary.[28]

His last letter of the month was to Leykin, to whom he admitted his reluctance to lobby Suvorin for a review of a new novel by Leykin's and Chekhov's friend Palmin: "I will write to Suvorin about the review only if I'm writing him a business letter, writing à propos; otherwise, I'm not able to ask. People I know well, you, for example, or Bilibin, I can ask, but writing to people not connected with me in close acquaintance, about a favor, courtesy or service is blocked by my faintheartedness. In general asking for things I'm terribly shy, and so of course I don't gain anything and I lose a lot. Maybe in the middle of November I'll be in Peter and talk with Suvorin personally."[29]

Leykin answered that he would come down to Moscow himself to see Chekhov. They had a lot to talk over, he said.

Chekhov got over his shyness and wrote Suvorin on November 6 to ask him if *New Times* could review Palmin's book.

November 1886

—∿∿—

. . . while Tolstoy is in literature it is easy and pleasant
to be a writer; even to be aware that one has done
nothing and is doing nothing is not so terrible,
since Tolstoy does enough for all. His work serves as
the justification of all the hopes and anticipations built
upon literature. Thirdly, Tolstoy stands firmly, his
authority is immense, and while he lives, bad tastes
in literature, banality of every kind, impudent or
lachrymose, all the bristling, exasperated vanities will
remain far away, deep in the shade. His moral authority
alone is capable of maintaining on a certain height the
so-called literary moods and currents. Without him they
would all be a shepherdless flock, or a hotch-potch in
which it would be difficult to make out anything.

—Letter to a friend[1]

The Lodger" ("Zhilets," November 1), is ironically titled, as the lodger is the put-upon
husband of a woman who owns a lodging house. The house runs by her rules, so
when the husband tries to command the servants, they ignore him. He thus starts on his
way to being a drunk. "A Bad Night: Sketches" ("Nedobraya Noch': Nabroski," November 3)
includes a terrifying description of a fire that burns down the neighboring village:

Having driven five or six versts, the lady sees something unusually monstrous,
which not everyone ever sees even once in their life, and for the richest imagination is impossible to imagine. An enormous fire has the village ablaze. The

field of vision is obscured in a mass of creeping blinding flames, into which, like into a fog, sink the huts, trees and the church. Bright almost sunlike light mixes with puffs of black smoke and frosty steam; gold tongues glide with greedy crackings, smiling and merrily winking, and lick the black frameworks. Red clouds and golden dust quickly sweep to the sky, and, as if to increase the illusion, agitated pigeons dive into these clouds. In the air is a strange mix of laughing sounds: horrific cracklings, rustling flames, resembling the rustle of a thousand birds' wings, people's voices, bleatings, mooings, the scraping of wheels. The church is fearsome. Flames burst out of its windows and clouds of thick smoke. The bell tower stands like in a black ogre in a mass of light and gold dust; it is already burned over, but the bells hang on, and it's hard to understand what they're holding onto.[2]

Chekhov's narrator remarks, "Apparently misfortune attracts people."

He had kept his own "misfortune" with Efros quiet and out of sight. In his letter to Leykin on November 6, as he had effectively extinguished any possibility of marriage, Chekhov opened with a joke, possibly because he was using wedding stationery that had the letter (Ч) for Chekhov stamped on it: "I'm going to get married." He also wanted to tease Leykin, who was continually vexed by Chekhov's resistance to dating his letters. In the twelve-volume Soviet edition of Chekhov's letters, the editors often explain the various calculations they have made to provide possible or probable dates on the letters. The editors probably sympathized with Leykin's repeated complaint and sighed here at Chekhov's explanation:

> In the last letter I purposely didn't put the date on and made a bet with myself that you wouldn't leave such an incident without attention. For me, the date on letters is a prejudice and excessive embellishment. I understand the date on payments, business articles and letters, on checks, receipts, and so on, but on a letter, which goes to the address in only one day, it can go without a date.[3]

On November 10, Chekhov published the skit "Kalkhas" ("Kalkhas"), which he would rewrite in 1887 as a one-man one-act, "Swansong." A drunk fifty-eight-year-old actor delivers a monologue reviewing his life in the theater. Chekhov was now considering writing a full-length play.

"Dreams" ("Mechti," November 15) may be the most famous of this month's stories; it is, along with "Excellent People," concerned with Tolstoyan ideas about the meaning and purpose of life. The dreamer is a man in his thirties who, having refused to give his name, has been arrested for vagrancy and is being escorted to a transport to Siberia. He impresses his escorts, who are as moved by his life story as most readers will be. When Chekhov composes Tolstoy-inspired stories, he is not dominated or oppressed by Tolstoy; I see Chekhov even more distinctly. In all the ways that the story is not written by Tolstoy, there Chekhov is. For instance, the dreamer tells of his previous experience in prison:

> ". . . For four years I went about with my head shaved and fetters on my legs."
>
> "What for?"
>
> "For murder, my good man! When I was still a boy of eighteen or so, my mamma accidentally poured arsenic instead of soda and acid into my master's glass. There were boxes of all sorts in the storeroom, numbers of them; it was easy to make a mistake over them."
>
> The tramp sighed, shook his head, and said:
>
> "She was a pious woman, but, who knows? another man's soul is a slumbering forest! It may have been an accident, or maybe she could not endure the affront of seeing the master prefer another servant. . . . Perhaps she put it in on purpose, God knows! I was young then, and did not understand it all . . . now I remember that our master had taken another mistress and mamma was greatly disturbed. Our trial lasted nearly two years. . . . Mamma was condemned to penal servitude for twenty years, and I, on account of my youth, only to seven."[4]

Chekhov stands out from Tolstoy in his assertion that "another man's soul is a slumbering forest!" Tolstoy did not concede such ignorance; he saw into others' souls. The tramp admits to his curious escorts that he has run away from prison. By not giving his name, he can't be sent back to prison, only to a settlement in eastern Siberia.

And why is the story called "Dreams"?

> The tramp muttered and looked, not at his listeners, but away into the distance. Naïve as his dreams were, they were uttered in such a genuine and heartfelt tone that it was difficult not to believe in them. The tramp's little mouth was screwed up in a smile. His eyes and little nose and his whole face were fixed and blank with blissful anticipation of happiness in the distant future. The constables listened and looked at him gravely, not without sympathy. They, too, believed in his dreams.

"I am not afraid of Siberia," the tramp went on muttering. "Siberia is just as much Russia and has the same God and Tsar as here. They are just as orthodox Christians as you and I. Only there is more freedom there and people are better off. . . ."

In 1890, Chekhov would see Siberia for himself, as he traveled across its entire width to the Pacific prison island of Sakhalin.

But the tramp's beautiful dreams of the life there, thousands of miles away from the mud through which they are walking to a local lockup, are made of smoke.

Whether [one of the escorts] envied the tramp's transparent happiness, or whether he felt in his heart that dreams of happiness were out of keeping with the gray fog and the dirty brown mud—anyway, he looked sternly at the tramp and said:

"It's all very well, to be sure, only you won't reach those plenteous regions, brother. How could you? Before you'd gone two hundred miles you'd give up your soul to God. Just look what a weakling you are! Here you've hardly gone five miles and you can't get your breath."

Tolstoy may well have found a sober and profound conclusion to such a story, but he would not have popped the tramp's bubble. Chekhov anyway does bring us to think about those pacifying, inspiring dreams that come to us in the most hopeless times. Dispirited for the moment, perhaps the tramp will dream another dream.

Chekhov enjoyed making fun of creative artists' self-importance, including their need for peace and quiet. He needed it too! I will include a discussion of "Hush!" (November 15) in the next chapter, when he, writing on deadline as usual, would compose an additional tale of a writer working on deadline.

He had Leykin, the pestering deadline-reminder, as company in Moscow from November 16 to 19. Leykin stayed with the Chekhov family the last night before returning by train to Petersburg. What they did and talked about is unknown.

Though I enjoy seeing the connections between what Chekhov was writing and what was going on in his life, most enjoyable of all is simply rereading the stories again in the midst of a particular month. He would exclude "At the Mill" ("Na Mel'nitse," November 17) from his *Collected Works*, which led to Constance Garnett's overlooking it. Or maybe she read it and didn't care for this tale about a terribly miserly, grumbling, kvetching miller. The miller's mother comes to beg for a little money. The monks who are already there for the milling of their grain, and who themselves have been insulted by the miller for among other things having gone fishing in what he thinks of as his river, are appalled by the miller's rudeness.

We can enjoy this story because we do not have suffer the miller's inventive and relentless cynical abuse. One of the monks exclaims, "Holy Lord, there is nothing harder for me to obey than to come to the mill! It is real hell! Hell, truly hell!"[5] I find myself thinking that at some point the miller will bend. But no, he has figured out the world, and he self-righteously abuses one and all for their offenses against him, against life, against his ideas of fairness. "It was evident that to scold or to swear was as much a habit with him, as the sucking of his pipe."

As the miller's mother appeals to him to help his brother, I wonder: Was this passage also about the desperate circumstances of Chekhov's brother Alexander?

> "Looking at him I'm terribly worried. . . . There's nothing to eat, the children in tatters, he himself is ashamed to show his nose in the street, his trousers are all in holes and he has no boots. . . . All six of us sleep in one room. Such poverty, such poverty! Nothing worse can be imagined. I have come to ask you to help. Aleshenka, in consideration of an old woman, help Vasili. . . . Remember, he's your brother!"

She compares the miller's circumstances to his brother's, just as, I imagine, Chekhov's down-on-their-luck older brothers compared theirs to his miraculous success:

> "He is poor, but you thank the Lord! The mill is your own, and you have kitchen-gardens and you trade in fish. The Lord has given you wisdom and exalted you above others, and bestowed on you plenty. . . . You are also alone. . . . But Vasya has four children, and I, accursed old thing, am a weight on his neck, and his wages are only seven rubles. How can he feed us all? Help us! . . ."

Though he himself was ever generous, the character Chekhov is closest to in this story is, of all people, the horrible miller.

His brother Alexander was in bad straits, and, like the miller's brother Vasili, a drinker. Alexander did not have his mother Evgenia Chekhova living with him, but he did have a wife and three (not four) children, and Chekhov was actively trying to help Alexander get a job in the publishing world in Petersburg. Alexander was writing and sending pieces to Leykin again. Chekhov, sitting pretty in Moscow in the red house that looked like a chest of drawers, had to support the immediate family and also come up with money sometimes to bail out his brother in the provinces.

The mean miller, after his mother rues having come when he refuses her anything, nevertheless has had his hard heart touched for a second and almost gives her the money she would need. But his heart rehardens and he gives her instead a twenty-kopeck coin.

And why did Chekhov exclude from his *Collected Works* this incisive story, so much more powerful and moving than others he included? There's no telling.

He *did* include "Excellent People" ("Khoroshie Lyudi," November 22), an analytical portrait presented by an unnamed first-person narrator about two siblings, Vladimir, a well-to-do critic, and Vera, his doctor-sister. Vladimir "was a literary man all over when with an inspired face he laid a wreath on the coffin of some celebrity, or with a grave and solemn face collected signatures for some address; his passion for making the acquaintance of distinguished literary men, his faculty for finding talent even where it was absent, his perpetual enthusiasm, his pulse that went at one hundred and twenty a minute, his ignorance of life, the genuinely feminine flutter with which he threw himself into concerts and literary evenings for the benefit of destitute students, the way in which he gravitated toward the young—all this would have created for him the reputation of a writer even if he had not written his articles."[6]

Vera, who lost her husband to typhus and attempted suicide after that tragedy, worships her brother:

> She gave up medicine, and, silent and unoccupied, as though she were a prisoner, spent the remainder of her youth in colorless apathy, with bowed head and hanging hands. The only thing to which she was not completely indifferent, and which brought some brightness into the twilight of her life, was the presence of her brother, whom she loved. She loved him himself and his programme, she was full of reverence for his articles; and when she was asked what her brother was doing, she would answer in a subdued voice as though afraid of waking or distracting him: "He is writing. . . ." Usually when he was at his work she used to sit beside him, her eyes fixed on his writing hand. She used at such moments to look like a sick animal warming itself in the sun. . . .

Chekhov's friends would observe such displays of reverence toward him from both his mother and sister.

The story also shows Chekhov's scorn for know-nothing critics:

On the table near the writing hand there lay open a freshly cut volume of a thick magazine, containing a story of peasant life, signed with two initials. Vladimir Semyonich was enthusiastic; he thought the author was admirable in his handling of the subject, suggested Turgenev in his descriptions of nature, was truthful, and had an excellent knowledge of the life of the peasantry. The critic himself knew nothing of peasant life except from books and hearsay, but his feelings and his inner convictions forced him to believe the story. He foretold a brilliant future for the author, assured him he should await the conclusion of the story with great impatience, and so on.

Chekhov was calling nonsense on the predictive power of critics, even of the critics that had predicted grand things for him.

That very night, in the story, it seems to have dawned on Vera that what Vladimir does isn't actually important at all. She asks him what he thinks about "nonresistance to evil," and as he splutters, she seems to see the same smug thoughtlessness that the narrator sees. The ensuing discussions of this idea divide them. She is becoming, it seems, a Tolstoyan and she soon leaves her brother's house. Not long after, Vladimir dies of an illness, soon to be forgotten by the literary community. "Excellent People" is a rehearsal for some of the famous plays Chekhov would write a decade later. Chekhov later shortened the version we know by more than three pages from the original in *New Times*, where he had titled the speech-heavy story "The Sister." In revision, he snipped the lone mention of Tolstoy.[7]

Chekhov would continue wrestling with Tolstoy's ideas until 1895, when he and the Grand Master of Literary Russia finally met in person at Tolstoy's estate. Ideas and philosophies were not the men, and, with insight into each other's character and appreciation of each other's art, they loved each other and were friends to the end of the younger man's life.

The *Letopis'* (Chronology) of Chekhov's life is ever helpful: letters and incidents in Chekhov's life are noted and excerpted. For November 21, the editors quote a sentence from Chekhov's letter of November 22 to Leykin, "Last night I accompanied a young lady in a cab and caught a cold." They speculate that the "young lady" referred to was "probably" Dunya Efros.[8]

Had he intercepted her somewhere and abjectly apologized for having hurt her feelings? I hope so. Where did he take her? There is no explanation by the editors of how they made their guess. What do they know of Efros's movements that the rest of us don't? Are there any clues in the stories? . . . No. Any other references in this period to Efros? . . . No, not until January 17, 1887, at his name day party.

Also in that November 22 letter to Leykin was the news that Chekhov would arrive in Petersburg in several days. He didn't mention that his sister Maria would join him on this late November, early December trip.

Maria and he and all the Chekhovs loved pets, and "The Incident" ("Sobytie," November 24) is about the benefits of children having pets, in this instance a cat. "Domestic animals play a scarcely noticed but undoubtedly beneficial part in the education and life of children. Which of us does not remember powerful but magnanimous dogs, lazy lapdogs, birds dying in captivity, dull-witted but haughty turkeys, mild old tabby cats, who forgave us when we trod on their tails for fun and caused them agonizing pain? I even fancy, sometimes, that the patience, the fidelity, the readiness to forgive, and the sincerity that are characteristic of our domestic animals have a far stronger and more definite effect on the mind of a child than the long exhortations of some dry, pale Karl Karlovich, or the misty expositions of a governess, trying to prove to children that water is made up of hydrogen and oxygen."[9] This story's cat has kittens, which delight the children. Unfortunately, their uncle and his dog come over and "the incident" of the title is that the dog eats the unminded kittens.

"The Playwright" ("Dramaturge," November 27) is a comic skit in which a doctor asks his patient, a playwright who drinks day and night, how and when he "writes." His work, the playwright says, is very difficult; that is, he has others translate foreign plays for him, and he adds a few Russian touches.

Though Chekhov was tired of writing comic pieces, he was still very funny. One of his funniest stories is "The Orator" ("Orator," November 29), about a young man named Zapoikin who is hired by acquaintances to speak at funerals: "He can speak [. . .] in his sleep, on an empty stomach, dead drunk or in a high fever. His words flow smoothly and evenly, like water out of a pipe, and in abundance; there are far more moving words in his oratorical dictionary than there are beetles [cockroaches] in any restaurant."[10] He is brought to the funeral of a collegiate assessor and delivers fulsome words about another man, who, Zapoikin discovers, is at the funeral.

––––⁓––––

Chekhov and his sister arrived in Petersburg on November 26th, and they stayed with Leykin through the first two days of December. "Leykin always listed the price of things to try to show his guests how much he liked them," remembered Mikhail

Chekhov, "and how generously they were being treated. 'Please eat this smoked fish; it cost two rubles and seventy-five kopecks a pound.'"[11] They also dined at Maria Kiseleva's sister's home and visited the Hermitage. Chekhov wrote Kiseleva when he had returned to Moscow, "I was relaxing in Peter, that is, I roamed around the city all day, paying visits and listening to compliments, which my soul doesn't tolerate."[12]

December 1886

※

"Why don't you write? One day, you will have blisters on your fingers, and you will become a writer. I will help you, if you wish. You should not wait for inspiration, but instead write every day. In about six years, you would be a good writer."

—In conversation with a young writer[1]

C hekhov would have finished writing and sent off "The Trouble" ("Beda," December 1) to Khudekov at the *Petersburg Gazette* before he and his sister Maria left for the capital on the 26th of November. Chekhov had personal reasons to work out his feelings about and remedies for alcoholism. In "The Trouble," an office worker, Putokhin, has been on a five-day binge, and as he comes out of it, he is fired by his boss. He then fears the hurt and disappointment his loving wife will express when he gets home. He is so ashamed he wonders if he should blow his brains out. To his amazement and delight, his wife forgives him: "God willing, we'll get through this trouble."[2] Her forgiveness reforms him, and now when he is out and sees drunks, he doesn't laugh at them or judge them. Putokhin concludes: "The vice isn't that we drink but that we don't raise drunkards up." And Chekhov, or his attentive narrator, adds: "Maybe he's right." As Chekhov believed at this time, to understand is to forgive.

Leykin wrote Chekhov on December 5 to ask him to send stories for the important year-end issue not later than December 21 and the New Year's pieces not later than December 28.[3] Chekhov probably didn't need reminding. On December 8, in the *Petersburg Gazette,* he published "The Order," which is about a writer working on deadline. (That same day he replied to Leykin and told him he had begun working on his

Christmas-issue story for *New Times*, which story, after an unusual two-week struggle, became "On the Road.")

Chekhov complained about deadlines and, thank goodness, wrote to deadline. What would he have written if he hadn't had to? How many great works by Mozart and Chekhov would we be deprived of if they hadn't needed to earn money? They were young and able, full of energy and genius, and if outside pressures nudged them to the table to compose, let us express our gratitude and appreciation for these deadline-inspired gems.

But Chekhov, though proud and self-critical of his work, didn't see or didn't like thinking of his stories as art. Writing at deadline does not inspire belief in one's work as art or genius. It's just got to be done. Chekhov was a pro.

In the middle of November he wrote a mocking story about a pretentious, overly precious writer who demands from his family awe and quiet, "Hush!" ("Tssst!" in Russian).

> "Shattered, soul-weary, a sick load of misery on the heart . . . and then to sit down and write. And this is called life! How is it nobody has described the agonizing discord in the soul of a writer who has to amuse the crowd when his heart is heavy or to shed tears at the word of command when his heart is light? I must be playful, coldly unconcerned, witty, but what if I am weighed down with misery, what if I am ill, or my child is dying or my wife in anguish!"
>
> He says this, brandishing his fists and rolling his eyes. . . .[4]

We are all unappreciated actors in the dramas of our lives. Chekhov is mocking Ivan, the writer, and also echoing his own complaints—minus the wife and child. At various times Leykin had heard all the rest from Chekhov, and Chekhov had heard absolutely all of it from Alexander. The protagonist is a prima donna:

> [. . .] he goes into the bedroom and wakes his wife.
>
> "Nadya," he says, "I am sitting down to write. . . . Please don't let anyone interrupt me. I can't write with children crying or cooks snoring. . . . See, too, that there's tea and . . . steak or something. . . . You know that I can't write without tea. . . . Tea is the one thing that gives me the energy for my work."

Thinking of himself, he thinks of nobody else.

Ivan Yegorich throws himself back in his chair, and closing his eyes concentrates himself on his subject. He hears his wife shuffling about in her slippers and splitting shavings to heat the samovar.

She is hardly awake, that is apparent from the way the knife and the lid of the samovar keep dropping from her hands. Soon the hissing of the samovar and the spluttering of the frying meat reaches him.

His wife is still splitting shavings and rattling with the doors and blowers of the stove.

In his mockery, Chekhov is not twitting Alexander or his other writer-friends so much as himself:

Like a girl who has been presented with a costly fan, he spends a long time coquetting, grimacing, and posing to himself before he writes the title. . . . He presses his temples, he wriggles, and draws his legs up under his chair as though he were in pain, or half closes his eyes languidly like a cat on the sofa. At last, not without hesitation, he stretches out his hand toward the inkstand, and with an expression as though he were signing a death-warrant, writes the title. . . .

Chekhov's titles changed occasionally from their first appearance in magazines and journals to their second in books or in the *Collected Works*. But his primary advice about titles was simplicity: "Put as plain a title as possible—any that occurs to your mind—and nothing else."[5]

He writes till four o'clock and would readily have written till six if his subject had not been exhausted. Coquetting and posing to himself and the inanimate objects about him, far from any indiscreet, critical eye, tyrannizing and domineering over the little anthill that fate has put in his power are the honey and the salt of his existence. And how different is this despot here at home from the humble, meek, dull-witted little man we are accustomed to see in the editor's offices!

"I am so exhausted that I am afraid I shan't sleep . . ." he says as he gets into bed. "Our work, this cursed, ungrateful hard labor, exhausts the soul even more than the body. . . . I had better take some bromide. . . . God knows, if it were not for my family I'd throw up the work. . . . To write to order! It is awful."

It is awful. It is. And yet Chekhov knew just as well the harsher demands of a full-time doctor's life. If he had had to earn his bread by medical work, he would have died even younger.

> He sleeps till twelve or one o'clock in the day, sleeps a sound, healthy sleep. . . . Ah! how he would sleep, what dreams he would have, how he would spread himself if he were to become a well-known writer, an editor, or even a sub-editor!

This description would have nudged his brother Alexander; Chekhov was using his connections to help Alexander settle in Petersburg and get a sub-editor job at *New Times*.

> "He has been writing all night," whispers his wife with a scared expression on her face. "Sh!"
>
> No one dares to speak or move or make a sound. His sleep is something sacred, and the culprit who offends against it will pay dearly for his fault.
>
> "Hush!" floats over the flat. "Hush!"

Chekhov was acknowledging here the kind of respect he received in his own household. A friend, Zakhar Pichugin, remembered Chekhov's mother as her son's sentry:

> I visited the Chekhov family. As I came in, I greeted the father of Anton Pavlovich, and heard in reply the words which he whispered in a mysterious tone, "Hush, please don't make noise, Anton is working!"
>
> "Yes, dear, our Anton is working," Evgenia Yakovlevna the mother added, making a gesture indicating to the door of his room. I went further, Maria Pavlovna, his sister, told me in a subdued voice, "Anton is working now."
>
> In the next room, in a low voice, Nikolay Pavlovich told me, "Hello, my dear friend. You know, Anton is working now," he whispered . . . Everyone was afraid to break the silence, and you could see that the members of the family had a great deal of respect for the creative process of the young writer.[6]

And in this bit from "Excellent People" we see what Chekhov would have considered ridiculous reverence:

> One winter evening Vladimir Semyonich was sitting at his table writing a critical article for his newspaper: Vera Semyonovna was sitting beside him,

staring as usual at his writing hand. The critic wrote rapidly, without erasures or corrections. The pen scratched and squeaked.[7]

And there, reflected in the glass of the window in front of which Chekhov was sitting, was himself, writing "without erasures or corrections" (usually). The biographer Ronald Hingley writes that Maria Chekhova said "she could always tell from his mood when he was in the throes of creation. 'His way of walking and his voice changed, a sort of absent-mindedness appeared, and he often answered questions at random. . . . This continued until he began writing, when he became his old self again . . .'"[8]

Chekhov and the narrator of "Excellent People" disdain the critic, but Chekhov as usual sees himself even in the people he mocks. Just like Vladimir the critic, Chekhov was proud of the speed at which he wrote; he could focus in such a fashion that some of his short pieces could spin along in one continuous, uncorrected strip. "He is a strange writer," said Tolstoy. "He throws words about as though at random, and yet everything in his writings is alive. And what great understanding! He never has any superfluous details, every one of them is either essential or beautiful."[9]

"The Assignment" ("Zakaz," December 8) is a comedy that describes the situation in which Chekhov wrote so many of his stories in these busy years. Here, the freelancer Pavel Sergeich needs to finish writing a story on deadline before he joins the informal party that his wife is hosting in the next room. He keeps getting interrupted by her or by the distracting conversations he overhears. He joins the party for a few minutes and then returns to his uninspired murder story. He is either focused enough or unengaged enough that the party's activities do not intrude into the story.

"Pavel Sergeich!" they cried out in the living room. "Come here!"

Pavel Sergeich hopped up and ran to the ladies.

"Sing a duet with Michel!" said his wife. "You sing lead, and he'll sing second."

"Fine! Give the key!"

Pavel Sergeich waved his pen, on which still shone some ink, tapped his toe, and, making a passionate face, sang "Thoughtless Nights" with the student.

"Bravo!" he chortled, having finished singing and seizing the student by the waist. "You and I are such young men! I would sing another something but, the devil take it, I've got to write!"

"But toss it aside! It's up to you!"

"No-no-no . . . I promised! And there's no hiding! The story's got to be ready today!"[10]

I imagine Chekhov imagining Leykin reading that line in the *Petersburg Gazette*. Leykin smiles, appreciative of the writer's dedication, while Chekhov calls out, laughing, "See, see what I have to do to produce stories for you!"

Pavel Sergeich waved his hands, ran back into his study and resumed writing [. . .]

"The Assignment" is light, but not fine, as Chekhov, who never seemed to miss a comic opportunity, did miss some here. The tale that Pavel Sergeich writes is neither comical nor coordinated with the atmosphere in which he writes it. Chekhov is interested in the comedy of the writer being distracted; what the writer writes, however, doesn't reflect his distractions. Could Chekhov have written the story around a dead little piece he had thrown out? A translator[11] calls it a "Halloween" story, perhaps because of the murder in Pavel's tale. At the conclusion, the party is leaving the house for a pretty drive, which doesn't fit the time when Chekhov was submitting the story, early December. There are no variants of "The Assignment." When Chekhov was readying his collected works he wrote on the "clerical copy": "N.B.: it will not go in the collected works."

Though out of its seasonal place, "The Assignment" does fit the kind of activities that were going on around Chekhov in his house. Mikhail Chekhov believed that his older brother liked very much to have social activity going on while he wrote: "Anton drew inspiration from all the sounds and people and spent a lot of time at work in his study downstairs. He would sometimes take a break to come upstairs and joke or horse around with the rest of us. During the day when everybody was otherwise occupied and there were no visitors, he would often say to me, 'Misha, play something, would you? I can't write like this.' I did play for him—sometimes for half an hour straight. I'd play songs from popular musicals and did it with as much frenetic zeal as a sanguine second-year university student could muster."[12] The biographer David Magarshack adds: "In the drawing room his sister's friends used to gather almost every evening, playing the piano and singing, and Chekhov would occasionally interrupt his work and join them upstairs."[13]

Chekhov's friend Ignati Potapenko recalled that in these years, "When he was in the presence of guests he would repeatedly slip away to his study, write two or three lines in private, and then rejoin the company a few minutes later."[14]

In the next two weeks of December, Chekhov described his franticness, his feeling of being lazy, his feeling of pressure while trying to write his Christmas story for *New Times*.

In the midst of that unusual struggle, he wrote three other pieces, including "A Work of Art" ("Proizvedenie Iskusstva," December 13), a clever situation-comedy episode, and "Who Was to Blame?" ("Kto Vinovat?," December 20) for Leykin's *Fragments*, and "The Anniversary" ("Yubiley," December 15) for *Petersburg Gazette*.

Chekhov was like any persistent, duty-bound freelancer: he knocked off the shorter pieces that he could while chipping away at the bigger and more lucrative assignment.

Leykin wrote him on December 11 that he liked "A Work of Art," but that the censor made him take out two words, "Paradise" (the censor objected that there shouldn't be a snake in Paradise, with which Adam and Eve would have agreed) and "obscene."[15] That is, a young man brings a doctor "a work of art" in appreciation from him and his mother for having saved his life. The antique candelabra features two naked women. He apologizes that it's one of an incomplete pair of candelabras. The doctor knows he can't show it in the office or at home. He gives it away to his lawyer. The lawyer gives it to an actor. The actor sells it to an antiques dealer, where it's bought by the woman to "complete the set," which she then sends to the doctor.

Chekhov continued his correspondence with Maria Kiseleva on December 13. He sent her the fateful story "Mire" with his letter and meanwhile defended himself from her teasing about his love life. He was paid 115 rubles for that story about a Jew, he told her, so "how after this not incline toward the Hebrew tribe?"[16] I sure wish he hadn't said that.

He added, because she had joshed him about his busy love life: "You cruelly insult me, reproaching me for Yashen'ka, Madame Sakharova and so on. Weren't you informed that I long ago turned away from the world's bustle, from earthly pleasures, and gave up everything but medicine and literature? A better-intentioned and more restrained person than I is hard to find in the world. I suppose that even the Archimandrite Veniam is a bigger sinner than I."

Kiseleva would find other sins to charge him with in "Mire."

He was definitely unhappy with his first Christmas-issue story for *New Times*, but he was perhaps the only person unhappy with it. On December 21, he wrote to Suvorin: "I began the yuletide story ["On the Road"] two weeks ago and haven't at all finished it. An evil spirit has nudged me toward a theme with which I can't cope. After two weeks I succeeded in getting acquainted with the theme and the story and now I don't understand what's good and what's bad. Simply a disaster! Tomorrow, I hope, I'll finish it and send it to you. You'll receive it the 24th, at three o'clock. If you take a look at the story you'll understand the effort with which it was written and excuse that I was late and didn't keep my promise."[17]

He kept his promise; on Christmas Day "On the Road" ("Na Puti") was published. His brother Alexander read it and reported on the "sensation" that it had produced in Petersburg; while Alexander had been visiting the *New Times* offices, he had even been introduced around as "the author's brother." The young women office-workers there told him they had been delighted by Anton's Christmas card.[18]

Chekhov sent his Christmas and New Year's greetings with friendly jokes to Leykin and a request for an immediate payout for his December contributions to *Fragments*: "Excuse me that I'm breaking your law of bookkeeping, but . . . what am I to do?"[19]

The hero of "On the Road" (December 25) is even harder pressed than Chekhov was. The story's play-like setting might remind us of "The Witch," except instead of a posting station, we have a tavern, snowed in during a Christmas-season blizzard: "Something frantic and wrathful, but profoundly unhappy, seemed to be flinging itself about the tavern with the ferocity of a wild beast and trying to break in." In a traveler's room, Likharev, an idealistic but impoverished forty-two-year-old ex-landowner, and his eight-year-old daughter are waiting out the storm when a young woman landowner traveling with a sledge driver stops for refuge. Likharev is a widower whose charisma is infectious:

> "I say this from hard, bitter experience: the proudest, most independent women, if I have succeeded in communicating to them my enthusiasm, have followed me without criticism, without question, and done anything I chose; I have turned a nun into a Nihilist who, as I heard afterward, shot a gendarme; my wife never left me for a minute in my wanderings, and like a weathercock changed her faith in step with my changing enthusiasms."

As he converses with the young woman, his intellectual vitality revives:

> "There, you see," cried Likharev delighted, and he even stamped with his foot. "Oh dear! How glad I am that I have met you! Fate is kind to me, I am always meeting splendid people. Not a day passes but one makes acquaintance with somebody one would give one's soul for. There are ever so many more good people than bad in this world. Here, see, for instance, how openly and from our hearts we have been talking as though we had known each other a hundred

years. Sometimes, I assure you, one restrains oneself for ten years and holds
one's tongue, is reserved with one's friends and one's wife, and meets some
cadet in a train and babbles one's whole soul out to him. It is the first time I
have the honor of seeing you, and yet I have confessed to you as I have never
confessed in my life. Why is it?"[20]

Her reaction shows him that he has gone too far again:

Miss Ilovaisky got up slowly, took a step toward Likharev, and fixed her
eyes upon his face. From the tears that glittered on his eyelashes, from his
quivering, passionate voice, from the flush on his cheeks, it was clear to her
that women were not a chance, not a simple subject of conversation. They
were the object of his new enthusiasm, or, as he said himself, his new faith!
For the first time in her life she saw a man carried away, fervently believing.
With his gesticulations, with his flashing eyes he seemed to her mad, frantic,
but there was a feeling of such beauty in the fire of his eyes, in his words,
in all the movements of his huge body, that without noticing what she was
doing she stood facing him as though rooted to the spot, and gazed into
his face with delight.

He realizes he has bewitched her: "Whether his finely intuitive soul were really able to
read that look, or whether his imagination deceived him, it suddenly began to seem
to him that with another touch or two that girl would have forgiven him his failures, his
age, his desolate position, and would have followed him without question or reasonings."
Likharev is unconsciously seductive the way Raissa in "The Witch" is, but he is a good
man, and this is a Christmas story, and he deliberately sends the young woman on her
way. Likharev is like Chekhov in this way, that he unintentionally attracted women who
sensibly lost their heads over him.

As a medical student Chekhov himself had been swept off his feet by another of
Likharev's enthusiasms:

"When you set to work to study any science, what strikes you first of all is its
beginning. I assure you there is nothing more attractive and grander, nothing
is so staggering, nothing takes a man's breath away like the beginning of any
science. From the first five or six lectures you are soaring on wings of the
brightest hopes, you already seem to yourself to be welcoming truth with

open arms. And I gave myself up to science, heart and soul, passionately, as to the woman one loves. I was its slave; I found it the sun of my existence, and asked for no other."

As a wayward and awkward postscript to this story, last year I was editing a collection of Chekhov's love stories for an anthology. I included "On the Road," as I had also fallen for Likharev. However, in the midst of the story, Chekhov includes a popular Russian Christmas carol that a group of children sing for the guests at the tavern. It goes like this:

> *Hi, you Little Russian lad,*
> *Bring your sharp knife,*
> *We will kill the Jew, we will kill him,*
> *The son of tribulation . . .*

Happy holidays and murder? It is not Chekhov's fault, is it, that perversity and cruelty had made tormenting and murdering Jews a Christian custom? It's not his fault, but he might, just might, have excised it from a Christmas story in a right-wing anti-Semitic newspaper. I cut it from the Dover anthology, and I, in a failure of scrupulousness, didn't note the excision.

Chekhov's Christmas story for *Petersburg Gazette* was "Vanka," about a nine-year-old orphan apprenticed to a shoemaker in Moscow. Vanka writes his grandfather begging him to bring him back home. He complains: "They make me sleep in the vestibule, and when their brat cries, I don't sleep at all, but have to rock the cradle. Dear Grandpapa, for Heaven's sake, take me away from here, home to our village, I can't bear this any more. . . . I bow to the ground to you, and will pray to God for ever and ever, take me from here or I shall die. . . ."[21] When he mails his heartsick letter, he carefully addresses it "To grandfather in the village."

So that we don't take Vanka for a simpleton, Chekhov adds: "Then he scratched his head, thought a little, and added: Konstantin Makarich. Glad that he had not been prevented from writing, he put on his cap and, without putting on his little greatcoat, ran out into the street as he was in his shirt. . . . The shopmen at the butcher's, whom he had questioned the day before, told him that letters were put in post-boxes, and from the boxes were carried about all over the earth in mailcarts with drunken drivers and ringing bells. Vanka ran to the nearest post-box, and thrust the precious letter in the slit. . . ."

Vanka mailing his letter to his grandfather.

Chekhov, meanwhile, had mailed off in the slit two comic pieces for *Fragments'* Christmas issue, and no doubt they were better addressed than Vanka's letter, as they were received and published on December 27. "The Person: A Bit of Philosophy" ("Chelovek: Nemnozhko Filosofii") is about a philosopher of life who is seemingly above everything; however, when a beautiful woman orders him to bring her some water, he hops to and gets it. "Who Was She?" ("To Bila Ona?") is a longer tale about an old coot who tells the young ladies a story of his long-ago "affair" in a haunted house. He disappoints them—revealing their hypocrisy—by telling them the mysterious woman was his wife. So he switches back and says no, it was his steward's wife, which pleases them. I won't mention the unpleasant remarks about Jews that the old man makes.[22]

Chekhov answered his brother Alexander's complimentary December 26 letter sometime in the next few days. He in return was abrupt and scolding: he didn't like Alexander's new story and was annoyed that Alexander didn't inform the Moscow family about his family's new apartment in Petersburg and his new job at *New Times*:

> You write me about your goose, about Tan'ka, about the fiancée without a profile, but you don't say a word about your new place, about the new people and so on.
>
> Right this minute write me everything from beginning to end, not leaving anything out and not reducing it. I'm waiting with impatience and I'm not writing to you until you send me a letter.
>
> [. . .] Don't sign the trifles by your full name. "Theme by Al. Chekhov." What's that for? You want to be ashamed?

That is, the Chekhov brothers were only to use pen names in *Fragments*.

—⁂—

We have reached the end of 1886. Did Chekhov take stock of what he had done? Or did he only feel it in his head and bones? Was he wondering when he could slow down? Did he assume, as other young people have, that he could keep burning through life, that if his family needed him for financial support and stability, then that's just what he would have to keep doing? As a doctor, he recognized stress and exhaustion. He knew his own illnesses and afflictions. He could not keep going like this. He had to find a new way or other ways to bring in the money and ease the pace.

PART FOUR

Friends and "Enemies"

Having so thoroughly followed in Chekhov's footsteps during 1886, I blinked and blanked at the prospects of the year ahead, as if I no longer knew any better than Chekhov did what was going to happen in 1887. Maybe this happens whenever we reread a long novel. We know what's coming, but so immersed are we in the present-day of the novel that it feels as if we don't have knowledge of the future. We hope, for example, that things will get better for Anna Karenina, that Elizabeth Bennet will have a chance to make up for her mistakes, or that Karl Ove will find peace and contentment. For Chekhov in 1887, I hope he gets some rest. (He will.) I hope he finds someone to fall in love with. (He won't.) I hope his financial worries disappear. (Not quite.) I hope he somehow keeps writing great stories. (He will.) I hope he stays healthy. (Nope.) I hope there are no more anti-Semitic references or jokes. (I'm not sure. Wait, I just remembered *Ivanov*, his play. Ivanov's put-upon wife is Jewish.)

I have a note from an earlier draft of this book that says, "in the second half of 1887 something happened, and Chekhov wasn't interested in writing freshly about romantic relationships."

What happened?

Chekhov, 1887.

January 1887

—◊—

I was always amused when I heard conversations
about Chekhov's purported indifference, or about his
cold-bloodedness, his apathy or homochromatism: I,
for one, knew how brilliant and crafty this striking
artist was under his modest exterior, who spent his
entire lifetime mercilessly training and drilling just
one pupil—himself.

—Dina Rubina[1]

New Year's Day was spent at home in conversation with a young writer (only a year
younger than Chekhov), Alexander Lazarev (pen name, Gruzinskiy), the journalist
Vladimir Gilyarovskiy, and A. Kurepin, *The Alarm Clock's* editor. Lazarev and Kurepin
were keeping company with Chekhov for the first time (Lazarev had met him in March
at the *Alarm Clock* office).[2] The *Letopis'* notes: "Conversations about *Fragments*, about
N. A. Leykin, V. V. Bilibin, A. V. Nasonov. In an argument with Kurepin, Chekhov
'showed that it's necessary to well investigate the Tolstoyan theory of resistance to evil,
but then it's impossible to honestly speak for or against it . . .'"[3] Tolstoy insisted that one
must commit oneself to nonresistance to evil; Chekhov would show in various stories
that he was attracted to the idea, or to the people who committed to that idea, but that
for many reasons such nonresistance was impractical or constraining.

I'm guessing that the topic of Leykin occupied more of their time and most definitely
more of their enjoyment. Leykin was one of those bosses who the people who work for
them like to complain about. This New Year's, when Leykin was in Petersburg or at his
estate across the river from the capital, his ears, which seem to have been sensitively tuned

to gossip, were probably burning. The young men would all have agreed that Leykin was exasperating and frustrating, nudgy and persistent. He published young writers, but he paid them a pittance.

Chekhov treated Lazarev like a little brother, encouraging him and teasing him and scolding him forward on his literary path. Lazarev wrote: "I sat at his place the whole long winter's night until 12:00. The impression produced on me for this first meeting with Chekhov was unusual. I was shaken. Returning home I began remembering our conversations, Chekhov's words, his laugh, his smile, and I didn't sleep until morning."[4]

What Chekhov knew of Lazarev's previous writing is not stated, but Lazarev says that Chekhov recommended he "write something for *New Times*." The biographer David Magarshack describes a joshing moment of that evening: "Chekhov said, pointing to the furniture, the aquarium and the piano: 'It's good to be a writer: literature has given me all that!' And seeing how greatly impressed his visitor was, Chekhov laughed and explained that the piano was on hire and that part of the furniture Nikolay had received in payment for his illustrations in *The Alarm Clock*."[5]

Lazarev and his friend, Nikolay Ezhov, revered their mentor.[6] Ezhov remembered: "Chekhov treated me and Lazarev very warmly; he guided our work, gave advice, pointing out and underlining successes and mistakes, and all this he did with special Chekhovian simplicity and delicacy."[7]

Chekhov received New Year's greetings from Alexander in Petersburg, who passed along a remark Suvorin made in conversation to him and Bilibin and Golike: "Why does Anton Pavlovich write so much? It's very very dangerous."

Chekhov wrote to Bilibin and his uncle Mitrofan this New Year's week, but these letters haven't survived.

January's stories seem dark and unhappy, even those that are comical.

In "New Year's Torture" ("Novogodnyaya Pitka," January 4), Chekhov writes, unusually, in the second person about making required New Year's calls around Moscow: to the narrator's wife's rich but boring uncle; to a friend to whom they owe money; on the sly to a girlfriend; then to his wife's brother's; and finally to a drinking friend. The story begins: "You deck yourself out in a tailcoat, you put, if you have one, a Stanislaus [medal] on your neck, you spritz a handkerchief with cologne, twist up your moustache—and all this with such angry, fitful movements, as if you were dressing not yourself but your most vicious enemy."[8] At the end the narrator glumly returns to his shrewish wife. If you were to ask what this had to do with Chekhov's life, I would shrug. . . . And then, I might point out that when Mikhail, the narrator, is at his brother-in-law Petya's, Petya's desperate pleas for a loan sound a lot like Chekhov's: "Before the holidays, you understand, I spent all my money, and now I'm without a kopeck . . . It's a disgusting situation . . . You're my only hope . . . If you don't give me 25 rubles, you're stabbing me without a knife . . ."

"Champagne: A Wayfarer's Story" ("Shampanskoe: Rasskaz Prokhodimtsa," January 5), on the other hand, is humorless and despairing enough to make anyone groan. Garnett translates the word for the story's narrator as "Wayfarer," but "Bum" or "Transient" would be more in keeping with the narrator's self-judgment:

> Upon me, a native of the north, the steppe produced the effect of a deserted Tatar cemetery. In the summer the steppe with its solemn calm, the monotonous chur of the grasshoppers, the transparent moonlight from which one could not hide, reduced me to listless melancholy; and in the winter the irreproachable whiteness of the steppe, its cold distance, long nights, and howling wolves oppressed me like a heavy nightmare. There were several people living at the station: my wife and I, a deaf and scrofulous telegraph clerk, and three watchmen. My assistant, a young man who was in consumption, used to go for treatment to the town, where he stayed for months at a time, leaving his duties to me together with the right of pocketing his salary. I had no children, no cake would have tempted visitors to come and see me, and I could only visit other officials on the line, and that no oftener than once a month.[9]

During his and his wife's quiet New Year's celebration, she sees a spilled bottle as a bad omen. He wondered at the time, how could things get worse? "What further harm can you do a fish which has been caught and fried and served up with sauce?" The narrator remembers having the blues and reflects with a clarity and depth that it is unlikely he could muster, but that Chekhov certainly could and did express: "Melancholy thoughts haunted me still. Painful as it was to me, yet I remember I tried as it were to make my thoughts still gloomier and more melancholy. You know people who are vain and not very clever have moments when the consciousness that they are miserable affords them positive satisfaction, and they even coquet with their misery for their own entertainment. There was a great deal of truth in what I thought, but there was also a great deal that was absurd and conceited, and there was something boyishly defiant in my question: 'What could happen worse?'" And he recounts how a seductive woman, his wife's uncle's young wife, arrived that New Year's night. Chekhov knew this was a relentlessly despairing story. He moderated it not a wit: "Everything went head over heels to the devil. I remember a fearful, frantic whirlwind which sent me flying around like a feather. It lasted a long while, and swept from the face of the earth my wife and my aunt herself and my strength. From the little station in the steppe it has flung me, as you see, into this dark street."

———

From January 4 to January 11, Chekhov occupied at least part of his time attending a medical conference in Moscow. He went to a talk given by Pavel Rozanov, at whose wedding he had been the best man the previous January. On January 8, Chekhov wrote Alexander to thank him for his New Year's letter and to coax him, as soon as possible, to go to the offices of *New Times* and *Petersburg Gazette* and forward him the payments that he was due from them. He offered his brother a commission of 1/40th, a grand total of about five rubles.

The writer Lazarev met with Chekhov again on January 11; about this meeting Lazarev immediately wrote his friend Ezhov. The two friends' visits with Chekhov were treasured by each and shared with each other at the time, so even today their accounts have a freshness and undusty believability: "Chekhov is a lovely guy. We talked and chatted a lot. He told me plenty of interesting things. Chekhov had a harsh school of life, was in a chorus, worked in a shop, froze in the cold and so on and so on. [. . .] Chekhov terribly cursed Leykin, but says that one should feel sorry for him [. . .] Chekhov is a most absolutely simple guy [. . .] Chekhov says for anyone who wants to have an independent existence it's necessary to work, work, and work."[10]

The next day's annual drunken Tatyana Day bash served as Chekhov's excuse to Leykin about why he wouldn't immediately be coming up with a new piece for *Fragments*. He would in fact give Leykin only fourteen pieces all year:[11]

> My head has detached from my hand and refuses to create . . . The entire holidays, my brain has strained; I puffed and sniffed, a hundred times I sat down to write, but every time, from my "lively" pen, long things or sour ones, or nauseated ones poured out, which doesn't go over for *Fragments*, and they were so bad, I decided not to send them to you so as not to embarrass my family name.[12]

He knew Leykin would scoff at his excuses, so he piled it on:

> I didn't send *New Times* a single story, to the *Gazette* some sort of 2 stories, and how on such dough I will live in February, God knows . . . You are generally a skeptic, and you don't believe in human incapability, but I assure you by

honest word, yesterday from morning to night, the whole day I toiled over a
story for *Fragments*, lost the time, and lay down to sleep, not having written
a page . . . Laziness or a lack of desire is out of the discussion . . . If you will
be resentful and scold, you'll be wrong. I'm guilty, but I deserve indulgence!

[. . .] The holidays in Moscow were loud. I didn't have a single peaceful
day: guests, doctors' conference, long conversations, etc. . . .

He recommended, by the way, that Leykin use work by Lazarev: "He's quiet, like
Bilibin, but through his quietness it's sometimes possible to detect the man." Chekhov
knew already that Leykin didn't appreciate his recommendations of writers to replace
him, but he regularly tried anyway.

Now about a ticklish matter. [. . .] Considering that I am beginning to lose
my value as a constant, correct, and dependable employee for *Fragments*, in
view of that, that even in the full swing of literary energy, I'm caused to miss
up to 1–2 pieces in each month almost, it would be right to eliminate the
extra ones. Right? Agree with me and make the fitting arrangement. I will
work as before, trying not to miss a single week, but I can't swear that cases
of craziness won't again be repeated.

He offered to go off the retainer and receive the freelancers' usual per-line pay.

He was looking forward, he went on, to Leykin and his wife's arrival on the 17th
for Chekhov's name day party at 1:00 in the afternoon. In the P.S. Chekhov suggested
they work out a simpler line of communication regarding his submissions. Chekhov
liked efficiency in telegraph messages; no use paying extra for needless words. He could
write Leykin a telegram whenever he didn't have that week's submission with the simple
unmistakable message: "No. Chekhov."

Leykin, nettled, replied on the 14th that he and his wife would indeed arrive in
Moscow on the 16th, and that he and Chekhov could continue the conversation on the
17th, but . . . "You write that you didn't write over the holidays. But apparently you did
write over the holidays for *The Alarm Clock*. [. . .] I've already received 3–4 letters asking
why Chekhonte's not writing." Leykin didn't hesitate to call him out. How the devil did
Leykin know about a pseudonymous piece in the Moscow humor magazine? As for the
complaint letters Leykin received, Chekhov didn't believe that.

The scenes in Chekhov's stories sometimes seem as if they were staged in his head. One very particular place is animated by its sights and smells, and there are two or three characters who move about and talk. In "Frost" ("Moroz," January 12), a garrulous and generous mayor and two of his guests recall, with some bit of pleasure, the misery of being young, poor, and cold: "I've a fur coat now, and at home I have a stove and rums and punches of all sorts. The frost means nothing to me now; I take no notice of it, I don't care to know of it, but how it used to be in old days, Holy Mother! It's dreadful to recall it! My memory is failing me with years and I have forgotten everything; my enemies, and my sins and troubles of all sorts—I forget them all, but the frost—ough! How I remember it!"

Nostalgia kicks in: "The governor and the mayor grew lively and good-humored, and, interrupting each other, began recalling their experiences. And the bishop told them how, when he was serving in Siberia, he had traveled in a sledge drawn by dogs; how one day, being drowsy, in a time of sharp frost he had fallen out of the sledge and been nearly frozen; when the Tunguses turned back and found him he was barely alive. Then, as by common agreement, the old men suddenly sank into silence, sat side by side, and mused."

How much pleasure Chekhov, this young man full of redolent memories, had in *recollection*. How generous our Chekhov was to be imagining the happy reminiscences of old men. With whom did quiet, modest, young Chekhov most closely identify? The generous, gabby old mayor, who, seeing the suffering of the musicians at the town's bitter-cold celebration, dismisses them hours early and treats them all to drinks.

~~~

One of the letters reproduced in nearly every selection of Chekhov's letters is his spirited January 14 refutation of his friend and mentee Maria Kiseleva's disappointed and moralistic criticisms of "Mire." She had written in late December. His delayed response was unusual. His reply letters usually followed immediately, without much mulling over.

What had set him mulling was this:

Beginning with that piece you sent me, good Anton Pavlovich, I so so do not like it, despite that I am convinced that few will join with my opinion. It is written well—male readers are pitying themselves if their fate does not collide with someone like Susanna, which might unleash their licentiousness; women will in secret envy her, and a big part of the public will read it with interest and say: "This Chekhov writes in a lively way, what a fellow!"

Maybe the 115 rubles in pay please you, but[13] I am personally chagrined that a writer of *your* caliber, i.e., not shortchanged by God, shows me nothing but a "manure pile." The world is teeming with villains and villainesses and the impression they produce is not new; therefore, one is all the more grateful to a writer who, having led you through all the stench of the manure pile, will suddenly extract a pearl from it. You are not myopic, you are perfectly capable of finding this pearl, so why do we get only a manure pile? Give me that pearl, so that the filth of the surroundings may be effaced from my memory; I have a right to demand this of you. As for the others, the ones who are unable to find and to defend a human being among the quadruped animals—I'd just as soon not read them. Perhaps it might have been better to remain silent, but I could not resist an overpowering desire to give a piece of my mind to you and to your vile editors who allow you to wreck your talent with such equanimity. If I were your editor, I would have returned the story to you for your own good. No matter what you may say, the story is utterly disgusting! Leave such stories (such subjects) to hacks like Okreyts, Pince-nez, Aloe and *tutti quanti* mediocrities, who are poor in spirit and have been shortchanged by fate.

Give Kiseleva credit: she called out herself by her nickname Pince-nez as one of the "mediocrities." She, further on in the letter, credited herself for valuing and having liked, on the other hand, "On the Road." She understood *that*, a young woman losing her head over an idealistic man. She, the prim mother and author of children's stories, had lost her head over Chekhov, I believe.

His reply to her letter is the story of their relationship and an example of how seriously and how deeply Chekhov contemplated art. Whatever literary or moral sins he had committed in "Mire," the self-censorship that Kiseleva was advocating in her letter was a trap for any honest writer. Before arguing with her, he praised her short story, which though "uneven" was good enough for him to recommend for publication in *New Times*, whose editors she had maligned:

Your "Larka" is very nice, honored Maria Vladimirovna; there are roughnesses, but the conciseness and masculine manner of the story redeem everything. Not wishing to be the sole judge of your offspring, I am sending it to Suvorin, who is a very understanding man. His opinion I will let you know in due time. And now allow me to snap at your criticism.[14] Even your praise of "On the Road" has not softened my anger as an author, and I hasten to avenge myself

for "Mire." Be on your guard, and catch hold of the back of a chair that you
may not faint. Well, I begin. . . .

One meets every critical article with a silent bow even if it is abusive and
unjust—such is the literary etiquette. It is not the thing to answer, and all who
do answer are justly blamed for excessive vanity. But since your criticism has the
nature of "an evening conversation on the steps of the Babkino lodge" [. . .][15]
and as, without touching on the literary aspects of the story, it raises general
questions of principle, I shall not be sinning against the etiquette if I allow
myself to continue our conversation.

She invited his conversational response, so here it was. He started with her prudery.
He pointed out that the great writers show both sides of life, the good and the bad. He
reminded her that landscape painters have to show the defects of the landscape.

He refused her premise that there are purities. What is is. In chemistry as in human life:

In the first place, I, like you, do not like literature of the kind we are discussing. As a reader and "a private resident" I am glad to avoid it, but if you
ask my honest and sincere opinion about it, I shall say that it is still an open
question whether it has a right to exist, and no one has yet settled it [. . . [16]].
Neither you nor I, nor all the critics in the world, have any trustworthy
data that would give them the right to reject such literature. I do not know
which are right: Homer, Shakespeare, Lope de Vega, and, speaking generally, the ancients who were not afraid to rummage in the "muck heap," but
were morally far more stable than we are, or the modern writers, priggish on
paper but coldly cynical in their souls and in life. I do not know which has
bad taste—the Greeks who were not ashamed to describe love as it really is
in beautiful nature, or the readers of Gaboriau, Marlitz, Pierre Bobo.[17] Like
the problems of nonresistance to evil, of free will, etc., this question can only
be settled in the future. We can only refer to it, but are not competent to decide
it. Reference to Turgenev and Tolstoy—who avoided the "muck heap"—does
not throw light on the question. Their fastidiousness does not prove anything;
why, before them there was a generation of writers who regarded as dirty not
only accounts of "the dregs and scum," but even descriptions of peasants and
of officials below the rank of titular councillor. Besides, one period, however
brilliant, does not entitle us to draw conclusions in favor of this or that literary
tendency. Reference to the demoralizing effects of the literary tendency we

are discussing does not decide the question, either. Everything in this world is relative and approximate. There are people who can be demoralized even by children's books, and who read with particular pleasure the piquant passages in the Psalms and in Solomon's Proverbs, while there are others who become only the purer from closer knowledge of the filthy side of life. Political and social writers, lawyers, and doctors who are initiated into all the mysteries of human sinfulness are not reputed to be immoral; realistic writers are often more moral than archimandrites. And, finally, no literature can outdo real life in its cynicism, a wine-glassful won't make a man drunk when he has already emptied a barrel.

Most of us would throw in the towel by now and agree, saying, "Dear Anton, you're absolutely right." But Chekhov was piqued and anticipated that Kiseleva would not have conceded yet. He went on:

2. That the world swarms with "dregs and scum" is perfectly true. Human nature is imperfect, and it would therefore be strange to see none but righteous ones on earth. But to think that the duty of literature is to unearth the pearl from the refuse heap means to reject literature itself. "Artistic" literature is only "art" in so far as it paints life as it really is. Its vocation is to be absolutely true and honest. To narrow down its function to the particular task of finding "pearls" is as deadly for it as it would be to make Levitan draw a tree without including the dirty bark and the yellow leaves. I agree that "pearls" are a good thing, but then a writer is not a confectioner, not a provider of cosmetics, not an entertainer; he is a man bound, under contract, by his sense of duty and his conscience; having put his hand to the plough he mustn't turn back, and, however distasteful, he must conquer his squeamishness and soil his imagination with the dirt of life. He is just like any ordinary reporter. What would you say if a newspaper correspondent out of a feeling of fastidiousness or from a wish to please his readers would describe only honest mayors, high-minded ladies, and virtuous railway contractors?

To a chemist nothing on earth is unclean. A writer must be as objective as a chemist, he must lay aside his personal subjective standpoint and must understand that muck heaps play a very respectable part in a landscape, and that the evil passions are as inherent in life as the good ones.

He would say something like this again a few years later, but to Suvorin: "You abuse me for objectivity, calling it indifference to good and evil, lack of ideals and ideas, and so on. You would have me, when I describe horse-thieves, say: 'Stealing horses is an evil.' But that has been known for ages without my saying so. Let the jury judge them; it's my job simply to show what sort of people they are. I write: you are dealing with horse-thieves, so let me tell you that they are not beggars but well-fed people, that they are people of a special cult, and that horse-stealing is not simply theft but a passion. Of course it would be pleasant to combine art with a sermon, but for me personally it is extremely difficult and almost impossible, owing to the conditions of technique. You see, to depict horse-thieves in seven hundred lines I must all the time speak and think in their tone and feel in their spirit, otherwise, if I introduce subjectivity, the image becomes blurred and the story will not be as compact as all short stories ought to be. When I write, I reckon entirely upon the reader to add for himself the subjective elements that are lacking in the story."[18]

To Kiseleva, he continued:

> 3. Writers are the children of their age, and therefore, like everybody else, must submit to the external conditions of the life of the community. Thus, they must be perfectly decent. This is the only thing we have a right to ask of realistic writers. But you say nothing against the form and executions of "Mire." . . . And so, I suppose I have been decent.
>
> 4. I confess I seldom commune with my conscience when I write. This is due to habit and the brevity of my work. And so when I express this or that opinion about literature, I do not take myself into account.

I would make a case for Chekhov here: He freed himself of "community standards" when he wrote. He did not fight or promote existing social mores. Those were entanglements that a social or political conscience would bring—and to write at speed and to write seriously he needed to eliminate obstacles: social or moral purposes. Nonetheless, his stories are usually and naturally very moral because he continuously communed with his conscience. He and his art shared a conscience. To our and Chekhov's amazement, Kiseleva had advocated for censorship and questioned his editor's judgment. She also begrudged him the money!

> 5. You write: "If I were the editor I would have returned this feuilleton to you for your own good." Why not go further? Why not muzzle the editors themselves who publish such stories? Why not send a reprimand to the Head-quarters of the Press Department for not suppressing immoral newspapers?

The fate of literature would be sad indeed if it were at the mercy of individual views. That is the first thing. Secondly, there is no police which could consider itself competent in literary matters. I agree that one can't dispense with the reins and the whip altogether, for knaves find their way even into literature, but no thinking will discover a better police for literature than the critics and the author's own conscience. People have been trying to discover such a police since the creation of the world, but they have found nothing better.

Here you would like me to lose one hundred and fifteen rubles and be put to shame by the editor; others, your father among them, are delighted with the story. Some send insulting letters to Suvorin, pouring abuse on the paper and on me, etc. Who, then, is right? Who is the true judge?

But "Who is right?" . . . I'm going to stick my neck out on this one and assert regarding "Mire" that I'm right and a "true judge." Even if we didn't know Chekhov was trying to hurt Dunya Efros's feelings with "Mire," the story's anti-Semitic basis makes it immoral and bad.[19]

6. You also write, "Leave such writing to spiritless and unlucky scribblers such as Okreyts, Pince-Nez, or Aloe." Allah forgive you if you were sincere when you wrote those words! A condescending and contemptuous tone toward humble people simply because they are humble does no credit to the heart. In literature the lower ranks are as necessary as in the army—this is what the head says, and the heart ought to say still more.

Ough! I have wearied you with my drawn-out reflections. Had I known my criticism would turn out so long I would not have written it. Please forgive me! . . .

He had gone through a list of six points, to his own surprise, and then characteristically wound up apologizing for having written at such length.

Over the decades, every time I read Chekhov's reply, I shook my head with annoyance at Kiseleva. *Idiot! She's thinks she's bigger than her britches.* . . . I haven't enjoyed seeing my disapproval intersect with hers, because it means that either I, too, am getting bigger than my britches in regard to Chekhov or that the energy and power of his response had its roots in his own misgivings about the story's anti-Semitism and mockery of Efros. That is, Kiseleva's attack on the story may have missed its target (she doesn't object to the anti-Semitism as such) but it touched a sore spot. The story wasn't Chekhov at his best, and his heart had been in the wrong place. She provoked him, anyway, into spelling out some of his artistic principles.

Even as I am wincing over his deflections, he then pulled himself together and restored balance and made peace with Kiseleva with jokes and jokey immodesty. This Chekhov is Chekhov. This Chekhov is as mature as humankind will ever be.

> We are coming. We wanted to leave on the fifth, but . . . we were held up by a medical congress. Then came St. Tatyana's Day, and on the seventeenth we're having a party: it's "his" [that is, Chekhov's] name day!! It will be a dazzling ball with all sorts of Jewesses, roast turkeys and Yashenkas. After the seventeenth we'll fix a date for the Babkino trip.[20]
>
> You have read my "On the Road." Well, how do you like my courage? I write of "intellectual" subjects and am not afraid. In Petersburg I excite a regular furor. A short time ago I discoursed upon nonresistance to evil, and also surprised the public. On New Year's Day all the papers presented me with a compliment, and in the December number of the *Russkoye Bogatstvo*, in which Tolstoy writes, there is an article thirty-two pages long by Obolenskiy titled "Chekhov and Korolenko." The fellow goes into raptures over me and proves that I am more of an artist than Korolenko. He is probably talking rot, but, anyway, I am beginning to be conscious of one merit of mine: I am the only writer who, without ever publishing anything in the thick monthlies, has merely on the strength of writing newspaper rubbish won the attention of the lop-eared critics—there has been no instance of this before. [. . .]
>
> I have written a play on four sheets of paper.[21] It will take fifteen to twenty minutes to act. [. . .] It is much better to write small things than big ones: they are unpretentious and successful. . . . What more would you have? I wrote my play in an hour and five minutes. I began another, but have not finished it, for I have no time.[22]

He, this man with "no time," was writing like gangbusters.

In Petersburg, Alexander, not being able to get to Moscow for his brother's name day, wrote him beforehand and was full of beans, catching him up on literary matters at *New Times*, where Alexander was now working in the evenings as a sub-editor: For one thing, Grigorovich had come to the office and excitedly greeted Alexander, mistaking him for Anton. Alexander was amused and now teased Anton, "I'm the brother of that Chekhov, who and so on, in a word, *his brother*. Always and everywhere I'm introduced, recommended and known primarily under this title. My individuality has fallen away. Menelaus—the husband of the queen, and I—the brother of Anton."[23]

On the day after his 27th birthday, Anton answered Alexander with his usual liveliness and teasing: thanking him, first off, for sending the money owed to him from the Petersburg periodicals. He had found himself almost out of money again and was again bewildered about where it all went, and groused—in a fashion of grousing he only shared with Alexander—about the labor of his writing: "Please tell me, dear heart, when shall I live like a human being, that is, work and not be out of pocket? At present I slave and am hard up, and I ruin my reputation by having to produce trash,"[24] namely the short pieces for *Fragments*.

Anton was probably writing Alexander in the morning, as the party was set for 1:00 P.M., and he was anticipating and dreading Leykin's arrival: "With a sinking heart I am waiting for Leykin. He will again wear me out. I am not getting along with this Quasimodo. I refused a raise and also refused punctual delivery of contributions, and he bombards me with tearful-pompous letters, accusing me of the shrinkage of subscriptions, perfidy, duplicity, and the like. He lies, saying that he receives letters from subscribers asking why Chekhonte does no writing. He is cross with you for not contributing."

Anton asked Alexander about his work and greeted and congratulated his nephews. Chekhov was in good spirits, despite the money worries and the pending confrontation with Leykin. He concluded in a postscript: "Besides a wife—medicine—I also have literature—a lover, but I don't mention her, since those living without laws will be destroyed without the law." (This concluding phrase, says Donald Rayfield, mimicked their father Pavel.)[25]

Can we imagine that name-day party in the red Moscow house in midwinter? Chekhov wrote his uncle Mitrofan the next day that they had had a violin and zither (played by his maternal cousin Aleksei Dolzhenko). Among the other guests at the "crowded and merry" party[26] were his brother Nikolay, Levitan, and Schechtel, the old poet Palmin and the forgiving Dunya Efros.

He thanked Mitrofan for the birthday letter and explained how busy he had been. Knowing what would most impress his uncle, he told him once again about his fame and financial success: "During the holidays I was so overwhelmed with work that on Mother's name-day I was almost dropping with exhaustion. I must tell you that in Petersburg I am now the most fashionable writer. One can see that from papers and magazines, which at the end of 1886 were taken up with me, bandied my name about, and praised me beyond my deserts. The result of this growth of my literary reputation is that I get a number of orders and invitations—and this is followed by work at high pressure and exhaustion. My work is nervous, disturbing, and involving strain. It is public and responsible, which makes it doubly hard. Every newspaper report about me agitates both me and my family. . . . My stories are read at public recitations, wherever I go people point at me, I am overwhelmed with acquaintances, and so on, and so on. I have not a day of peace, and feel as though I were on thorns every moment."[27]

He was unabashedly proud of the man who would become his best friend: "My good acquaintance Suvorin, the editor-publisher of the *New Times*, will publish Pushkin's works on January 29 [the 50th anniversary of Pushkin's death], at a fabulously cheap price—two rubles, postage included. [. . .] Such things can be done only by such a great and wise man as Suvorin, for he spares nothing for literature." Chekhov was not being sarcastic. "He has five book shops, a daily paper, a monthly, a tremendous publishing concern, a fortune of a million—and all this he gained by honest, sympathetic work. He comes from Voronezh, where he was a teacher in the country school."[28] He wanted Suvorin to be admired by Mitrofan and was laying out the reasons, concluding with one that would most resonate, *the pay*. For his Christmas story ("On the Road"), Chekhov (knowing his uncle's skepticism), sent the receipt showing "I was paid 111 rubles."

He told Mitrofan (and the extended family reading or hearing the letter) that he had given up writing the humorous stories. "I'm sending you my book [*Motley Stories*]—a collection of my unserious fluff, which I chose not so much for reading as for remembering the beginning of my literary work. . . . Those I like in my book I marked in the contents with a blue pencil. The rest don't require attention."

Chekhov was also in a philosophical mood. He seems to have seen his uncle as someone with whom it was worth discussing serious matters. Mitrofan's son Volodya had apparently brought up the matter of excess letters in the Russian alphabet and the matter of insincerity or even irreverence in addressing people as "great" or "exalted." Chekhov took a surprising but convincing opposing tack: "Peoples and history have the right to call their elect by whatever name they like, without fear of offending the greatness of God or of raising man to God. The point is that we extol not the man but his virtues, the divine principle which he succeeded in developing in himself to a high degree. [. . .] In using these titles we do not lie, do not exaggerate, but express our ecstasy, as a mother does not lie when she says to her child: 'My golden one!' A sense of beauty speaks in us, and beauty does not suffer the common and banal; beauty permits us to make these comparisons, which Volodya can with his mind analyze into powder, but will understand them with his heart. [. . .] The sense of beauty in man knows no bounds, no limitations. That is why the Russian prince may be called the 'Lord of the World'; my friend Volodya also bears that name, for names are not given for merits but in honor and in memory of remarkable men who once lived. [. . .] in extolling man, even to God, we do not sin against love but, on the contrary, express it."

And then Chekhov sneaked in a principle that he tried to observe in his fiction: "Don't belittle people, that's the main thing. It's better to say 'my angel' to a person than label him 'an idiot,' though a person more resembles an idiot than an angel."[29] Truly, there are many idiots in Chekhov's stories, and some of them turn out to seem more like angels.

Leykin told Chekhov sometime during the visit to Moscow that he would be recommending Chekhov for membership in the prestigious Literary Fund. A week later Leykin wrote him that he and Bilibin would be voted on as members on February 2, and then, during the second week of Lent, Chekhov would be asked to come and read "something" to the assembled group.[30] Sensing Chekhov's eagerness to fly the coop, Leykin continued trying to keep him cooped. The thought of having to speak in public, however, would fluster Chekhov for weeks.

Chekhov was a do-gooder. He believed that we help others through generous acts and sympathy rather than through well-meaning advice and admonitions. "The Beggar" ("Nishchiy," January 19) is a good and probably familiar story to most Chekhov readers: A drunken beggar is apparently reformed by taking on odd jobs that a lawyer has offered him. Although Chekhov had been on a kind of campaign against lying in 1886, he makes us think twice about its absolute prohibition when the lawyer, having detected the lies in the educated beggar's sob-story, says, "You are poor and hungry, but that does not give you the right to lie so shamelessly!"[31]

But doesn't it *actually* give him the right? The lawyer's sense of justice is too harsh for Chekhov:

> The beggar at first defended himself, protested with oaths, then he sank into silence and hung his head, overcome with shame.
>
> "Sir!" he said, laying his hand on his heart, "I really was . . . lying! I am not a student and not a village schoolmaster. All that's mere invention! I used to be in the Russian choir, and I was turned out of it for drunkenness. But what can I do? Believe me, in God's name, I can't get on without lying—when I tell the truth no one will give me anything. With the truth one may die of hunger and freeze without a night's lodging! What you say is true, I understand that, but . . . what am I to do?"

Even the lawyer is won over by this argument, and he offers an alternative: payment for chopping wood. Chekhov was no pushover, though. He well understood the beggar's laziness and lack of discipline—it was quite similar to Chekhov's brother Nikolay's. The beggar, anyway, agrees to the work:

> It was evident from his demeanor that he had consented to go and chop wood, not because he was hungry and wanted to earn money, but simply from shame and *amour propre*, because he had been taken at his word. It was clear, too, that he was suffering from the effects of vodka, that he was unwell, and felt not the faintest inclination to work.

The lawyer hires him for monthly work. Eventually the lawyer moves away. Two years later he and the ex-beggar run into each other at the ticket window of a theater. The beggar is respectably dressed and has a real job. The proud lawyer learns now, however, the true story of the beggar's remarkable conversion:

> "I used to come to you to chop wood and she [the cook] would begin: 'Ah, you drunkard! You God-forsaken man! And yet death does not take you!' and then she would sit opposite me, lamenting, looking into my face and wailing: 'You unlucky fellow! You have no gladness in this world, and in the next you will burn in hell, poor drunkard! You poor sorrowful creature!' and she always went on in that style, you know. How often she upset herself, and how many tears she shed over me I can't tell you. But what affected me most—she chopped the wood for me! Do you know, sir, I never chopped a single log for you—she did it all! How it was she saved me, how it was I changed, looking at her, and gave up drinking, I can't explain. I only know that what she said and the noble way she behaved brought about a change in my soul, and I shall never forget it."

I wonder if Chekhov had seen or was only hoping to see this change in his older brothers? Perhaps, he had decided, all the righteous scolding wouldn't do as much for Alexander or Nikolay as a self-conversion inspired by someone's unexpected kindness.

———

The heaviest of this month's heavy stories, "Enemies" ("Vragi," January 20), is Chekhov's greatest and most disturbing story of the winter. Where did it come from? He had probably just finished "Enemies" on January 14 when he was responding to Kiseleva's letter objecting to the contents of "Mire."

Before I started to reread it again, what I remembered is . . .

. . . a doctor and his wife are grieving. Their young son, their lone child, has just died. They are devastated.

Someone arrives to ask for the doctor's services.

The doctor explains the situation.

The someone, a landowner, understands but insists that his wife has a serious illness and requires help right away.

The doctor explains again why he can't leave his wife right now.

The man insists, and threatens to report him for not doing his duty.

The estate is "not far," he says and the miserable doctor gives in.

They get there and the landowner finds a letter from his wife that she has run away with her lover.

He is wretched and dramatic and wants sympathy, and the doctor blows up at him.

They say terrible things at each other.

The landowner sends the doctor home in his carriage.

Both of them are out of their minds with hatred of each other, which Chekhov directly points at and explains that both of them, in any other circumstances, would have been decent and sympathetic to the other.

My sympathy is not at all with the landowner: So what? His wife left him.

The doctor and his wife—the tragedy of their son's death is the darkest of clouds that will never leave them. They will never recover. They will live but not recover.

The landowner? He has money. He'll remarry and maybe to someone who loves him and he'll think of himself as better off.

Now I'll read it in Russian. Why? If I say, "to go as far as possible as I can into the story," I would be skeptical of my claim. Will I really take in any more of it through Russian than I do in English?

And why focus on this story?

It's not characteristic of Chekhov, is it?

It's not *un*characteristic, how about that?

The anger, the fury, the disgusting hatred the enemies fling at each other—had Chekhov felt it or only witnessed it?

Before starting the Russian, I check the "Variants" page in the back of the volume and see that Chekhov made almost no changes in it after its initial publication. Just a few rephrasings . . .

I've now read the Russian. It is so full of surprises. I did not misrepresent the plot in my memory above, but the effects and surprises abound.

The first paragraph is two sentences, but they contain so much; they do what everyone who ever wrote a short story wants to do in the opening paragraph. It's tempting to say the beginning is too polished. It's the kind of beginning, it's better to say, that everyone would want to be able to write. Like a story by Heinrich von Kleist: at the moment the story starts, you know the dramatic situation and the setting and the impending next action. (I will be quoting Constance Garnett's translation rather than my herky-jerky reading of the Russian.)

> Between nine and ten on a dark September evening the only son of the district
> doctor, Kirilov, a child of six, called Andrey, died of diphtheria. Just as the doc-
> tor's wife sank on her knees by the dead child's bedside and was overwhelmed
> by the first rush of despair there came a sharp ring at the bell in the entry.

I've already summarized the story, so let me just comment where surprises come up or there are interesting details I didn't note. I didn't remember, for instance, that Dr. Kirilov and the estate-owner Abogin have met once before. They're in the dark of the house, however, and can't see each other's faces.

I forgot that when the doctor tells him his son has just now died, Abogin reacts like a human being:

> "Is it possible!" whispered Abogin, stepping back a pace. "My God, at what an
> unlucky moment I have come! A wonderfully unhappy day . . . wonderfully.
> What a coincidence. . . . It's as though it were on purpose!"
>
> Abogin took hold of the door-handle and bowed his head. He was evidently
> hesitating and did not know what to do—whether to go away or to continue
> entreating the doctor.
>
> "Listen," he said fervently, catching hold of Kirilov's sleeve. "I well under-
> stand your position! God is my witness that I am ashamed of attempting at
> such a moment to intrude on your attention, but what am I to do? Only think,
> to whom can I go? There is no other doctor here, you know. For God's sake
> come! I am not asking you for myself. . . . I am not the patient!"

I hated Abogin in my memory, but there's no reason to hate him now (or, as Chekhov would argue, ever). I understand his argument: he is asking a favor for someone else; he wouldn't ask it for himself.

But Dr. Kirilov doesn't take in Abogin's words! He turns and walks away, first into the drawing room and then into the bedroom. Chekhov reveals in telling details the short recent history of the boy's diphtheria.

> Here in the bedroom reigned a dead silence. Everything to the smallest detail was eloquent of the storm that had been passed through, of exhaustion, and everything was at rest. A candle standing among a crowd of bottles, boxes, and pots on a stool and a big lamp on the chest of drawers threw a brilliant light over all the room.

Chekhov, like his hero Tolstoy, lays out very simple phrasings at the most dramatic moments: "On the bed near the window lay a boy with open eyes and a look of wonder on his face." As I am reading it in Russian, I am not translating but reading; it flows, unrearranged, like this, "In bed, by lone window, lay boy with open eyes and amazed expression on his face."[32]

Chekhov notes the smell of the room:

> The bedclothes, the rags and bowls, the splashes of water on the floor, the little paint-brushes and spoons thrown down here and there, the white bottle of lime water, the very air, heavy and stifling—were all hushed and seemed plunged in repose.

But he discreetly (considerately) avoids letting us stare at the doctor's wife.

Having fully described the death-room and the parents, Chekhov becomes *lyrical*. I had forgotten the editorializing, which doesn't usually come up for comment when people write or talk about Chekhov. We assume that he is always letting the actions and events speak for themselves, which is an explicit credo of his writing-advice, but in this story and in other great stories, he occasionally steps forward to comment:

> That repellent horror which is thought of when we speak of death was absent from the room. In the numbness of everything, in the mother's attitude, in the indifference on the doctor's face there was something that attracted and touched the heart, that subtle, almost elusive beauty of human sorrow which men will not for a long time learn to understand and describe, and which it seems only music can convey. There was a feeling of beauty, too, in the austere stillness. Kirilov and his wife were silent and not weeping, as though besides

the bitterness of their loss they were conscious, too, of all the tragedy of their position; just as once their youth had passed away, so now together with this boy their right to have children had gone for ever to all eternity! The doctor was forty-four, his hair was gray and he looked like an old man; his faded and invalid wife was thirty-five. Andrey was not merely the only child, but also the last child.

I can imagine a criticism: Chekhov has set up the situation too neatly; the couple is in absolute despair. There is no possible consolation, no possible new baby to be had.

The doctor is forty-four and Chekhov will be forty-four when he dies. His wife Olga Knipper will be thirty-five when he dies. And they will have been childless. That's just a coincidence. Anyway, the doctor here is not dying.

We find out that Kirilov has forgotten about Abogin, who is waiting for him. Abogin thinks Kirilov has been changing his clothes in order to come with him.

Kirilov is bewildered to discover Abogin is still there and tells him he certainly is not and won't come with him. He can't leave his wife. Because of the disease their servants have been sent away for a time, and if he left she would be alone.

Abogin is persistent. Kirilov tells him he knows it's his legal duty to help him, but he just can't. Abogin says he won't hold him to his legal duty, but he is annoying in his manner and words. He ends his argument by saying: "You were just speaking of the death of your son. Who should understand my horror if not you?"

And now something happens that reverses Kirilov's decision. Chekhov steps forward again to editorialize an interesting explanation that contains one of Chekhov's rules of writing, which I have italicized:

> Abogin's voice quivered with emotion; that quiver and his tone were far more persuasive than his words. Abogin was sincere, but it was remarkable that whatever he said his words sounded stilted, soulless, and inappropriately flowery, and even seemed an outrage on the atmosphere of the doctor's home and on the woman who was somewhere dying. He felt this himself, and so, afraid of not being understood, did his utmost to put softness and tenderness into his voice so that the sincerity of his tone might prevail if his words did not. *As a rule, however fine and deep a phrase may be, it only affects the indifferent, and cannot fully satisfy those who are happy or unhappy; that is why dumbness is most often the highest expression of happiness or unhappiness; lovers understand each other better when they are silent, and a fervent,*

passionate speech delivered by the grave only touches outsiders, while to the widow
and children of the dead man it seems cold and trivial.

This should remind us that Chekhov is continually showing us conversations running on different tracks and why he is suspicious of speeches.

But maybe it also shows us some of his own medical experience. He was often run down and exhausted, suffering from minor complaints and also the more harrowing symptoms of tuberculosis. He had daily office hours, but he saw anyone who knocked at the door for medical care, and he did house calls when he had to. Perhaps he had noticed this too; after he had resolved not to go out, someone's shaky voice or simple unaffected argument got to him and persuaded him to go.

> Kirilov stood in silence. When Abogin uttered a few more phrases concerning the noble calling of a doctor, self-sacrifice, and so on, the doctor asked sullenly: "Is it far?"
>
> "Something like eight or nine miles. I have capital horses, doctor! I give you my word of honor that I will get you there and back in an hour. Only one hour."
>
> These words had more effect on Kirilov than the appeals to humanity or the noble calling of the doctor. He thought a moment and said with a sigh: "Very well, let us go!"

Again, Chekhov has us think of those everyday appeals we all hear, but that what motivates us to comply is a surprise, even to us. As they set out in Abogin's carriage toward his estate, Kirilov takes in the dark world, and the dark world takes in him. The two protagonists have not yet fully taken in each other, however; they have not seen each other in full light.

And why is this? What does this show us about how Chekhov was imagining and creating the story? It's important that neither man quite sees the other as something besides a role: doctor and patient-advocate. There are only a few particular details they have picked up about each other:

> It was dark out of doors, though lighter than in the entry. The tall, stooping figure of the doctor, with his long, narrow beard and aquiline nose, stood out distinctly in the darkness. Abogin's big head and the little student's cap that barely covered it could be seen now as well as his pale face. The scarf showed white only in front, behind it was hidden by his long hair.

I had forgotten there's a driver; there is, and Abogin encourages him to drive as fast as possible.

Abogin, whose words are so annoying, manages to keep himself from talking most of the way.

But on that way, with few visual impressions, there are smells and sounds. It's September: the riders can smell the "dampness and mushrooms." Unusually in these years, Chekhov does not tie the events of this story to the time of year in which the story is being published, which is the middle of winter. On the other hand, Chekhov had attended that medical conference the week before he began writing the story and had listened to various speakers, including one about the difficult working conditions for doctors in Russia and the lack of accessible health care.[33] Chekhov would have talked to more doctors than usual and heard work-life stories. "The life of a rural doctor in the 19th century was hard and unremitting, and required great physical and emotional stamina," writes Dr. John Coope. "As Astrov [in *Uncle Vanya*] relates to Marina, the old nurse: 'On my feet from morning to night with never a moment's peace, and then lying under the bedclothes afraid of being dragged out to a patient. All the time we've known each other I haven't had one day off.'"[34]

These characters take in the impressions each in his own way: ". . . the crows, awakened by the noise of the wheels, stirred among the foliage and uttered prolonged plaintive cries as though they knew the doctor's son was dead and that Abogin's wife was ill."

When Abogin breaks the silence, we understand why he says it and why Kirilov would say nothing in reply:

> "It's an agonizing state! One never loves those who are near one so much as when one is in danger of losing them."

Not because of Abogin's words but because the carriage crosses a river does Kirilov come to—realizing he really should not have left his wife on her own.

But it's too late. They've come too far to go back. They continue on their way through the dimness.

> In all nature there seemed to be a feeling of hopelessness and pain. The earth, like a ruined woman sitting alone in a dark room and trying not to think of the past, was brooding over memories of spring and summer and apathetically waiting for the inevitable winter. Wherever one looked, on all sides, nature seemed like a dark, infinitely deep, cold pit from which neither Kirilov nor Abogin nor the red half-moon could escape. . . .

Again, though separate from each other, unrealizing of the other, the same mood has descended on them. Or is it mostly Chekhov's mood?

Abogin anticipates being crushed, while Kirilov already has been. Arriving at the house, Abogin says: "'If anything happens . . . I shall not survive it.'"

They enter the quiet house:

> Now the doctor and Abogin, who till then had been in darkness, could see each other clearly. The doctor was tall and stooped, was untidily dressed and not good-looking. There was an unpleasantly harsh, morose, and unfriendly look about his lips, thick as a negro's, his aquiline nose, and listless, apathetic eyes. His unkempt head and sunken temples, the premature grayness of his long, narrow beard through which his chin was visible, the pale gray hue of his skin and his careless, uncouth manners—the harshness of all this was suggestive of years of poverty, of ill fortune, of weariness with life and with men. Looking at his frigid figure one could hardly believe that this man had a wife, that he was capable of weeping over his child.

We see why Abogin doesn't fully sympathize with Kirilov's tragedy: he can't see the suffering of the doctor, which has been internalized. The doctor is someone he needs but is not quite fully realized as a person to him. On the flip side:

> Abogin presented a very different appearance. He was a thick-set, sturdy-looking, fair man with a big head and large, soft features; he was elegantly dressed in the very latest fashion. In his carriage, his closely buttoned coat, his long hair, and his face there was a suggestion of something generous, leonine; he walked with his head erect and his chest squared, he spoke in an agreeable baritone, and there was a shade of refined almost feminine elegance in the manner in which he took off his scarf and smoothed his hair. Even his paleness and the childlike terror with which he looked up at the stairs as he took off his coat did not detract from his dignity nor diminish the air of sleekness, health, and aplomb which characterized his whole figure.

Kirilov perceives the vitality—the unattractive vitality of Abogin. Why should *he* have so much life? But he does! He has so much vitality and takes it for granted. It's appalling! There is a limitation in this view, but under the circumstances it is too much to ask of Kirilov to appreciate Abogin as a complete human being.

The first time reading this story, or the first time coming back to it after a decade or two, a reader of Chekhov might not anticipate or remember what happens next—but Chekhov keeps us so much on our toes that we feel anything could happen. Abogin is prepared for one kind of tragedy: She has died! But the lack of bustle in the house seems to preclude that possibility.

> "There is nobody and no sound," he said going up the stairs. "There is no commotion. God grant all is well."

He has the doctor wait in the fancy drawing room. (I wonder why he wouldn't have the doctor rush up the stairs with him?) Kirilov, not letting himself think, takes in the details of the room. Eventually, "Somewhere far away in the adjoining rooms someone uttered a loud exclamation . . ." We don't know and Kirilov doesn't know what's happened, but we know we'll soon find out.

Five minutes later:

> In the doorway stood Abogin, but he was not the same as when he had gone out. The look of sleekness and refined elegance had disappeared—his face, his hands, his attitude were contorted by a revolting expression of something between horror and agonizing physical pain. His nose, his lips, his moustache, all his features were moving and seemed trying to tear themselves from his face, his eyes looked as though they were laughing with agony. . . .
>
> Abogin took a heavy stride into the drawing room, bent forward, moaned, and shook his fists.
>
> "She has deceived me," he cried, with a strong emphasis on the second syllable of the verb. "Deceived me, gone away. She fell ill and sent me for the doctor only to run away with that clown Papchinsky! My God!"

And Abogin goes on and on, in naked agony before the doctor. He has been transformed by his grief—it is grief, though on a different order, almost anyone would say, from that of Kirilov. Chekhov does not say this. And of course we sympathize with Abogin, to a point. We sympathize as humans for someone genuinely suffering, but if we imagine being in Kirilov's shoes, comparing griefs, Abogin's would seem mockable.

> Abogin took a heavy step toward the doctor, held out his soft white fists in his face, and shaking them went on yelling:

"Gone away! Deceived me! But why this deception? My God! My God! What need of this dirty, scoundrelly trick, this diabolical, snakish farce? What have I done to her? Gone away!"

Tears gushed from his eyes. He turned on one foot and began pacing up and down the drawing room. Now in his short coat, his fashionable narrow trousers which made his legs look disproportionately slim, with his big head and long mane he was extremely like a lion.

I had misread the story. Kirilov does *not* understand what Abogin has been saying. At the beginning of the story, Chekhov told us: "Kirilov listened and said nothing, as though he did not understand Russian." He is in that state again.

> A gleam of curiosity came into the apathetic face of the doctor. He got up and looked at Abogin.
>
> "Excuse me, where is the patient?" he said.
>
> "The patient! The patient!" cried Abogin, laughing, crying, and still brandishing his fists. "She is not ill, but accursed! The baseness! The vileness! The devil himself could not have imagined anything more loathsome! She sent me off that she might run away with a buffoon, a dull-witted clown, an Alphonse! Oh God, better she had died! I cannot bear it! I cannot bear it!"

Now Kirilov gets it. Now it all sinks in. He should or could have just walked out the door back to the carriage. Maybe that is what Chekhov would have done. But Chekhov shows us why this man, about whom we know little beyond his strained life and the brand-new tragedy that marks the end of the rest of his life, instead makes a stand that brings about his loss of self-control:

> The doctor drew himself up. His eyes blinked and filled with tears, his narrow beard began moving to right and to left together with his jaw.
>
> "Allow me to ask what's the meaning of this?" he asked, looking around him with curiosity. "My child is dead, my wife is in grief alone in the whole house. . . . I myself can scarcely stand up, I have not slept for three nights. . . . And here I am forced to play a part in some vulgar farce, to play the part of a stage property! I don't . . . don't understand it!"

But Abogin is not listening to *him*:

Abogin unclenched one fist, flung a crumpled note on the floor, and stamped on it as though it were an insect he wanted to crush.

"And I didn't see, didn't understand," he said through his clenched teeth, brandishing one fist before his face with an expression as though someone had trodden on his corns. "I did not notice that he came every day! I did not notice that he came today in a closed carriage! What did he come in a closed carriage for? And I did not see it! Noodle!"

"I don't understand . . ." muttered the doctor. "Why, what's the meaning of it? Why, it's an outrage on personal dignity, a mockery of human suffering! It's incredible. . . . It's the first time in my life I have had such an experience!"

With the dull surprise of a man who has only just realized that he has been bitterly insulted the doctor shrugged his shoulders, flung wide his arms, and not knowing what to do or to say sank helplessly into a chair.

Abogin, privileged, self-consumed, human, grieves for himself and doesn't hear or perceive the man to whom he is pouring out his heart.

"If you have ceased to love me and love another—so be it; but why this deceit, why this vulgar, treacherous trick?" Abogin said in a tearful voice. "What is the object of it? And what is there to justify it? And what have I done to you? Listen, doctor," he said hotly, going up to Kirilov. "You have been the involuntary witness of my misfortune and I am not going to conceal the truth from you. I swear that I loved the woman, loved her devotedly, like a slave! I have sacrificed everything for her; I have quarrelled with my own people, I have given up the service and music, I have forgiven her what I could not have forgiven my own mother or sister. . . I have never looked askance at her. . . . I have never gainsaid her in anything. Why this deception? I do not demand love, but why this loathsome duplicity? If she did not love me, why did she not say so openly, honestly, especially as she knows my views on the subject? . . ."

With tears in his eyes, trembling all over, Abogin opened his heart to the doctor with perfect sincerity. He spoke warmly, pressing both hands on his heart, exposing the secrets of his private life without the faintest hesitation, and even seemed to be glad that at last these secrets were no longer pent up in his breast.

When Chekhov turned twenty-eight in 1888, the date of this photo,
he had just completed the most productive two years of his literary life.

The concluding image from "Misery" (published January 27, 1886), illustrated in 1903 by M. Efimov.

V. F. Vasil'ev's illustration of "Agafya" (published March 15, 1886) shows the title character unable to yet cross the river to her husband after her rendezvous with Savka.

Alexander Chekhov (1855–1913), Chekhov's oldest brother, was demonstrably intense and vulnerable in ways that Anton was not.

Anton and his brother Nikolay Chekhov (1858–1891) pose in review of the drawings that Nikolay has made to illustrate Anton's little book of stories *The Prank* (1882).

Maria Chekhova (1863–1957),
Chekhov's lone sister, became a teacher
and, after his death in 1904, the archivist
of her brother's writings.

Mikhail Chekhov (1865–1936), the
youngest of six surviving Chekhov
siblings, wrote an ever-interesting and
admiring memoir of Anton.

Evgenia Chekhova (1835–1919), Chekhov's tenderhearted, loving mother, in about 1880, after the family had moved to Moscow from Taganrog.

Pavel Chekhov (1825–1898), in a photo from about 1880, was born a serf. As Anton's father, he was heavy-handed and rough-tongued. He believed in education and in the arts, though he never expressed in writing any appreciation of or interest in Anton's stories or plays.

The Chekhovs in Taganrog in 1874, when Anton was fourteen. Standing: brother Ivan, Anton, brother Nikolay, brother Alexander, Uncle Mitrofan Chekhov. Sitting: brother Mikhail, sister Maria, father Pavel, mother Evgenia, Aunt Liudmila, cousin Georgy.

Chekhov, armed only with a giant quill, was well enough known as a young writer to be parodied in magazines. (Illustrator unknown.)

Nikolay Chekhov, a talented but irresponsible artist, never finished this oil painting of Anton that he began in 1884. Anton's right ear awaits completion.

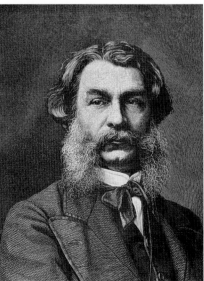

ABOVE: Isaac Levitan (1860–1900), one of Russia's most renown landscape painters, was introduced to the Chekhov family by his art-school classmate Nikolay. He became particularly close to Anton and Maria. This sketch was drawn by Aleksey Stepanov in 1888.

RIGHT: Dmitry Grigorovich (1822–1900) is better known today as what he wasn't, "the man who discovered Chekhov," than for what he was, a novelist considered at the time in the same league as Dostoevsky, Turgenev, and Tolstoy.

The artist and architect Franz Schechtel (1859-1926) was among Chekhov's closest friends in the mid-1880s. He designed the frontispiece of Chekhov's first big collection, *Motley Stories* (1886).

The wealthy right wing publisher of *New Times*, Aleksei Suvorin (1834–1912), opened his newspaper's literary supplement to Chekhov's contributions in 1886, and a few years later became Chekhov's best friend and confidant.

ABOVE LEFT: The frontispiece of *Motley Stories* (*Piostrye Rasskazy*), most of which were stories originally published in Moscow and St. Petersburg humor magazines in 1884–1885, was drawn by Chekhov's friend Franz Schechtel. BOTTOM LEFT: The children's story author Maria Kiseleva (1847–1922) was Chekhov's first writing mentee. Though she resisted much of his advice and rejected many of his opinions about literature, she cultivated and valued their friendship. ABOVE RIGHT: The Chekhov House Museum, located on Sadovaya-Kudrinskaya Street in Moscow, faces a busy boulevard today.

ABOVE: Chekhov hesitated to post the nameplate ("Doctor A. P. Chekhov") on the door of the house when he became overwhelmed by patients and deadlines in the fall of 1886. BELOW: Chekhov's study as recreated in his Moscow house museum.

ABOVE: The primary characters of "The Dependents" (September 8, 1887): Mikhail Petrovich Zotov, the dog Lyska, the unnamed "priceless steed." Illustration by N. Nikonov (1903). BELOW: In "Vanka," Chekhov's 1886 Christmas story, illustrated here by S. S. Boim, the nine-year-old, apprenticed to a shoemaker in the city, writes to his grandfather "in the village."

ABOVE: The anonymous illustrator of "Enemies" lingers over the deathbed scene of Dr. Kirilov's only son. BELOW LEFT: The composer Peter Ilyich Tchaikovsky delighted in Chekhov's short stories. Meeting in 1889, Tchaikovsky suggested they write an opera libretto together (this suggestion did not bear fruit). BELOW TOP RIGHT: Alexander Lazarev (1861–1927) was a humor writer (pen name Gruzinskiy) mentored by Chekhov in 1887. BELOW BOTTOM RIGHT: The author Ivan Leont'ev (pen name, Shcheglov, nicknamed "Jean" by Chekhov) met Chekhov in St. Petersburg in December 1887, when they became fast, lifelong friends.

ABOVE: The November 19, 1887 opening night poster announcement of Chekhov's *Ivanov*. It was performed in Moscow's Korsh Theater's "Barbershop Hall."

LEFT: Though embarrassed about the modest fee he collected for the second-level stories in *Innocent Speeches* (*Nevinnye Rechi*), Chekhov acknowledged the high quality of the volume's artistic production. The book's cover illustration is by Nikolay Chekhov; the author is "A. Chekhonte."

The actor Olga Knipper (1868–1959) became Chekhov's wife in 1901. She performed in Chekhov's plays in Stanislavsky's Moscow Art Theater.

Chekhov in 1904, in the last photograph of him before his death in July.

Chekhov's grave at the Novodevichy Cemetery in
Moscow. Photograph by Ross Robins (2009).

Amazing! Abogin, in *his* grief, loses sight of Kirilov's. Chekhov does something no other writer in the world would do: he admires Abogin's "perfect sincerity." Abogin has opened himself up: This is a quality. We understand why. But Chekhov also has us standing (now sitting) there in Kirilov's shoes. Abogin's confession is out of place. It is a burden on someone carrying his own burden. Chekhov reflects:

> If he had talked in this way for an hour or two, and opened his heart, he would undoubtedly have felt better. Who knows, if the doctor had listened to him and had sympathized with him like a friend, he might perhaps, as often happens, have reconciled himself to his trouble without protest, without doing anything needless and absurd. . . . But what happened was quite different.

And as all professionals know, yes, if we do our duty, if we do not involve our own troubles with those sharing theirs with us, all will go more smoothly. We can dislike them later at our leisure, but not now, not now. Now we must suffer them and say and do the right things. If Kirilov could have viewed Abogin as a patient . . . But that's unreasonable to ask of him, given his grief. And Abogin, taking for granted his rights as a patient, doesn't understand why Kirilov can't keep performing his role as doctor. He only sees him as a doctor.

> While Abogin was speaking the outraged doctor perceptibly changed. The indifference and wonder on his face gradually gave way to an expression of bitter resentment, indignation, and anger. The features of his face became even harsher, coarser, and more unpleasant. When Abogin held out before his eyes the photograph of a young woman with a handsome face as cold and expressionless as a nun's and asked him whether, looking at that face, one could conceive that it was capable of duplicity, the doctor suddenly flew out, and with flashing eyes said, rudely rapping out each word:
>
> "What are you telling me all this for? I have no desire to hear it! I have no desire to!" he shouted and brought his fist down on the table. "I don't want your vulgar secrets! Damnation take them! Don't dare to tell me of such vulgar doings! Do you consider that I have not been insulted enough already? That I am a flunky whom you can insult without restraint? Is that it?"
>
> Abogin staggered back from Kirilov and stared at him in amazement.
>
> "Why did you bring me here?" the doctor went on, his beard quivering. "If you are so puffed up with good living that you go and get married and

then act a farce like this, how do I come in? What have I to do with your love affairs? Leave me in peace! Go on squeezing money out of the poor in your gentlemanly way. Make a display of humane ideas, play (the doctor looked sideways at the violoncello case) play the bassoon and the trombone, grow as fat as capons, but don't dare to insult personal dignity! If you cannot respect it, you might at least spare it your attention!"

Abogin is us, in our amazement at someone else's blow-up—especially when the blow-up is directed at us:

"Excuse me, what does all this mean?" Abogin asked, flushing red.

"It means that it's base and low to play with people like this! I am a doctor; you look upon doctors and people generally who work and don't stink of perfume and prostitution as your menials and *mauvais ton*; well, you may look upon them so, but no one has given you the right to treat a man who is suffering as a stage property!"

"How dare you say that to me!" Abogin said quietly, and his face began working again, and this time unmistakably from anger.

"No, how dared you, knowing of my sorrow, bring me here to listen to these vulgarities!" shouted the doctor, and he again banged on the table with his fist. "Who has given you the right to make a mockery of another man's sorrow?"

Chekhov won't let me be settled in my complete sympathy with Kirilov, even though we understand his anger at and contempt for Abogin. Chekhov himself insisted on preserving his dignity as a man, as a doctor. He resented or mocked superiority in manner or treatment. But he also didn't let himself blow up.

Is this why I find the story so compelling, so powerful? That it doesn't let me sit in my justification of anger and hatred, as Kirilov does? Kirilov will hate this fool Abogin forever, perhaps, but there will be a feeling of shame, too, in his recollection. Chekhov won't let me have complacency in my hatred. It will wear at me until, perhaps, it arrives at Chekhov's level of understanding. All the same, understanding doesn't mean sympathy. Abogin's a plump, self-satisfied dope. His heart is broken, but he sees his undisguised grief as its own excuse. Why shouldn't he wail and carry on? As Chekhov says, he would have eventually, probably, come around, and would have eventually, probably, weighed Kirilov's grief and circumstances with his own. And he would have thought: "My God! Compared to him, I am very lucky. I can start over. I can find someone my family will love and respect. I will be free. I will have children."

But Abogin won't have time to do that, now that Kirilov has blown up at him.

> "You have taken leave of your senses," shouted Abogin. "It is ungenerous. I am intensely unhappy myself and . . . and . . ."
>
> "Unhappy!" said the doctor, with a smile of contempt. "Don't utter that word, it does not concern you. The spendthrift who cannot raise a loan calls himself unhappy, too. The capon, sluggish from overfeeding, is unhappy, too. Worthless people!"
>
> "Sir, you forget yourself," shrieked Abogin. "For saying things like that . . . people are thrashed! Do you understand?"

Abogin says everything wrong. He scarcely restrains himself. He is a "gentleman," and suggests that Kirilov is a nobody, one of the "people," someone Abogin feels he would have the right to "thrash." He even seems to think much of himself for offering to pay Kirilov for his time, but that, too, is, as Kirilov feels, insulting.

Finally:

> Abogin and the doctor stood face to face, and in their wrath continued flinging undeserved insults at each other.

So now I don't understand my previous misunderstandings of the story. This standoff reminds me of the beginning of *The Iliad*, Achilles and Agamemnon, throwing their furious words at each other, ready to resort to swords. Homer understands both men and doesn't let us pick sides: What's terrible is that two men who are nominally on the same side would love to kill the other.

Chekhov explains:

> I believe that never in their lives, even in delirium, had they uttered so much that was unjust, cruel, and absurd. The egoism of the unhappy was conspicuous in both. The unhappy are egoistic, spiteful, unjust, cruel, and less capable of understanding each other than fools. Unhappiness does not bring people together but draws them apart, and even where one would fancy people should be united by the similarity of their sorrow, far more injustice and cruelty is generated than in comparatively placid surroundings.

Chekhov even gives us the long perspective on their lives. They never did worse than what we have just witnessed. We understand why they fight in this ugly way. And somehow Chekhov realizes in this story, or shows us what he has before realized, about "the egoism of the unhappy." And what an unhappy family he arose from.

But now to the ending. The doctor demands that Abogin send him back home, and Abogin orders that to be done, but he is so beside himself that he screams at and threatens the driver.

To my surprise (once again), Abogin, the bigger offender, shows Kirilov and us that he can pull himself together:

> Abogin and the doctor remained in silence waiting for the carriage. The first regained his expression of sleekness and his refined elegance. He paced up and down the room, tossed his head elegantly, and was evidently meditating on something. His anger had not cooled, but he tried to appear not to notice his enemy. . . . The doctor stood, leaning with one hand on the edge of the table, and looked at Abogin with that profound and somewhat cynical, ugly contempt only to be found in the eyes of sorrow and indigence when they are confronted with well-nourished comfort and elegance.

Robust health! As a doctor, Kirilov sees and appreciates it—wasted on Abogin! And again, Chekhov argues about why the hatred and spite have been foolhardy:

> All the way home the doctor thought not of his wife, nor of his Andrey, but of Abogin and the people in the house he had just left. His thoughts were unjust and inhumanly cruel. He condemned Abogin and his wife and Papchinsky and all who lived in rosy, subdued light among sweet perfumes, and all the way home he hated and despised them till his head ached. And a firm conviction concerning those people took shape in his mind.

Chekhov must have argued with someone about this. He must have known a *doctor* who had justified himself this way. This is a reaction story. Chekhov shows us that for his part he sympathizes with both sides, and that there were alternatives, and that our self-justifying hatreds cost us:

> Time will pass and Kirilov's sorrow will pass, but that conviction, unjust and unworthy of the human heart, will not pass, but will remain in the doctor's mind to the grave.

Chekhov had multiple opportunities to revise this story. He did not. He tacked on the moral and left it there, forever.

———~~~———

I know of no classic Russian fiction so mocking of Germans as an episode in *Crime and Punishment*, where Dostoevsky delights in Marmeladov's landlady's grammatical and vocabulary errors:

> "Listen to the owl!" Katerina Ivanovna whispered at once, her good-humor almost restored, "she meant to say he kept his hands in his pockets, but she said he put his hands in people's pockets. (Cough-cough.) And have you noticed, Rodion Romanovich, that all these Petersburg foreigners, the Germans especially, are all stupider than we! Can you fancy anyone of us telling how 'Karl from the chemist's' 'pierced his heart from fear' and that the idiot, instead of punishing the cabman, 'clasped his hands and wept, and much begged.' Ah, the fool! And you know she fancies it's very touching and does not suspect how stupid she is!"[35]

Every time I read it, I blush for my clumsy, lousy Russian.

Chekhov was nicer. There are, however, a few mockings of "foreign" accents, including unfortunately of Jewish ones, and Chekhov regularly mocked his own incapacity with foreign languages, though he occasionally used common French, Latin, and German phrases. "The Good German" ("Dobriy Nemets," January 24) is about Ivan Karlovich Schwei, a German immigrant with a good job in a steel mill who has married a poor Russian woman. He speaks like so: "Cabman, you good cabman! I love Russian peoples! You are a Russian man, my wife is a Russian man, and I am a Russian man."[36] Toiling away in Tver, he misses his wife in Moscow and returns home unannounced to see her and discovers a man in their bed. After writing an angry ungrammatical letter to her parents, he learns that his admirably frugal wife has rented out their former bedroom to a locksmith and his wife. Chekhov has fun with the German's language, but Ivan Karlovich's challenges with Russian have nothing to do with his honest mistake.

After that light fare, Chekhov ended his very dark January publications with "Darkness" ("Temnota," January 26): A peasant begs a doctor to intervene for the peasant's convict brother to get him released. The doctor can do nothing about that, which the peasant, dim and frustrated, has trouble understanding. "What right have I?" asks the exasperated doctor. "Am I a jailer or what? They brought him to the hospital for me to treat him, but I have as much right to let him out as I have to put you in prison, silly fellow!" As the story goes on to its hopeless end, all of Chekhov's sympathy is directed to the convict's brother, whose family suffers the relentless and incomprehensible rules of the Russian justice system.

Chekhov felt obliged on January 26 to write Leykin to thank him for the payment for "The Good German" and offer excuses again for not writing for *Fragments*. "My whole body is achy and weak. I need to work, but it's not working, and everything I write is bad."[37] He had gone to the famous doctor Zakharin's ninety-minute lecture on syphilis that day and standing there had exhausted him. "Concerning a trip to Petersburg the second week of Lent, I don't know what to tell you." He fretted that after forty or fifty lines of reading aloud at the Literary Fund ceremony his voice would become dry and hissy. Leykin shrugged at that but let him know that there would be a free round-trip ticket for him.

Chekhov also wrote to Alexander that day, sighing, "It's probable we'll see each other the second week of Lent. [. . .] I'm sick, living boringly, but I'm starting to write lousily, or I'm tired and can't follow Levitan's example of turning the pictures upside down and averting my critical eye . . . "[38]

Alexander replied a few days later, telling him that he was constantly hearing praise about Anton, that, for example, "You have the divine spark in you and that they expect from you—what exactly they expect they don't know, but they expect it."[39]

At the end of the month, Chekhov, still anxious about the speech that Leykin expected him to make in Petersburg, wrote and requested Alexander to ask around and find out if it would be good after all for him to go ahead and do it.[40] Fortunately, he never had to, as the event was canceled.

February 1887

—◦◦◦—

Creativity—that state when ideas seem to organize themselves into a swift, tightly woven flow, with a feeling of gorgeous clarity and meaning emerging— seems to me physiologically distinctive, and I think if we had the ability to make fine enough brain images, these would show an unusual and widespread activity with innumerable connections and synchronizations occurring. At such times, when I am writing, thoughts seem to organize themselves in spontaneous succession and to clothe themselves instantly in appropriate words. I feel I can bypass or transcend much of my own personality, my neuroses. It is at once not me and the innermost part of me, certainly the best part of me.

—Dr. Oliver Sacks, "The Creative Self"[1]

Chekhov's money problems were not disappearing. At the beginning of February Anton was scolding Alexander about a missing ruble or two in the last dispatch.[2]

On February 2nd, both Alexander and Leykin wrote Chekhov to let him know he had been officially elected to the Literary Fund.

"Polinka" ("Polin'ka," February 2) is one of Chekhov's few love stories of 1887. It is a model of simple design. Polinka is a dressmaker who has recently left behind her admirer, the fabric shopman Nikolay Timofeich, for a student of medicine or law. She has come to the store to order materials she and her mother need for their clients' dresses and to wonder about the cessation of Nikolay's friendly visits. Because he is working, they must discuss their relationship while she shops:

"The black's from eighty kopecks and the colored from two and a half rubles. I shall never come and see you again," Nikolay Timofeich adds in an undertone.

"Why?"

"Why? It's very simple. You must understand that yourself. Why should I distress myself? It's a queer business! Do you suppose it's a pleasure to me to see that student carrying on with you? I see it all and I understand. Ever since autumn he's been hanging about you and you go for a walk with him almost every day; and when he is with you, you gaze at him as though he were an angel. You are in love with him; there's no one to beat him in your eyes. Well, all right, then, it's no good talking."

Polinka remains dumb and moves her finger on the counter in embarrassment.

"I see it all," the shopman goes on. "What inducement have I to come and see you? I've got some pride. It's not everyone likes to play gooseberry. What was it you asked for?"

"Mamma told me to get a lot of things, but I've forgotten. I want some feather trimming, too."

"What kind would you like?"[3]

Chekhov describes a situation that cannot be happily resolved. What Nikolay wants, he cannot have. What Polinka wants, Nikolay's former regard and friendship, she cannot have. Neither wants to be miserable and both are, and we understand it perfectly and sympathize with both:

"I want . . . I want . . . size forty-eight centimetres. Only she wanted one, lined . . . with real whalebone . . . I must talk to you, Nikolay Timofeich. Come today!"

"Talk? What about? There's nothing to talk about."

"You are the only person who . . . cares about me, and I've no one to talk to but you."

"These are not reed or steel, but real whalebone. . . . What is there for us to talk about? It's no use talking. . . . You are going for a walk with him today, I suppose?"

"Yes; I . . . I am."

"Then what's the use of talking? Talk won't help. . . . You are in love, aren't you?"

"Yes . . ." Polinka whispers hesitatingly, and big tears gush from her eyes.

Though in tears during this painful interaction, Polinka will no doubt be happy when she takes her afternoon walk with the student.

There are no happy love stories in Chekhov's fiction, but there are plenty of comic ones, and of them this is one of his most touching.

Pushkin, on the other hand, did write at least one happy love story ("The Amateur Peasant-Girl"), and the biggest publishing sensation of 1887 was Suvorin's publishing company's edition of Pushkin's collected works. Even today, Pushkin's works unapologetically include his unfinished works, marvelous drafts of what would have or could have been marvelous complete pieces. Pushkin really was lazy. More brilliant, an even greater writer of short fiction than Chekhov, but a hundred times lazier! The publication of this edition marked the fiftieth anniversary of his death from injuries that he sustained in a duel over his wife's honor.

On the 3rd or 4th of February Anton wrote to ask Alexander to get him twenty copies of the Pushkin edition, as they had all been sold out in Moscow. But the publication was so popular that Alexander discovered Petersburg's booksellers were also sold out. Chekhov would soon learn that not even Suvorin himself could get Chekhov any copies for now.

Having written a *Fragments* story, "Inadvertence," Chekhov was proud of himself when he wrote Leykin on the 8th: "The whole day I was interrupted writing it, but all the same I wrote it. . . . I'm beginning to get back to normal and I'm working more regularly than in January." It was the middle of winter, but, wrote Chekhov, "It smells of spring. You'll soon leave for Tosna, but where I'll be in summer is unknown to me."

Why he didn't want to return to Babkino and the Kiselevs' estate is not clear, but when alternatives did not pan out, the family ended up there in May anyway.

———⁓———

How many drunks are there in Chekhov? No one, as far as I know, has counted, but they are not rare. In "Drunk" ("P'yanie," February 9), a rich, self-loathing man and his lawyer are dining at a restaurant after a ball. The rich man asks rhetorically: "Why is it [. . .] that people don't invent some other pleasure besides drunkenness and debauchery?" He drunkenly insults the waitstaff, the musicians, and his companion. He wretchedly declares that he hates his wife:

> "What for?"
> "I don't know myself! I've only been married two years. I married as you know for love, and now I hate her like a mortal enemy, like this parasite here,

saving your presence. And there is no cause, no sort of cause! When she sits by me, eats, or says anything, my whole soul boils, I can scarcely restrain myself from being rude to her. It's something one can't describe. To leave her or tell her the truth is utterly impossible because it would be a scandal, and living with her is worse than hell for me. I can't stay at home! I spend my days at business and in the restaurants and spend my nights in dissipation. Come, how is one to explain this hatred? She is not an ordinary woman, but handsome, clever, quiet."[4]

That he hates his wife is not the cause of his wretchedness, seemingly, just a byproduct of it. Nothing satisfies him. He goes on to admit that once he got the idea into his head that his wife married him for his money, he could not shake it: "I keep fancying I am being flattered for my money. I trust no one! I am a difficult man, my boy, very difficult!" He is proud of his obnoxiousness, and his pride is that he knows it and announces it. The most important thing about "Drunk" is that the director Josef Heifitz included two events from it in his superb 1960 film version of Chekhov's "The Lady with the Dog."

Despite his unhappiness with Maria Kiseleva's criticism of "Mire," Chekhov followed through, as he said he would, in submitting her story "Larka-Gerkules" to Suvorin on February 10 for *New Times*. He was still humble, careful, and polite with Suvorin, which means they weren't quite friends yet. He explained in apology about his own work that "All January I was sick, lazy and wrote nonsense."[5] He told him he was planning to go south at the end of March. "There, I think, the work will go with more liveliness." He added that his friends and acquaintances were seeking out the Pushkin edition and so he had been asked by them to ask Suvorin about it. By the end of 1887, Chekhov would be writing Suvorin more directly and comfortably and amusingly.

He rather contorted himself when he wrote to old Grigorovich on February 12 about a story of Grigorovich's that he had just read in the *Petersburg Gazette*, "Karelin's Dream" (a reviewer had called it "irreproachable").[6] "Karelin's Dream" was presented as a section of a novel, *Petersburg of Past Time*, but Grigorovich never completed the novel. There are no English translations of "Karelin's Dream," so (reminding myself that this is one of the reasons I learned Russian), I read the excerpt that Chekhov had read and began a makeshift translation.

Chekhov's restrained, all-too-careful questioning observations on it suggest that Grigorovich's pre-cinematic cinematic representations of Karelin's dream made Chekhov wonder if he himself was representing dreams correctly. Because if what Grigorovich had written was right and true to actual dreams, then Chekhov's dreams were not. The critic

Gleb Struve notes that in the midst of "Karelin's Dream," "the reader almost forgets that all this is supposed to be happening in a dream."[7] In the letter, Chekhov ventured into a discussion of dreams, an area where his own representations, from which he demanded faithfulness to psychology and physiology, excelled.

Chekhov dashed off letters, but he didn't dash off this one; he made himself copy it over from a rough, heavily edited draft.[8] Chekhov dipped a toe in and then splashed about:

> I have just read "Karelin's Dream," and I am very much interested to know how far the dream you describe really is a dream.[9]

The essence of Chekhov's criticism is there: *You call this a "dream," but is it?*

> I think your description of the workings of the brain and of the general feeling of a person who is asleep is physiologically correct and remarkably artistic.

"Remarkably artistic" is his acknowledgment of Grigorovich's effort to make it so. But Chekhov does not as a rule praise attempts to make writing *look* artistic. Grigorovich might have been vain, but I believe he would have understood this as criticism. Chekhov makes a plainer compliment: "the sensation of cold is given by you with remarkable subtlety."

Maybe Chekhov was indicating this next passage, which to my mind is excessive and literary rather than "subtle":

> The wind increased and began tearing unbearably at my face. It was so cold, so unbearably cold, that it seemed all of the Arctic Ocean had moved from its place, moving and remaining there, somewhere beyond Vasilevsky Island. I finally came out from under the collar of my coat. In a moment, lifting my eyelids, I saw to my right the statue of Peter. The rider and the horse under him running so fast on the cliff, it seemed frozen in granite; the very cliff seemed to me frozen to the depth of its heart. On the outside of the statue, in the simple expanse with the covered bronze shell of the horse and rider, there was a thick layer of icy needles; on the outside, on the protruding parts of the statue, the bronze shone with a cold gloss [. . .]

Chekhov was very much interested in an individual's experience of dreaming, but he doesn't assert rank or privilege over Grigorovich on the basis of his medical knowledge. Instead, he makes it very personal and as usual is very particular:

When at night the quilt falls off I begin to dream of huge slippery stones, of cold autumnal water, naked banks—and all this dim, misty, without a patch of blue sky; sad and dejected like one who has lost his way, I look at the stones and feel that for some reason I cannot avoid crossing a deep river; I see then small tugs that drag huge barges, floating beams. . . . All this is infinitely gray, damp, and dismal. When I run from the river I come across the fallen cemetery gates, funerals, my school-teachers. . . . And all the time I am cold through and through with that oppressive nightmare-like cold which is impossible in waking life, and which is only felt by those who are asleep. The first pages of "Karelin's Dream" vividly brought it to my memory—especially the first half of page five, where you speak of the cold and loneliness of the grave.

In "Karelin's Dream," Grigorovich muddies the actual dreamlike core of the dream. In contrast, to clarify the point for himself at least, Chekhov returns to unusually personal experiences:

One does dream of people, and always of unpleasant ones. . . . I, for instance, when I feel cold, always dream of my teacher of scripture, a learned priest of imposing appearance, who insulted my mother when I was a little boy; I dream of vindictive, implacable, intriguing people, smiling with spiteful glee—such as one can never see in waking life. The laughter at the carriage window is a characteristic symptom of Karelin's nightmare. When in dreams one feels the presence of some evil will, the inevitable ruin brought about by some outside force, one always hears something like such laughter. . . . One dreams of people one loves, too, but they generally appear to suffer together with the dreamer.

Chekhov is now sharing something never elsewhere revealed about his personal and domestic life:

But when my body gets accustomed to the cold, or one of my family covers me up, the sensation of cold, of loneliness, and of an oppressive evil will, gradually disappears. . . .

This midwinter, who came in and covered chilly Anton? Mama? Maria? Mikhail?

> With the returning warmth I begin to feel that I walk on soft carpets or on grass, I see sunshine, women, children. . . . The pictures change gradually, but more rapidly than they do in waking life, so that on awaking it is difficult to remember the transitions from one scene to another.

He was laying bare the kinds of particular experiences he only usually described in fiction. Chekhov did not often describe his personal experiences in his letters with the precision that he used in the fiction.

Having ventured far into a critical discussion of Grigorovich's story, he returned to humble mode:

> Forgive me, I so like your story that I am ready to write you a dozen sheets, though I know I can tell you nothing new or good. . . . I restrain myself and am silent, fearing to bore you and to say something silly. I will say once more that your story is magnificent. [. . .] Hard as I tried I could detect only two small blots, even those are rather farfetched! (1) the characteristics of the people interrupt the picture of the dream and give the impression of explanation notes, which in gardens botanists nail on trees and spoil the scenery;[10] (2) at the beginning of the story the feeling of cold is soon blunted in the reader and becomes too usual, owing to the frequent repetition of the word "cold."
>
> There is nothing else I could find, and I feel that as one is always feeling the need of refreshing models, "Karelin's Dream" is a splendid event in my existence as an author.

There is more feeling of apology in that sentence than praise. It's as if the more Chekhov looked and wrote about the story, the less satisfactory it became.

In further apology and to assure Grigorovich that he was not asserting any superiority of artistic judgment, Chekhov defamed himself:

> There is little good I can say about myself. I write not what I want to be writing, and I have not enough energy or solitude to write as you advised me. . . . There are many good subjects jostling in my head—and that is all. I am sustained by hopes of the future, and watch the present slip fruitlessly away.
>
> Forgive this long letter, and accept the sincere good wishes of your devoted [signature]

Chekhov, the greater artist by a mile and a half, could only defer to Grigorovich on the basis of age and prestige. He would eventually resent the crouching that he was expected to do. Two years later he would write to Suvorin: "I am very fond of Grigorovich, but I do not believe that he really is anxious about me. He is a tendentious writer himself and only pretends to be an enemy of tendentiousness. I can't help thinking that he is terrified of losing the respect of people he likes, hence his quite amazing insincerity."[11] The biographer David Magarshack notes that "Chekhov never really regarded Grigorovich as a major writer, and as time passed he got tired of being lectured by him. He certainly never accepted the generally held view that Grigorovich had 'discovered' him."[12]

Grigorovich's reply to this letter suggests he may well have been offended: "You praise particularly that which I least of all thought about when I wrote." He continued, however, very interestingly: "A true portrayal of the process of dreaming as such and its impressions occupied me incomparably less than the idea of giving the outward and social picture of a certain milieu in Petersburg [. . .] In our profession, is it not, however, often the case that that about which one bothers comes out weakest of all, while that which has been sung unconsciously, like a bird sings, comes off best? You must have experienced this yourself more than once."[13]

A month later, Chekhov would visit Grigorovich in Petersburg, when it seemed Grigorovich might be on his deathbed. And then, this very summer, Chekhov emphatically dedicated his first book of "serious" stories to him.

———〜———

On the evening of February 15, after a gathering with Schechtel and Nikolay at home, Chekhov and Lazarev went to vespers at the church of Christ the Savior, where, according to Lazarev, they heard miraculous singers. A couple of weeks later, Lazarev wrote Ezhov about their mentor's habits and writing routine:

> He has few acquaintances, he goes rarely to the theater, and constantly writes, writes, and writes! There's not a day when he doesn't write or continue writing something. Now he's so proficient that he writes the *Fragments* stories *straight on white* and without errors. I saw it myself. Every time when I've gone to see him I've found him at work, every time without exception. This Chekhov is a great talent. Little reading (he doesn't read magazines constantly, but occasionally glances at them), that is, the little reading replenishes him with enormous observations and talent, and then perseverance. (We think about

them—Chekhov and Palmin—with envy, but they work so terribly much, ten times more than we do.) His family (father, mother, sister and, it seems, student-brother) are on his hands. He says that if for a month he didn't hold a pen in his hand, he would be bankrupt, a person destroyed by poverty. [. . .] He also hardly reads *Fragments*. He doesn't read Leykin, and it seems not even his brother does, either. "You, I read," he told me [. . .] as his alternate at *Fragments*. "You should work, become my replacement. I'm not going to work for long!" [. . .] He complained that new forces in humor are not appearing, though of course there are talented ones.[14]

The same day, Chekhov heard from his friend Bilibin, Leykin's sub-editor, who, unlike Lazarev, wasn't impressed at all, telling Chekhov that his pieces in *Fragments* were "unworthy of him." Was this a general assessment? Chekhov hadn't published anything in *Fragments* in weeks, ever since "The Good German." A new story, "An Inadvertence," had been at the *Fragments* office since February 10 but would not come out until February 21, and then Bilibin and Leykin would praise it.

Anton, impatient with his brother Alexander's reticence, goaded him in a letter on the 19th or 20th: "How come you don't describe your work? How do you spend your time in the evenings in the [*New Times*] editorial office?" On the 21st Alexander was happy to oblige, explaining, in the third person, that "From one in the afternoon to five he translates foreign newspapers, helps set up the issue, reads through the correspondents' mail and plans the chronicle. At five he goes home to eat and, having quickly eaten, leaves home at 7 in order not to be late for various groups' meetings, the reports of which he is charged with. From the meetings he goes again to the editorial office (making sometimes ten-page finishes), writes a report and until three in the morning makes corrections, revisions, and sorts and lays out the issue. At four in the morning, sometimes later, he returns home."[15] Anton replied a few days later that Alexander's salary was too small and that he should ask Suvorin for more money.

"An Inadvertence" ("Neostorojhnost'," February 21) is a perfect farce, which Bilibin, Leykin, and Tolstoy would praise and enjoy. A man comes home quite drunk from a christening and drinks, by accident, a squirreled away bottle of his sister-in-law's paraffin, which she berates him for while he is the midst of believing that he's going to die.

His *New Times* story this month (February 21) was "Verochka," about a shy twenty-nine-year-old researcher, Ivan Alexeich Ognev: "Having been in the N—District from the early spring, and having been almost every day at the friendly Kuznetsovs', Ivan Alexeich had become as much at home with the old man, his daughter [Verochka], and the servants as though they were his own people; he had grown familiar with the whole house to the smallest detail, with the cozy verandah, the windings of the avenues, the silhouettes of the trees over the kitchen and the bath-house; but as soon as he was out of the gate all this would be changed to memory and would lose its meaning as reality for ever, and in a year or two all these dear images would grow as dim in his consciousness as stories he had read or things he had imagined."[16]

Do we learn something from this next passage, seemingly personally related by the otherwise inconspicuous narrator, about feminine aspects that particularly attracted Chekhov?

> Girls who are dreamy and spend whole days lying down, lazily reading whatever they come across, who are bored and melancholy, are usually careless in their dress. To those of them who have been endowed by nature with taste and an instinct of beauty, the slight carelessness adds a special charm. When Ognev later on remembered her, he could not picture pretty Verochka except in a full blouse which was crumpled in deep folds at the belt and yet did not touch her waist; without her hair done up high and a curl that had come loose from it on her forehead; without the knitted red shawl with ball fringe at the edge which hung disconsolately on Vera's shoulders in the evenings, like a flag on a windless day, and in the daytime lay about, crushed up, in the hall near the men's hats or on a box in the dining-room, where the old cat did not hesitate to sleep on it. This shawl and the folds of her blouse suggested a feeling of freedom and laziness, of good-nature and sitting at home. Perhaps because Vera attracted Ognev he saw in every frill and button something warm, naïve, cozy, something nice and poetical, just what is lacking in cold, insincere women that have no instinct for beauty.

I think we are hearing Chekhov's opinion here, not just Ognev's naïve, unconscious perceptions.

Who those "cold, insincere women" Chekhov had in mind, however, is a mystery.

Ognev is not in love with the sweet provincial Kuznetsov daughter, who is in love with him and who, at his imminent departure, declares herself.

> "I . . . love you!"
>
> These words, so simple and ordinary, were uttered in ordinary human language, but Ognev, in acute embarrassment, turned away from Vera, and got up, while his confusion was followed by terror.

[. . .]

Telling him of her love, Vera was enchantingly beautiful; she spoke eloquently and passionately, but he felt neither pleasure nor gladness, as he would
have liked to; he felt nothing but compassion for Vera, pity and regret that
a good girl should be distressed on his account. Whether he was affected by
generalizations from reading or by the insuperable habit of looking at things
objectively, which so often hinders people from living, but Vera's ecstasies and
suffering struck him as affected, not to be taken seriously, and at the same time
rebellious feeling whispered to him that all he was hearing and seeing now,
from the point of view of nature and personal happiness, was more important
than any statistics and books and truths. . . . And he raged and blamed himself,
though he did not understand exactly where he was in fault.

After second thoughts, objective Ognev almost decides to marry her:

He looked for Vera's footprints on the road, and could not believe that the
girl who had so attracted him had just declared her love, and that he had so
clumsily and bluntly "refused" her. For the first time in his life it was his lot
to learn by experience how little that a man does depends on his own will,
and to suffer in his own person the feelings of a decent kindly man who has
against his will caused his neighbor cruel, undeserved anguish.

Chekhov knew how love stories usually go. His brother-in-detachment Ognev also
knows. And even if it's not the ultimate love story, the absolutely mutually satisfying love
story it should be, isn't *almost* enough enough?

His conscience tormented him, and when Vera disappeared he felt as though
he had lost something very precious, something very near and dear which he
could never find again. He felt that with Vera a part of his youth had slipped
away from him, and that the moments which he had passed through so fruit-
lessly would never be repeated.

Chekhov then suddenly gives us the present tense; for Ognev this story has long ended:
"And Ivan Alexeich remembers that he went back again." What he remembers only brings
him more shame: that is, he remembers that he walked around the outside of her house
and then retreated.

That might be our metaphor for Chekhov's relationship with Dunya Efros.

⌇

Chekhov was dependable for providing periodicals with Lent stories. In "Shrove Tuesday" ("Nakanune Posta," February 25), the last day before Lent, a family, having shared the last non-Lenten meal, is tired, stuffed, but the mother tells the father to go tutor their frustrated son, who has to prepare for the next day's lessons.

> "Are you working?" asks Pavel Vassilich, sitting down to the table and yawning. "Yes, my boy. . . . We have enjoyed ourselves, slept, and eaten pancakes, and tomorrow comes Lenten fare, repentance, and going to work. Every period of time has its limits. Why are your eyes so red? Are you sick of learning your lessons? To be sure, after pancakes, lessons are nasty to swallow. That's about it."

Because it's the last night before Lent, "Faces and gestures betray the sloth and repletion that comes when the stomach is full, and yet one must go on eating." The story concludes: "No one is hungry, everyone's stomach is overfull, but yet they must eat."

For Chekhov, Shrove Tuesday was a comic holiday.

How did the Chekhov family celebrate it? There is nothing in the chronicle of his life that indicates a special get-together, but the stories last year and this suggest they were a happily satiated time in the Chekhov household.

⌇

Chekhov wrote Leykin a casual, wandering letter on February 25, as he had responsibly sent *Fragments* "A Defenseless Creature" ("Bezzashchitnoe Sushchestvo") the day before for the next issue (February 28). He asked about *Motley Stories*. "How's my book doing?"[17] He mentioned that at the end of March he would be going south, alone, for a month. He was being hopeful, as he did not have the funds to do so and didn't know how he would get them.

A couple of days later, Leykin replied that as for *Motley Stories*, nobody's books were selling except the Pushkin edition by Suvorin. He suggested that Chekhov get Suvorin to publicize the book in *New Times*.

On February 27, Leykin wrote Chekhov about his previous story for *Fragments*, "An Inadvertence," which was "superb," but that "Verochka" (in *New Times*) was "an unsuccessful little thing." (Alexander, in Petersburg with Leykin, wrote to say "Verochka" was being praised.)[18] "Your *short* stories succeed better," Leykin wrote, by which he meant the very short ones for *Fragments* and the *Petersburg Gazette*. "I'm not the only one saying this. . . . On Tuesday I was at Mikhnevich's [. . .] and there were many writing brothers there, and a conversation came up about you, and they all said the same."[19]

Leykin was apparently sincerely baffled by Chekhov's success as a "serious" writer. "In subsequent years, with the spread of Chekhov's fame, note Heim and Karlinsky, Leykin repeatedly claimed to have been the first to discern his talent. But, as his published diaries demonstrate, he was actually incapable of appreciating Chekhov's mature work and, like many Russians in his day, admired the early humorous sketches [. . .] while being quite baffled by *The Seagull* and 'The Lady with the Dog.'"[20]

Though Chekhov was modest about his talent, he knew he was at least among the first rank of young Russian fiction writers. The writer Vladimir Korolenko was the one peer that Chekhov rated higher than himself. Chekhov did not note the date they met and neither did Korolenko. Writing his memoirs, Korolenko placed the date "at the end of 1886," but "the exact date escapes my memory." Scholars figured out it had to be sometime in February 1887. The two young literary stars, who had already admired each other's work from afar, hit it off. Korolenko recalled: "Thinking back to the first time we met in his living room, I see Chekhov's mother, who always sat by his side."[21]

Chekhov told Korolenko that he wanted to write a play, and, in an interesting lack of nerve, or perhaps simply imagining that having a writing partner would make the task less daunting, "suggested writing it together (in Nizhni Novgorod): 'We will work together. Let's write a play. In four acts. In two weeks.' Korolenko refused: 'No, Anton Pavlovich. I can't chase after you. You'll write a play alone, and you'll come still to Nizhni.'"[22] Korolenko was right, and Chekhov would follow through on his own and in less than two weeks in September would write a four-act play.

March 1887

—〰—

> Noah had three sons: Shem, Ham, and—was it Aphet?
> All Ham could see was that his father was a drunkard;
> he completely disregarded the fact that Noah was a
> genius, that he had built the Ark and saved the world.
> Writers must avoid imitating Ham. Mull that one
> over for a while. [. . .] I do dare remind you of justice,
> which is more precious for an objective writer than air.
>
> —Letter to a young writer[1]

Chekhov believed in nightmares and hallucinations, but not in ghosts. "A Bad Business" ("Nedobroe Delo," March 2) creates as eerie an atmosphere as a nightmare. The story begins:

> "Who goes there?"
>   No answer. The watchman sees nothing, but through the roar of the wind and the trees distinctly hears someone walking along the avenue ahead of him. A March night, cloudy and foggy, envelops the earth, and it seems to the watchman that the earth, the sky, and he himself with his thoughts are all merged together into something vast and impenetrably black. He can only grope his way.[2]

Now that I have read Grigorovich's pseudo-dream story, it occurs to me that this story, though realistic, is more actually dreamlike than Grigorovich's. When I read it a few years ago in Russian, I found myself more deeply spooked than when I was breezing through it in English. It's as if I was groping through the same apprehension as the watchman. Chekhov resorts again to the present tense, which perhaps lends itself to the narration of scary stories:

The watchman stops for a minute to light his pipe. He stoops down behind the traveler's back and lights several matches. The gleam of the first match lights up for one instant a bit of the avenue on the right, a white tombstone with an angel, and a dark cross; the light of the second match, flaring up brightly and extinguished by the wind, flashes like lightning on the left side, and from the darkness nothing stands out but the angle of some sort of trellis; the third match throws light to right and to left, revealing the white tombstone, the dark cross, and the trellis around a child's grave.

The "traveler" is in fact a lookout for a gang of thieves. But while still in the disguise of darkness he is all too candid and truthful:

"Our doings are wicked, our thoughts are deceitful! Sins, sins! My soul accursed, ever covetous, my belly greedy and lustful! I have angered the Lord and there is no salvation for me in this world and the next. I am deep in sins like a worm in the earth."

He is also a wickedly teasing philosopher: "'There are pilgrims of different sorts. There are the real ones who are God-fearing men and watch over their own souls, and there are such as stray about the graveyard at night and are a delight to the devils. . . Ye-es! There's one who is a pilgrim could give you a crack on the pate with an axe if he liked and knock the breath out of you.'"

With that, the watchman has a renewed sense of apprehension. And his apprehension only increases as the one thief holds him to prevent him from raising an alarm while the other thieves ransack the church.

⁓

On March 2, Petya Kravtsov, knowing Chekhov had been under the weather, invited him to stay with his family in the village of Rogozin Ravine, the "best air" to be found in the Crimea and Caucasus.[3] Chekhov had been Petya's tutor in Taganrog when the Chekhov family, fleeing creditors, left him behind and relocated to Moscow in 1876. As a teenager, Chekhov had spent a few summers there in the countryside with Petya's family.

This was yet another reason to go south. But how to pay for it?

⁓

In "Home" ("Doma," March 7), Chekhov seems to elude any attempt by me to link the story to his life. Bykovsky, a weary prosecutor and the recently widowed father of a seven-year-old son, comes home to an annoyed governess; she complains that the boy, Seryozha, has been smoking cigarettes: "'When I began to expostulate with him, he put his fingers in his ears as usual, and sang loudly to drown my voice.'"[4] Yes, Chekhov had been a tutor, but of course he wasn't a lawyer, he was never widowed, and he had no children. But . . . otherwise . . . let's see. Chekhov had once been a child and seemed to understand childhood and children at a psychological depth reached by few writers. Bykovsky is amused by the thought of his little boy smoking, but he realizes he has a responsibility to the governess. The trouble is: he doesn't really know his son, much less children. He is used to thinking about law and its consequences; now he "remembered the head-master of the high school, a very cultured and good-natured old man, who was so appalled when he found a high-school boy with a cigarette in his mouth that he turned pale, immediately summoned an emergency committee of the teachers, and sentenced the sinner to expulsion. This was probably a law of social life: the less an evil was understood, the more fiercely and coarsely it was attacked."

Chekhov was a smoker. It was a "vice," and Chekhov knew he should have avoided it. He was in a period of weighing the benefits versus the drawbacks of punishment. Punish drinkers? He didn't think that worked. Bykovsky, meanwhile, ponders the situation:

> The prosecutor remembered two or three boys who had been expelled and their subsequent life, and could not help thinking that very often the punishment did a great deal more harm than the crime itself. The living organism has the power of rapidly adapting itself, growing accustomed and inured to any atmosphere whatever, otherwise man would be bound to feel at every moment what an irrational basis there often is underlying his rational activity, and how little of established truth and certainty there is even in work so responsible and so terrible in its effects as that of the teacher, of the lawyer, of the writer. . . .

Before he has prepared himself, the governess sends Seryozha to him. He scolds the boy with harsh words but little feeling:

> "I am very, very much displeased with you! You used to be a good boy, but now I see you are spoiled and have become a bad one."
>
> Yevgeny Petrovich smoothed down Seryozha's collar and thought:
>
> "What more am I to say to him!"

"Yes, it's not right," he continued. "I did not expect it of you. In the first place, you ought not to take tobacco that does not belong to you. Every person has only the right to make use of his own property; if he takes anyone else's . . . he is a bad man!" ("I am not saying the right thing!" thought Yevgeny Petrovich.) "For instance, Natalya Semyonovna has a box with her clothes in it. That's her box, and we—that is, you and I—dare not touch it, as it is not ours. That's right, isn't it? You've got toy horses and pictures. . . . I don't take them, do I? Perhaps I might like to take them, but . . . they are not mine, but yours!"

"Take them if you like!" said Seryozha, raising his eyebrows. "Please don't hesitate, papa, take them! That yellow dog on your table is mine, but I don't mind. . . . Let it stay."

The prosecutor realizes he cannot even explain law to his son. But he continues to try, desperately seeking the proper level. He returns to the smoking topic, one perfectly in accord with Chekhov's views:

"Though I smoke it does not follow that you may. I smoke and know that it is stupid, I blame myself and don't like myself for it." ("A clever teacher, I am!" he thought.) "Tobacco is very bad for the health, and anyone who smokes dies earlier than he should. It's particularly bad for boys like you to smoke. Your chest is weak, you haven't reached your full strength yet, and smoking leads to consumption and other illness in weak people. Uncle Ignat died of consumption, you know. If he hadn't smoked, perhaps he would have lived till now."

Seryozha looked pensively at the lamp, touched the lamp-shade with his finger, and heaved a sigh.

"Uncle Ignat played the violin splendidly!" he said. "His violin is at the Grigoryevs' now."

Seryozha leaned his elbows on the edge of the table again, and sank into thought.

True enough about smoking and Chekhov's own consumption (tuberculosis), but the father thinks he has still not connected with Seryozha. But, just as Tolstoy showed the depths of thought and feeling in Anna Karenina's nine-year-old son Seryozha, Chekhov shows us his younger Seryozha's, whose actual thoughts Chekhov insists he can only guess at:

His white face wore a fixed expression, as though he were listening or following a train of thought of his own; distress and something like fear came into his big staring eyes. He was most likely thinking now of death, which had so lately carried off his mother and Uncle Ignat. Death carries mothers and uncles off to the other world, while their children and violins remain upon the earth. The dead live somewhere in the sky beside the stars, and look down from there upon the earth. Can they endure the parting?

Most assuredly, Chekhov describes what the contemplative boy now does, which is draw pictures and chatter:

"Cook was chopping up cabbage today and she cut her finger," he said, drawing a little house and moving his eyebrows. "She gave such a scream that we were all frightened and ran into the kitchen. Stupid thing! Natalya Semyonovna told her to dip her finger in cold water, but she sucked it . . . And how could she put a dirty finger in her mouth! That's not proper, you know, papa!"

Then he went on to describe how, while they were having dinner, a man with a hurdy-gurdy had come into the yard with a little girl, who had danced and sung to the music.

Chekhov puts us not in Seryozha's but in the father's shoes:

"He has his own train of thought!" thought the prosecutor. "He has a little world of his own in his head, and he has his own ideas of what is important and unimportant. To gain possession of his attention, it's not enough to imitate his language, one must also be able to think in the way he does. He would understand me perfectly if I really were sorry for the loss of the tobacco, if I felt injured and cried. . . . That's why no one can take the place of a mother in bringing up a child, because she can feel, cry, and laugh together with the child. One can do nothing by logic and morality. What more shall I say to him? What?"

This story is Bykovsky's reckoning: "'[. . .] in school and in court, of course, all these wretched questions are far more simply settled than at home; here one has to do with people whom one loves beyond everything, and love is exacting and complicates the question. If this boy were not my son, but my pupil, or a prisoner on his trial, I should not be so cowardly, and my thoughts would not be racing all over the place!'"

Is Chekhov offering a "moral of the story," or is this only Bykovsky's? . . . The story is not over. It goes on continuously marvelously and surprisingly. But, I'll answer before proceeding: it *is* Chekhov's moral: "all these wretched questions are far more simply settled than at home." All the hardest questions are easy to answer if they don't actually involve ourselves and our loved ones. This is a theme in one story after another. Chekhov already knew it; Bykovsky is only understanding it at this instant.

In Babkino, Chekhov occasionally made pictures and stories for Maria Kiseleva's children. This child Seryozha's pictures, however, are an artifact of the boy's imagination that puzzle the father:

> Yevgeny Petrovich sat down to the table and pulled one of Seryozha's drawings to him. In it there was a house with a crooked roof, and smoke which came out of the chimney like a flash of lightning in zigzags up to the very edge of the paper; beside the house stood a soldier with dots for eyes and a bayonet that looked like the figure 4.
>
> "A man can't be taller than a house," said the prosecutor.

We don't groan too much over Yevgeny's misplay here; he's a father learning on the job.

> Seryozha got on his knee, and moved about for some time to get comfortably settled there.
>
> "No, papa!" he said, looking at his drawing. "If you were to draw the soldier small you would not see his eyes."

How often our loved ones reveal themselves, and how often instead of appreciating the revelation we strive to get them to cover themselves back up. Papa wonders:

> Ought he to argue with him? From daily observation of his son the prosecutor had become convinced that children, like savages, have their own artistic standpoints and requirements peculiar to them, beyond the grasp of grown-up people.

Chekhov shoulders Papa aside now and opens the floor to the rest of us:

> Had he been attentively observed, Seryozha might have struck a grown-up person as abnormal. He thought it possible and reasonable to draw men taller than houses, and to represent in pencil, not only objects, but even his

sensations. Thus he would depict the sounds of an orchestra in the form of smoke like spherical blurs, a whistle in the form of a spiral thread. . . . To his mind sound was closely connected with form and color, so that when he painted letters he invariably painted the letter L yellow, M red, A black, and so on.

Papa hasn't "attentively observed" Seryozha. But someone like Chekhov, our scientist-writer, has. *He* noticed those amazing depictions, described as synesthesia, one manifestation of which is associating sounds to numbers or letters or particular colors.

Papa is puzzled, in new territory as a parent. The next moment is as intimate as he might have ever been with his son:

The prosecutor felt the child's breathing on his face, he was continually touching his hair with his cheek, and there was a warm soft feeling in his soul, as soft as though not only his hands but his whole soul were lying on the velvet of Seryozha's jacket.

He looked at the boy's big dark eyes, and it seemed to him as though from those wide pupils there looked out at him his mother and his wife and everything that he had ever loved.

And still this remarkable, heartbreaking story is not over. Chekhov's genius renews and renews. After the prosecutor repents to himself over having thought of punishing the boy, he means to send the boy to bed, but Seryozha objects, insisting on a story.

And here in the final two pages of "Home," following Papa's random, rambling improvisation, we might learn more about how Chekhov wrote his stories than from his claim to Korolenko that he could create a new story from the most random item, an ashtray:[5]

Yevgeny Petrovich on his free evenings was in the habit of telling Seryozha stories. Like most people engaged in practical affairs, he did not know a single poem by heart, and could not remember a single fairy tale, so he had to improvise. As a rule he began with the stereotyped: "In a certain country, in a certain kingdom," then he heaped up all kinds of innocent nonsense and had no notion as he told the beginning how the story would go on, and how it would end. Scenes, characters, and situations were taken at random, impromptu, and the plot and the moral came of itself as it were, with no plan on the part of the storyteller.

Had Chekhov "planned" this very story he was writing? I don't think so, though he scarcely changed a word of it in its many republishings. I think he discovered depths in "Home" as he composed it. He had written to Alexander on February 22 or 23 that the story was "very 'clever' (*vumniy*[6]) but not very smart." It's clever all right:

> Seryozha was very fond of this improvisation, and the prosecutor noticed that the simpler and the less ingenious the plot, the stronger the impression it made on the child.

Chekhov had noticed this, too.

> "Listen," he said, raising his eyes to the ceiling. "Once upon a time, in a certain country, in a certain kingdom, there lived an old, very old emperor with a long gray beard, and . . . and with great gray moustaches like this. Well, he lived in a glass palace which sparkled and glittered in the sun, like a great piece of clear ice. The palace, my boy, stood in a huge garden, in which there grew oranges, you know . . . bergamots, cherries . . . tulips, roses, and lilies-of-the-valley were in flower in it, and birds of different colors sang there. . . . Yes. . . . On the trees there hung little glass bells, and, when the wind blew, they rang so sweetly that one was never tired of hearing them. Glass gives a softer, tenderer note than metals. . . . Well, what next? There were fountains in the garden. . . . Do you remember you saw a fountain at Auntie Sonya's summer villa? Well, there were fountains just like that in the emperor's garden, only ever so much bigger, and the jets of water reached to the top of the highest poplar."

What's happened for Papa and I believe what happened hundreds and hundreds of times for Chekhov is that he conjured up for himself one flash after another of connections and associations. Not fancy, but clear, visual connections between the imagination and memory. Like dreams.

> Yevgeny Petrovich thought a moment, and went on:
> "The old emperor had an only son and heir of his kingdom—a boy as little as you. He was a good boy. He was never naughty, he went to bed early, he never touched anything on the table, and altogether he was a sensible boy. He had only one fault, he used to smoke. . . ."

Seryozha listened attentively, and looked into his father's eyes without
blinking.

The prosecutor went on, thinking: "What next?"

I think Papa, having noticed Seryozha's raptness, experiences a moment of self-
consciousness. Now how does he end this nonsense? Like other stymied storytellers, he
decides death is a fitting conclusion:

He spun out a long rigmarole, and ended like this:

"The emperor's son fell ill with consumption through smoking, and died when
he was twenty. His infirm and sick old father was left without anyone to help him.
There was no one to govern the kingdom and defend the palace. Enemies came,
killed the old man, and destroyed the palace, and now there are neither cherries,
nor birds, nor little bells in the garden. . . . That's what happened."

This ending struck Yevgeny Petrovich as absurd and naïve, but the whole
story made an intense impression on Seryozha. Again his eyes were clouded
by mournfulness and something like fear; for a minute he looked pensively at
the dark window, shuddered, and said, in a sinking voice:

"I am not going to smoke any more. . . ."

When he had said good-night and gone away his father walked up and
down the room and smiled to himself.

"They would tell me it was the influence of beauty, artistic form," he meditated.
"It may be so, but that's no comfort. It's not the right way, all the same. . . . Why
must morality and truth never be offered in their crude form, but only with embel-
lishments, sweetened and gilded like pills? It's not normal. . . . It's falsification . . .
deception . . . tricks . . . ."

He thought of the jurymen to whom it was absolutely necessary to make
a "speech," of the general public who absorb history only from legends and
historical novels, and of himself and how he had gathered an understanding
of life not from sermons and laws, but from fables, novels, poems.

"Medicine should be sweet, truth beautiful, and man has had this foolish
habit since the days of Adam . . . though, indeed, perhaps it is all natural,
and ought to be so. . . . There are many deceptions and delusions in nature
that serve a purpose."

Amen.

On March 8, Chekhov got on the train to St. Petersburg to see his brother Alexander and his publisher Suvorin. Alexander had beckoned him there via telegram to treat him for typhus, his presumed "dangerous illness." Chekhov's consolation was reading *Anna Karenina* on the unusually long, slow, crowded ride north, arriving on March 9.

Petersburg was in the midst of a typhus epidemic, and once Chekhov arrived at his brother's, he discovered that Alexander was symptomless but that his wife Anna had typhus. Petersburg gave Chekhov the impression of being "a city of death." After spending the first night in Alexander's crowded apartment, Chekhov accepted a medical colleague's invitation to stay at his house.

Besides fear of typhus, money worries were more than usual preying on Chekhov, and his next three stories were about characters desperately seeking money. "The Lottery Ticket" ("Viigrishniy Bilet," March 9) is a trick story. The first sentence provides the conventional fiction setup information:

> Ivan Dmitrich, a middle-class man who lived with his family on an income
> of twelve hundred a year and was very well satisfied with his lot, sat down on
> the sofa after supper and began reading the newspaper.[7]

A real story by Chekhov seems alive, because, as in "Home," it was alive as he created it. He didn't have to be alert to work through "The Lottery Ticket." He could've handed off the idea to Alexander or any of his mentees and have had them do it. As soon as Ivan and his wife Masha start daydreaming about winning the lottery on the ticket Masha holds, they begin hating each other with a passion they haven't until now realized: "And he looked at his wife, not with a smile now, but with hatred. She glanced at him, too, and also with hatred and anger. She had her own daydreams, her own plans, her own reflections; she understood perfectly well what her husband's dreams were. She knew who would be the first to try to grab her winnings." The ticket doesn't win, however, but the couple maintains their newfound hatred.

The next story, "Too Early!" ("Rano!" March 16), is slight, but Chekhov was imaginatively engaged in picturing it to himself, daydreaming himself out of the city. The present tense in this story allows Chekhov to paint the setting's picture as his painter-friends might have:

> In Semyon's pothouse [. . .] two peasant sportsmen are sitting. One of them
> is called Filimon Slyunka; he is an old man of sixty, formerly a house-serf,

belonging to the Counts Zavalin, by trade a carpenter. He has at one time been employed in a nail factory, has been turned off for drunkenness and idleness, and now lives upon his old wife, who begs for alms. He is thin and weak, with a mangy-looking little beard, speaks with a hissing sound, and after every word twitches the right side of his face and jerkily shrugs his right shoulder. The other, Ignat Ryabov, a sturdy, broad-shouldered peasant who never does anything and is everlastingly silent, is sitting in the corner under a big string of bread rings. The door, opening inward, throws a thick shadow upon him, so that Slyunka and Semyon the publican can see nothing but his patched knees, his long fleshy nose, and a big tuft of hair which has escaped from the thick uncombed tangle covering his head. Semyon, a sickly little man, with a pale face and a long sinewy neck, stands behind his counter, looks mournfully at the string of bread rings, and coughs meekly.

The two idlers, who "haven't got a ruble," try to badger Semyon to give them back the gun that Slyunka pawned with him so they can hunt birds. He refuses and they grumble and wander outside into the muddy winter. They, like Chekhov, see signs of spring. The author conjures up a beautiful scene for them and himself: "The sun has set and left behind it a red streak like the glow of a fire, scattered here and there with clouds; there is no catching the colors of those clouds: their edges are red, but they themselves are one minute gray, at the next lilac, at the next ashen." Slyunka and Ryabov wouldn't have needed the gun anyway; it's "too early!" for snipe.

—·—

On the 10th, Chekhov dined with Leykin and then went to see the printer Golike. From a hotel room he wrote home: "Alexander is in fact perfectly well. All that had happened was that he imagined he was ill, became depressed and frightened, and that's why he sent that telegram. Anna Ivanovna actually does have typhoid fever, but not very severely. I consulted with the other doctor. We agreed to treat her according to my regime. [. . .] The typhoid fever that is raging throughout Petersburg at the moment is a particularly virulent form. The commissionaire at Leykin's offices, a tall, thin old man whom you may remember, Masha, died of it yesterday."[8]

On March 11, he treated for tuberculosis the dying mother of an office worker at *Fragments*. He was "hanging between the heavens and earth," he wrote to his sister Maria on the 11th or early on the 12th. He was sending her ten rubles but asked her to spend as little as possible. He didn't know yet when he was coming back, but probably by the 15th. Alexander, he reported, was well but low-spirited. He tossed in a greeting, of sorts, to Dunya, "Homage to the Nose with Efros,"[9] and Maria's friend Yashenka.

In the next day or two, almost as anxious at the moment about money as about typhus, he wrote his friend Schechtel, who had connections with the railroad, telling him he just had to go south, and could Schechtel get him a free round-trip ticket to Taganrog?[10] "Everywhere I am made much of, but no one has the bright idea of handing me one or two thousand rubles."[11] He didn't ask Schechtel for a loan but mentioned: "Right now I am sitting in the boring hotel room about to make a clean copy of a finished story." The editors of the Soviet edition of the letters say that "probably" that story was "Too Early!" which would be published in the *Petersburg Gazette* on the 16th. "An Encounter" would come out on the 18th in *New Times*.

Both "Early!" and "An Encounter" are about needing money; this letter is about needing money. Because he didn't ask Schechtel for a loan, that means, I think, he might have been expecting that Suvorin would give him the loan or advance on the night of the 12th. Chekhov could have written "Too Early!" in one sitting; it's short, simple, uninvolving. Probably Chekhov was rewriting "An Encounter." Garnett did not translate "An Encounter," so I found the story in the Russian edition, which includes a reproduction of a manuscript draft page of the first page of the story (there are very few handwritten manuscripts of Chekhov's creative work). The page has a lot of cross-outs. There are a great number of differences between the manuscript and the published copy. So it must have been "An Encounter" that he was making "a clean copy of"; otherwise, why would he revise a completely finished story? Most likely the draft, which, unusually, survived, is the first draft, and the published story is the second draft. He was already in Petersburg and he could have walked the second draft to the office, greeted his weary but mostly well brother, handed him the story, and *New Times* printed it from that.

Let's imagine encountering the fresh final draft of "An Encounter" (March 18), one of his best stories so far this year, a few days ahead of the date of publication, and definitely in the week of its writing.[12] I imagine Chekhov, pen in hand, deadline looming, financial needs pressing, anxiously looking around: "Yefrem Denisov anxiously looked around." First sentence, *done*. Chekhov was thirsty, he was achy: "He was tormented by thirst and he ached all over."

In the third sentence, Chekhov mentions the hero's horse, who is also suffering. "His horse, who had not eaten for a long time and was miserable with the heat, drooped his head sadly."

As I imagine Chekhov imagining this story, there's the hero, Yefrem Denisov, but the other living creature also has to live. This characterization of the horse is not how Tolstoy would do it, but Tolstoy would also do it. Chekhov characteristically sees and feels his way into a scene.

He concludes the first paragraph: "The forest, a green monster, climbed up a terraced hill, and seemed endless." This is so simple, so childlike a perception, but to notice such things, to feel the vitality of the world, is a childlike and artistic perspective.

And now the explanation of the situation, after the scene-setting: "Yefrem was traveling about to collect money for the building of a church to replace the one that had burned down in his native village in the province of Kursk." Chekhov further and clearly explains Yefrem's humble quest, and then his naturally despairing feeling: "Yefrem did not know where he was, and the forest, which swallowed the road, held out no promise of a settlement nearby."

Chekhov describes the woods and the smell of the air.

Did he naturally turn on all his senses as he wrote? He suggested, in a letter the following winter, that taking in the smell of an imagined scene was what he strove to do: "I am writing a steppe story. I am writing, but I don't get the smell of hay . . ."[13] He was like a hungry hunter entering and proceeding through an alien forest. All his senses were up and attentive in expectation and wariness.

This is when the crook suddenly appears, voice first. Yefrem has been looking, seemingly, with attention into the woods. Someone addressing a passing stranger without first making himself seen means he is someone to be leery of.

Now Yefrem takes him in: "Close to the road, his head propped on an ant-hill, lay a lanky peasant of about thirty wearing a cotton shirt and tight citified trousers tucked into reddish boots. Near his head was a cap that went with some uniform, now so faded that its original color could only be guessed from the spot that had once flaunted a cockade."

Yefrem makes conversation, addressing the odd-faced stranger as "Fellow Christian," and asking how far to the next village. Though the stranger may have served in the military, he speaks uneducatedly: "'Not so far. Maloye ain't no more'n three or four miles from here.'"

They exchange names. The crook is Kuzma. We don't yet know he's a crook, but one of his first questions makes one suspicious: "'You're collecting for a church?'"

And when Yefrem explains that the church burned down, Kuzma says exactly the thing to put anyone on the alert: "'How did that happen?'"

Yefrem tells the unhappy but fateful story.

"Kuzma strode alongside and listened. He was sober"—This is, I assume, Yefrem's steady, clear-eyed perception of Kuzma and not Chekhov telling us from narrative omniscience. A drunk man is one kind of a menace, a sober man another. Anyway,

> He was sober, but he walked as though he were drunk, waving his arms and tramping now beside the cart, now in front of it . . .
> "And what do *you* get out of it? They pay you wages?" he asked.
> "What wages? I am traveling for the salvation of my soul, the community sent me . . ."
> "So you're traveling for nothing?"
> "Who's to pay me wages? The community sent me, you know—they'll harvest my crops, sow the rye, pay the taxes for me . . . So it's not for nothing!"
> "And how do you eat?"
> "I beg my bread."

Yefrem grows leerier. He is surprised that Kuzma has no immediate appreciation of the idea of someone going out into the world to serve his community.

> And Kuzma inquired further, what would happen to the horse and the money if Yefrem himself died, where would people put their contributions if the box were suddenly filled, and what if the bottom of the box fell out, and so on.

Does Kuzma purposefully give himself away? Or is he, as suggested by the epigraph, just a "savage predatory animal"?

> Yefrem, getting no chance to answer all these questions, merely panted and stared at his fellow traveler in wonder.

Yefrem and Kuzma spend the night in the village, where Kuzma has chatted up the locals, and in the morning the old man sees that the money is gone. Kuzma returns to their shared quarters and feigns outrage when Yefrem accuses him. Yefrem, perhaps from having dealt with such criminals before, says, "Fine, then you didn't steal it."

Kuzma can't stand that Yefrem accepts his denial. He pesters Yefrem as they go on their way. But Yefrem won't rise to the bait and Kuzma angrily throws the remaining money at him and says it was all a joke. He explains away the missing money and excuses

himself for it. Then, guiltily, Kuzma asks how he can make up for it, and Yefrem tells him
to go back and confess to the priest, and then send the money when he has it to Yefrem's
village for the church. Kuzma seems to enjoy the thought of having an opportunity to
make up for his theft, but as soon as they get to the next village, he is completely himself
again, a charismatic lying cheat.

In 1899, a dozen years after composing "An Encounter," having passed it over for
inclusion in any of his collections, Chekhov remembered the story and considered it
for the collected edition, but he decided not to try to revise it. Even shortly after it was
published this month, he said he didn't like it.

How can I disagree so often with Chekhov's assessments of his stories? Lazarev wrote
to Ezhov that Chekhov thought the story "Home" was "bad. It stretches out (too much)."
As for "An Encounter," which Lazarev called (rightly) "a beautiful story," he confided to
his pal that "Chekhov doesn't like it, that is, partly and correctly in that he doesn't and I
don't like the moral attached to the end. That ought not to be. A moral ought not to be
'expressed,' but if it's there ought to be unnoticed."[14]

The story ends:

> At noon, when the cart stopped at Telibeyevo, Kuzma disappeared in the pot-
> house. Yefrem rested for about two hours and all that time Kuzma stayed in the
> pot-house. One could hear him swearing in there and bragging, pounding
> the bar with his fist, and the drunken peasants jeering at him. And when Yefrem
> was leaving Telibeyevo, a brawl had started in the pot-house, and Kuzma was
> shrilly threatening someone and shouting that he would send for the police.

The moral is . . . don't start fights in Telibeyevo bars? I and readers of the *Collected
Works* must not be seeing the moral ending Lazarev and Chekhov saw.[15]

———

What seems to have completely sealed Chekhov's devotion to Suvorin was spending
several hours with him on the evening of March 12. Suvorin asked him to put together a
collection of his *New Times* stories for publication as a book. The rich, fond, and generous
editor gave Chekhov an advance on his pay for his continued contributions to *New Times*,
so that Chekhov could definitely make his long-desired spring trip to Taganrog.

Chekhov wrote home again on the 13th. Money problems solved, he had a whole
new mood:

I'm hereby informing you that I'm alive and well and I haven't contracted typhus. At first I was depressed, as I was bored and feared an impoverished future, but now I feel positive and in character. Surprises rain on my head: 1) the whole time it's been spring weather, and only being without a coat has prevented me from wandering about, 2) everywhere I'm greeted here with open arms, 3) Suvorin, speaking like a Jew, loaned me money (a secret: 300 rubles) and asked me to send him material for a book edition of my *New Times* stories. The book will be published by the summer, under conditions quite beneficial for me. And so on. [. . .] I'm going to the south on the 31st or earlier.[16]

On the 14th, Chekhov visited Grigorovich, who seemed to him to be dying: "The old man kissed me on the forehead, hugged me, began crying [. . .]" Chekhov sat by the writer's bedside for two and a half hours and found himself "cursing the whole time my worthless medicine." He only left when Grigorovich's own doctor arrived.[17]

Chekhov departed for Moscow the next day.

Between the train ride home from Petersburg and the 18th, Chekhov selected and edited sixteen of his *New Times* stories[18] for the collection that Suvorin had just solicited. Quick and efficient, Chekhov suggested the format and layout that he had seen in Suvorin's edition of Edgar Allan Poe, whose stories had become popular in literary Russia. Unlike Poe, Chekhov couldn't think up a good title, so he suggested "My Stories" or "Stories."[19] Alexander, now in good standing with Suvorin, would be the supervising editor. There were eventually nineteen stories in this collection, *In the Twilight*; it included three stories from the *Petersburg Gazette*.[20]

On March 17, safe and sound in Moscow, Chekhov wrote to Maria Kiseleva about his trip. He had talked to a textbook publisher in Petersburg about her children's book, which he now encouraged her to publish as soon as possible. As for himself, he had received that "big advance" from Suvorin. Chekhov, not one to crow, actually crowed: "Petersburg recognizes only one writer right now: me!"[21]

He told her also, on the other hand: "I went there with a frightened imagination; on the way, I encountered two coffins." Death was everywhere he went. He saw children dying in agony from croup. Dispirited, he remarked, "True, one could start drinking. However, they say everything is usable in belle lettres." Indeed. By March 21, Chekhov had finished the 1,850-word "Typhus" and sent it to the *Petersburg Gazette,* where it was published on March 23. Several years later, he would tell Yelena Shavrova, one of his young writing mentees, "For myself, I stand by the following rule: I write about sickness only when it forms part of the characters or adds color to them. I am afraid of frightening people with diseases."[22]

It seems that Chekhov was able to communicate all the reasons anyone could have to be sensibly frightened of typhus. I began translating "Typhus" ("Tif") at the start of the COVID-19 pandemic.[23] Sentence 1: "Young Lieutenant Klimov was riding in the smoking car on the post train from Petersburg to Moscow." Chekhov had just been on this train. Klimov is coming down with typhus but doesn't realize it. He becomes cranky and discombobulated. A fellow passenger, an old man, a "foreigner," smokes a stinky pipe. Klimov "daydreamed about how good it would be to rip the raspy pipe from his hand, toss it under the stuffed seat, and drive the Finn away into another car. 'Disgusting people these Finns . . . and Greeks!' he thought. 'Absolutely worthless, good for nothing, rotten people, they're only taking up space on the planet. What use are they?'"

> And the thought of Finns and Greeks produced something like nausea throughout his entire body. For comparison, he wanted to think about the French and Italians, but the memory of those people somehow only evoked images of organ-grinders, naked women, and the foreign oleographs that hung over the dresser at his aunt's house.

Chekhov reminds us that such reflexive Dostoevskian prejudices say nothing about Finns, Greeks, the French, or Italians. Expressed prejudices such as these by Klimov are signs of weakness and confusion. They're ranklings inspired by weariness and sickness:

> The officer didn't feel right at all. His arms and legs somehow didn't fit on the seat, despite the whole seat being available; his mouth was dry and sticky, and his head was filled with a heavy fog. His thoughts, it seemed, roamed not only through his mind but out beyond his skull, among the seats and the people shrouded in the nighttime haze. Through his head-sludge, as if it were in a dream, he heard a murmur of voices, the knocking of wheels, the clomping of doors. Bells, the conductor's whistling, passengers rushing along the platform, resounded more often than usual. Time passed swiftly, unnoticeably, and so it

seemed as if the train was stopping at a new station every minute, and metallic voices floated into the carriage.

Chekhov gives us such a keen, fine description of physical discomfort and mental derangement. Upon arrival in Moscow, Klimov makes his way home to the apartment that he shares with his aunt and younger sister, who is studying to become a teacher, just as Maria Chekhova was.

When Katya greeted him, she had in her hands a notebook and a pencil, and he recalled that she was preparing for her teacher's exam. Not answering their questions or greetings, only gasping from the heat, he aimlessly passed through all the rooms and, reaching his bed, fell onto his pillow. The Finn, the red coat, the woman with the white teeth, the stink of the frying meat, and the blinking spots occupied his consciousness, and he didn't know where he was, and he didn't hear the excited voices.

Chekhov knew the long train ride and the tedium firsthand; he knew the various illnesses from medical literature and practice.

Awakening, he saw he was in his bed, undressed; he saw the carafe with the water and Pavel, but none of this made him either cooler, more relaxed, or more comfortable. As before, his legs and arms would not settle down. His tongue stuck to the roof of his mouth, and he heard the sobbing of the Finn's pipe. Near the bed, a black-bearded doctor was fussing about and bumping Pavel with his broad back.

He has a bad few days. "As in the train, at home time flew by astoundingly fast. . . In the bedroom, daylight every now and then turned into dusk."
Finally:

When Klimov awoke from oblivion, there was not a soul in his bedroom. The morning sun slid through the window beneath the lowered curtain, and a trembling ray of light, thin and airy like a blade, played on the carafe. There was the clatter of wheels—this meant there was no longer snow outside. The lieutenant looked at the light, the familiar furniture, at the door, and the first thing he did was laugh. His chest and belly shook with tickling laughter from the sweetness, the happiness. His whole being, from his head to his toes, was overpowered by unlimited happiness and joy of life, which probably the first human felt when he became conscious and saw the world.

Unfortunately, his typhus infected his sister and she has died. How often had Chekhov witnessed such tragedies? Every time he saw Yanova, her family's tragedy, which he as the fussing doctor had not been able to prevent, would have come to mind.

The infector survives his family:

> Only a week later, when he was in his robe and supported by Pavel, and when he went to the window and looked out at the cloudy spring sky and was hearing the unpleasant banging of the old railway that ran past, did his heart seize up from pain; he began to cry and he leaned his forehead on the window-frame.
>
> "How unhappy I am!" he moaned. "God, how unhappy!"
>
> And joy gave way to mundane tedium and the feeling of irreversible loss.

———

With a happier and healthier family in Moscow than poor Klimov's, Chekhov wrote warmly to Suvorin on March 18 to update him on Grigorovich's health. Striking while the iron was hot, he was sending a list of sixteen stories for the book that Suvorin would publish this summer; meanwhile, he said, he would be trying to write the Easter story to send soon.

Anton followed up in a letter to Alexander on March 19, his first point being that his brother was an ass for not updating them on his family's health. The letter was full of jokes and banter and directions about the book, which Alexander would be in charge of overseeing. "Size and font and so on—just like 'Unusual Stories' by Poe." He still wanted the simple title, and he set up an order of presentation of the stories. He told his brother which ones to take out if there were too many ("An Incident," "In the Court," "A Trivial Incident") and if more were needed, which ones they might include. He provided the text of an advertisement for his *Motley Stories* to be printed on the book cover.

He was in happy high-efficiency mode as he prepared for departure and freedom. He wrote to Maria Kiseleva and Leykin on March 21. For Kiseleva, he advised her about royalties and explained the tricks that publishers used so that their authors would not have the right to republish elsewhere. But keep in mind, he said, that publishers take all the risk, so authors should be grateful: "After all, a bad sparrow in hand is better than a paradise bird in paradise."[24] He teased her, as if in revenge for her criticisms of "Mire": "Ach! In summer, reading a critic on your book, I will feel happy! As I will be gloating and maliciously rubbing my hands!" His teasing was funny and fast. She had teased him about a gift Dunya Efros had given him, which means that Efros was continuing to socialize with him. Most important, as Kiseleva's unpaid agent, he had an update on "Larka," Kiseleva's story that he had submitted for her to *New Times*: Suvorin hadn't read it yet. Also, Chekhov's colleague with typhus had asked him to visit: "I'm not going!" (How would Chekhov have borne infecting his sister or mother!)

He wrote Leykin to tell him, among other things, that he had sent "Typhus" to the *Petersburg Gazette*. "I'm *really* leaving the 31st."[25] He asked Leykin to write him when he was down south, but he warned that he wouldn't answer him. "I'll describe for you in detail my trip, which in all probability will turn out strange and wild." He kept trying to suggest to Leykin that their publishing relationship was essentially over but that their friendship should be fine, please!

He wrote to his Taganrog cousin Georgy Chekhov with his arrival time on April 4, but he asked him to keep it secret. On March 25 and 27 he reminded Alexander about keeping their mother informed about the health of his family; she was worried about Alexander's children. Anton told him the typhus that Anna, Alexander's wife, had would show its effects for one to two months. Alexander responded that Anna had been in the hospital; her typhus was less bad but she had a cough and was spitting more. But he also joked: "All the work on your book has been laid on me. [I'll fix] places I don't like and redo in my way the style corrections . . ."[26]

Chekhov wrote Leykin again on March 28 to give him fair warning again: "In the south I'll be trying to write less. That means I'll write little things from which the good half I'll send you." He encouraged Leykin to do better advertising for *Motley Stories*. Leykin denied any fault in promoting the book, however, insisting again that the only thing readers wanted then was Surovin's Pushkin edition.[27] In fact, Leykin had only placed one advertisement for *Motley Stories*, nearly ten months before. Was Leykin dishonest, as the Chekhov brothers complained, or just cagey? Why should Leykin, after all, help promote his star who was leaving him?

Chekhov was certainly bolting from his domestic life; in "Everyday Troubles"[28] ("Zhit-eyskie Nevzrody," March 28), he describes the atmosphere of a noisy apartment: a bellowing wife with a toothache; a conservatory student banging out a piece by Liszt on the piano upstairs; a medical student next door pacing the floor while memorizing information. Amid the continual distractions, the hero focuses on doing his accounting for future earnings. Finally, he cracks. The story concludes, "In the morning they brought him to the hospital."[29]

"In Passion Week" ("Na Strastnoy Nedele," March 30) Chekhov tells in the first-person present tense the experiences of an eight-year-old, Fedya, going to confession during Lent. He and Chekhov notice signs of spring: "The roads are all covered with brownish slush, in which future paths are already beginning to show; the roofs and sidewalks are dry; the fresh young green is piercing through the rotting grass of last year, under the fences. In the gutters there is the merry gurgling and foaming of dirty water, in which the sunbeams do not disdain to bathe. Chips, straws, the husks of sunflower seeds are carried rapidly along in the water, whirling around and sticking in the dirty foam. Where, where are those chips swimming to? It may well be that from the gutter they may pass into the river, from the river into the sea, and from the sea into the ocean. I try to imagine to myself that long terrible journey, but my fancy stops short before reaching the sea."[30] The boy's imagination about the journey fails him; Chekhov's imagination also failed to picture what his "long terrible journey" to Taganrog and the steppe would actually be like.

The precocious eight-year-old, meanwhile, wears guilt like a heavy coat (as probably Chekhov did, too), though we see that he is actually sinless: "The Mother of God and the beloved disciple of Jesus Christ, depicted in profile, gaze in silence at the insufferable agony and do not observe my presence; I feel that to them I am alien, superfluous, unnoticed, that I can be no help to them by word or deed, that I am a loathsome, dishonest boy, only capable of mischief, rudeness, and tale-bearing. I think of all the people I know, and they all seem to me petty, stupid, and wicked, and incapable of bringing one drop of relief to that intolerable sorrow which I now behold."

Having seen a woman ahead confessed and forgiven, the boy thinks to himself: "But how happy the man must be who has the right to forgive sins!" The unbelieving but forgiving Chekhov would have been this kind of happy man. Before the boy has his turn to confess, he has a scuffle with the local bully. After confession, he feels clean and duly reverent. The next day in church, he notices "the lady I saw yesterday looks lovely. She is wearing a light blue dress, and a big sparkling brooch in the shape of a horse-shoe. I admire her, and think that, when I am grown-up, I will certainly marry a woman like that, but remembering that getting married is shameful, I leave off thinking about it, and go into the choir [. . .]"

Chekhov saw no shame in marrying, but he put it off himself until he was forty-one years old.

Leykin on the 29th suggested to Chekhov that his story "The Cat" (retitled "Spring") would be better at half the length. Was Leykin baiting Chekhov or just being a good editor? It wasn't published for another four weeks. On the 30th, Chekhov wrote back to tell Leykin the story was "at his disposal." Chekhov's other editors almost never suggested or demanded changes in his stories.

Meanwhile, in the offices of *New Times*, Alexander and Suvorin were discussing Chekhov's collection of stories. Alexander wished Anton a peaceful journey.[31] During the last two days of March, before his departure southward, Chekhov was hurrying to finish his Easter story, "The Letter," for *New Times*.[32]

PART FIVE

To the South and Back

The sun had risen, but whether it was dancing or not Torchakov did not see. He remained silent all the way home, thinking and keeping his eyes fixed on the horse's black tail. For some unknown reason he felt overcome by depression, and not a trace of the holiday gladness was left in his heart.

—Chekhov, "The Cossack"[1]

Chekhov was to be disappointed by what he found in Taganrog. He hadn't realized how much his own perspective had changed after living in Moscow for nearly eight years. In letters and in his stories during this time, he mocked his hometown: its pace, the people, and their customs. "Threading my way through the New Bazaar, I became aware of how dirty, drab, empty, lazy, and illiterate is Taganrog," he wrote his family shortly after his arrival for Easter weekend. "There isn't a single grammatical signboard and there is even a 'Rushian Inn'; the streets are deserted; the dumb faces of the dock-workers are smugly satisfied; the dandies are arrayed in long overcoats and caps. All this thrust before the eyes is so disheartening that even Moscow with its grime and typhus seems attractive."[2]

He was happier if less comfortable while visiting with friends on the southern steppe. In later years Taganrog's cultural development became one of Chekhov's charitable social projects; he funded the city's libraries and hospitals. The return north in mid-May, however, did not bring him peace of mind. Except for a few trips to Moscow and performing medical duties nearby, he was with his family at Babkino for the entire summer. He was fulfilling his obligations of supplying short stories to *New Times* and the *Petersburg Gazette*, but he was not settling down. Marriage with Dunya Efros still crossed his mind. By September, his spirits were lower than they had ever been.

April 1887

"What is there to teach? There is nothing to teach. Sit
down and write."

—"The Letter"

While on the road, Chekhov wanted and had a light month of writing; it was Holy
Season, and the first three pieces he published, "A Mystery" ("Tayna," April 11),
"The Cossack" ("Kazak," April 13), and "The Letter" ("Pis'mo," April 18), were appropri-
ately religiously themed for the periodicals. Only "The Letter" inspired him to sublimity.

By April 1, Chekhov had sent "The Letter" to Suvorin. On April 2, Lazarev accompanied Chekhov to Moscow's Kursky terminal, where Chekhov boarded the train headed
south. Usually he did not date his letters, but he now recounted this leg of the trip to his
family with, sometimes, hour by hour notations. For the next several weeks, he reported
the events and his movements in a "diary" for the family's entertainment. He was glad to
share his impressions with his "Gentle readers and devout listeners."[1]

He began writing his sister while on the train on April 3. He wrote that he hadn't had
an envelope, so sent a postcard at 4:50 in the morning from Orel ("I'm drinking coffee
that tastes like smoked whitefish");[2] he wasn't able to mail the first installment of the
diary until April 7, the day after he arrived in Taganrog.

He wrote one unhappy short story on the way, but in his letters his observations of
life on the train and out the window were relaxed, amusing and happy. On April 4 the
train was on familiar territory:

> . . . Twelve o'clock. Lovely weather. There is a scent of the steppe and one hears
> the birds sing. I see my old friends the ravens flying over the steppe.

The barrows, the water-towers, the buildings—everything is familiar and well-remembered. At the station I have a helping of remarkably good and rich sorrel soup. Then I walk along the platform. Young ladies. At an upper window at the far end of the station sits a young girl (or a married lady, goodness knows which) in a white blouse, beautiful and languid. I look at her, she looks at me. . . . I put on my glasses, she does the same. . . . Oh, lovely vision! I caught a catarrh of the heart and continued my journey. The weather is devilishly, revoltingly fine. Little Russians, oxen, ravens, white huts, rivers, the line of the Donets railway with one telegraph wire, daughters of landowners and farmers, red dogs, the trees—it all flits by like a dream. . . . It is hot. The inspector begins to bore me. The rissoles and pies, half of which I have not gotten through, begin to smell [. . .].[3]

On the 6th, he was in Taganrog for Good Friday, but he was disappointed by his homecoming; he wrote his family on April 7:

It gives one the impression of Herculaneum and Pompeii; there are no people, and instead of mummies there are sleepy drishpaks [Garnett's footnote: "Uneducated young men in the jargon of Taganrog"] and melon-shaped heads. All the houses look flattened out, and as though they had long needed replastering, the roofs want painting, the shutters are closed. . . .

At eight o'clock in the evening my uncle [Mitrofan], his family, Irina, the dogs, the rats that live in the storeroom, the rabbits were fast asleep. There was nothing for it but to go to bed, too. I sleep on the drawing room sofa. The sofa has not increased in length, and is as short as it was before, and so when I go to bed I have either to stick up my legs in an unseemly way or to let them hang down to the floor. I think of Procrustes and his bed. I cover myself with a pink quilt, stiff and stuffy, which becomes intolerably obnoxious at night when the stoves lit by Irina make their presence felt. A Yakov Andreyevich [a nickname for a chamber pot] is a fond but unattainable dream. Only two persons permit themselves this luxury in Taganrog: the mayor and Alferaki. All the rest must either pee in bed or take a trip to God's outdoors.[4] [. . .]

He had a sore on his leg and diarrhea: "There is no end to my ailments. The biblical saying that in sorrow thou shalt bring forth children is being fulfilled so far as I am concerned, for my children are my stories, and I cannot bear to think of them now. The very idea of writing is repugnant to me."

Chekhov caught up on mail; he read letters from Leykin, who wrote from his estate near Petersburg: "We had a houseguest last week [. . .] and she kept asking me about you. I told her what kind of person you are: how tall, skin color, how fat. Come to Tosna in June and we'll show her to you, and we'll show you to her. Why not? Maybe . . ."[5]

Leykin hadn't guessed how sour Chekhov was feeling about marriage. Chekhov replied on April 7, sour mostly on Taganrog:

> Stark Asia! All around there's such Asia that I can't believe my eyes. Sixty thousand inhabitants busy themselves exclusively with eating, drinking, pro-creating, and they have no other interests, none at all. Wherever you go there are Easter cakes, eggs, local wine, infants, but no newspapers, no books. . . . The site of the city is in every respect magnificent, the climate glorious, the fruits of the earth abound, but the people are devilishly apathetic. [. . .]
>
> On Saturday I am going to Novocherkassk, where I act as best man at the wedding of a wealthy Cossack girl. [. . .][6]

Chekhov received a letter from his father written April 7, the first such correspondence from Pavel that exists in this period. With Chekhov out of town, perhaps the actual father of the family felt the need to take charge. Pavel knew that payment for his son's latest publications was due from Petersburg, but it still hadn't arrived. The family had spent Easter alone: "It was boring without you."[7]

But Chekhov himself was already bored in Taganrog. He wrote his parents and siblings over April 10–11:

> Frightfully dull. It is cold and gray. . . . During all my stay in Taganrog I could only do justice to the following things: remarkably good ring-rolls sold at the market, the Santurninsky wine, fresh caviar, excellent crabs and uncle's genuine hospi-tality. Everything else is poor and not to be envied. The young ladies here are not bad, but it takes some time to get used to them. They are abrupt in their movements, frivolous in their attitude to men, run away from their parents with actors, laugh loudly, easily fall in love, whistle to dogs, drink wine, etc. [. . .]
>
> The devil only knows what I haven't spent a night on: on beds with bugs, on sofas, settees, boxes. Last night I spent in a long and narrow parlor on a sofa under a looking-glass. . . .[8]

On the 11th, Chekhov wrote his sister to tell her that the delay in their receiving his payment had been Alexander's fault: "Between you and me: I'm afraid he's sick or drinking." As usual in his letters to Maria, he sent acknowledgments to Dunya Efros.

Chekhov's heart and soul seem to have not been fully engaged in the comic "A Mystery" (April 11), which he had dispatched to Leykin on March 31: An official is perplexed by a mysterious guest signature that doesn't seem to belong to any of his yearly party attendees. After taking up spiritualism whole hog, the official then finds out his priest likes to sign guestbooks with his former nonreligious name.

Chekhov had written "The Cossack" ("Kazak," April 13) while on the train south; the steppe, viewed dreamily and beautifully, was just outside the window: "The sun had not yet risen, but the east was all tinged with red and gold and had dissipated the haze which usually, in the early morning, screens the blue of the sky from the eyes. It was quiet. . . . The birds were hardly yet awake. . . . The corncrake uttered its clear note, and far away above a little tumulus, a sleepy kite floated, heavily flapping its wings, and no other living creature could be seen all over the steppe."[9] Chekhov loved Easter and so does his young newlywed hero: "Torchakov drove on and thought that there was no better nor happier holiday than the Feast of Christ's Resurrection." The plot, however, is solemn and its moral as heavy as lead. Torchakov's young wife won't let her husband give a sick Cossack any of their whole and pretty Easter cake. For once, the religious stories of Tolstoy did not inspire but instead dampened Chekhov. Torchakov gives in to his wife's fussy lack of charitableness but then repents and feels tortured:

> "I can't get that Cossack out of my head, do what you will!" he said to his wife. "He gives me no peace. I keep thinking: what if God meant to try us, and sent some saint or angel in the form of a Cossack? It does happen, you know. It's bad, Lizaveta; we were unkind to the man!"

This leads to the newlyweds' first but definitely not last fight:

> Maxim got up from the table and began reproaching his young wife for hard-heartedness and stupidity. She, getting angry too, answered his reproaches with reproaches, burst into tears, and went away into their bedroom, declaring she would go home to her father's.
>
> This was the first matrimonial squabble that had happened in the Torchakovs' married life. He walked about the yard till the evening, picturing his wife's face, and it seemed to him now spiteful and ugly. And as though to torment him the

Cossack haunted his brain, and Maxim seemed to see now his sick eyes, now his unsteady walk.

"Ah, we were unkind to the man," he muttered.

When the day ends without Maxim able to find the Cossack to whom he wanted to make up for his unkindness, "he was overcome by an insufferable depression such as he had never felt before."

Feeling so dreary, and being angry with his wife, he got drunk, as he had sometimes done before he was married. In his drunkenness he used bad language and shouted to his wife that she had a spiteful, ugly face, and that next day he would send her packing to her father's. On the morning of Easter Monday, he drank some more to sober himself, and got drunk again.

And with that his downfall began.

His horses, cows, sheep, and hives disappeared one by one from the yard; Maxim was more and more often drunk, debts mounted up, he felt an aversion for his wife. Maxim put down all his misfortunes to the fact that he had an unkind wife, and above all, that God was angry with him on account of the sick Cossack.

Lizaveta saw their ruin, but who was to blame for it she did not understand.

So their despairing, miserable story ends. But there is a bigger story than theirs. Chekhov himself had enjoyed the pretty sunrise over the steppe, and, unlike Lizaveta, his narrator doesn't begrudge sharing it: "In the east the first rays of the rising sun shone out, cutting their way through the feathery clouds, and the song of the lark was heard in the sky. Now not one but three kites were hovering over the steppe at a respectful distance from one another. Grasshoppers began churring in the young grass." This is Chekhov's odd Thomas Hardy-like moment, where the world shines in its glory while the abject humans crawl across it.

But what stories was Chekhov writing now that he was bouncing around the environs of Taganrog? In the next letter to his family, he stated again, as he had last week, that his offspring were his creative works: "My children aren't Yegor or Little Vladimir," he wrote his family, "but stories and tales, about which I'm unable to think . . . To write disgusts me."[10] He was restless and unhappily unproductive. He was wondering if his long multi-day letters hadn't gone astray: "I've sent you twice 16pp of diary and I'm amazed that you still haven't received it."

To Leykin he wrote a letter on the 17th explaining or excusing himself in list-form for not writing to him (or thereby for *Fragments*) because of how sick he was feeling; among his other afflictions were hemorrhoids, coughing, a bad leg. He also diagnosed and questioned Leykin's doctor's remedies for Leykin and offered his own medical advice, qualified only by "Such is my opinion."[11]

On the 18th of April, he was on the road to his friends on the steppe at Rogozin Ravine and on the 19th sent the next installment of his diary-letter.

On the 18th, Surovin published Chekhov's "The Letter" ("Pis'mo," then known as "Laypeople"), which the composer Peter Ilyich Tchaikovsky read through "twice in a row" and loved. This story led to these Russian titans meeting in October of 1889 and their friendship.

Here's the first paragraph:

> The clerical superintendent of the district, His Reverence Father Fyodor Orlov, a handsome, well-nourished man of fifty, grave and important as he always was, with an habitual expression of dignity that never left his face, was walking to and fro in his little drawing room, extremely exhausted, and thinking intensely about the same thing: "When would his visitor go?"

Besides the marvelous immediate characterization of Father Orlov, there's the excitement of the suspenseful situation: wishing one's visitor would leave.

> The thought worried him and did not leave him for a minute. The visitor, Father Anastasy, the priest of one of the villages near the town, had come to him three hours before on some very unpleasant and dreary business of his own, had stayed on and on, was now sitting in the corner at a little round table with his elbow on a thick account book, and apparently had no thought of going, though it was getting on for nine o'clock in the evening.

I wonder if either of Chekhov's new friends Lazarev and Ezhov reading the next paragraph wouldn't have tried to keep it in mind the next time they dropped in on Chekhov:

> Not everyone knows when to be silent and when to go. It not infrequently happens that even diplomatic persons of good worldly breeding fail to observe that their presence is arousing a feeling akin to hatred in their exhausted or busy host, and that this feeling is being concealed with an effort and disguised with a lie. But Father Anastasy perceived it clearly, and realized that his presence was burdensome and inappropriate, that His Reverence, who had taken an early morning service in the night and a long mass at midday, was exhausted

and longing for repose; every minute he was meaning to get up and go, but he did not get up, he sat on as though he were waiting for something.

The third and final character arrives, the deacon Liubimov, and this is where I will begin a summary of the middle of the story, and save the end for further quotations, commentary, and revelations of Chekhov's moral bearings.

The deacon has family problems—a wayward son—and can confide the problem to Father Orlov in a way that the latter can give counsel in a tried-and-true fashion. It's Lent, and the deacon's son is violating the fast. . . . But that's not all! Liubimov's son has been living with a married woman for three years, and they socialize as if they are indeed married! They have not produced any children, he says, at which Father Anastasy most inappropriately remarks:

> "I suppose they have been living in chastity!" chuckled Father Anastasy, coughing huskily. "There are children, Father Deacon—there are, but they don't keep them at home! They send them to the Foundling! He-he-he! . . ."
> Anastasy went on coughing till he choked.

"His Reverence" tells Anastasy to butt out, and the deacon continues his story. We don't know if Anastasy's comment is true; it's ignored as if it is true or too cynical to bother refuting. Orlov, we learn from Chekhov, is not an impartial judge of Liubimov's son Pyotr. He has known Pyotr since he was a noisy, difficult boy who avoided church "and had been given to raising delicate and insoluble questions with a peculiarly provoking zest."

I would suggest Pyotr had something in common with the Taganrog Chekhov boys, except for one little turn: as a boy he "had taken up a contemptuous and critical attitude to fishing, a pursuit to which both His Reverence and the deacon were greatly addicted." The story's author was addicted to fishing as well. We see Chekhov "switching up"—personally identifying in different aspects with characters very different from himself and disassociating from characters otherwise similar.[12]

This story is a play that we are watching with the comic genius who wrote it. Chekhov glances here and over there and now again over here. He knows what each character is thinking and feeling, but for the most part he has the confidence in us that we can figure out—with his occasional comments and from the dialogue—the hearts and minds of these three men.

The deacon begs His Reverence to direct the composition of the letter to his wayward son. Though the deacon is neither clever nor calculating, he knows how to persuade Orlov:

"Father Fyodor!" said the deacon, putting his head on one side and pressing his hand to his heart. "I am an uneducated slow-witted man, while the Lord has vouchsafed you judgment and wisdom. You know everything and understand everything. You can master anything, while I don't know how to put my words together sensibly. Be generous. Instruct me how to write the letter. Teach me what to say and how to say it. . . ."

"What is there to teach? There is nothing to teach. Sit down and write."

And maybe here, in Father Fyodor, we see Chekhov's own matter-of-fact reflex: The secret to writing is to sit down and write. *That's all there is to it!* But we and the deacon know that some people are masterfully bold writers, and for the rest of us it's not easy to write a reproachful letter to someone we adore.

"Oh, do me the favor, Father Fyodor! I beseech you! I know he will be frightened and will attend to your letter, because, you see, you are a cultivated man, too. Do be so good! I'll sit down, and you'll dictate to me. It will be a sin to write tomorrow, but now would be the very time; my mind would be set at rest."

His Reverence looked at the deacon's imploring face, thought of the disagreeable Pyotr, and consented to dictate. He made the deacon sit down to his table and began.

The deacon and Father Anastasy exult over the letter's fiery excellence and leave His Reverence to a well-earned nap.

The scene changes, even seemingly to Chekhov's relief and pleasure. Chekhov, we know, loved the Easter season.

As is always the case on Easter Eve, it was dark in the street, but the whole sky was sparkling with bright luminous stars. There was a scent of spring and holiday in the soft still air.

"How long was he dictating?" the deacon said admiringly. "Ten minutes, not more! It would have taken someone else a month to compose such a letter. Eh! What a mind! Such a mind that I don't know what to call it! It's a marvel! It's really a marvel!"

Yes, "a marvel," and even Anastasy agrees and heaps on the praise of His Reverence. The deacon continues to exult, as if his problem with Pyotr has been solved:

The deacon laughed gaily and loudly. Since the letter had been written to Pyotr he had become serene and more cheerful. The consciousness of having performed his duty as a father and his faith in the power of the letter had brought back his mirthfulness and good-humor.

"It's a splendid letter, only you know I wouldn't send it, Father Deacon. Let him alone."

"What?" said the deacon, disconcerted.

"Why . . . Don't send it, deacon! What's the sense of it? Suppose you send it; he reads it, and . . . and what then? You'll only upset him. Forgive him. Let him alone!"

I think even some of us readers are surprised by Father Anastasy's advice. And maybe it's the surprise of a simply stated moral opinion in the face of logical arguments to the contrary that most effectively convinces us (and eventually the deacon) that he's right.

The deacon looked in surprise at Anastasy's dark face, at his unbuttoned cassock, which looked in the dusk like wings, and shrugged his shoulders.

"How can I forgive him like that?" he asked. "Why I shall have to answer for him to God!"

"Even so, forgive him all the same. Really! And God will forgive you for your kindness to him."

"But he is my son, isn't he? Ought I not to teach him?"

"Teach him? Of course—why not? You can teach him, but why call him a heathen? It will hurt his feelings, you know, deacon. . . ."

They arrive at the deacon's "little house with three windows." We learn the deacon is a widower living with his invalid sister.

Father Anastasy went in with him. Seeing his table already laid with Easter cakes and red eggs, he began weeping for some reason, probably thinking of his own home, and to turn these tears into a jest, he at once laughed huskily.

"Yes, we shall soon be breaking the fast," he said. "Yes . . . it wouldn't come amiss, deacon, to have a little glass now. Can we? I'll drink it so that the old lady does not hear," he whispered, glancing sideways toward the door.

Without a word the deacon moved a decanter and wineglass toward him.

Chekhov reminds us that Father Anastasy has his own problems, and that his drinking is connected to the disappointment and shame of his life. And to get a drink, he's cagey.

The deacon reads the letter aloud, admiring it once again.

Anastasy, despite his dissipation and need to get drunk, reasserts his advice, but even more inspiringly:

> "Do you know, deacon, don't send it!" said Anastasy, pouring himself out a second glass of vodka as though unconsciously. "Forgive him, let him alone! I am telling you . . . what I really think. If his own father can't forgive him, who will forgive him? And so he'll live without forgiveness. Think, deacon: there will be plenty to chastise him without you, but you should look out for some who will show mercy to your son! I'll . . . I'll . . . have just one more. The last, old man. . . . Just sit down and write straight off to him, 'I forgive you Pyotr!' He will under-sta-and! He will fe-el it! I understand it from myself, you see old man . . . deacon, I mean. When I lived like other people, I hadn't much to trouble about, but now since I lost the image and semblance, there is only one thing I care about, that good people should forgive me. And remember, too, it's not the righteous but sinners we must forgive. Why should you forgive your old woman if she is not sinful? No, you must forgive a man when he is a sad sight to look at . . . yes!"

As great as Tolstoy is, even greater an artist than Chekhov (both Chekhov and I would say), I can't help feeling that Tolstoy writing this story would give in to me and to himself—and let us have a sentimental hero. Only Chekhov can resist this big opportunity for sentimentality. In Tolstoy's story, Anastasy would not be getting drunk.

> Anastasy leaned his head on his fist and sank into thought.
>
> "It's a terrible thing, deacon," he sighed, evidently struggling with the desire to take another glass—"a terrible thing! In sin my mother bore me, in sin I have lived, in sin I shall die. . . . God forgive me, a sinner! I have gone astray, deacon! There is no salvation for me! And it's not as though I had gone astray in my life, but in old age—at death's door . . . I . . ."
>
> The old man, with a hopeless gesture, drank off another glass, then got up and moved to another seat.

And now the burden of decision about the letter rests on the deacon's soft shoulders.

> The deacon, still keeping the letter in his hand, was walking up and down the
> room. He was thinking of his son. Displeasure, distress, and anxiety no longer
> troubled him; all that had gone into the letter. Now he was simply picturing
> Pyotr; he imagined his face, he thought of the past years when his son used
> to come to stay with him for the holidays. His thoughts were only of what
> was good, warm, touching, of which one might think for a whole lifetime
> without wearying. Longing for his son, he read the letter through once more
> and looked questioningly at Anastasy.

Rereading this, I get tears in my eyes, as I'll bet Tchaikovsky did too: "His thoughts
were only of what was good, warm, touching, of which one might think for a whole
lifetime without wearying. Longing for his son [. . .]"! How can we not finally love the
deacon? But will he or won't he heed Anastasy's advice?

"Don't send it," said the latter, with a wave of his hand.

And again, while revealing to me my own sentimental impulses, Chekhov won't let
readers mush up the story. The deacon is obedient; he admires His Reverence. He has
committed to sending the letter.

Just as with the Greek gods, however, the gift of the letter cannot be ungifted, but there
can be conditions and qualifiers attached that completely alter its quality:

> The deacon took an envelope from the table, but before putting the letter
> into it he sat down to the table, smiled, and added on his own account at the
> bottom of the letter:
>
> "They have sent us a new inspector. He's much friskier than the old one.
> He's a great one for dancing and talking, and there's nothing he can't do, so
> that all the Govorovsky girls are crazy over him. Our military chief, Kostyrev,
> will soon get the sack too, they say. High time he did!" And very well pleased,
> without the faintest idea that with this postscript he had completely spoiled
> the stern letter, the deacon addressed the envelope and laid it in the most
> conspicuous place on the table.

Chekhov made the Psychology of Forgiveness the god of this story.

On the road on April 20 to a wedding in Zverevo, Chekhov wrote a note to Alexander: "I'm alive and well. [. . .] Why don't you write?"[13]

In these two years, Chekhov was so productive that he only very rarely looked back at old work and recycled it. With a new title and revisions, probably submitted to the *Petersburg Gazette* before he left Moscow, "Boa Constrictor and Rabbit" ("Udav i Krolik," April 20) is a story he wrote for *Fragments* ("The Behavior of Husbands" ["K Svedeniyu Muzhei"]) that had been blocked by a censor in January of 1886 and been given up on by Leykin. An old Don Juan advises his listener how to lead a husband into preparing his wife to be seducible: "According to this method, if you're trying to seduce a man's wife, you should keep as far away from her as possible. [. . .] It's all a matter of hypnosis. She must not see you but feel you, just as a rabbit feels the gaze of the boa constrictor."[14] The speaker's cynical, knowing voice, it seems to me, is Chekhov's brother Nikolay's or their friend Levitan's; part of the seduction, in any case, depends on the wife beginning to study herself in the mirror with the eye of a head over heels admirer.

On the 23rd, Chekhov wrote his sister from Zverevo to assure her he would be writing a lot about his visit to the Kravtsovs' in Novocherkassk. Their brother Ivan wrote Chekhov on this date that "The Letter" was so popular that the issue of *New Times* it was in was unavailable to buy, even from Suvorin's own bookshops.[15] Though Chekhov had been having a terrible time trying to write fiction, on the 24th he mailed to the *Petersburg Gazette* the exciting, seemingly un-Chekhovlike murder story "An Adventure." On the 25th, he wrote up his adventures about the previous day's event in Zverevo: "A real Cossack wedding with music, feminine bleating, and revolting drunkenness. . . . The bride is sixteen. They were married in the cathedral. I acted as best man, and was dressed in somebody else's evening suit with fearfully wide trousers, and not a single stud on my shirt. In Moscow such a best man would have been kicked out, but here I looked smarter than anyone."[16]

> I saw lots of rich prospective brides. An enormous choice, but I was so drunk all the time that I took bottles for girls and girls for bottles. Owing to my drunken condition, probably, the local girls found I was witty and "sarcastical." The girls here are absolute sheep: if one gets up to leave a room, the others follow after. The boldest and "smartest" of them, who wanted to show that she was not unaware of subtle niceties of behavior and the social graces, kept tapping me on the arm with her fan and saying, "You bad boy!" though she kept on darting timid glances at me all the time. I taught her to repeat to the local cavaliers, "How naïve you are!"

[. . .] I have many themes in mind for *New Times* but the heat is such that even letter-writing is a chore.[17]

At Zverevo I shall have to wait from nine in the evening till five in the morning. Last time I spent the night there in a second-class railway-carriage on the siding. I went out of the carriage in the night [for a pee][18] and outside I found veritable marvels: the moon, the limitless steppe, the barrows, the wilderness; deathly stillness, and the carriages and the railway lines sharply standing out from the dusk. It seemed as though the world were dead. . . . It was a picture one would not forget for ages and ages.

Chekhov's "Spring: Monologue Scene" ("Vesnoy," April 25), the monologue of a cat, had been at *Fragments* for a month, but after Leykin abridged it, as he had asked Chekhov's permission to do, he held it and renamed it "Spring" to conform to the season. Leykin cut, as far the *Collected Works* editors can figure, specific references to Moscow, as the original piece had been written for Moscow's *Alarm Clock*. It reads simply and clearly, with no evidence of abridgment: In the early morning, a young gray cat with a big scratch on his nose speaks on a variety of topics, but the first one is love: "Here before you is the happiest of mortals! Oh, love! O, sweet moments! Oh, when I am dead and they take me by the tail and fling me in the garbage pit, even then I won't forget the first encounter beside the toppled barrel. I won't forget the glance of her sharp eyes, her velvety, furry tail. For one twitch of that graceful unearthly tail, I'm ready to reject the whole world."[19]

I was tempted to put Chekhov into the cat's shoes (or paws), but there seems no particular connection and necessarily no immediate connection to his adventures in Taganrog or on the steppe, as he had written the story more than a month before. In his letters, Chekhov did not share news of any liaisons this trip, but perhaps that was only because most of the letters were to his sister or entire family.

While in Taganrog the previous week, Chekhov sent "The Critic" ("Kritik," April 27) to the *Petersburg Gazette*. There had probably never been a story about a critic who is sympathetic, much less a hero. And there still isn't one. There are two critics in "The Critic": At the buffet of a theater, a drama-loving priest and a newspaper man drink, argue, get drunk, and on principal cut down to size any actor the other appreciates.

From April 26 to May 6 Chekhov was in Ragozin Ravine.

While there he had his eye on his return north; he wrote to Maria on the 29th. She and their mother and eventually the whole family were heading for Babkino before Anton would get back.

Alexander wrote that Suvorin wanted to put Anton on a 200-ruble-a-month retainer, twice as much as Leykin had paid him in 1886.[20]

Chekhov wrote the whole family on the 30th: "The evening is warm. There are storm-clouds about, and so one cannot see a thing. The air is close and there is a smell of grass."[21]

> I am staying in Ragozin Ravine at K.'s. There is a small house with a thatched roof, and barns made of flat stone. There are three rooms, with earthen floors, crooked ceilings, and windows that lift up and down instead of opening out-ward. [. . .] The first necessaries [outhouses] are conspicuous by their absence, and one has in all weathers to slip out to the ravine, and one is warned to make sure there is not a viper or some other creature under the bushes. [. . .]
>
> Now about food. In the morning there is tea, eggs, ham and bacon fat. At midday, soup with goose, roast goose with pickled sloes, or a turkey, roast chicken, milk pudding, and sour milk. No vodka or pepper allowed. At five o'clock they make on a camp fire in the wood a porridge of millet and bacon fat. In the evening there is tea, ham, and all that has been left over from dinner.
>
> The entertainments are: shooting bustards, making bonfires, going to Ivanovka, shooting at a mark, setting the dogs at one another, preparing gun-powder paste for fireworks, talking politics, building turrets of stone, etc. [. . .]
>
> . . . The coal mines are not far off. Tomorrow morning early I am going on a one-horse droshky to Ivanovka (twenty-three versts) to fetch my letters from the post.
>
> . . . We eat turkeys' eggs. Turkeys lay eggs in the wood on last year's leaves. They kill hens, geese, pigs, etc., by shooting here. The shooting is incessant.

Chekhov, far from finding peace and quiet, also detailed the agonized state of his hemorrhoids.

May 1887

—◦◦◦—

> I have peasant blood flowing in my veins, and I'm not
> one to be impressed with peasant virtues. I acquired
> my belief in progress when still a child; I couldn't help
> believing in it, because the difference between the
> period when they flogged me and the period when
> they stopped flogging me was enormous. . . . Prudence
> and justice tell me there is more love for mankind in
> electricity and steam than in chastity and abstention
> from meat.
>
> —Letter to a friend[1]

While Chekhov was still at Ragozin Ravine, his brother Alexander wrote him a postcard on the 1st of May in Latin to disguise and hide his news from any eavesdroppers: Suvorin's son Vladimir had killed himself. Chekhov seems to have received this postcard on May 5.

On May 4, Chekhov received two peeved letters from Leykin, to which he replied the next day, as usual leading off with an excuse about why he hadn't written anything for *Fragments* lately: "You're mad at me at my silence for nothing. I'd be glad to write, but there's no postal service." He was leaving now for Holy Mountains for three or four days. He asked, with more courage than the son in "Difficult People," for a loan of 200–300 rubles.

Mikhail Chekhov informed his brother, "Everybody reads your diary with pleasure." When their friends read sections of it aloud, "there were many laughs."[2] That had to be just what Chekhov intended to happen when his family received his long letters.

He had sent off to *New Times* at the end of April "An Adventure: A Driver's Story" ("Proisshestvie: Rasskaz Yamshchika," May 4), which, like all of Chekhov's stories of murder, is especially shocking. Murders don't happen in Chekhov . . . except when they do.

Unusually, the story is told in the first person by someone of a lower educational class than Chekhov. No one thinks of Chekhov as an experimentalist, maybe because his experiments are too subtle for the likes of us. To tell this story, Chekhov probably figured out in a moment's flash of inspiration that the third person wouldn't do. For all the knowledge the story depends on, the tale has to be told by an intelligent, perceptive but not highly cultured person:

> To tell the truth, all our family have a great taste for vodka. I can read and
> write, I served for six years at a tobacconist's in the town, and I can talk to any
> educated gentleman, and can use very fine language, but, it is perfectly true,
> sir, as I read in a book, that vodka is the blood of Satan. Through vodka my
> face has darkened. And there is nothing seemly about me, and here, as you
> may see, sir, I am a cab-driver like an ignorant, uneducated peasant.[3]

The narrator's father needed his children to accompany him to keep him awake after his bouts of drinking. On this fateful adventure, he brought the narrator's little sister. His drunken bragging in an inn about the money he has on him leads to him being pursued on the wooded road by robbers. Before the robbers arrive, he gives his daughter the money and instructs her to hide, and then, if there's more trouble, to run home. Perhaps because Chekhov thought a hero should not tell her own tale, the heroine's older brother tells the tale of the traumatized and heroic seven- or eight-year-old Anyutka. The story has a neatness and finish that is unusual in Chekhov's fiction, perhaps because of its being presented as a spoken tale that has been repeated many times.

Fleeing after witnessing her father's torture, Anyutka finds her way to a forester's cabin. A seemingly kindly mother listens to the girl's story and promises to help her get home in the morning.

> The woman took the money, and put Anyutka to sleep on the stove where at
> the time the brooms were drying. And on the same stove, on the brooms, the
> forester's daughter, a girl as small as our Anyutka, was asleep. And Anyutka
> used to tell us afterward that there was such a scent from the brooms, they
> smelt of honey!

How comfortable or uncomfortable sleeping on brooms is, Chekhov doesn't say. During his month in the south, traveling here and there, he often slept uncomfortably. The detail of the honey-scent surprises the narrator and pleases Chekhov and us. Chekhov continually makes us aware of our senses pulling in impressions, even if, seemingly, they have nothing to do with the plot of the story. But it's our senses that give us the atmosphere, our awareness of imagining an absolutely particular place.

> Anyutka lay down, but she could not get to sleep, she kept crying quietly; she was sorry for Father, and terrified. But, sir, an hour or two passed, and she saw those very three robbers who had tortured Father walk into the hut; and the one in the crimson shirt, with big jaws, their leader, went up to the woman and said:
> "Well, wife, we have simply murdered a man for nothing. Today we killed a man at dinner-time, we killed him all right, but not a farthing did we find."
> So this fellow in the crimson shirt turned out to be the forester, the woman's husband.
> "The man's dead for nothing," said his ragged companions. "In vain we have taken a sin on our souls."
> The forester's wife looked at all three and laughed.
> "What are you laughing at, silly?"
> "I am laughing because I haven't murdered anyone, and I have not taken any sin on my soul, but I have found the money."

Through Anyutka's telling and her brother's retelling of her clever escape ("For all she was so simple, she thought of something that, I must say, not many an educated man would have thought of"), it feels almost like a fairy tale. But this is enough summary. I won't tell the rest.

While in Slavyansk, on his way to Holy Mountains, Chekhov ran into Alexandra Selivanova, whom he had tutored when he was in high school in Taganrog. Small world! "She was happy, she works in some kind of factory school, dressed luxuriously and produced a very positive impression."[4] He wrote to her later, "I remember the impression you made on me in Slavyansk (I wanted to throw myself under the train)." She did not, however, inspire him to write any love stories.

In sights, sounds and smells, he sketched his impressions in his letter-diary for his family:

I came to Slavyansk on a dark evening. The cabmen refuse to take me to the
Holy Mountains at night and advise me to spend the night at Slavyansk, which
I did very willingly, for I felt broken and lame with pain. . . . The town is
something like Gogol's *Mirgorod*; there is a hairdresser and a watchmaker, so
that one may hope that in another thousand years there will be a telephone.
The walls and fences are pasted with the advertisements of a menagerie. . . .
On green and dusty streets walk pigs, cows, and other domestic creatures. The
houses look cordial and friendly, rather like kindly grandmothers; the pave-
ments are soft, the streets are wide, there is a smell of lilac and acacia in the
air; from the distance come the singing of a nightingale, the croaking of frogs,
barking, and sounds of a harmonium, of a woman screeching. . . . I stopped
in Kulikov's hotel, where I took a room for seventy-five kopecks.

After sleeping on wooden sofas and washtubs *[Maybe the bed of brooms
from "An Adventure" was a dream image?]* it was a voluptuous sight to see a bed
with a mattress, a washstand. . . . Fragrant breezes came in at the wide-open
window and green branches thrust themselves in. It was a glorious morning.
It was a holiday (May 6th) and the bells were ringing in the cathedral. People
were coming out from mass. I saw police officers, justices of the peace, military
superintendents, and other principalities and powers come out of the church.
I bought two kopecks' worth of sunflower seeds, and hired for six rubles a
carriage on springs to take me to the Holy Mountains and back (in two days'
time). I drove out of the town through little streets literally drowned in the
green of cherry, apricot, and apple trees. The birds sang unceasingly. Little
Russians whom I met took off their caps, taking me probably for Turgenev;
my driver jumped every minute off the box to put the harness to rights, or to
crack his whip at the boys who ran after the carriage. . . . There were strings
of pilgrims along the road. On all sides there were white hills, big and small.
The horizon was bluish-white, the rye was tall, oak copses were met with here
and there—the only things lacking were crocodiles and rattlesnakes.

I came to the Holy Mountains at twelve o'clock.

He wrote the family about his two days at this holiday gathering, and this account
from his travels is one of the rare instances where he gives as vivid a description in his
correspondence as in his fiction:

It is a remarkably beautiful and unique place. The monastery stands on the bank of the river Donets at the foot of a huge white rock covered with gardens, oaks, and ancient pines crowded together and over-hanging, one above another. It seems as if the trees had not enough room on the rock, and as if some force were driving them upward. . . . The pines literally hang in the air and look as though they might fall any minute. Cuckoos and nightingales sing night and day.

The monks, very pleasant people, gave me a very unpleasant room with a pancake-like mattress. I spent two nights at the monastery and gathered a mass of impressions. While I was there some fifteen thousand pilgrims assembled because of St. Nicolas' Day; eight-ninths of them were old women. I did not know before that there were so many old women in the world; had I known, I would have shot myself long ago. About the monks, my acquaintance with them and how I gave medical advice to the monks and the old women, I will write to [*New Times*] and tell you when we meet. The services are endless: at midnight they ring for matins, at five for early mass, at nine for late mass, at three for the song of praise, at five for vespers, at six for the special prayers. Before every service one hears in the corridors the weeping sound of a bell, and a monk runs along crying in the voice of a creditor who implores his debtor to pay him at least five kopecks for a ruble:

"Lord Jesus Christ, have mercy upon us! Please come to matins!"

It is awkward to stay in one's room, and so one gets up and goes out. I have chosen a spot on the bank of the Donets, where I sit during all the services. I have bought an ikon for Auntie [his mother's sister]. The food is provided gratis by the monastery for all the fifteen thousand: cabbage soup with dried fresh-water fish and porridge. Both are good, and so is the rye bread. The church bells are wonderful. The choir is not up to much. I took part in a religious procession on boats.[5]

In July he would write up this scene again in "Uprooted: An Incident from My Travels" ("Perekati-Pole"). As the subtitle indicates, the story is told in the first person and begins "on my way back from evening service."[6]

Comparing Chekhov's letter to Chekhov's fictional representation, I retreat from trying to figure out which is better: his voice in the letter is looser, funnier; the narrator of "Uprooted" is more grounded and focused. Through these two voices, Chekhov gives us a fascinating picture of this cultural event:

More than ten thousand people flocked to the Holy Mountains for the festivals of St. John the Divine and St. Nikolay the wonder-worker. Not only the hostel buildings, but even the bakehouse, the tailoring room, the carpenter's shop, the carriage house, were filled to overflowing. . . . Those who had arrived toward night clustered like flies in autumn, by the walls, around the wells in the yard, or in the narrow passages of the hostel, waiting to be shown a resting-place for the night. The lay brothers, young and old, were in an incessant movement, with no rest or hope of being relieved. By day or late at night they produced the same impression of men hastening somewhere and agitated by something, yet, in spite of their extreme exhaustion, their faces remained full of courage and kindly welcome, their voices friendly, their movements rapid. [. . .] Watching them during the course of twenty-four hours, I found it hard to imagine when these black moving figures sat down and when they slept.

The biggest difference, of course, is that in the letter to his family Chekhov had to be out in front, speaking as himself, maintaining his family's impression of him as their joking guide. Here, his narrator wants us to focus not on himself but on appreciating the overlooked, overwhelmed but kindly priests.

In dreams and in fiction, Chekhov went straight at what caught his attention. "Unlocking the little padlock on my door," writes the narrator of "Uprooted," "I was always, whether I wanted to or not, obliged to look at the picture that hung on the doorpost on a level with my face. This picture with the title, 'A Meditation on Death,' depicted a monk on his knees, gazing at a coffin and at a skeleton laying in it. Behind the man's back stood another skeleton, somewhat more solid and carrying a scythe."

The story then becomes about the Jewish convert who a priest has asked the narrator to share his room with. The hunting out of "Jewish" characteristics was, as Donald Rayfield has noted, a reflex Chekhov had developed growing up in Taganrog.[7]

He was a young man of two-and-twenty, with a round and pleasing face, dark childlike eyes, dressed like a townsman in gray cheap clothes, and as one could judge from his complexion and narrow shoulders, not used to manual labor. He was of a very indefinite type; one could take him neither for a student nor for a man in trade, still less for a workman. But looking at his attractive face and childlike friendly eyes, I was unwilling to believe he was one of those vagabond impostors with whom every conventual establishment where they give food and lodging is flooded, and who give themselves

out as divinity students, expelled for standing up for justice, or for church
singers who have lost their voice. . . . There was something characteristic,
typical, very familiar in his face, but what exactly, I could not remember
nor make out.[. . .]

In his language, too, there was something typical that had a very great deal
in common with what was characteristic in his face, but what it was exactly
I still could not decide. [. . .]

"You know I am a convert."

"You mean?"

"I am a Jew baptized. . . . Only lately I have embraced orthodoxy."

Now I understood what I had before been utterly unable to understand
from his face: his thick lips, and his way of twitching up the right corner of
his mouth and his right eyebrow, when he was talking, and that peculiar oily
brilliance of his eyes which is only found in Jews. I understood, too, his phrase-
ology. . . . From further conversation I learned that his name was Alexander
Ivanich, and had in the past been Isaac, that he was a native of the Mogilev
province, and that he had come to the Holy Mountains from Novocherkassk,
where he had adopted the orthodox faith.

In spite of his prejudices, the narrator is fascinated by the convert's story:

"From early childhood I cherished a love for learning," he began in a tone
which suggested he was not speaking of himself, but of some great man
of the past. "My parents were poor Hebrews; they exist by buying and
selling in a small way; they live like beggars, you know, in filth. In fact,
all the people there are poor and superstitious; they don't like education,
because education, very naturally, turns a man away from religion. . . .
They are fearful fanatics. . . . Nothing would induce my parents to let
me be educated, and they wanted me to take to trade, too, and to know
nothing but the Talmud. . . . But you will agree, it is not everyone who
can spend his whole life struggling for a crust of bread, wallowing in filth,
and mumbling the Talmud. At times officers and country gentlemen would
put up at papa's inn, and they used to talk a great deal of things which
in those days I had never dreamed of; and, of course, it was alluring and
moved me to envy. I used to cry and entreat them to send me to school,
but they taught me to read Hebrew and nothing more. Once I found a

Russian newspaper, and took it home with me to make a kite of it. I was
beaten for it, though I couldn't read Russian. Of course, fanaticism is
inevitable, for every people instinctively strives to preserve its nationality, but
I did not know that then and was very indignant. . . ."

Chekhov himself was a convert, educated away from his faith into a belief in Science
and Progress, and Alexander Ivanich's experiences in his family were not so different
from Chekhov's as a boy under the hand and fist of Pavel. This declaration by Alexander
Ivanich is not a pretext for anti-Semitism but for "freedom from lies," from superstition.
Chekhov had nothing against an intellectually curious teenager rebelling against the law
of the father.

Alexander Ivanich goes on and on about his life and travails, with the narrator at various
times noting his "Semitic" characteristics. And Chekhov, having allowed his narrator to
make Alexander Ivanich a distinctly foreign entity, has his own artistic counterweights
kicking in. Alexander Ivanich is afflicted with Chekhov's own troubles. After a mining
accident, says Alexander, "the doctors there said I should go into consumption. I always
have a cough now and a pain in my chest. And my psychic condition is terrible. . . . When
I am alone in a room I feel overcome with terror."

There is no serious character, it seems, who does not have a dose of Chekhov's own
mind or body.

The narrator, however, is suspicious of conversion. He doesn't buy Alexander Ivanich's
rationalization of it: "There was nothing for it but to accept the idea that my companion
had been impelled to change his religion by the same restless spirit that had flung him
like a chip of wood from town to town, and that he, using the generally accepted formula,
called the craving for enlightenment. [. . .] Picking out his phrases, he seemed to be trying
to put together the forces of his conviction and to smother with them the uneasiness of
his soul, and to prove to himself that in giving up the religion of his fathers he had done
nothing dreadful or peculiar, but had acted as a thinking man free from prejudice, and
that therefore he could boldly remain in a room all alone with his conscience. He was
trying to convince himself, and with his eyes besought my assistance."

The narrator isn't sympathetic to Alexander Ivanich, but I think we are. And so was
Chekhov, who was never smug about his atheism.

The narrator's conscience, as dawn comes on and they lie down to sleep, is awakened, and he muses: "some hundreds of such homeless wanderers were waiting for
the morning, and further away, if one could picture to oneself the whole of Russia, a vast
multitude of such uprooted creatures was pacing at that moment along highroads and

side-tracks, seeking something better, or were waiting for the dawn, asleep in wayside inns and little taverns, or on the grass under the open sky. . . . As I fell asleep I imagined how amazed and perhaps even overjoyed all these people would have been if reasoning and words could be found to prove to them that their life was as little in need of justification as any other."

On either side of the presentation of Alexander Ivanich is the narrator's recollection of his glorious time in Holy Mountains:

> When I woke up my companion was not in the room. It was sunny and there was a murmur of the crowds through the window. Going out, I learned that mass was over and that the procession had set off for the Hermitage some time before. The people were wandering in crowds upon the river bank [. . .] One boat with rugs on the seats was destined for the clergy and the singers, the other without rugs for the public. When the procession was returning I found myself among the elect who had succeeded in squeezing themselves into the second. [. . .] The singing of the Easter hymns, the ringing of the bells, the splash of the oars in the water, the calls of the birds, all mingled in the air into something tender and harmonious. [. . .]

The narrator is intercepted by Alexander Ivanich, who then tags along with him. The insecure convert should distinctly remind us of Chekhov himself, as he, Alexander Ivanich, starts describing "how hard it was to eradicate in the boy the habitual tendency to evil and superstition, to make him think honestly and independently, to instill into him true religion, the ideas of personal dignity, of freedom, and so on."

—―∿∿∿—―

On his way back to Taganrog from Holy Mountains on May 8, Chekhov, without the company of the fictional Alexander Ivanich, waited six hours for a train. One benefit this trip had been giving him was the luxury of not having to make efficient use of his time. Had there been Wi-Fi and email, he could have read at the train station this note from his sister:

> We're all doing well. There's money and we're soon going to the dacha [at the Kiselevs']. We're expecting you as soon as possible; we're bored without you. The only unpleasantness is poor Alexander; his whole family is sick again.

Anna Ivanovna, you know, is in the hospital, Annushka is also in the hospital, little Kolya is sick with catarrh of the intestines, and little Antosha [Anton's namesake one-year-old nephew] has a rash and a further something, I don't remember—last night we got a telegram. We were getting ready to send mother, but Alexander took in some sort of nurse. [. . .]

Everyone reads your diary with pleasure. A few days ago Maria Vladi-mirovna and Aleksei Sergeevich [the Kiselevs] were here, and they read excerpts from your diary; there was a lot of laughter. Write when you come back. On May 10 we're going to Babkino. Be well.

P.S. Don't forget about the money, darling.

Levitan's on the Volga. We're bored, come as soon as possible from Marfa Ivanovna; we will be glad.[8]

For his last week in the south, May 9–15, he was based in Taganrog at his uncle's, but he also ventured out of town to see friends.

———

"The Examining Magistrate" ("Sledovatel'," May 11) is one of the stories that could fairly be called Maupassantian. Guy de Maupassant is, of all of Chekhov's contemporaries, the one to whom he is most often compared, if just for quality and quantity of short stories.[9] They both had periods where they wrote as fast as journalists. I was about to summarize the story, but again the opening sets up the situation better than I can describe it:

A district doctor and an examining magistrate were driving one fine spring day to an inquest. The examining magistrate, a man of five and thirty, looked dreamily at the horses and said:

"There is a great deal that is enigmatic and obscure in nature; and even in everyday life, doctor, one must often come upon phenomena which are absolutely incapable of explanation. I know, for instance, of several strange, mysterious deaths, the cause of which only spiritualists and mystics will undertake to explain; a clear-headed man can only lift up his hands in perplexity. For example, I know of a highly cultured lady who foretold her own death and died without any apparent reason on the very day she had predicted. She said that she would die on a certain day, and she did die."

The rest of the story is about how the examining magistrate, under the curious and careful questions of the doctor, further unfolds the details. Maupassant couldn't have written it better. Anyone who has read dozens of stories by each author would know it's a Chekhov story, however, because . . . No, except for a description of a "Russian" face, I wouldn't be able to tell.

Perhaps "The Examining Magistrate" is also less characteristic of Chekhov in that he had to have worked out the plot before he wrote it: the cautious revelation of a medical mystery.

Chekhov's medical school classmate doctor Grigory Rossolimo remembered what a good listener Chekhov was with his patients: "Chekhov did not go to work as an average medical student. He collected the elements of the case history together with surprising ease and accuracy. But it was where one had to touch on the ordinary life of the patient, uncovering its intimate details, about how the illness developed into its present state that Chekhov seemed to bowl along effortlessly without forcing himself, in contrast to many students and even doctors who find it difficult to relate to the vivid statements emerging from the unique circumstances of patients' lives."[10]

––––––

On May 14, Chekhov wrote to Leykin: "I got your letter [of April 24] today, dear Nikolay Aleksandrovich! It's so hot and stuffy that I have no strength to write, but I have to write because tomorrow, the 15th, I'm returning to Moscow, and on the evening of the 17th I'll already be in Voskresensk at the dacha."[11] He thanked Leykin for the offer of a puppy from Leykin's dog's litter and would come and pick it up. "There were so many impressions and so much material," Chekhov explained, "that I'm not regretting that I've spent a month and a half on the trip." Unfortunately, he was completely broke, "without a kopeck." Could he get a loan? Could Leykin send forty rubles to him at Voskresensk? And, finally, he had to postpone his visit to Leykin's estate until he wrote two or three stories for *New Times*. He would try to get there by June 10.

Chekhov arrived in Moscow on the 17th and arranged seeing his friend Schechtel, from whom he hoped to get a small loan, before he got on the train to Babkino on the 18th.

––––––

"Aborigines" ("Obivateli," May 18) was the first story he wrote about his time in Taganrog, though he didn't name it Taganrog as such ("in a town in one of the southern provinces").

A Polish officer, the invalid Ivan Lyashkevsky, "who has at some time or other been wounded in the head," hysterically rants to his German architect companion (Chekhov was meeting with his "German" architect friend Schechtel on the very day of the story's publication):

> "Extraordinary people, I tell you," grumbled Lyashkevsky, looking angrily at the native [townsperson outside], "here he has sat down on the bench, and so he will sit, damn the fellow, with his hands folded till evening. They do absolutely nothing. The wastrels and loafers! It would be all right, you scoundrel, if you had money lying in the bank, or had a farm of your own where others would be working for you, but here you have not a penny to your name, you eat the bread of others, you are in debt all around, and you starve your family—devil take you! [. . .]"
>
> [. . .] Lyashkevsky is gradually roused to fury, and gets so excited that he actually foams at the mouth. He speaks with a Polish accent, rapping out each syllable venomously, till at last the little bags under his eyes swell, and he abandons the Russian "scoundrels, blackguards, and rascals," and rolling his eyes, begins pouring out a shower of Polish oaths, coughing from his efforts. "Lazy dogs, race of curs. May the devil take them!"

It's impossible to associate Chekhov with the Pole's further furious denunciations of Taganrog's citizens, except that just a month before on his arrival in Taganrog, Chekhov had expressed himself similarly, only slightly more mildly ("Passing through the New Market, I could see how filthy, empty, lazy, illiterate and uninteresting Taganrog is"[12]). In life and letters, Chekhov didn't let himself go like Lyashkevsky, that is, in the manner of his father and older brothers. Yet the author so well understood and described the anger and frustration of sick people that in the midst of this story we discount the denunciations that the suffering Lyashkevsky makes, most of which criticisms Chekhov wholly agreed with at the time, and sympathize only with his German friend and the inoffensive natives.

Ensconced at Babkino with his family, where it was unusually and uncomfortably cold, Chekhov was writing "Happiness" for *New Times*. "I am sitting in my autumn coat trying to produce a Saturday story, but my brains seem to be able to disgorge nothing but icicles,"[13] he wrote Leykin on May 22. He was answering Leykin's letter that was full of complaints about why when Chekhov was down south he had written for *Petersburg Gazette* but not for *Fragments*. "Your anger will turn," Chekhov predicted, "when you find my letter from Taganrog. You're an amazingly ungracious and cruel person! You reproach me that I, wandering through the south, didn't write anything for *Fragments*."[14] It was true that he had written those six stories for the *Gazette*, but the family had needed the money!

Even with his sore, hurt-feelings complaints, Leykin repeated his invitation to Chekhov to visit his summer house.

On May 25, Alexander wrote from the *New Times* office to greet Anton after his trip. Alexander updated him on his wife's health and on the state of the book; he asked Anton to let him include "The Examining Magistrate" in order to get the number to twenty stories. Also, couldn't Anton modify the title of the book? "In the Twilight" seemed too dark and bleak. And, as if to avoid being overheard in a crowded room, mentioned about Suvorin: "He is distressed about the revolver business [his son's suicide]."

Within the next week, Anton wrote back from Babkino, shrugging off the story-count: "If it's not twenty stories, the readers won't die." (In reply Alexander explained that with the increased size of the book, by including that twentieth story, the volume would bypass censorship.) Chekhov justified the title and meanwhile mentioned remedies for Alexander's wife's post-typhus symptoms: "Milk and more milk" and various specific drops of elixirs. He would be in Petersburg on June 8–10 and then onto Leykin's unless his legs were bothering him.

June 1887

—∾—

During his work on the topic "General Larionov's Rout
of Zhloba's Cavalry Corps," the young historian had
decided to compile a maximally precise, inasmuch
as was possible, hourly account of the activity of
both commanders during the month of June 20th.
Many of Solovyov's colleagues regarded that work as
deliberately unachievable, so suggested for starters he
write down his own hourly life in June (during the
previous year, for example) and then later set his sights
on events seventy-six years in the past.

—Eugene Vodolazkin, *Solovyov and Larionov*[1]

On June 1, "Volodya" appeared in the *Petersburg Gazette*. As I read it, I winced and
gasped, wondering how Chekhov, after *Aleksei Suvorin's son Volodya had just died
of suicide,* could have published a story about a fragile seventeen-year-old named *Volodya*
who kills himself. What was Chekhov, who was ever considerate, ever conscious, thinking?
How could this story possibly have consoled a grieving father?

Suvorin had poured out his heart in his diary back on May 2 about his twenty-two-
year-old son's suicide. "Yesterday Volodya shot himself," he begins. "I never was able
to anticipate anything; this is my misery, my curse. I noticed that on the previous day
he was somewhat especially sad after dinner, and I wanted to ask him about it, but I
didn't."[2]

On May 4, Suvorin's *New Times* newspaper published an account of the suicide. At
11:00 A.M. on May 1, Vladimir (Volodya) ate breakfast with his family, "was merry and
lively." He went out in his student uniform but returned shortly after and went to his room

and ten or fifteen minutes later shot himself in the heart.[3] Volodya left a note, blaming no one and explaining that life had become uninteresting and that existence in the other world would be incomparably more attractive; because of his religious convictions it had taken him a long time to decide on suicide. He had studied at the university only one year, but the second semester he had failed, "and this," added the *New Times* article, "it is said, made a strong impression on him." Indeed, after Suvorin's own death, Volodya's older brother, Aleksei Alekseevich Suvorin, would blame their father for Volodya's tardy return to school one fall, which resulted in his failure and thus his suicide.[4]

Volodya's mother Anna Ivanovna had died fourteen years before, shot in the head by her lover, who then killed himself. In his diary of May 2, Suvorin reviews that connection and describes her death.

What Suvorin wrote or told Chekhov about the tragedy is unknown, but by May 5 Chekhov had heard from Alexander about Volodya Suvorin's death. What condolences Chekhov wrote or expressed to Suvorin is also unknown. Perhaps, I ignorantly speculated, Chekhov's story was intended to show Suvorin his son's possible state of mind? But even that would be presumptuous and tactless. It was too soon!

To summarize: Chekhov's Volodya is plain and unhappy, a failure at school, embarrassed by his widowed mother, who sponges off a rich distant relative. At the relative's house, he becomes infatuated with a plain but sexy thirty-year-old married woman. Her flirtation leads them to an embarrassing sexual encounter ("Then it seemed to Volodya that the room, Nyuta, the sunrise and himself—all melted together in one sensation of acute, extraordinary, incredible bliss, for which one might give up one's whole life and face eternal torments. . . . But half a minute passed and all that vanished. Volodya saw only a fat, plain face, distorted by an expression of repulsion, and he himself suddenly felt a loathing for what had happened"), and his shame over failing at his exams and his anger at his mother's lack of shame at being a sponging relative results in Chekhov imagining a suicide to its conclusion:

> Volodya put the muzzle of the revolver to his mouth, felt something like a trigger or spring, and pressed it with his finger. . . . Then felt something else projecting, and once more pressed it. Taking the muzzle out of his mouth, he wiped it with the lapel of his coat, looked at the lock. He had never in his life taken a weapon in his hand before. . . .
>
> "I believe one ought to raise this . . ." he reflected. "Yes, it seems so."
>
> [. . .] Volodya put the muzzle in his mouth again, pressed it with his teeth, and pressed something with his fingers. There was a sound of a shot. . . .

Something hit Volodya in the back of his head with terrible violence, and he
fell on the table with his face downward among the bottles and glasses. Then
he saw his father, as in Mentone, in a top-hat with a wide black band on it,
wearing mourning for some lady, suddenly seize him by both hands, and they
fell headlong into a very deep, dark pit.

Then everything was blurred and vanished.

What did the grieving Suvorin think? What did Chekhov hope to awaken in Suvorin
or in himself with this terribly vividly imagined suicide?

The answer is less than a misfire. If Suvorin did indeed read "Volodya" in the *Petersburg
Gazette*, he wouldn't have blinked. The story as published on June 1, 1887, is subtitled,
"His First Love," and ends with Volodya's angry denunciation of his mother while they
are riding in a coach from the relative's estate to the station. Volodya shoots off his mouth
but does not shoot himself. There are many reasons Chekhov provides for why Volodya
behaves so rudely to his mother: "dirty memories, a sleepless night, the Little Russian
outfit with a bustle" that his mother wears, "exclusion, a remorseful conscience—all this
came together in him as a heavy dark anger." He is furious with his poor mother, whom
he doesn't love, which declaration embarrasses her in front of the driver. The story ends,
with her declaring, "He can hear everything!"[5]

It wasn't until three years later, when Chekhov was preparing a volume of stories
titled *Gloomy People*, that he substantially revised "Volodya" and developed it to its most
gloomy of conclusions.

Chekhov wrote to thank Leykin on June 4 for the loan of forty rubles and to arrange for
his trip to Leykin's summer place at Lake Ladoga. The weather continued to be lousy at
Babkino. Chekhov often kvetched at Leykin about Leykin's kvetching: "You write that
if while I'd been traveling in the south I'd sent you the stories that were published in
the *Gazette*, I wouldn't have received any less and they would've been in the spirit of the
magazine! Oh, come on!"[6]

He also wrote to his younger brother Ivan to see if Ivan would join him on his trip
to Leykin's. He started one more letter that day to Schechtel and continued it the next,
mostly about being busy with writing at chilly Babkino and hoping to cross paths with
him in Petersburg in a few days. In the Soviet edition there is a footnote explaining that
some words to Schechtel had been crossed out. The inveterate researcher (and biographer)

Donald Rayfield deciphered the censored sentence: "In Babkino there's still nobody to screw. So much work that there's no time even for a quiet fart."[7]

Chekhov had been busily writing, making up for the lull during his spring adventure. On June 6 "Happiness" ("Schast'e"), a story full of the south, appeared. In the early morning on the steppe, there are two shepherds and an overseer; more notably, though, are the sheep themselves, whose brains, perhaps to their surprise, Chekhov glances into:

> The sheep were asleep. Against the gray background of the dawn, already beginning to cover the eastern part of the sky, the silhouettes of sheep that were not asleep could be seen here and there; they stood with drooping heads, thinking. Their thoughts, tedious and oppressive, called forth by images of nothing but the broad steppe and the sky, the days and the nights, probably weighed upon them themselves, crushing them into apathy; and, standing there as though rooted to the earth, they noticed neither the presence of a stranger nor the uneasiness of the dogs.[8]

When the eager and superstitious old shepherd and the dispassionate, well-read overseer reach a standstill in their conversation about their surroundings and memories, Chekhov meditates: "In the bluish distance where the furthest visible hillock melted into the mist nothing was stirring; the ancient barrows, once watch-mounds and tombs, which rose here and there above the horizon and the boundless steppe had a sullen and death-like look; there was a feeling of endless time and utter indifference to man in their immobility and silence; another thousand years would pass, myriads of men would die, while they would still stand as they had stood, with no regret for the dead nor interest in the living, and no soul would ever know why they stood there, and what secret of the steppes was hidden under them."

After the overseer rides away, Chekhov muses: "The old shepherd and Sanka stood with their crooks on opposite sides of the flock, stood without stirring, like fakirs at their prayers, absorbed in thought. They did not heed each other; each of them was living in his own life. The sheep were pondering, too."

Alexander wrote on June 14 to say that "Happiness" was being praised all around: "I'm convinced that you yourself were a sheep when you experienced and described all those sheepy feelings."[9]

There had been bad weather at Babkino for a while, and on June 8 "Bad Weather" ("Nenast'e"), a dacha story, came out in the *Petersburg Gazette*: "Big raindrops were pattering on the dark windows. It was one of those disgusting summer holiday rains which, when they have begun, last a long time—for weeks, till the frozen holiday maker grows used to it, and sinks into complete apathy. It was cold; there was a feeling of raw, unpleasant dampness."[10] A good, kind young wife and her mother worry about her husband, who, working in the city, insists that he can't be at the dacha in rainy weather; when his innocent wife goes to the city to relieve him of his boredom, she learns he hasn't been to their apartment in days. She realizes he has been deceiving them and returns miserably to the dacha; but the weather changes, and he shows up and tells them an elaborate story about his whereabouts; she and her mother believe him (that dirty liar!) and are relieved.

Before Chekhov could set out on June 8 to stay with Leykin at Lake Ladoga, he was asked by Dr. Uspensky to fill in for him, just as he had last year, at the Zvenigorod District Hospital for a few days from June 13 on. Chekhov wrote Leykin the next day to tell him he was sorry, but he probably had to substitute for a medical colleague. Besides which, he was sick, the family was sick, and the fish weren't biting. "If I don't come, curse, but don't get angry. I think that you understand my situation and, being in my situation, you wouldn't do otherwise."[11]

Leykin seemed to think that Chekhov was happy to have an excuse not to come, and instead of replying went silent.

<center>~~~</center>

"A Play" ("Drama," June 13), one of Tolstoy's favorite stories,[12] is about an imperious woman author who forces her work and herself upon a leery critic: "I will not venture to call myself an authoress, but . . . still I have added my little quota . . . I have published at different times three stories for children."[13] Chekhov gave Madame Murashkin the same literary background as Maria Kiseleva, which his friend would have taken as amusing, as she and Chekhov had once exchanged just as absurd a drama in miniature as that which Murashkin reads at the critic.[14] Chekhov and Kiseleva would also have shared a laugh here:

> "You see . . . (the lady cast down her eyes and turned redder) I know your talents . . . your views, Pavel Vassilyevich, and I have been longing to learn your opinion, or more exactly . . . to ask your advice. I must tell you I have perpetrated a play, my firstborn—*pardon pour l'expression!*—and before sending it to the Censor I should like above all things to have your opinion on it."
>
> Nervously, with the flutter of a captured bird, the lady fumbled in her skirt and drew out a fat manuscript.

Pavel wants her to leave it, but she is too clever for him and insists on giving him a sample, just a half-hour's worth . . . before dumping the whole heap over him. As the hours pass, he begins daydreaming and dozing:

> Like a man condemned to be executed and convinced of the impossibility of a reprieve, Pavel Vassilyevich gave up expecting the end, abandoned all hope, and simply tried to prevent his eyes from closing, and to retain an expression of attention on his face. . . . The future when the lady would finish her play and depart seemed to him so remote that he did not even think of it.
>
> "Trooo—too—too—too . . ." the lady's voice sounded in his ears. "Troo—too—too . . . sh—sh—sh—sh . . ."

The ending cannot be summarized.

Chekhov had been able to get back to producing stories, but except for "Happiness," which he and his readers particularly enjoyed, he doesn't seem to have been fully activated or inspired. "One of Many" ("Odin iz Mnogikh," June 15) is another dacha story. "The father of the family" (otherwise unnamed), who works in the city and commutes back and forth to the dacha, wants to shoot himself for weariness and irritation over all the petty errands his family demands of him. "What am I living for? For what?"[15] he demands of his friend. Having detailed the items he's asked to pick up for family, friends, acquaintances, and his wife, he rants: "You're the husband, but the word 'husband' in translation to a lady's language means a wimp, an idiot, and voiceless beast on whom you're able to ride and burden, as much as she likes, not fearing intervention by the animal welfare society." Now that he has got it all off his chest, the father of the family asks for his friend's sympathy. The friend sympathizes . . . and asks him if he could just do him one little favor.

Anton cursed out Alexander in his letter of June 16, because Alexander, editing *In the Twilight*, had monkeyed with the galleys' dedication to Grigorovich. Chekhov was touchy or anxious and didn't catch that Alexander had been joking. Anton congratulated his brother on his debut story the week before in *New Times*, but wondered why he wouldn't take a serious subject. He wrote Alexander again on June 21 to explain that Anna's poor health would or could continue for a while because of the typhus. And then more jokes and insults. His postscript: "In 50 years you can publish this letter in 'Old Russia.'"

Right about now Chekhov seems to have developed a worry that the contents of his letters were going too far afield. In his very next letter, two days later, to his cousin Georgy, he declared unusually seriously: "besides to your own family, don't read my letters to anyone; private correspondence is a family secret with which nobody has any business."[16] Letters were where Chekhov could cut loose and clown around, and thus were private, to be shared only with the particular people he had in mind while writing them; this in itself distinguishes his letters from his fiction. But here we are, minding his business, joining a happy world of Chekhov correspondence readers. The best essay I have encountered about reading Chekhov's collected letters is by the Russian-Israeli novelist Dina Rubina. She explains her and our attraction to the personal Chekhov:

> I was ten years old, and was not yet aware that reading other people's corre-spondence was boring [. . .] I simply read everything, one letter after another, skipping over things that I didn't understand, circling languidly over the mar-velous images in them, returning over and over to things I found funny—and there were so many [. . .]. Circling like a goat tied to a stake who eats the grass within his reach, gathering *sustenance*, I entered the world of Chekhov's friends, relatives, correspondents, and lovers, making it my own. I was intoxicated by the intonation of his voice, which was something unique unto itself, unlike any other person or thing I knew, conveying dignity, irony, warmth, and at the same time a remarkably serious attitude toward life.
>
> I often tried to picture him as he was when he wrote these letters: his slightly slanting handwriting unfurling in long lines, one following after another . . . I pictured him reaching the end of a page; without looking, he reaches for his ink blotter and rolls it across the damp lines in an accustomed gesture before turning to the next page . . .
>
> I hereby attest: long before I began writing short stories, I knew everything about the life of this writer—not in the sense of dates, but in the most precise sense—his moods, his tastes, the life of his heart.[17]

In "First Aid"[18] ("Skoraya Pomoshch'," June 22) the title is ironic, as Chekhov describes peasants trying to bring back to his senses an old drunk man they rescued from a river. A grand lady decides that he was drowning and orders her coachman to intervene with "rubbing" and artificial respiration. This intervention kills the man. Perhaps Chekhov intended this story as a public service announcement: *Don't do this!*

Chekhov was private but liked bustle, and he continually asked friends to visit and no one ever complained of him as a host. On June 27 or 28 he cajoled Lazarev to come to Babkino, the sooner the better. He would send the coachman Aleksei to pick him up: "You'll recognize him by 1) stupidity 2) a distracted look and 3) a NT [*New Times*] I'll tell him to hold in his hand."[19] He asked Lazarev to bring various sausages from Moscow. Instead of Lazarev, two of Chekhov's cousins arrived at Babkino on June 28.

In "An Unpleasant Story" ("Nepryatnaya Istoriya," June 29), the philandering protagonist Zhirkov learns that different cultures have different customs. In the rain he arrives at a house for a rendezvous with his married lover, but when the maid answers the door, she mentions that the master has just returned home. "At the word 'master' Zhirkov made a step back from the door, and in a moment faintheartedness covered him, a pure boyish terror, which even brave people experience when they unexpectedly bump into the possibility of meeting a husband."[20] He flees, but his driver has left. It's pouring, so he returns to get help from the maid, but this time the husband answers the door.

Zhirkov panics and lies to the husband, who is thoroughly French and unfamiliar with Russian customs, that he is a messenger from the dressmaker. Just then, his mistress enters the room and expresses her delight to see him. "Oh, I see! Probably you're scared of Jacques?" she laughs. Her husband thinks nothing of her boyfriend's visit, and Zhirkov spends the night with her.

By the end of June, Chekhov wasn't mentioning the bad weather anymore. Perhaps he was able to fish again. "His hobbies were also silent," recalled Vassily Maklakov. "First and foremost was fishing. He used to lie down, having a nap on the grass of a riverbank, and wait for the fish in complete silence. . . . You should have seen him—so childish and happy—when he caught his fish. He cried out, 'Hurray, hurray!' He was very happy and joyful as if he had just won a lottery or bet."[21]

July 1887

—⁓—

> You express disappointment that your story is
> uninteresting. Let me tell you that if only one of
> your five stories has the power to entertain the reader,
> you may thank God for that. It is not the writing of
> uninteresting attempts that is terrible, but it is terrible
> when one feels it a boring task to write, and hateful
> tedium. . . .
>
> —To a young writer[1]

This was the Chekhov family's last summer at Babkino. The two families had apparently continued to enjoy one another's company, and usually the Kiselevs managed not to step on the plebian Chekhovs' toes. Maria Kiseleva's younger sister Natalia Gubareva was married to a Russian senator, who would in 1890 attempt to help advocate through government channels for Chekhov's travel to Sakhalin Island. Gubareva recalled visiting her sister "quite often" this summer. At gatherings, she remembered, "Chekhov was making such funny jokes we could not stop laughing. Everyone was laughing except for him."[2] This was characteristic of him as an artist: amusing others while maintaining a poker-face.

The topic of marriage had settled back into being only a comedy. In "A Transgression" ("Bezzakonie," July 4), a guilt-ridden husband, finding a baby on the doorstep of his dacha, believes it is the baby he has in fact fathered with his wife's former maid.

> He was numb with terror, anger, and shame . . . What was he to do now? What would his wife say if she found out? What would his colleagues at the office say? His Excellency would be sure to dig him in the ribs, guffaw, and say: "I

congratulate you! . . . He-he-he! Though your beard is gray, your heart is gay. . . .
You are a rogue, Semyon Erastovich!" The whole colony of summer visitors would know his secret now, and probably the respectable mothers of
families would shut their doors to him. Such incidents always get into the papers,
and the humble name of Miguev would be published all over Russia. . . .[3]

He finds out only after he has confessed his transgression to his wife that the baby he
found is that of a visiting woman he has had nothing to do with.

"From the Diary of a Violent-Tempered Man" ("Iz Zapisok Vspil'chivogo Cheloveka,"
July 5) is a joke on Chekhov himself. Ever mild, ever restrained, Chekhov's narrator,
having been roped into a romance and consequently marriage, is—to no one's in the
summer community's knowledge, because there is absolutely no outward indication of
it—dangerously "violent-tempered."

> When the duty of walking arm-in-arm with a lady falls to my lot, for some
> reason or other I always feel like a peg with a heavy cloak hanging on it.
> Nadenka (or Varenka), between ourselves, of an ardent temperament (her
> grandfather was an Armenian), has a peculiar art of throwing her whole weight
> on one's arm and clinging to one's side like a leech. And so we walk along.[4]

When he tries to escape the social scene, he is blocked:

> Varenka's *maman*, Varenka herself, and the variegated young ladies sur-
> round me, and declare that I cannot possibly go, because I promised
> yesterday to dine with them and go to the woods to look for mushrooms.
> I bow and sit down again. My soul is boiling with rage, and I feel that in
> another moment I may not be able to answer for myself, that there may
> be an explosion, but gentlemanly feeling and the fear of committing a
> breach of good manners compels me to obey the ladies. And I obey them.

No matter his stony indifference, Varenka and the other females see in his manner the
sadness of unrequited love:

> "Nicolas," sighs Nadenka [the narrator continually varies her unknown name],
> and her nose begins to turn red, "Nicolas, I see you are trying to avoid being
> open with me. . . . You seem to wish to punish me by your silence. Your

feeling is not returned, and you wish to suffer in silence, in solitude . . . it is
too awful, Nicolas!" she cries impulsively seizing my hand, and I see her nose
beginning to swell. "What would you say if the girl you love were to offer you
her eternal friendship?"

I mutter something incoherent, for I really can't think what to say to her.

In the first place, I'm not in love with any girl at all; in the second, what
could I possibly want her eternal friendship for? and, thirdly, I have a violent
temper.

Chekhov, being a professional writer with an eye on the calendar as well as a scientist, plays a future-events card: "Next morning. Typical holiday weather. Temperature
below freezing, a cutting wind, rain, mud, and a smell of naphthalene, because my
maman has taken all her wraps out of her trunks. A devilish morning! It is the 7th
of August, 1887, the date of the solar eclipse. I may here remark that at the time of
an eclipse every one of us may, without special astronomical knowledge, be of the
greatest service. Thus, for example, anyone of us can (1) take the measurement of
the diameters of the sun and the moon; (2) sketch the corona of the sun; (3) take the
temperature; (4) take observations of plants and animals during the eclipse; (5) note
down his own impressions, and so on."

This summer's eclipse was indeed a special event, and for the educated Russian community it was promoted as such. This was the first published of Chekhov's four stories
that concern or mention the eclipse.

The narrator means to clarify matters with the ridiculous Varenka: "To begin with, I
will tell her that she is mistaken in supposing that I am in love with her. That's a thing
one does not say to a lady as a rule, though. To tell a lady that one's not in love with her,
is almost as rude as to tell an author he can't write." The violent-tempered man concludes
his tale on the day of his wedding: "To lead a violent, desperate man to the altar is as
unwise as to thrust one's hand into the cage of a ferocious tiger."

Similarly Chekhov didn't want to marry, but impulses stronger than he, as unstoppable
as the eclipse, seem to have been pressing on him.

While they were both at Babkino, crossing paths seemingly every day between the
two domiciles, he wrote Maria Kiseleva about his "A Transgression": "If my Agniya's
language doesn't sustain itself, it still gives a most definite impression [. . .]. The story
is not bad and is worth a thousand 'Stray Bullets' [the title of Kiseleva's story]. [. . .] A
stray shot through the temple helps toothache and love. Such a bullet gives a particular
impression."[5]

Their flirtatious yet testy friendship continued as he critiqued Kiseleva's stories up and down, and she had the confidence to criticize his.

Chekhov went to Moscow on July 8. Leykin had not written him since Chekhov wrote that he probably wouldn't be visiting him at Lake Ladoga. Chekhov spent a week in Moscow before returning to Babkino, but what he did, besides meet up with his friend Lazarev, is not recorded. He didn't like Moscow in the summer; a dozen years later, he wrote his future wife: "It is impossible to live worse or more disgustingly than the Muscovites live in summer. The only amusements are provided by the Aquarium and the farces, and in the streets everybody is suffocated by the smoke from the asphalt."[6]

While he was in Moscow, he wrote to Alexander about *In the Twilight*. What was the hold-up? Could Alexander get him the money for his July 14 *New Times* story ("Uprooted")? In reply, Alexander told him, "The book is completely ready and was sent to Suvorin at his dacha for him to determine the price. For two weeks there's been no answer."[7] Once Alexander had an answer, the cover could be printed. Neither brother mentioned the reason for Suvorin's withdrawal from society and business, Volodya's suicide.

Chekhov and Lazarev took the train to Babkino on July 15. Lazarev was all ears, raptly taking in Chekhov's description of the first chapter of "a novel" that Chekhov had commenced: "Imagine a quiet railroad station on the steppe, not far from the estate of a general's widow. A bright evening. The train arrives at the platform with two steam-engines. Then, standing at the station for five minutes, one train goes on with one engine, but the other moves little by little to the platform with one cargo wagon. The wagon stops. It opens. In the wagon is a coffin containing the only son of the general's widow."[8]

Chekhov showed him his notebook and advised him "to get one like it." (Lazarev, living in 2022, would have ordered one on his phone the first second Chekhov glanced out the window.) Lazarev writes: "the little book was in miniature size; I remember it was handmade, out of writing paper; in it were very finely handwritten themes, witty thoughts, aphorisms, things that came to Chekhov's head. One remark was about the special barks of red dogs—'all red dogs bark as tenors'—I soon found this on the last pages of [1888's] 'The Steppe.'"[9]

Lazarev remembered from his first Babkino visit that "at the time, two-three times a week, Chekhov was strictly connected to magazine-newspaper work, but in his free hours he had a reception time for sick ones, and the surrounding peasants came to Chekhov for advice. He treated them for free."[10]

Chekhov was anxious about his impending book, and he was anxious about Leykin, to whom he wrote again on July 17: "Where are you, and what's with you, kind Nikolay

Aleksandrovich? I positively don't know how to explain your continued silence in answer to my last letter. It's one of these three: either you've gone away, you're sick, or you're angry. If you went to Finland, it's been long since you were due to return; if you were sick, I would have found out about that from Bilibin. Apparently you're angry. If so, for what? I hope that the reasons of my not coming, laid out in my last letter (which you received by June 12), were valid enough and could not be the reason of your silence. . . . Why are you angry? I await your answer, and meanwhile I wish you health and I bow to your family."[11] In a postscript he said he had sent a story for *Fragments* to Bilibin. This was his usual peace offering, a new story.

He wasn't accustomed to Leykin's silence.

On July 22, Leykin answered that, yes, he was mad because Chekhov hadn't come to Lake Ladoga.[12] And it turned out Leykin didn't like Chekhov sending the new story to Bilibin rather than to him.[13]

Despite their wrangling, Chekhov had a better father-son relationship with Leykin than he had with his own father, who Chekhov continued to prefer not to mention. But Pavel, like a nightmare, seemingly infused himself into Chekhov's dissipated, infuriating characters. "A Father" ("Otets," July 20) is about a leech whose three sons and daughter are so good and considerate that they never scold him for being a lying drunk; they support him and give him money whenever he comes begging for it. He shows up at the summer villa where his son Boris is staying to shake him down for money . . . and a beer. (Despite his other weaknesses, Pavel Chekhov was not a drinker.)

The father is conscious of and even amazed by what a disgusting creature he has been:

> "I blackguarded you poor children for all I was worth. I abused you, and complained that you had abandoned me. I wanted, you see, to [. . .] pose as an unhappy father. It's my way, you know, when I want to screen my vices I throw all the blame on my innocent children. I can't tell lies and hide things from you, Borenka. I came to see you as proud as a peacock, but when I saw your gentleness and kind heart, my tongue clave to the roof of my mouth, and it upset my conscience completely."
>
> "Hush, father, let's talk of something else."
>
> "Mother of God, what children I have," the old man went on, not heeding his son. "What wealth God has bestowed on me. Such children ought not to have had a black sheep like me for a father, but a real man with soul and feeling! I am not worthy of you!"[14]

There's no evidence that Pavel ever expressed himself this way and admitted his failings to his children. Chekhov, I suspect, searched for his father's conscience, and gave voice to it in the hopes that it did in fact exist.

What terrific children the wretched father has, though:

"You are all pure gold, you and Grisha and Sasha and Sonya. I worry you, torment you, disgrace you, rob you, and all my life I have not heard one word of reproach from you, you have never given me one cross look. It would be all very well if I had been a decent father to you—but as it is! You have had nothing from me but harm. I am a bad, dissipated man. . . . Now, thank God, I am quieter and I have no strength of will, but in old days when you were little I had determination, will. Whatever I said or did I always thought it was right. Sometimes I'd come home from the club at night, drunk and ill-humored, and scold at your poor mother for spending money. The whole night I would be railing at her, and think it the right thing too; you would get up in the morning and go to school, while I'd still be venting my temper upon her. Heavens! I did torture her, poor martyr! When you came back from school and I was asleep you didn't dare to have dinner till I got up. At dinner again there would be a flare up. I daresay you remember. I wish no one such a father; God sent me to you for a trial. Yes, for a trial! Hold out, children, to the end! Honor thy father and thy days shall be long. Perhaps for your noble conduct God will grant you long life. [. . .]"

"The Father" by P. Pinkievich.

The father brings one of his sons home, where he lives with a shrew. It could be that his wife, the children's mother, has died of mistreatment and woe. He shows off in front of the shrew and taunts the son for thinking he's better than his old man. The father is proud of his children, because he has done everything to make himself loathsome, but they hang in there with him.

In "A Happy Ending" ("Khoroshiy Konets," July 25) a fifty-two-year-old passenger train guard (who describes himself as "a strict, respectable, practical man," just as sixty-two-year-old Pavel Chekhov would have described himself) goes to a matchmaker; he wants to settle down. Noting the matchmaker's pleasing plumpness and money-making talent, he pitches for the matchmaker herself. If Chekhov himself was still weighing marriage, it was as a joke.

At the end of July Alexander sent his brother the cover of *In the Twilight*, noting, however, that the publication date was still up in the air.[15]

Title page of *In the Twilight*.

August 1887

—⁂—

"Why write,"—he wondered—"about a man getting
into a submarine and going to the North Pole to
reconcile himself with the world, while his beloved at
that moment throws herself with a hysterical shriek
from the belfry? All this is untrue and does not happen
in reality. One must write about simple things: how
Peter Semionovich married Marie Ivanovna."

—In conversation with a fellow writer[1]

On August 3, *In the Twilight* was advertised as published by Suvorin's *New Times*
press. It wasn't available to buy, however, for another three days,[2] and Chekhov
himself would not even see a copy for another couple of weeks. Suvorin had told Alexander
to hold onto Chekhov's copies until he, Suvorin, returned to Petersburg.

Sometime early this month, Chekhov invited Lazarev to return to Babkino: "Come as
soon as you receive this letter." He gave him a list of groceries to bring: "1 pound of pork
sausage, 5 lemons, 4 heads of cabbage."[3] (Lazarev wasn't able to deliver until the 20th.)

I thought I was going to notice that now, by the end of a dull, rainy, cool summer,
Chekhov had lost creative steam. I wanted to point out evidence that the stories were
not drawing him out. Because I knew his full-length play, *Ivanov*, was on the horizon, I
wanted to show that while he was professional enough to write, he had reached a plateau
and needed to find something else, a new genre, a new challenge.

Instead, as I reread "In the Coach-House" ("V Sarae," August 3) I decided that
Chekhov was just as creative and ingenious as ever. Why had I doubted him? What I've
learned is that Chekhov wrote so many gems that I took them for granted and couldn't

keep track of them all. The story is about servants of a grand house discussing the suicide of a married father, a "gentleman." But before we know or realize any of that, Chekhov presents the coach-house as a kind of stage set: the light, the darkness, the people, the smell:

> It was between nine and ten o'clock in the evening. Stepan the coachman, Mihailo the house-porter, Alyoshka the coachman's grandson, who had come up from the village to stay with his grandfather, and Nikandr, an old man of seventy, who used to come into the yard every evening to sell salt herrings, were sitting around a lantern in the big coach-house, playing "kings." Through the wide-open door could be seen the whole yard, the big house, where the master's family lived, the gates, the cellars, and the porter's lodge. It was all shrouded in the darkness of night, and only the four windows of one of the lodges which was let were brightly lit up. The shadows of the coaches and sledges with their shafts tipped upward stretched from the walls to the doors, quivering and cutting across the shadows cast by the lantern and the players . . . . On the other side of the thin partition that divided the coach-house from the stable were the horses. There was a scent of hay, and a disagreeable smell of salt herrings coming from old Nikandr.

Once Chekhov has the scene vibrant to all his senses, he can move the story in seemingly any direction. Only in the midst of the card game do we learn of the incident in the "big house."

> "It's a nasty business," said the porter, sitting down to the cards again. "I have just let the doctors out. They have not extracted it."
>
> "How could they? Just think, they would have to pick open the brains. If there is a bullet in the head, of what use are doctors?"
>
> "He is lying unconscious," the porter went on. "He is bound to die. Alyoshka, don't look at the cards, you little puppy, or I will pull your ears! Yes, I let the doctors out, and the father and mother in. . . . They have only just arrived. Such crying and wailing, Lord preserve us! They say he is the only son. . . . It's a grief!"

Was Volodya Suvorin's suicide in Chekhov's thoughts? A month ago Chekhov had teased Maria Kiseleva about her story "Stray Bullets" and putting a gun to one's head. We have noticed Chekhov continually joking about wanting to shoot himself in despair, and it has happened in this story. But instead of relating it in a context that was familiar to him as a doctor and a friend, he tells it from the point of view of the servants.

The porter sums up the suicide for his companions:

> "I have orders to go to the police station tomorrow," said the porter. "There will be an inquiry . . . But what do I know about it? I saw nothing of it. He called me this morning, gave me a letter, and said: 'Put it in the letter-box for me.' And his eyes were red with crying. His wife and children were not at home. They had gone out for a walk. So when I had gone with the letter, he put a bullet into his forehead from a revolver. When I came back his cook was wailing for the whole yard to hear."
>
> "It's a great sin," said the fish-hawker in a husky voice, and he shook his head, "a great sin!"

They agree on that judgment, and they speculate on the suicide's reasoning:

> "From too much learning," said the porter, taking a trick; "his wits outstripped his wisdom. Sometimes he would sit writing papers all night. . . . Play, peasant! . . . But he was a nice gentleman. And so white skinned, black-haired and tall! . . . He was a good lodger."
>
> "It seems the fair sex is at the bottom of it," said the coachman, slapping the nine of trumps on the king of diamonds. "It seems he was fond of another man's wife and disliked his own; it does happen."

With Maria Kiseleva in mind, Chekhov could have written this as a lesson: If she was going to attempt to write about suicide, and if someone shoots himself in the head, then *this* is what happens. Grief overwhelms the family and the terror of death infects others. The old man remembers the old days:

> "It was the same thing at our lady's," he said, pulling his cap on further. "We were serfs in those days; the younger son of our mistress, the General's lady, shot himself through the mouth with a pistol, from too much learning, too. It seems that by law such have to be buried outside the cemetery, without priests, without a requiem service; but to save disgrace our lady, you know, bribed the police and the doctors, and they gave her a paper to say her son had done it when delirious, not knowing what he was doing. You can do anything with

money. So he had a funeral with priests and every honor, the music played, and
he was buried in the church; for the deceased General had built that church
with his own money, and all his family were buried there. Only this is what
happened, friends. One month passed, and then another, and it was all right.
In the third month they informed the General's lady that the watchmen had
come from that same church. What did they want? They were brought to her,
they fell at her feet. 'We can't go on serving, your excellency,' they said. 'Look
out for other watchmen and graciously dismiss us.' 'What for?' 'No,' they said,
'we can't possibly; your son howls under the church all night.'"

We see in the prohibition of burying suicides in the church cemetery the natural
birth of a ghost story. As the account of that incident goes on, the men and the boy get
the creeps; the boy becomes almost hysterical with fear. "The General's lady" eventually
believed various testimonials about the howling and she ordered that her son be reburied
outside the cemetery.

The old man tells of an intriguing custom concerning the lone exception to the prohibition against praying for the souls of those who have committed suicide:

"There is only one day in the year when one may pray for such people: the
Saturday before Trinity. . . . You mustn't give alms to beggars for their sake,
it is a sin, but you may feed the birds for the rest of their souls."[4]

Chekhov knows eerie and what it is to be spooked:

"The man was living and is dead!" said the coachman, looking toward the
windows where shadows were still flitting to and fro. "Only this morning he
was walking about the yard, and now he is lying dead."

"The time will come and we shall die too," said the porter, walking away
with the fish-hawker, and at once they both vanished from sight in the
darkness.

Chekhov has us and himself stand at a respectful distance from the family's grief. This
may as well be the Suvorin family:

The coachman, and Alyoshka after him, somewhat timidly went up to
the lighted windows. A very pale lady with large tear-stained eyes, and a

fine-looking gray-headed man were moving two card-tables into the middle of the room, probably with the intention of laying the dead man upon them, and on the green cloth of the table numbers could still be seen written in chalk. The cook who had run about the yard wailing in the morning was now standing on a chair, stretching up to try and cover the looking glass with a towel.

"Grandfather, what are they doing?" asked Alyoshka in a whisper.

"They are just going to lay him on the tables," answered his grandfather. "Let us go, child, it is bedtime."

There is more grieving and more howling by the parents. After the card game resumes, the terrified Alyoshka falls asleep, has a nightmare, but wakes up to comforting daylight.

"Who would've thought that out of an outhouse would come such a genius?"[5] Chekhov wrote Alexander, repeating that family joke-line. He had last used it in his correspondence to refer to himself. Now it was Alexander's turn at geniushood:

> Your last story, "At the Lighthouse," is beautiful and miraculous. Probably you stole it from some great writer. I read it through myself, then asked Mikhail to read it aloud, then I gave it to Masha to read, and in all cases, I was convinced that in this lighthouse you had outdone yourself. A blinding spark in the darkness of ignorance! A smart word after 30 stupid years. I'm in ecstasy, so I'm writing so that you wouldn't be long expecting my letter . . . (lazy!).

He went through a list of the characters with praise and criticism: "Olya is not at all successful, like all of your women. You sure don't know women!"

But Chekhov was otherwise enthusiastic and encouraging, assuring Alexander that with a dozen such high-quality stories, he would have a book of stories himself. Chekhov meanwhile wondered where his *In the Twilight* was. Had it been published or not?

Having expressed himself kindly and intimately, he concluded, as Alexander would have thought proper, with insults: "I bow to all your people, but not to you. You are not a genius, and there is nothing in common between us."

Chekhov had two more solar eclipse stories up his sleeve. He played one, "The Intruders: An Eyewitness Account" ("Zloumyshlenniki: Rasskaz Ochevidtsev," August 8) in *Fragments*, and "Before the Eclipse: Snippets from the Spectacle" ("Pered Zatmeium: Otryvok iz Feerii," August 9) in *Alarm Clock*, one and two days after the actual eclipse, which Chekhov himself wanted to witness but couldn't, as a dense cloud-cover intervened. "The darkness, very formidable, continued a minute," he later wrote Leykin.[6]

"The Intruders" are scientists who have appeared out of nowhere in a provincial town; the eyewitness is a poorly educated townsman who suspiciously scrutinizes them as they sit to a meal in a grubby tavern and make plans, sometimes in French, which the eyewitness doesn't understand. They talk about the next morning, when they would like the waiter to have tea ready for them that doesn't have flies or cockroaches in it.

"Are you aware of what's happening tomorrow morning?" one intruder asks the waiter.

"Not at all," he replies.

"Well! Tomorrow morning you will be struck and amazed."[7]

The townspeople watch as the next morning the scientist-observers set up their table outside the tavern and lay out their charts and papers and telescopes.

Suddenly the sun disappears and the night begins "and where the day went, no one knows." The citizens and the animals, there at the town square for market day, panic.

When daylight returns, the intruders (perhaps Austrians, the eyewitness wonders) pack up and leave, who knows where.

"Before the Eclipse," on the other hand, is in the format of a dialogue between the sun and the moon, "sitting on the horizon and drinking a beer." They part after several exchanges, agreeing if they're too drunk to perform the eclipse in August that they'll cover themselves with clouds.[8]

"Zinochka" ("Zinochka," August 10) is another Maupassant-like tale: a group of hunters, resting one evening, have been telling various rounds of stories (which we don't get to read) until one suggests a new topic:

> "It is nothing much to be loved; the ladies are created for the purpose of loving us men. But, tell me, has any one of you fellows been hated—passionately, furiously hated? Has any one of you watched the ecstasies of hatred? Eh?"[9]

He is met by silence, so he proceeds and recalls that as a bratty child, he tattled on his young governess, who was having a romance with his older brother. Chekhov was aware of fashions and cliches in storytelling, and he regularly scolded his brother Alexander for not noticing which were worn-out topics and where there might be room for discovery. "The ecstasies of hatred" was a clever and original topic.

It looks and sounds like a love story:

> "At the edge of the pond, between the thick stumps of two old willows, stood my elder brother, Sasha [. . .]. He looked toward Zinochka as she approached him, and his whole figure was lighted up by an expression of happiness as though by sunshine. And Zinochka, as though she were being driven into the Cave of Dogs, and were being forced to breathe carbonic acid gas, walked toward him, scarcely able to move one leg before the other, breathing hard, with her head thrown back.[10] . . . To judge from appearances she was going to a rendezvous for the first time in her life. But at last she reached him. . . . For half a minute they gazed at each other in silence, as though they could not believe their eyes. Thereupon some force seemed to shove Zinochka; she laid her hands on Sasha's shoulders and let her head droop upon his waistcoat. Sasha laughed, muttered something incoherent, and with the clumsiness of a man head over ears in love, laid both hands on Zinochka's face. [. . .]"

This appreciation of Sasha and Zinochka's joyful encounter makes me hope Chekhov had experienced such a moment for himself and not just as a bystander. The hunter recalls himself taunting her and his brother with his secret knowledge and how he exploited her fear of his tattling by refusing to do his schoolwork. He was overwhelmed by his power. After he nearly spilled the beans in front of his mother, the tormented Zinochka gave up trying to propitiate little Petya.

> "At our evening lessons that day I noticed a striking change in Zinochka's face. It looked sterner, colder, as it were, more like marble, while her eyes gazed strangely straight into my face, and I give you my word of honor I have never seen such terrible, annihilating eyes, even in hounds when they overtake the wolf. I understood their expression perfectly, when in the middle of a lesson she suddenly clenched her teeth and hissed through them:
>
> "'I hate you! Oh, you vile, loathsome creature, if you knew how I hate you, how I detest your cropped head, your vulgar, prominent ears!'"

He eventually ratted her out, which led to his mother firing her. But Chekhov surprises us:

"Zinochka soon afterward became my brother's wife. She is the Zinaida Niko-laevna whom you know. The next time I met her I was already an ensign. In spite of all her efforts she could not recognize the hated Petya in the ensign with his moustache, but still she did not treat me quite like a relation. . . . And even now, in spite of my good-humored baldness, meek corpulence, and unassuming air, she still looks askance at me, and feels put out when I go to see my brother. Hatred it seems can no more be forgotten than love. . . ."

Did Chekhov have anyone in mind? Was there a woman who hated him or was it someone *he* hated? . . . As Chekhov did not cultivate his hatreds of individual people, it's more likely he had seen rather than experienced the feeling.

Chekhov wrote Leykin on August 11 to try once again to explain their missed connections and miscommunications: the mail didn't come every day to Voskresensk and hence to Babkino; he had sent the story to Bilibin because he didn't know where Leykin was. As for safe, non-debatable topics, the weather was lousy; there had not been a sunny week. But then Chekhov got back to his usual mode with Leykin. He defended Gruzinskiy (Lazarev) for complaining about Leykin's shortening one of Lazarev's pieces: "If you take the editorial right to correct and not insert pieces, why not recognize the correspondent's right to protest?"[11]

As for *In the Twilight*, "Judging by the ad in [*New Times*], my Suvorin book came out 9 days ago, but I haven't heard anything about it, even though Alexander oversees the publication."

Chekhov was tactful and polite, usually, but not now. He asked, "Speak frankly: Aren't you sick of editing *Fragments* yet? If I were in your place, I would toss it all to hell, put my money in a side pocket and go on an around-the-world cruise. [. . .] Life is short."

Leykin was sharp and would have recognized that Chekhov was baiting him. He wasn't going anywhere, and he would continue using any tricks he could to keep Chekhov from leaving him.

Chekhov would return to Moscow in early September, but for now he was occupied. He wrote his friend Schechtel: "I'm dreaming of winter, as I'm sick of summer. For me, after all, summer began April 1." His letters to Schechtel were invariably easy-breezy: "Find me a fiancée."[12] In a postscript, he noted a distraction: "I've gone mad on mushrooms. I wander in the woods for days, looking under my feet. I shall have to give it up, for this pleasure is interfering with my work."[13]

Another distraction was wanting to see his book, finally. "Goose!" he wrote Alexander. "If you believe the Monday book ads, my book came out 9 days back already. Not a word or a peep about it."[14]

In "The Doctor" ("Doktor," August 17) the protagonist-doctor wants a confession from the mother of a dying nine-year-old boy that he is not the boy's father. There is no hope for the boy, who has a brain tumor.

The boy is dreamy and passive, possibly hallucinating.

> "Misha, does your head ache?" he asked.
> Misha answered, not at once: "Yes. I keep dreaming."
> "What do you dream?"
> "All sorts of things. . . ."[15]

The doctor has been paying the mother for support of the boy, as have two other men. He asks her, at this crucial time, to confess that she knows the boy is not his. She insists the boy is his. He argues: "A father's rights to the boy are equally shared with me by Petrov and Kurovsky the lawyer, who still make you an allowance for their son's education, just as I do! Yes, indeed! I know all that quite well! I forgive your lying in the past, what does it matter? But now when you have grown older, at this moment when the boy is dying, your lying stifles me!"

He is cracking, but she, grieving over her son's impending death, is not. He only wants her to tell him the truth. Chekhov doesn't tell us that the doctor is correct in his surmise, only that the doctor is sure she is lying. But there is no way for him to know and he is frustrated with his powerlessness. The story concludes with him uttering to himself on his way home: "What a pity that I don't know how to speak! I haven't the gift of persuading and convincing. It's evident she does not understand me since she lies! It's evident! How can I make her see? How?"

Lazarev returned to Babkino on August 20, and Chekhov wrote Leykin on August 21 to continue trying to mediate between his friend and Leykin. Chekhov explained that he had read a couple of lines of Leykin's complaints to Lazarev and that Lazarev had been amazed to learn he had offended Leykin. He invited Leykin to come to Babkino. He added: "Well, I burden the end of this letter with requests"—could Leykin place an announcement of *In the Twilight* in *Fragments*? . . . And, one more thing, could he have an advance, please? He apologized that Leykin hadn't received a copy of *In the Twilight*. "I'm not sending you my new book, as I don't have it."[16] As always, Leykin came through with the money; he printed an advertisement for *In the Twilight* and also had Bilibin write a review.

Meanwhile, Lazarev would describe Chekhov writing a story "all day" at Babkino; "finishing it, he turned to me with the request: 'Read "The Siren," A. S.! Did I leave out a word or comma? Is there any drivel? By the way, this is a record, the story was written without a single cross-out.'"[17] The comical "The Siren" ("Sirena," August 24) is about hungry judges awaiting one judge to finish writing his dissent. To pass the time, the others discuss, most distractingly, instances of "real appetite."[18] For example, "The richest odor is that of young onions when they just begin to get golden-brown, you know, and when the rascals fill the house with their sizzling."

Amid the lusty discussion, the dissenting judge finds it hard to concentrate and, unlike Chekhov in the story's errorless composition, keeps making mistakes, forcing him to start over.

The secretary, "a short man with sidewhiskers growing close to his ears and a sugary expression on his face," is the sweetest siren of all:

> He was so carried away that, like a nightingale singing, he heard only his own voice. "The meat pie must make your mouth water, it must lie there before you, naked, shameless, a temptation! You wink at it, you cut off a sizable slice, and you let your fingers just play over it, this way, out of excess of feeling. You eat, the butter drips from it like tears, and the filling is fat, juicy, rich, with eggs, giblets, onions . . ."

His quiet seductive voice sends one judge after another fleeing for a restaurant. The secretary reaches the end of the imagined meal:

> "Yes, my friend," the secretary continued. "And while you are sipping your brandy, it's not a bad thing to smoke a cigar, and you blow rings, and you begin to fancy that you are a generalissimo, or better still, you are married to the most beautiful woman in the world, and all day long she is floating under your windows in a kind of pool with goldfish in it. She floats there, and you call to her: 'Darling, come and give me a kiss.'"

The presiding judge finally flees too, tossing aside his work.

This is a variation on Chekhov's writer-on-deadline story from December 1886, "The Order." But it's better, neater, funnier. It would've made an appropriate gift for Leykin and *Fragments*, but Chekhov had sent it to the *Petersburg Gazette*. And, as noted by Lazarev, it was "written without a single cross-out."

As a counterweight to that farce, Chekhov followed with "The Pipe" ("Svirel'," August 29). Sitting at his desk at Babkino, Chekhov took one step into his imagination and conjured up this dreamlike scene:

> Meliton Shishkin, a bailiff from the Dementyev farm, exhausted by the sultry heat of the fir-wood and covered with spiders' webs and pine-needles, made his way with his gun to the edge of the wood. His Damka—a mongrel between a yard dog and a setter—an extremely thin bitch heavy with young, trailed after her master with her wet tail between her legs, doing all she could to avoid pricking her nose. It was a dull, overcast morning. Big drops dripped from the bracken and from the trees that were wrapped in a light mist; there was a pungent smell of decay from the dampness of the wood.[19]

Meliton's senses, though weary, are awake, as are Damka's.

> There were birch-trees ahead of him where the wood ended, and between their stems and branches he could see the misty distance. Beyond the birch-trees someone was playing on a shepherd's rustic pipe. The player produced no more than five or six notes, dragged them out languidly with no attempt at forming a tune, and yet there was something harsh and extremely dreary in the sound of the piping.

And so we follow the sound of the pipe and discover the piper, an old shepherd. Meliton, a bailiff, is chatty, but the shepherd is not.

> "What weather! God help us!" he said, and he turned his head from side to side. "Folk have not carried the oats yet, and the rain seems as though it had been taken on for good, God bless it."
>
> The shepherd looked at the sky, from which a drizzling rain was falling, at the wood, at the bailiff's wet clothes, pondered, and said nothing.
>
> "The whole summer has been the same," sighed Meliton. "A bad business for the peasants and no pleasure for the gentry."

This was Chekhov's dreary-weather summer at Babkino.

The shepherd offers no comfort. He sees the environmental destruction at the end of the 19th century that everyone ever since has been shocked to witness:

> "It's a wonder," he said, "what has become of them all! I remember twenty years ago there used to be geese here, and cranes and ducks and grouse—clouds and clouds of them! The gentry used to meet together for shooting, and one heard nothing but pouf-pouf-pouf! pouf-pouf-pouf! There was no end to the woodcocks, the snipe, and the little teals, and the water-snipe were as common as starlings, or let us say sparrows—lots and lots of them! And what has become of them all? We don't even see the birds of prey. The eagles, the hawks, and the owls have all gone. . . . There are fewer of every sort of wild beast, too. Nowadays, brother, even the wolf and the fox have grown rare, let alone the bear or the otter. And you know in old days there were even elks! For forty years I have been observing the works of God from year to year, and it is my opinion that everything is going the same way."
>
> "What way?"
>
> "To the bad, young man. To ruin, we must suppose . . . The time has come for God's world to perish."

The shepherd is undauntingly pessimistic. No matter the creature, the shepherd shakes his head and foresees its destruction:

> A silence followed. Meliton sank into thought, with his eyes fixed on one spot. He wanted to think of some one part of nature as yet untouched by the all-embracing ruin.

The shepherd, though he has started off to mind the cattle, brings up a recent event and then begins tooting away on his pipe!

> "Did you have an eclipse or not?" the shepherd called from the bushes.
>
> "Yes, we had," answered Meliton.
>
> "Ah! Folks are complaining all about that there was one. It shows there is disorder even in the heavens! It's not for nothing. . . . Hey-hey-hey! Hey!"
>
> Driving his herd together to the edge of the wood, the shepherd leaned against the birch-tree, looked up at the sky, without haste took his pipe from

his bosom and began playing. As before, he played mechanically and took no more than five or six notes; as though the pipe had come into his hands for the first time, the sounds floated from it uncertainly, with no regularity, not blending into a tune, but to Meliton, brooding on the destruction of the world, there was a sound in it of something very depressing and revolting which he would much rather not have heard. The highest, shrillest notes, which quivered and broke, seemed to be weeping disconsolately, as though the pipe were sick and frightened, while the lowest notes for some reason reminded him of the mist, the dejected trees, the gray sky. Such music seemed in keeping with the weather, the old man, and his sayings.

Chekhov drives the story on, the tension now being: When will a hint of hope appear? And Chekhov resists the demands of the genre, the demands of everyday conversation. . . . *No, there's no hope!*

<hr />

Lazarev remembered an episode at Babkino from that summer. There is no telling whether it was during his July visit or now, at the end of August: "One late evening, near midnight," writes Lazarev, "when Chekhov and I were about to go to bed, Maria Pavlovna returned in tears from the Kiselev house, and had scarcely entered the room when she went into hysterics. We got frightened and began giving her water and some kind of drops to help."

"But what's wrong with you, Masha? What's wrong with you?" Chekhov kept asking.

"I can't . . . I can't . . . Aleksei Sergeevich . . ."

"What about Aleksei Sergeevich?"

"What he says!"

With difficulty getting to the mystery, it came out that he had made a terrible statement. Amid bitter tears, Maria Pavlovna said that Aleksei Sergeevich Kiselev, distracted from a game of patience, for some reason brought up the ambition of the children of peasants and the cook to study, to go to school, and with outrage said that the government was inclined to allow them to do so instead of driving them away from schools and institutes . . . Kiselev said this sharply and rudely to the finish. In order to emphasize all the charm of this outburst by the head of a highly cultured family, it's necessary to remember that Chekhov's grandfather was a serf of Chertkov and that if Kiselev even in the smallest point didn't know this circumstance, he could not but know that the origins of the Chekhovs were in the peasantry.

Hearing his sister out, Chekhov shrugged his shoulders and said with annoyance: "And you wanted to listen to this idiot!" [. . .] In Chekhov's peaceful stories, in his even-keeled letters, sometimes for some reason, a sharp hatred flared up, uncharacteristic of his temperament. This is when Chekhov touches upon the rudeness and savagery of "cultured people."[20]

Yet he forgave the Kiselevs and they remained friends.

September 1887

———

You ask me what life is? It is like asking what a carrot
is. A carrot is a carrot, and nothing more is known.
—Letter to his wife, April 20, 1904[1]

Chekhov got to Moscow on September 2, and he wrote Leykin to thank him for the loan. He also wanted to clarify his role with *Fragments*, offering to write one or two stories a month; but it was time for new writers. He insisted that this arrangement would be fine, as Lazarev and Ezhov were already replacing him.[2]

He wrote Alexander a short note on September 3 to let him know where to send the next payment from *New Times*. Alexander wrote him a long letter on September 5, explaining, among other things, the delay in *In the Twilight*, ten copies of which were finally being sent to him that day. More important, he was responding to a depressed letter from Anton. This despairing letter has not survived. Alexander declared his sympathy:

> You write that you're all alone, there's no one to speak with, no one to write
> to [. . .] I repeat once more that I feel for you. You take on massive work, and
> I well understand that you're tired. [. . .] There's one thing I don't understand
> in your letter: the complaint that you hear and read lies and lies [. . .] You
> need to live and not work. You have overworked. The south inspired you and
> spurred you, but it didn't satisfy you.[3]

Alexander declined his brother's suggestion that he be his posthumous biographer and encouraged Anton to move to Petersburg and write his stories there. And he reminded Anton that Suvorin wanted to pay him 200 rubles a month to write for *New Times*. Anton could leave their parents behind. Finally, "I should call you the basest of pessimists if

I agreed with your phrase: 'My youth has been wasted.'"[4] Alexander described his own disappointed feelings of being cut out of serious editorial responsibility at *New Times*, and his own depressed feelings that had led to his reluctance to write Anton. Alexander knew quite well that he himself was dissipated and actually lazy, and perhaps that Anton's self-reproach was thus an even bigger reproach upon him.

Chekhov continually suggested to his brother and other correspondents that he was naturally lazy, that it wasn't in his character to be busy and hard-working. What was *their* excuse? Or was he reminding them (and us) that laziness can be a deep characteristic, yet allows, at times, exceptional effort?

On September 7 or 8 Anton replied with extra thanks for all the work Alexander had done on the book and continued their discussion of literary matters, including how to get along with Suvorin and shake up *New Times*.

With copies of *In the Twilight* finally in hand, Chekhov sent one on September 9 to the family's landlord, Yakov Korneev: "Instead of paying you for the apartment, I send you a volume of my excrement. . . . for rooms, alas!, I'll pay you in a hundred years." The Soviet editors explain, just in case the volume's readers have humor-deficiency-syndrome: "*Joke*. Chekhov paid 650 rubles a year for the apartment in the Korneev home."[5]

He confessed to Leykin on September 11 that he had been depressed: "For the last three weeks I gave myself up cravenly to a fit of melancholy. I lost all interest in life, my pen dropped out of my hand; in a word, 'nerves,' which you refuse to recognize. I was so disturbed mentally that I simply could not bring myself to sit down to work. There are all sorts of reasons for it: the bad weather, some family trouble, lack of money, moving into town from the country, etc."[6] He asked, by the way, about how Bilibin was doing.

Bilibin, working away at *Fragments*, and having just reviewed *In the Twilight*, wrote with exasperation to Chekhov on September 12. "In many letters you assail me because I write the wrong thing in the wrong way. That, obviously, is a misunderstanding. What do you want from me and what do you expect? I do what I can, and my literary conscience is at peace. Not everybody can be word-artists. I—I'm a craftsman, and in this there's nothing shameful. [. . .] I myself with full right might reproach you, blaming you for burying your talent, but I don't do this."[7]

Chekhov had been keen on Bilibin but, as with all his male friends, he joked coarsely to him. Bilibin seems to have been resistant or uncomfortable with that, never joking back in a similar manner. And he didn't like Chekhov's prodding him to write better. What was Bilibin protesting except, *I'm not as good as you, Anton Chekhov!*

Who was?

In "An Avenger" ("Mstitel'," September 12), "Shortly after finding his wife *in flagrante delicto* Fyodor Fyodorovich Sigaev was standing in Schmuck and Co.'s, the gunsmiths, selecting a suitable revolver. His countenance expressed wrath, grief, and unalterable determination." This is a *Fragments* comedy. The atmosphere is as authentic as a vaudeville stage-set. Sigaev's "unalterable determination" means that it *will* be altered. The shopman is a chatty foil, "a sprightly little Frenchified figure with rounded belly and white waist-coat." Sigaev is daunted by the price of a Smith & Wesson, and increasingly distracted by various thoughts about the proper form of vengeance:

> His imagination pictured how he would blow out their brains, how blood would flow in streams over the rug and the parquet, how the traitress's legs would twitch in her last agony. . . . But that was not enough for his indignant soul. The picture of blood, wailing, and horror did not satisfy him. He must think of something more terrible.
>
> "I know! I'll kill myself and him," he thought, "but I'll leave her alive. Let her pine away from the stings of conscience and the contempt of all surrounding her. For a sensitive nature like hers that will be far more agonizing than death."
>
> And he imagined his own funeral: he, the injured husband, lies in his coffin with a gentle smile on his lips, and she, pale, tortured by remorse, follows the coffin like a Niobe, not knowing where to hide herself to escape from the withering, contemptuous looks cast upon her by the indignant crowd.

He suffers finally from the awkwardness of changing his mind and having wasted the shopman's time. He instead buys a quail net.

Chekhov in the midst of his own despair and depression, mocked self-pity; such feelings eventually, *usually*, resulted in the consolation of buying oneself "a quail net." He had sent the story to Leykin on September 7, and perhaps, like "The Siren," he wrote it in one dash, without corrections. He liked it enough a dozen years later to include it in his *Collected Works*. It's pretty funny.

He wrote to Maria Kiseleva on September 13 in his usual jocular way, responding to her concern and sympathy for his low mood. What could he tell her? Chekhov looked at his desk and started there, opening with "I have a new lamp," which news he had conveyed at closing two days before to Leykin ("I bought (or, truer, I was given) a new room lamp"), "but all the rest is boring, gray and old."[8] After a couple of lines, he paused, mentally, though his pen went on: "There are no new thoughts, but the old things are tangled in my head and resemble worms in a green box that have been in the heat for five days. What's to write about? That I'm moneyless and deaf? You already know that." What didn't she know? He told her he had been reading reviews of *In the Twilight* and "cannot at all understand: are they praising me or complaining about my lost soul? 'Talent! Talent! But nonetheless the Lord rest his soul'—such is the implication of the reviews."

By the way, he went on newsily, "I've been twice at Korsh's theater and both times Korsh asked me to write him a play." Chekhov shrugged: "But of course I won't write plays." He mentioned a small publisher who would pay him a token sum and collect some of his old stories for a book. Dunya Efros had been over today, "in a new hat." As for the cat Fedor Timofeich, he "comes home to eat; all the rest of the time he strolls the roofs and dreamily looks at the sky. Apparently he came to the realization that life is without purpose." He had sent a couple of Kiseleva's joke-pieces to Leykin; in the meantime he greeted her family and told her everyone at the Chekhov house was well. He wound up, "The boredom is oppressive. Ought I get married?"

Joke, joke, joke. But Chekhov was still thinking about marriage . . . with Efros. He was always joking! But actually, in a week he would start writing a full-length play, *Ivanov*, and whatever Kiseleva's answer, he did not soon get married, and in three months the cat Fedor Timofeich would costar in a long story about a dog, "Kashtanka."

He seems to have got over the doldrums, but "The Post" ("Pochta," September 14) provides evidence of what those doldrums feel like. As usual, I try to sum up, but the neatest, quickest situational summary is Chekhov's own:

> It was three o'clock in the night. The postman, ready to set off, in his cap and his coat, with a rusty sword in his hand, was standing near the door, waiting for the driver to finish putting the mail bags into the cart which had just been brought around with three horses. The sleepy postmaster sat at his table, which was like a counter; he was filling up a form and saying:
>
> "My nephew, the student, wants to go to the station at once. So look here, Ignatyev, let him get into the mail cart and take him with you to the station: though it is against the regulations to take people with the mail, what's one to do? It's better for him to drive with you free than for me to hire horses for him."[9]

The scene becomes alive only once the journey begins, as Chekhov peers into the darkness and listens for the sounds and sniffs the air:

> The big bell clanged something to the little bells, the little bells gave it a friendly answer. The cart squeaked, moved. The big bell lamented, the little bells laughed. Standing up in his seat the driver lashed the restless tracehorse twice, and the cart rumbled with a hollow sound along the dusty road. The little town was asleep. Houses and trees stood black on each side of the broad street, and not a light was to be seen. Narrow clouds stretched here and there over the star-spangled sky, and where the dawn would soon be coming there was a narrow crescent moon; but neither the stars, of which there were many, nor the half-moon, which looked white, lighted up the night air. It was cold and damp, and there was a smell of autumn.

For the driver and the postman, the beauty of the sky and the adventure of being out on a dark fall night are too routine to be remarkable, but for the young student, everything is amusing and exciting:

> It was the first time in his life that he had driven by night in a mail cart, and the shaking he had just been through, the postman's having been thrown out, and the pain in his own back struck him as interesting adventures. He lighted a cigarette and said with a laugh:
>
> "Why you know, you might break your neck like that! I very nearly flew out, and I didn't even notice you had been thrown out. I can fancy what it is like driving in autumn!"
>
> The postman did not speak.
>
> "Have you been going with the post for long?" the student asked.
>
> "Eleven years."
>
> "Oho; every day?"
>
> "Yes, every day. I take this post and drive back again at once. Why?"
>
> Making the journey every day, he must have had a good many interesting adventures in eleven years. On bright summer and gloomy autumn nights, or in winter when a ferocious snowstorm whirled howling around the mail cart, it must have been hard to avoid feeling frightened and uncanny. No doubt more than once the horses had bolted, the mail cart had stuck in the mud, they had been attacked by highwaymen, or had lost their way in the blizzard. . . .

"I can fancy what adventures you must have had in eleven years!" said the student. "I expect it must be terrible driving?"

He said this and expected that the postman would tell him something, but the latter preserved a sullen silence and retreated into his collar.

The student's spirits are light. He can't imagine, however, anyone's spirits ever dampening or that his own excitement would not prove infectious. He receives the postman's brutal simple comeuppance:

"How fond you are of talking, upon my word!" he said. "Can't you keep quiet when you are traveling?"

Here's what Chekhov can do: simultaneously have us sympathize with the young man and completely understand the grouchy postman.

The sensitive student has been knocked into a grim mood. Chekhov makes us conscious of what has happened, but the boy doesn't know: "The chill of the morning and the surliness of the postman gradually infected the student. He looked apathetically at the country around him, waited for the warmth of the sun, and thought of nothing but how dreadful and horrible it must be for the poor trees and the grass to endure the cold nights."

Just before they arrive at the station, we realize that the postman has been wrestling with his feelings of discourtesy. He explains:

"It's against the regulations to take anyone with the post. . . ." the postman said unexpectedly. "It's not allowed! And since it is not allowed, people have no business . . . to get in. . . . Yes. It makes no difference to me, it's true, only I don't like it, and I don't wish it."

Chekhov doesn't allow us to simplify our conclusions about postmen or even about age versus youth. The violation of regulations has rankled the postman, and two people have been made unhappy. Chekhov concludes with questions, ones that the sore, put-out student isn't asking about the postman, but that we can: "With whom was he angry? Was it with people, with poverty, with the autumn nights?"

In a different mood, Chekhov describes the comically chaotic wedding-day preparations by a bride's parents in "The Wedding" ("Svadba," September 21). Chekhov seems to have taken in all the details from the weddings he attended during his trip in the spring; he describes the confusion of the elaborate but necessary marriage customs. When he himself finally married fourteen years later, he avoided absolutely all of it.

On or about September 21, Chekhov began writing the four-act *Ivanov*. Two weeks later, he had a complete draft, and in November it was staged. Probably he finished writing "The Runaway" ("Beglets," September 28) first. Chekhov had so far not mentioned any medical work since his return to Moscow from the summer house on September 2. The story is told for the most part from the point of view of seven-year-old Pashka, whose mother has led him on a long walk to a regional hospital clinic. (The age of most of the children, primarily boys, in the short stories these two years has been in the range of six to ten.) The presiding doctor is overwhelmed and sarcastic:

> The doctor began seeing the patients. He sat in his little room, and called up the patients in turn. Sounds were continually coming from the little room, piercing wails, a child's crying, or the doctor's angry words:
> "Come, why are you bawling? Am I murdering you, or what? Sit quiet!"

The doctor knows what's what and he cannot hold himself back from expressing his frustration. We should regard him as a bad guy. But he actually has Chekhov's sympathy. When the doctor realizes Pashka's situation, he blows up at the mother, who, we have learned, is husbandless, and, we will learn, very poor:

> The doctor examined his elbow, pressed it, heaved a sigh, clicked with his lips, then pressed it again.
> "You ought to be beaten, woman, but there is no one to do it," he said. "Why didn't you bring him before? Why, the whole arm is done for. Look, foolish woman. You see, the joint is diseased!"
> "You know best, kind sir . . ." sighed the woman.
> "Kind sir. . . . She's let the boy's arm rot, and now it is 'kind sir.' What kind of workman will he be without an arm? You'll be nursing him and looking after him for ages. I bet if you had had a pimple on your nose, you'd have run to the hospital quick enough, but you have left your boy to rot for six months. You are all like that."
> The doctor lighted a cigarette. While the cigarette smoked, he scolded the woman, and shook his head in time to the song he was humming inwardly, while he thought of something else.

Chekhov knows you can't say "You are all like that." It's not true. It's prejudiced.... *It's certainly not true!* But the doctor knows that if it's not the fault of life itself, it's the hard-pressed impoverished mother's fault. Knowing the doctor's situation, providing care every day to all and sundry, we cannot blame him for his agonized and accusatory response. Unlike the doctor in last month's "The Doctor," this doctor is "good" with children. He knows how to speak to them:

> "You stop with me, Pashka," said the doctor, slapping Pashka on the shoulder. "Let mother go home, and you and I will stop here, old man. It's nice with me, old boy, it's first-rate here. I'll tell you what we'll do, Pashka, we will go catching finches together. I will show you a fox! We will go visiting together! Shall we? And mother will come for you tomorrow! Eh?"
>
> Pashka looked inquiringly at his mother.
>
> "You stay, child!" she said.
>
> "He'll stay, he'll stay!" cried the doctor gleefully. "And there is no need to discuss it. I'll show him a live fox! We will go to the fair together to buy candy! Marya Denisovna, take him upstairs!"
>
> The doctor, apparently a light-hearted and friendly fellow, seemed glad to have company; Pashka wanted to oblige him, especially as he had never in his life been to a fair, and would have been glad to have a look at a live fox, but how could he do without his mother?

Unfortunately, knowing how to speak to children also means the doctor knows how to lie to them. Pashka is fed well and well-bedded, better than he has ever known. He observes the other patients, old and sick and damaged, and something of the direness of his situation seems to be dawning on him. A patient dies in the night, and amid the bustle of the hospital staff hauling the man away, Pashka and some of the other patients awaken.

We already know that Chekhov, according to his little brother Mikhail, had a fear of the dark and preferred having someone sleep in the same room or close by. Mikhail was that someone sleeping in an adjoining ground floor room at the house on Sadovaya in Moscow. "I positively cannot live without guests," Chekhov later wrote Suvorin. "When I'm alone, for some reason I become terrified, just as though I were alone in a frail little boat on a great ocean."[10] The following scene could have been inspired by one of his own nightmares:

> "Ma-a-mka!" he moaned [. . .].

And without waiting for an answer, he rushed into the next ward. There the darkness was dimly lighted up by a night-light and the ikon lamp; the patients, upset by the death of Mihailo, were sitting on their bedsteads: their dishevelled figures, mixed up with the shadows, looked broader, taller, and seemed to be growing bigger and bigger; on the furthest bedstead in the corner, where it was darkest, there sat the peasant moving his head and his hand.

Pashka, without noticing the doors, rushed into the smallpox ward, from there into the corridor, from the corridor he flew into a big room where monsters, with long hair and the faces of old women, were lying and sitting on the beds. Running through the women's wing he found himself again in the corridor, saw the banisters of the staircase he knew already, and ran downstairs. There he recognized the waiting-room in which he had sat that morning, and began looking for the door into the open air.

The latch creaked, there was a whiff of cold wind, and Pashka, stumbling, ran out into the yard. He had only one thought—to run, to run! He did not know the way, but felt convinced that if he ran he would be sure to find himself at home with his mother. The sky was overcast, but there was a moon behind the clouds. Pashka ran from the steps straight forward, went around the barn and stumbled into some thick bushes; after stopping for a minute and thinking, he dashed back again to the hospital, ran around it, and stopped again undecided; behind the hospital there were white crosses.

"Ma-a-mka!" he cried, and dashed back.

He sees a light in an out-building and discovers, through a window, the doctor himself peacefully reading inside, but suddenly for some reason, Pashka collapses and passes out, and wakes up in the morning, being scolded by the doctor for his escape. . . . But has the operation happened? Is Pashka about to notice that he has lost an arm? Or is that grim fate still ahead of him? Chekhov doesn't tell.

Tolstoy loved the story and read it aloud to guests.

Anton wrote Alexander on September 25 to ask him to go round up his fees for three stories at the *Petersburg Gazette.* He wanted Alexander to nudge a colleague, Burenin, about reviewing *In the Twilight,* which Burenin shortly thereafter did, publishing the review in *New Times* itself. Chekhov noted the book was selling "fairly well" in Moscow and that there would be an advertisement for it next week in the *Gazette*. And had Suvorin returned to the office?[11] (He had, but, according to Alexander, they hadn't yet conversed.)[12]

Meanwhile, Chekhov had discovered that he could knock out a play in two weeks, even with a few days off in those two weeks. There was money in plays, the way there might be money today in writing the script of a big-production movie. In Chekhov's Russia, every performance would bring in another payday for the author. He already wrote his short stories dramatically, and his comic pieces were often simple and stagy. He knew how to control a space and fill it with interesting people talking. He had written a full-length rambling play when he was twenty. His comic skits and dialogues were quick and funny. Why couldn't he write a successful money-making play?

He sealed himself off, and until he had proved to himself that he could do it, he seems to have told no one that he was writing *Ivanov*, except the contemporary he considered his literary equal, Korolenko. Korolenko came by the house to visit on September 26 or 27. It was only their second meeting. He was young, but seven years older than Chekhov. Korolenko remembered this as a business call on Chekhov to invite him to write for *Northern News*: "He came out of his study and held me by the arm, when I, not wanting to bother him, got ready to leave. 'I'm actually writing and undoubtedly am going to finish writing a play,' he said. 'Ivan Ivanovich Ivanov . . . You understand? There are thousands of Ivanovs . . . A regular person, certainly not a hero . . ."[13]

—⁓—

Chekhov was feeling better. He wrote Maria Kiseleva on September 28 about reading reviews of *In the Twilight* "almost every day"; he was "as used to them as, it must be, you are already to the sound of rain." He was proudly sending her the book.

He answered the poet Leonid Trefolev's letter on September 30 with a denial, however, of *In the Twilight* being, in Trefolev's words, worth twice its cost. Chekhov hadn't met Trefolev but knew him by reputation and from his photo being prominent at Leykin's and Palmin's; and in the meanwhile, he made an offer of free medical treatment if Trefolev was ever in Moscow: "About your illness that you write, I with pleasure will take up treating you and of course I will not cure you; I take patients every day, from 12 to 3; for literary people my doors are wide open day and night. At 6 o'clock I'm always at home."[14]

Chekhov's young friend and humor-writing mentee Nikolay Ezhov later remembered dropping by Chekhov's house unannounced one evening in late September or early October and pausing outside the ground floor window: "Chekhov was sitting alone behind the writing desk and writing something very very quickly. His pen ran across the paper. It had to be he was creating something new . . ."[15] It could well have been *Ivanov*; Chekhov would soon ask Ezhov to read it. "I looked at him a long while," writes the enamored Ezhov. "His beautiful wavy hair fell on his forehead, he steadied the pen, thought a bit, and suddenly . . . *smiled*. This smile was special, without his usual dab of irony, not humorous but tender, soft. And I understood that this was a smile of happiness—belles-lettres, creation, coming through in a fortunate style, form, phrase, and this gave him that joyful experience that only writers understand . . ."

However Ezhov reconstructed this pretty picture, we should appreciate his tact: "I did not want by my appearance to interfere with the work of a talented writer. I slowly redirected myself home and thought, along the way: 'Chekhov will be a great writer! He has everything: talent and intelligence working long and hard.'"

PART SIX

Ivanov
& Others

I failed in my attempt to write a play. It's a pity of course. Ivanov and Lvov seemed so alive in my imagination. I'm telling you the whole truth when I say that they weren't born in my head out of seafoam, or from preconceived notions or intellectual presentations or by accident. They are the result of observing and studying life. They are still there in my mind and I feel I haven't lied a bit or exaggerated an iota, and if they come out listless and blurred on paper, the fault lies not in them, but in my inability to convey my thoughts. Apparently it is too early for me to undertake playwriting.

—Letter to Suvorin[1]

After years of dashing off story after story and recovering from a bout of depression, Chekhov had set himself a task that would, if all went well, provide him the money so that he could slow down. At the end of September he had written *Ivanov*, his first major full-length play, but his hopes for it alternated with his misgivings about it. After all, *Ivanov* became a minor success, and he would revise it a year later. In the 1890s he resumed playwriting, having found his particular way in that line. *The Seagull*, *Uncle Vanya*, *Three Sisters*, and *The Cherry Orchard* became his most famous works. In the meantime, after the flush of excitement of *Ivanov*'s production, he made hay and finished off the year with a series of stories that would remain popular forever after.

October 1887

—⁓—

"Less than a year ago I was healthy and strong, full of pride and energy and enthusiasm, I worked with these hands here, and my words could move the dullest man to tears. I could weep with sorrow, and grow indignant at the sight of wrong. I could feel the glow of inspiration, and understand the beauty of romance of the silent nights which I used to watch through from evening until dawn, sitting at my worktable, and giving up my soul to dreams."

—*Ivanov*

I have found myself in the midst of writing this biography sometimes reading Chekhov's publication record like an accountant. At the end of September and the beginning of October, I worried that he certainly wasn't writing stories.

No, my inner-artist counters, but he wrote *a full-length play.*

And he began writing a novel. A novel!

But then Chekhov himself looked at the accounting and realized he needed money before the play could pay, and wrote four stories that were published in the second half of October.

On the 5th of October he wrote to Ezhov: "My play's ready. If you haven't changed your mind to help me, then tomorrow, if you would, Tuesday, at ten o'clock in the morning. You'll breakfast and lunch here. Be well." The postscript: "If you won't be here, then send."[1]

Ezhov didn't "send" and was there on the 6th: "Chekhov awaited me. On the table lay the fat notebook, clear, recopied in Chekhov's beautiful and personal handwriting. Anton Pavlovich was silent as if in bad spirits. No one bothered us. We sat, Chekhov opposite me. I read *Ivanov* from beginning to end, without stopping. The reading was finished. Chekhov, dark and thoughtful, didn't speak for a long time. Finally he spoke: 'I'm hoping for Davydov and Kiselevsky . . . These artists won't let me down.'"[2]

Ezhov doesn't say what approving remarks he made to Chekhov about the play or those famous actors. He kept his disapproving remarks to himself, "but privately reacted 'with amazement, since instead of the expected cheerful comedy in the Chekhov genre I found a gloomy drama crammed with depressing episodes . . . *Ivanov* seemed unconvincing.'"[3]

I myself remembered *Ivanov* as livelier than any of the other long plays. I remembered that I understood how Chekhov might have been amused by it and why it also could have been confusing to everyone in the audience. The translation I have read three times is by Marina Brodskaya, and she used the version Chekhov revised at the end of 1888 and was performed in 1889. The differences between the version of 1887 and Chekhov's revision do not seem of consequence to me.

Following Ezhov, I sit down to read *Ivanov* from beginning to end. Envying Ezhov, I decide to imagine that Chekhov is my friend and mentor, too. I, however, will be rereading it while pretending I have never read it before.

Scene: I walk into Chekhov's study, we shake hands, he asks about my sister, whose cough he treated last week, and he asks me to sit down. He nods to the chair at his desk. I sit and glance at the bookshelves. Am I sitting in his chair? I start to get up, I tell him he should sit in his own chair. He shakes his head and says he wants me to be comfortable. He'll sit across from me. I notice the lamp that he has been mentioning in his September letters. It shines onto a stack of manuscripts. Start? He nods. I make a humble smile. He doesn't smile. I try now to keep my expression blank and avoid his eyes as I read.

As a teacher, as a friend, as a writer, I know what it is to sit with someone while they read my work or I read theirs. And even though I am in Chekhov's presence, I am a reader first of all; I zone in, fully focused on the pages, but within a few minutes, I am wondering why *Ivanov* seems so dull. Without opening my mouth, I start to criticize and summarize: *The play reflects Ivanov's and Chekhov's disenchantment with women, who represent life, yet the "comedy" is that a bunch of difficult, unpleasant men know they're bums and that they're unworthy of the women. Anna/Sarra, the rich Jewish wife who converted to Christianity to marry Ivanov, but consequently lost her inheritance, is sympathetic but not interesting, and neither is Sasha, the young rich neighbor who is sadly in love with Ivanov. Does Chekhov not understand that his characters, untied from and unenlivened by his narration, are as dull as they think themselves to be? Should I say something? . . . Oh, and combined with the men's misogyny is the anti-Semitism again! Ivanov declares:* "My dear friend, you left college last year, and you are still young and brave. Being thirty-five years old I have the right to advise you. Don't marry a Jewess or a bluestocking or a woman who is queer in any way. Choose some nice, common-place girl without any strange and startling points in her character."[4]

By the end of Act 1, the questions the unsympathetic Dr. Lvov asks Anna/Sarra are, unfortunately, the ones I am asking myself. *Why am I here, wasting my time with these people?*

> Lvov: [. . .] Why are you here? What have you in common with such a cold and heartless—but enough of your husband! What have you in common with these wicked and vulgar surroundings? With that eternal grumbler, the crazy and decrepit Count? With that swindler, that prince of rascals, Misha, with his fool's face? Tell me, I say, how did you get here?

In Act 2, it seems to me that the characters are sometimes only Chekhov talking to himself. For example:

> 1) MARTHA [Martha is properly known as Babakina in Brodskaya's translation]. [*Aside*] Heavens! This is deadly! I shall die of ennui.

> 2) SASHA: Oh, dear! There is something wrong with you all! You are a lot of sleepy stick-in-the-muds! I have told you so a thousand times and shall always go on repeating it; there is something wrong with every one of you; something wrong, wrong, wrong!

> 3) SASHA: [*To Ivanov*] What makes you so depressed today?
> IVANOV: My head aches, little Sasha, and then I feel bored.

My imagination about reading this in front of Chekhov while he observes me begins to fail me. In real life, I realize it's evening, and I'm tired. What if I stop reading halfway through? I manage to rouse my imagination enough to picture Chekhov sighing, not saying anything though, as I clear my throat and apologize for my weariness. I ask him if he wouldn't mind if I came back tomorrow to finish. He looks glum but nods.

When I return in my imagination the next morning, I arrive at Chekhov's and knock and learn from a servant, a plump-faced young woman, that Anton Pavlovich is seeing a patient in his study, but that he has left instructions to lead me to his bedroom desk. I overhear the patient. She is a middle-aged woman by the sound of her voice; she goes on about a pain in her heel. She can't put pressure on it; pain shoots from the foot into her calf. Chekhov says, "Your shoe."

She says, "Lovely, aren't they?"

"Would you please take off that shoe?"

I sit down at his desk in front of the manuscript and take a glance around Chekhov's bedroom, sniffing the scent of books, tobacco, musty warmth. I sit up straight as the servant enters, bringing me a cup of tea. I thank her and resume reading.

I have been prepared for the worst, but Act 3 isn't so bad! I occasionally smile. I wonder if it has become better because the situation now has enough context and if my expectations have been properly diminished. Still, no character is sympathetic, and the humor is dry.

In the middle of Act 3 I think: *Okay, here is the play.* That is, *here* is the internal monologue, beyond which there is no need for any of the rest of the play:

> IVANOV: I am a worthless, miserable, useless man. Only a man equally miserable and suffering, as Pavel is, could love or esteem me now. Good God! How I loathe myself! How bitterly I hate my voice, my hands, my thoughts, these clothes, each step I take! How ridiculous it is, how disgusting! Less than a year ago I was healthy and strong, full of pride and energy and enthusiasm. I worked with these hands here, and my words could move the dullest man to tears. I could weep with sorrow, and grow indignant at the sight of wrong. I could feel the glow of inspiration, and understand the beauty and romance of the silent nights which I used to watch through from evening until dawn, sitting at my worktable, and giving up my soul to dreams. I believed in a bright future then, and looked into it as trustfully as a child looks into its mother's eyes. And now, oh, it is terrible! I am tired and without hope; I spend my days and nights in idleness; I have no control over my feet or brain. My estate is ruined, my woods are falling under the blows of the axe. [*He weeps*]

The speech, soliloquy, whatever you want to call it, goes on another . . . what, 300 words! It further describes Ivanov's shame, concluding with what is lately an all too typical refrain: "I can't, I can't understand it; the easiest way out would be a bullet through the head!" (Yes, a bullet would be the easiest way, and in Chekhov's revision next year, instead of Ivanov bringing down the curtain with a fatal heart attack, he does it with a shot to the head.)

As I sit at the desk, frowning over his manuscript, I wonder what my imaginary friend and mentor Chekhov is working out of his system. I go on:

> IVANOV: Sarah, stop at once and go away, or else I shall say something terrible. I long to say a dreadful, cruel thing. [*He shrieks*] Hold your tongue, Jewess!

[Brodskaya's translation: "I'm itching to say something dreadfully insulting . . . (*He yells*) Stop it, you Yid! . . . "]

Why does Chekhov have Ivanov throw the anti-Semitism in her face?[5]

The air is still. I look over my left shoulder, and Chekhov is standing there, leaning on the door-frame. Did he see me shake my head in disappointment?

I'm to Act 4, and feel as unhappy as the critic in "Drama." All that character did when the woman wouldn't stop reading her boring play was smash her in the head with a paperweight! . . . It's my own head I want to smash. I feign a smile at Chekhov, but inwardly wince as I read on through another of Ivanov's speeches. This time he is addressing his fiancée, as between Acts 3 and 4 his wife has died of tuberculosis. Chekhov, smoking a cigar, sits down across from me. Everyone says he's inscrutable, but he's not. He knows my feelings by my expressions and my quiet sighings; I read him while he reads me. He knows I'm hating his play!

> IVANOV: [. . .] We love each other, but we shall never be married. It makes no difference how I rave and grow bitter by myself, but I have no right to drag another down with me. My melancholy robbed my wife of the last year of her life. [. . .] Wherever I go, whether hunting or visiting, it makes no difference, I carry depression, dullness, and discontent along with me. [. . .] When I murmur at my fate everyone who hears me is seized with the same disgust of life and begins to grumble, too. [. . .]

Chekhov, I suspect again, was analyzing the play as he wrote it. I grumble to myself that it's not *my* fault I agree with the characters' self-assessments!

I turn over the last page and I smile.

"That bad, huh?" says Chekhov.

"No! . . ." Because, who am I to say? I love this guy! He is one of the greatest writers in the history of the world. In the English-speaking world, no one's plays except Shakespeare's are as admired and as often performed as his. Looking at my watch, I say, "Oh, my God! My wife's expecting me—the kids . . . they're supposed to call and . . . The play's *great*, Anton Pavlovich! Thanks for letting me read it."

Chekhov laughs. He sees me to the door and claps me on the back as I, ashamed of my cowardice, depart.

When *Ivanov* with slight revisions went into rehearsal at the end of 1888 in Petersburg, Chekhov wrote in exasperation to Suvorin: "The director sees Ivanov as a superfluous man in the Turgenev manner. Savina asks why Ivanov is such a blackguard. You write that 'Ivanov must be given something that makes it clear why two women throw themselves at him [. . .]' If all three of you have understood me this way, it means my *Ivanov* is a failure. I must have lost my mind and written something entirely different from what I had intended."[6]

All right, why shouldn't Chekhov have erred once in a long while? In the midst of the play's new production in Petersburg in January 1889, Chekhov reflected about the play: "I would very much have enjoyed delivering a paper to the Literary Society on where I found the idea for writing *Ivanov*. I would have publicly admitted my guilt. I cherished the audacious dream of summing up everything written thus far about whining, despondent people and of having my *Ivanov* put a stop to this sort of writing."[7]

But now in October 1887, Anton wrote to Alexander to ask him if *New Times* could put in a notice about *Ivanov* in the theater chronicle.[8] He told Alexander about chatting with Korolenko for three hours.

Writing to Leykin on October 7, he didn't tell him about having written *Ivanov*. That was his accomplishment of the last couple of weeks, and he wanted it advertised soon, but he didn't want Leykin to know. Instead, he pretended he hadn't been writing anything: "You're probably mad I'm not sending you stories. Alas, I sent them nowhere! I'm sick, then depressed, time wastes away, there's no money." He complimented Leykin's recent story and did mention he had sold old stories for a book to be published by the Verner Brothers, *Innocent Speeches*.

Why didn't he want Leykin to know about *Ivanov*? He didn't want Leykin's advice or he didn't want his envy? He hadn't told him in early 1886 about his new relationship with *New Times*, either. To inform Leykin about his other publishing opportunities was to tell him there would not be time to produce stories for *Fragments*—but that was a message he was continually trying to get across anyway. So why not fess up?

He wrote again on October 10 or 12 to Alexander, to whom he would continue to write frequently in the next two months: "Your letter is received; so as not to lie in bed and spit at the ceiling, I sit myself down at the table to answer."[9]

Chekhov's energy was often, understandably, depleted:

> I am ailing and depressed, like the son of a hen. The pen falls from my hand,
> and I do not write at all. I am expecting bankruptcy in the immediate future.
> If the play doesn't save me, then I am lost in the bloom of my years. The play

may bring me 600 or 700 rubles, but not before the middle of November, and what will happen until that middle I know not. I *cannot* work, and everything I write turns out rubbish. My energy—*fuit!* [. . .]

I am scratching a Saturday feuilleton, but merely so-so, and on an unattractive theme to me. ["The Cattle-Dealers"] will turn out bad, but still I will send it. [. . .]

I wrote the play *Ivanov* unexpectedly, after a talk with Korsh. I went to bed, thought out a theme, and wrote it. I spent a fortnight on it, or, rather, ten days, for there were days in the fortnight when I did not work or wrote something else. [. . .] It is a pity I cannot read the play to you. You are a light-minded man and have not seen much, but you are much fresher and keener-eared than all my Moscow praisers and accusers [the false-praising Ezhov and I would have to agree]. Your absence is no small loss to me.

Not only had weary, depressed Chekhov written *Ivanov*, he had composed, he told Alexander, a very long story:

Ask Suvorin or Burenin whether they will publish a thing of 1,500 lines. If so, I will send it, although personally I am against dailies publishing long dossiers and bringing over the train in the next number. I have a love story of 1,500 lines, not a tedious one, but no good for a serious monthly, for there figure in it a president and members of a military high court—that is, they are not Liberals. Ask them, and answer soon. On hearing from you I will make a clean copy and send it off.

Alexander replied on October 18 that "Suvorin was even amazed that you would ask about this."[10] Of course *New Times* would publish it. The editors of the *Collected Works* note that Chekhov's long story, a novel, was never found.

Sometime after October 10, Chekhov asked his friend Vladimir Gilyarovskiy if he wanted to go to the circus with him and his brother Ivan. Chekhov enjoyed the circus a lot, more than the fictional dog Kashtanka would in his upcoming Christmas story.

Chekhov wrote Korolenko on October 17: "it seems to me that if you and I live another ten or twenty years in this world, we shall not fail to find points of contact in the future. Among the Russians who are happily writing at the present day I am the most light-minded and least serious. I am under warning; poetically speaking, I have loved my pure muse but I have not respected her. I have been unfaithful to her more than once and taken her places unfit for her. But you are serious and sound and true."[11] He also told Korolenko about Thoreau's *Walden*, which was coming out in translation in an edition by *New Times*.[12] Chekhov had interesting and intelligent reservations about *Walden*: "The first chapter promises a great deal; he has ideas, freshness and originality, but he is hard to read. The architecture and composition are impossible. Ideas, beautiful and ugly, light and cumbrous, are piled on top of each other, crowded together, squeezing the juice out of each other, and at any moment the pressure may make them squeal."

On the same day, Chekhov wrote his cousin Georgy to apologize about the delay in communicating. He was busy writing "all day long" and his hand got tired. "I don't go to the theater or on visits, so Mama and Auntie call me homebound 'Grandpa.'"[13] (But he had gone quite a lot to Korsh's theater and he had just been to the circus!) Unusually, he mentioned his father: "With each year he becomes softer and kinder." Pavel was still working as a shop employee on the other side of Moscow and usually slept at Chekhov's brother Ivan's. Pavel's softening would have been information Georgy shared with his father, Anton's Uncle Mitrofan. Anton asked about everyone's health and set to rights all the family communications.

By the 19th, Chekhov was eager to assure Leykin: "In the last week I was fine, didn't feel depressed and worked";[14] he would submit a story again soon, if his health remained fine. (It did and within a couple of days he sent *Fragments* a semi-comic doctor story.) He also mentioned, perhaps suspecting that Leykin had already found out, that he had written a four-act play for Korsh. Wondering about Leykin's recent silence, he asked: "Isn't there any news about the literary world?"

Chekhov had managed to send *Petersburg Gazette* "A Problem" ("Zadacha," October 19). The problem, in a nutshell:

> The other side of the door, in the study, a family council was being held. The subject under discussion was an exceedingly disagreeable and delicate one. [Twenty-five-year-old] Sasha Uskov had cashed at one of the banks a false promissory note, and it had become due for payment three days before, and now his two paternal uncles and Ivan Markovich, the brother of his dead mother, were deciding the question whether they should pay the money and save the family honor, or wash their hands of it and leave the case to go for trial.

To outsiders who have no personal interest in the matter such questions seem simple; for those who are so unfortunate as to have to decide them in earnest they are extremely difficult. The uncles had been talking for a long time, but the problem seemed no nearer decision.

Chekhov liked to remind his readers that it takes a lot of thought, information, and imagination to appreciate the dynamics of a problem. If troubling family matters look simple to us, we're simply blind to all the circumstances.

In "A Problem," each uncle is confident and sure of himself and persuasive. The young man is a wretch, but Chekhov seems to not be taking sides:

> The maternal uncle, kind-hearted Ivan Markovich, spoke smoothly, softly, and with a tremor in his voice. He began with saying that youth has its rights and its peculiar temptations. Which of us has not been young, and who has not been led astray? To say nothing of ordinary mortals, even great men have not escaped errors and mistakes in their youth. Take, for instance, the biography of great writers. Did not every one of them gamble, drink, and draw down upon himself the anger of right-thinking people in his young days?

The family council goes on for hours, the resolution to let him go to trial breaks down and is reconsidered, and finally he is "forgiven."

His kindly uncle gives the conditions: repentance and reformation. Sasha, forgiven, immediately proves incorrigible.

A detail of Chekhov's biography that gets repeated again and again is his winning of the Pushkin Award in 1888. It's true that's the date of the award, but he knew this month, a year ahead of time, that he had won it. In response to Alexander's news, which had come to Alexander from Suvorin, who had the insider Grigorovich's knowledge of the voting, he replied on October 21:

> The Pushkin Prize cannot be given to me. That's first. Secondly, were it given to me, which I cannot believe, so many rebukes will come to me, in Moscow particularly, so many worries and perplexities will arise that even the 500 rubles won't make up for it. I could accept the prize only if it were divided between

me and Korolenko; but now, when it is still uncertain who is the better, when only ten or fifteen Petersburgians see talent in me, while all Petersburg and all Moscow see it in Korolenko, to give the prize to me would be to please a minority and to prick a majority. Don't say this to Suvorin, for he, as far as I know, does not read Korolenko, and therefore will not understand me.[15]

He gave his brother details about *Ivanov*'s future performances and payoffs: "If the censorship should not pass it, which is doubtful, then . . . most likely I will not shoot myself, though it will be bitter." He teased Alexander: "Please do my commissions without blinking. You will be superbly rewarded: the future historian will mention you in my biography: 'He had a brother Aleksei, who ran his errands, whereby he contributed not a little to the development of his talent.' My biographer is not obliged to know your right name, but from the signature 'Al. Chekhov' it will not be difficult for him to guess that your name is Aleksei."

Alexander replied on October 23 with an account of his conversation with Suvorin, wherein he had passed along Chekhov's wishes not to have his book entered in the Pushkin Prize contest. Suvorin told Alexander: "Don't worry, you, I'll write him myself. What a fellow! He wrote a play in 10 days! Truly, what a fellow!"[16]

Chekhov wrote Alexander again on October 24, having learned to his relief that the Pushkin Prize wouldn't be announced until the next year. He also gave Alexander this stern advice: "Damp for children is as dangerous as hunger. Hack this on your nose and find a drier apartment."[17]

> You invite me to stay in your flat. . . . Rather! Everybody should be pleased to give shelter to a man of genius! Well, I'll do you that favor. But one condition: cook for me soup with herbs, which you do nicely, and offer me vodka not before 11 P.M. I am not afraid of the children's singing.

—⁓—

Chekhov wrote "Intrigues" ("Intrigi," October 24) for Leykin. A conniving doctor plans to slander his way out of a hearing—but his face seems to be betraying him. Chekhov's recent doctor characters have been frustrated or difficult. In *Ivanov*, most of the characters despise Dr. Lvov, whose moral bearing is correct but insufferable. In "Intrigues," Dr. Shelestov may well be the most competent of doctors, but he is also a cheat. Chekhov tells the story from Shelestov's point of view; Shelestov regards himself as superior to the doctors intriguing against him. He imagines his cool unruffled response to "a whole series of new accusations [. . .] being leveled against me".[18]

At this point, carelessly twirling a pencil or a chain, he would say that yes, in actual fact it was true that during consultations he had sometimes been known to raise his voice and attack colleagues, regardless of who was present. It was also true that once, during a consultation, in the presence of doctors and family members, he had asked the patient, "Who was the idiot who prescribed opium for you?" Rare was a consultation without incident . . . But why was this? The answer was simple! In these consultations he, Shelestov, was always saddled with colleagues whose knowledge left much to be desired. There were thirty-two doctors in town, most of whom knew less than a first-year medical student.

Shelestov continues imagining his unflustered, condescending self-defense: "He would go on expounding, and his supporters would applaud and clasp their hands together in exultation." But when he is finally about to set out for the actual meeting, Shelestov loses his composure before the mirror.

Shelestov looks at his face, flies into a rage, and begins sensing that his face is plotting against him. He goes out into the hall, and as he is putting on his coat, his galoshes, and his hat, he feels that they are intriguing against him, too.

Chekhov leaves it to us to imagine how the meeting will go.

—⁄⁄⁄—

While he was proud of and anxious about the publication of *In the Twilight*, Chekhov was defensive and embarrassed about the content of and the chintzy payment he received for *Innocent Speeches*, which was published on October 27. He downplayed his involvement in it. While the brothers Evgeny and Mikhail Verner, the editors of *The Cricket*, one of the humor periodicals Chekhov used to contribute to, had asked him to select a dozen stories, which Chekhov variously described as a dozen or fifteen or a dozen and a half, Chekhov gave them eventually twenty-one stories, which he lightly edited. The Verners' payment was only slightly more than he would receive for a typical story at *New Times*. Still, 150 rubles was *something*, rent, for example, for almost three months. The only money Chekhov seemed to pass up in these years was for his medical work.[19]

Even to Alexander, he disparaged the contents of *Innocent Speeches*: "the stories are so bad you have the right to hit me on the back of the head"; he blamed himself and the Verners for exploiting his "poverty"; he asked Alexander to put the kibosh on any request by the Verners for notice of the book in *New Times*. "In silence I see the greatest favor."[20] Alexander replied that in fact two of his colleagues wanted to review the book.

Despite Chekhov's momentary embarrassment, most of the stories went into the *Collected Works*, which inclusion a dozen years later had to survive Chekhov's steely criticism. Perhaps this fall he was embarrassed about exploiting his own fame—*In the Twilight* was very recent and popular—or about the Verners exploiting his fame, or that he was not (and never would be) a good negotiator, only receiving 150 rubles.

On the other hand, Chekhov had so many fine stories in his archives, so why not publish them while they were wanted?

—⁘—

Chekhov had pep in his step when he wrote to first reader Ezhov on October 27: "You, as the groomsman of my *Ivanov*, I regard it as not out of place to communicate the following: *Ivanov* will definitely go on at the end of November or early December."[21] Ivanov would be played by Davydov, with whom Chekhov had sat until three in the morning the night before. Davydov had told Chekhov he had done by instinct all that makes a play correct. Chekhov beamed: "From this comes the moral: 'Don't be shy, young people!'"

And so, Ezhov's friend and mentor continued, "Of course it's bad that you're lazy and write little. You're a 'beginner' in the full meaning of that word and ought not to forget under the fear of a death sentence that each line in the present establishes capital for the future. If now you don't train your hand and your head to discipline and forced marches, if you don't hurry and tune yourself, in 3–4 years it will be already too late." He scolded him and Lazarev for not making hay: "You both work too little." He pestered Ezhov to submit pieces to every issue of *Fragments*. As a sidenote, he confided: "For example, my brother Agafopod [Alexander] wrote meagerly and now already feels written out. . . . You know that whoever's a little and lazy cockroach begins impotence early. I say this to you on a scientific basis." He invited little lazy Ezhov, who was teaching outside of Moscow, to visit at Christmas. Chekhov, meanwhile, had persuaded Lazarev to start working on a play about *Hamlet* with him; Chekhov had started it, all Lazarev had to do was finish it.[22]

Lazarev wrote Ezhov about this conversation, and then years later wrote it up in a memoir:

> On one of my latest meetings with him, he gave me "Hamlet, Prince of Danes."
> "Take the play with you to Kirzhach, A. S.! I began, but I'm too lazy to finish it. I'm too busy and tormented by *Ivanov*. Write the end, we'll work it over together."

I countered that I had never written a play and I was afraid I could not justify the hopes that he raised on me as a playwright.

"Nonsense, nonsense! You have to begin, my dear. Plays—they're the bread for our brother. Write twenty plays, they'll make you a fortune!"[23]

What's compelling about this recollection is hearing Chekhov's energetic, encouraging, irrefutable voice: his boldness about taking on projects. The joint manuscript was lost, but Lazarev's description of the play sounds plausible and modern:

> The play's action took place behind scenes at a provincial theater at the time of rehearsing *Hamlet*. [. . .] The first act began with preparing for the rehearsal. [. . .]
> The first act was supposed to end with a scandal and general confusion.
> In the second act it was suggested to give a scene from "Hamlet."
> Thinking over the first act, I sketched out some combinations and a plan for the first act to the end. [. . .] Making for myself a copy of the original Hamlet, Prince of Denmark, together with my sketches, I sent them to Chekhov [. . .]

Chekhov replied in the middle of November with several comments and directives.

If one writes to a confidant about one's mood, perhaps the mood is likely to be low? On October 27, the same day he wrote cheerfully to Ezhov, he wrote to Alexander, kvetching about Alexander not having yet sent a fee from the *Petersburg Gazette*; he didn't have any money! "I've fallen into a depression again; I'm not working. I sit all day in my armchair looking at the ceiling. However, there's the practice."[24] By which, did Chekhov mean that being a doctor was comparatively satisfying? Alexander invited him to come to Petersburg for a couple of months and liven up.

Chekhov's distraction was *Ivanov*. Rehearsals were starting.

On October 29, "The Old House: A Story Told by a Houseowner" ("Stariy Dom") was published. In this sociological tale of poverty and criminality, Chekhov is unrelenting. Surveying the rooms in the house that is about to be knocked down to be replaced by a new house, the narrator grimly notes:

The door at the end of the corridor leads to the wash-house, where by day they washed clothes and at night made an uproar and drank beer. And in that flat of three rooms everything is saturated with bacteria and bacilli. It's not nice there. Many lodgers have died there, and I can positively assert that that flat was at some time cursed by someone, and that together with its human lodgers there was always another lodger, unseen, living in it.[25]

He recalls the funeral of a mother and relates the pitiful story of her family, who lived in that flat:

It seemed to me that he [the widower] himself, his children, the grandmother and Yegorich, were already marked down by that unseen being which lived with them in that flat. I am a thoroughly superstitious man, perhaps, because I am a houseowner and for forty years have had to do with lodgers. I believe if you don't win at cards from the beginning you will go on losing to the end; when fate wants to wipe you and your family off the face of the earth, it remains inexorable in its persecution, and the first misfortune is commonly only the first of a long series. . . . Misfortunes are like stones. One stone has only to drop from a high cliff for others to be set rolling after it.

This narrator is unusual. An older man, he likes the way he sounds: he concludes there with a nice folksy, wise summation. He writes *quotably*. Chekhov determinedly resisted writing fine quotable sentences. Wit and wisdom were to be suppressed in the service of description, so that only the description left its impression.

The father of the family loses his job, becomes a drunk, the family disintegrates.

Chekhov in his service as a doctor saw such lodgings; witnessing such poverty, he despaired.

———

"The Cattle-Dealers" ("Kholodnaya Krov,'" October 31 and November 3): Over the course of several days a father and son ride railroad cars with the cattle they're bringing to a city. Malahin, the father, has to keep bribing railroad officials, track inspectors, everyone who has anything to do with letting the eight cattle-cars pass. He's a drinker, but he is meticulous in teaching his son Yasha the ropes of this peculiar business.

Malahin, laying out a complaint in the midst of the frequently delayed journey, seeks to achieve as a storyteller what only an artist can give a sense of: "he wants to describe in the protocol not any separate episode but his whole journey, with all his losses and conversations with station-masters—to describe it lengthily and vindictively."

The primary description of "his whole journey," could Malahin have done it, is this:

> The van is quite full. If one glances in through the dim light of the lantern, for the first moment the eyes receive an impression of something shapeless, monstrous, and unmistakably alive, something very much like gigantic crabs which move their claws and feelers, crowd together, and noiselessly climb up the walls to the ceiling; but if one looks more closely, horns and their shadows, long lean backs, dirty hides, tails, eyes begin to stand out in the dusk. They are cattle and their shadows. There are eight of them in the van. Some turn around and stare at the men and swing their tails. Others try to stand or lie down more comfortably. They are crowded. If one lies down the others must stand and huddle closer. No manger, no halter, no litter, not a wisp of hay. . . .

Malahin (usually referred to as "the old man") has to metaphorically grease the wheels to get the train moving:

> "God be my judge, I have reckoned it and even jotted it down in a notebook; we have wasted thirty-four hours standing still on the journey. If you go on like this, either the cattle will die, or they won't pay me two rubles for the meat when I do get there. It's not traveling, but ruination."
>
> The guard raises his eyebrows and sighs with an air that seems to say: "All that is unhappily true!" The engine-driver sits silent, dreamily looking at the cap. From their faces one can see that they have a secret thought in common, which they do not utter, not because they want to conceal it, but because such thoughts are much better expressed by signs than by words. And the old man understands. He feels in his pocket, takes out a ten-ruble note, and without preliminary words, without any change in the tone of his voice or the expression of his face, but with the confidence and directness with which probably only Russians give and take bribes, he gives the guard the note. The latter takes it, folds it in four, and without undue haste puts it in his pocket. After that all three go out of the room, and waking the sleeping guard on the way, go on to the platform.

(The story was too long to fit into the space in that Saturday's literary section of *New Times*, so its conclusion, when Malahin's cattle's journey ends, followed three days later.)[26]

At last the bullocks are sold to a dealer. Malahin hires drovers. The cattle are divided into herds, ten in each, and driven to the other end of the town. The bullocks, exhausted, go with drooping heads through the noisy streets, and look indifferently at what they see for the first and last time in their lives. The tattered drovers walk after them, their heads drooping, too. They are bored. . . . Now and then some drover starts out of his brooding, remembers that there are cattle in front of him entrusted to his charge, and to show that he is doing his duty brings a stick down full swing on a bullock's back. The bullock staggers with the pain, runs forward a dozen paces, and looks about him as though he were ashamed at being beaten before people.

Having read only this one story, the Russian literary world would have had to sit up straight and wonder, "Who's this Chekhov? Whatever outhouse he emerged from, he's a genius!" Titled "Cold Blood" in Russian, "The Cattle-Dealers" "won an accolade from the Petersburg Society for the Protection of Animals."[27]

From the end of October to November 19, Chekhov attended four rehearsals of *Ivanov*.[28] An actor remembered his presence at one: "I saw a mechanical toy moving across the floor at me, and I noticed Anton Pavlovich walking toward us. The other actors told me later that all of Chekhov's pockets were packed with mechanical toys. Anton Pavlovich explained, apologizing, that he was a doctor, and that earlier that day he had some children among his patients, and that they stuffed his pockets with toys. 'Look at this! I have too many toys . . .'" Alexandra Glama-Mesherskaya, who played Sarra, says that during rehearsals, Chekhov "never interrupted the director's work. He never made a single remark on the actors at all. I never saw a more humble author in my life."[29]

November 1887

—⁓—

To the question of what he would do, if he became
rich, Chekhov answered with perfect seriousness: "I
would write the tiniest possible stories . . ."

—Reminiscences[1]

T rust the action, not the words. In the first week of November, Chekhov and his
brother Alexander began giving out copies of *Innocent Speeches* to friends and
family.[2] It was a well-designed, good-looking volume, in Chekhov's opinion,[3] and full of
funny stories that had enjoyed a wide audience. A book's publication has been known to
soften an author's view of it.

Cover of *Innocent Speeches.*

At Korsh's request, he went to the theater on November 2 to answer the actors' questions about *Ivanov*, and the next night he watched a rehearsal. He wrote to Leykin on November 4: "Forgive me, kind Nikolay Aleksandrovich, that for so long I didn't answer your letter. My play, of the highest expectations—that it be simple!—has so taken me and tormented me that I lost the ability to orient the time, it knocked me off my legs, and probably I'll soon become a psycho. Writing it was not hard, but putting it on demands not only expenditures on cabs and time, but so much nervous work."[4] He complained, in a comically outraged list, about his unhappiness with Moscow, actors, Korsh, the women in Korsh's troupe. He had wanted to take his play back, so he said, but Korsh wouldn't let him.

Maria Kiseleva, having received his invitation to the premiere performance, wrote him on November 4: "I'm worried for you and imagine—if the play is liked and they call you up—how you will bow. Your forelock will fall on your head . . . Will you be embarrassed? I'm already embarrassed to death, though I desire that you are often and much called up . . ."[5] Kiseleva's attraction to Chekhov seems beyond latent to me. Virginia Llewellyn Smith writes that Kiseleva "took a vicarious interest in Chekhov's flirtations. In a letter to Chekhov of 1887 [Nov. 4] she wrote: 'The other day I dreamt of you as Dunya's bridegroom. Your face was sad and you admitted that you didn't want to marry, but Mama Efros commanded it . . . they dragged you both to the synagogue, and I was so sorry I wept . . .'; but, Kiseleva added, had it been real, she would have laughed and said: 'He got what was coming to him! Serves him right!' Chekhov in her opinion had carried the flirtation far enough to warrant Dunya's having some claim on him: but he had not intended to commit himself to her."[6]

The only story Chekhov published this month was "Expensive Lessons" ("Dorogie Uroki," November 9), which is about a dull, self-deceiving twenty-six-year-old who decides he should learn French ("For a cultivated man to be ignorant of foreign languages is a great inconvenience. Vorotov became acutely conscious of it when, after taking his degree, he began upon a piece of research work");[7] Chekhov liked to make fun of himself for not knowing foreign languages. A young and pretty French-Russian woman comes to Vorotov's house, expecting to teach a child; she agrees to teach the man, because, like Chekhov, she needs the money:

"French grammar has twenty-six letters. The first letter is called A, the second B . . ."

"Excuse me," Vorotov interrupted, smiling. "I must warn you, mademoiselle, that you must change your method a little in my case. You see, I know Russian, Greek, and Latin well. . . . I've studied comparative philology, and I think we might omit Margot [a textbook] and pass straight to reading some author."

And he explained to the French girl how grown-up people learn languages.

"A friend of mine," he said, "wanting to learn modern languages, laid before him the French, German, and Latin gospels, and read them side by side, carefully analyzing each word, and would you believe it, he attained his object in less than a year. Let us do the same. We'll take some author and read him."

The French girl looked at him in perplexity. Evidently the suggestion seemed to her very naïve and ridiculous. If this strange proposal had been made to her by a child, she would certainly have been angry and have scolded it, but as he was a grown-up man and very stout and she could not scold him, she only shrugged her shoulders hardly perceptibly and said:

"As you please."

Some of us who have tried to learn a new language after leaving school will recognize ourselves in Vorotov.

With a good-natured smile, breathing hard, he spent a quarter of an hour over the word "Mémoires," and as much over the word *de*, and this wearied the young lady. She answered his questions languidly, grew confused, and evidently did not understand her pupil well, and did not attempt to understand him. Vorotov asked her questions, and at the same time kept looking at her fair hair and thinking:

"Her hair isn't naturally curly; she curls it. It's a strange thing! She works from morning to night, and yet she has time to curl her hair."

After several lessons, wherein he has only learned the word "memoir," he decides she doesn't know what she's doing. (Is it possible she doesn't know what she's doing? Or is it more likely that he's hopeless? . . . I ask, unrhetorically, because I had Russian tutors who thought the same about me: "Idiot!" And my only way out was to accept my hopelessness and nevertheless slowly stumble toward being regarded by them as "very slow" or "as competent grammatically as a little boy.") He resolves to give her a week's pay and fire her. But when he notices that she, having guessed his intentions, is upset, and that she must really count on the money, he changes his mind. Like distracted students everywhere, he amuses himself as he can:

> The lessons began again. Vorotov felt no interest in them. Realizing that he would gain nothing from the lessons, he gave the French girl liberty to do as she liked, asking her nothing and not interrupting her. She translated away as she pleased ten pages during a lesson, and he did not listen, breathed hard, and having nothing better to do, gazed at her curly head, or her soft white hands or her neck and sniffed the fragrance of her clothes.

He is smitten, but she has absolutely no interest in him. He continues to pay her for her incomprehensible, useless lessons of reading and translating to him.

Though the neat, clever, amusing, story resounds for me as a teacher and student, there does not seem to be any special or immediate biographical connection to Chekhov. He would have earned sixty rubles from the *Petersburg Gazette* for it. What he and "Alice," the French teacher, needed was money, whether or not readers were paying attention to a good story.

He followed up on his first invitation to the Kiselevs to the November 19 premiere of *Ivanov* in Moscow with another, to Aleksei Kiselev, on November 10: "If you don't come I'll give you such a pill in the newspapers shaming you that you'll flee to America. Important reasons for not appearing might be: a) dysentery, b) rivers overflowing the banks, c) bankruptcy, d) people's unrest, e) doomsday and f) a visit to Babkino by the shah of Persia. I don't recognize other reasons. Hear that? [. . .] If Maria Vladimirovna doesn't come, then I, first, will not give her story to *Spring*, and, second, I will my whole life campaign against children's magazines."[8]

He also wrote to Alexander on November 10, the day of *Ivanov*'s first staging in distant Saratov, to ask him to send him the payment as soon as possible for "The Cattle-Dealers." He was out of money. He wouldn't get paid for out-of-town performances of *Ivanov* until he joined (for fifteen rubles) the Society of Playwrights. (He did so on November 16.)[9]

Chekhov was abuzz with *Ivanov* and queried a confused and insecure Lazarev about how he was doing with their "vaudeville" *Hamlet*. They needed, he wrote Lazarev on November 15, to "pound while the iron is hot." If all went well, the Korsh actors could begin performing it by January. Among Chekhov's suggestions for Lazarev was that there be a "a complete jumble," "each person has to be a character and speak in his own language," "continuous movement," roles for eleven actors, and "no longwindedness." "In expectation of your quick answer, I recommend to you, kind sir, to lie down on the bed, take your brain in your hands, and partake in contemplation; after a long contemplation, sit at the table and sketch out your plan."

On November 15 he also wrote to Leykin:

Forgive me, kind Nikolay Aleksandrovich, for not sending you a story this time around. Wait a bit. My play is opening on Thursday, and as soon as that is over with, I'll sit myself down and hack away.[10]

After the apology and promise, he took to testy argument:

Your lines about production of plays puzzle me. You write that the author only gets in the production's way, makes the actors uncomfortable, and more often than not contributes only the most inane comments. Let me answer you thusly: (1) the play is the author's property, not the actors'; (2) where the author is present, casting the play is his responsibility; (3) *all* my comments to date have improved the production, and they have all been put into practice, as I indicated; (4) the actors themselves ask for my comments [. . .]

You write that Suvorin agrees with you. I'm surprised. Suvorin wrote me not long ago that I should "take my actors in hand" and advised me how to go about the in-hand-taking process.

In any case, thank you for bringing up the subject. I'll write Suvorin and raise the question of the limits of an author's competence in such matters.

You also write, "Why the blazes don't you forget about your play?" An eye for an eye: "Why the hell don't you forget about your shareholding operations?" Dropping the play means dropping my hopes for a profitable deal.

But since all this whining of mine must be getting on your nerves, let's move on to more timely affairs.

Of those "timely affairs," wrote Chekhov, "We have a lot to talk about." He would be arriving in Petersburg at the end of the month. "I don't know what to say to your remark about Davydov [the actor playing Ivanov]. Maybe you're right [Leykin had written that Davydov wasn't to be trusted]. My opinion about him is based not so much on my personal impression as on Suvorin's recommendation. 'You can trust Davydov,' he writes."

Leykin had to know he had been supplanted.

Opening night for *Ivanov* poster.

November 19 was *Ivanov*'s opening night. Anton reported on the action to Alexander the next day:

Well, the first performance is over. I will tell you all about it in detail. To begin with, Korsh promised me ten rehearsals, but gave me only four, of which only two could be called rehearsals, for the other two were tournaments in which *messieurs les artistes* exercised themselves in altercation and abuse. Davydov and Glama were the only two who knew their parts; the others trusted to the prompter and their own inner conviction.

Act One.—I am behind the stage in a small box that looks like a prison cell. My family is in a box of the benoire and is trembling. Contrary to my expectations, I am cool and am conscious of no agitation. The actors are nervous and excited, and cross themselves. The curtain goes up . . . the actor whose benefit night it is comes on. His uncertainty, the way that he forgets his part, and the wreath that is presented to him make the play unrecognizable to me from the first sentences. Kiselevsky, of whom I had great hopes, did not deliver a single phrase correctly—literally *not a single one*. He said things of his own composition. In spite of this and of the stage manager's blunders, the first act was a great success. There were many calls.

Act Two.—A lot of people on the stage. Visitors. They don't know their parts, make mistakes, talk nonsense. Every word cuts me like a knife in my back. But—o Muse!—this act, too, was a success. There were calls for all the actors, and I was called before the curtain twice. Congratulations and success.

Act Three.—The acting is not bad. Enormous success. I had to come before the curtain three times, and as I did so Davydov was shaking my hand, and Glama, like Manilov, was pressing my other hand to her heart. The triumph of talent and virtue.

Act Four, Scene One.—It does not go badly. Calls before the curtain again. Then a long, wearisome interval. The audience, not used to leaving their seats and going to the refreshment bar between two scenes, murmur. The curtain goes up. Fine: through the arch one can see the supper table (the wedding). The band plays flourishes. The groomsmen come out: they are drunk, and so you see they think they must behave like clowns and cut capers. The horseplay and pot-house atmosphere reduce me to despair. Then Kiselevsky comes out: it is a poetical, moving passage, but my Kiselevsky does not know his part, is drunk as a cobbler, and a short poetical dialogue is transformed into something tedious and disgusting: the public is perplexed. At the end of the play the hero dies because he cannot get over the insult he has received. The audience, grown cold and tired, does not understand this death (the actors insisted on it; I have another version). There are calls for the actors and for me. During one of the calls I hear sounds of open hissing, drowned by the clapping and stamping.

On the whole I feel tired and annoyed. It was sickening though the play had considerable success. [. . .] Theater-goers say that they had never seen such a ferment in a theater, such universal clapping and hissing, nor heard such discussions among the audience as they saw and heard at my play. And it has never happened before at Korsh's that the author has been called after the second act. [. . .][11]

Chekhov's account of the performance is for me (and maybe for Ezhov) incomparably more amusing than the actual play. He asked Alexander to tell his fellow editor Burenin that as soon as the play ended he sat down to work on his next *New Times* short story, which he didn't finish until December 13, "The Kiss."

Lazarev, who couldn't make it to the premiere of *Ivanov*, sent Chekhov his work on "Hamlet, Prince of Danes" on November 21.[12] Ezhov, Nikolay Chekhov, and Isaac Levitan made it to the second performance of the play on November 23. Anton wrote Alexander on November 24; his report on the second night was briefer:

> Well, dearest Gusev, the dust has finally settled and everything has calmed down. Here I am as usual, sitting at my desk and placidly writing stories. You can't possibly imagine what it was like! The devil only knows what they've made out of so insignificant a piece of junk as my miserable little play. [. . .]
>
> The second performance went well [. . .] Reading the play won't tell you what all the excitement was about; you won't find anything special in it.[13]

He asked Alexander to note the performance in *New Times* and congratulated him on his promotion to Suvorin's secretary. Chekhov would be arriving in Petersburg on November 30.

Finally, he apologized: "Have I been getting on your nerves? I've felt like a psychopath all November. [. . .] Keep well and forgive the psychopathy. I'm over it now. Today I'm normal." He signed himself "Schiller Shakespearovich Goethe."

———

On November 26 Chekhov was dealing with Lazarev's collaboration on their play. He didn't like it: "1) Your 'Hamlet' consists entirely of dialogues that don't have organic connections. The dialogues are unthinkable. [. . .] 5) The end of the first act is stilted. You can't end it that way. [. . .] . . . 8) I'm afraid I'm making you sick of me and you will curse me as a swine in a yarmulke . . . But I take comfort in the thought that fussing with vaudeville will be useful to you. You have your hands full. 9) After the play I was so tormented that I lost the ability to rightly think or to speak sensibly."[14]

This was the end of their work together, and the manuscript disappeared.

Chekhov got on the train in Moscow on November 29. He wrote to his sister the next day to say he would be sending money. He was at Alexander's dirty, stinky, stuffy apartment, and Alexander's wife Anna was sick.

December 1887

The Lord gave you a kind and tender heart, so why
not put it to good use? Write with a gentle pen and
a carefree spirit. Don't think about the wrongs that
have been done you. . . . Be objective, take a look at
everything with the eye of a good, kind man, with
your own eye, I mean, and sit down and write a story
or play about life in Russia—not a criticism of Russian
life, simply a joyous song, the song of the Goldfinch,
about Russian life and life in general. Our life comes
only once, and there is no point, honestly there isn't,
in wasting it . . . Dear Jean, be fair for once to yourself
and your talent. . . . Forgive everyone who has offended
you, forget about them, and, I repeat, sit down and
write.

—Letter to a friend[1]

Chekhov was free, clear of Moscow, clear of his domestic responsibilities, clear of
the pressures of *Ivanov*. He wrote to Davydov on December 1 to thank him for his
portrayal of Ivanov and to share his misgivings and pride about the play and about how
it was being discussed and reviewed there in Petersburg.

He wrote to his family on December 3 about what a great time he was having, despite
staying in Alexander's filthy apartment; at least Anna was getting better and the children
were well. The night before, he had had a respite from Alexander's and had eaten and
stayed at Leykin's.

He was meeting sometimes with Korolenko and every day with Suvorin: "I feel I'm in seventh heaven." The food, the people, the "ladies," the encouragement for him to bring *Ivanov* to the capital. "How I wish I could live here always!" He would be leaving on December 15.

It was probably on December 3, when he was sitting in the *Fragments* office writing to his family, that he submitted "The Lion and the Sun" ("Lev i Solntse," December 5). There is nothing final or significant about this good comic story, but it was in fact the last story Chekhov would write for *Fragments* until 1892. Chekhov had arrived in Petersburg and been feted, and in "The Lion and the Sun" a Persian magnate arrives in a Russian town, where he is similarly feted by a medal-hungry mayor:

> It is well known that the more orders and medals you have the more you want—and the mayor had long been desirous of receiving the Persian order of The Lion and the Sun; he desired it passionately, madly. He knew very well that there was no need to fight, or to subscribe to an asylum, or to serve on committees to obtain this order; all that was needed was a favorable opportunity. And now it seemed to him that this opportunity had come.[2]

Like Chekhov, the mayor is not a linguist; he doesn't understand Persian or French, but he still lays on his welcome pretty thick:

> "The frontiers of Persia"—Kutsyn continued the greeting he had previously learned by heart—"are in close contact with the borders of our spacious fatherland, and therefore mutual sympathies impel me, so to speak, to express my solidarity with you."
>
> The illustrious Persian got up and again muttered something in a wooden tongue. Kutsyn, who knew no foreign language, shook his head to show that he did not understand.
>
> "Well, how am I to talk to him?" he thought. "It would be a good thing to send for an interpreter at once, but it is a delicate matter, I can't talk before witnesses. The interpreter would be chattering all over the town afterward."
>
> And Kutsyn tried to recall the foreign words he had picked up from the newspapers.
>
> "I am the mayor of the town," he muttered. "That is the lord mayor . . . municipalais . . . Vwee? Kompreney?"

He wanted to express his social position in words or in gesture, and did not know how. A picture hanging on the wall with an inscription in large letters, "The Town of Venice," helped him out of his difficulties. He pointed with his finger at the town, then at his own head, and in that way obtained, as he imagined, the phrase: "I am the head of the town." The Persian did not understand, but he gave a smile, and said:

"Goot, monsieur . . . goot. . . ." Half-an-hour later the mayor was slapping the Persian, first on the knee and then on the shoulder [. . .]

The mayor shows the Persian quite a good time and eventually secures himself the coveted medal.

In "A Problem," the uncles let off their criminally inclined nephew, but in "In Trouble" ("Beda"), which Chekhov wrote for the *Petersburg Gazette* (December 7), an auditor who apparently innocently (at least negligently) signed off on fraudulent deals does not anticipate being charged with fraud himself. But he is charged and his life falls apart: "His conscience was clear, and he ascribed his position to mistake and misunderstanding; to his mind, it was all due to the fact that the officials and the examining magistrates were young men and inexperienced. It seemed to him that if he were to talk it over in detail and open his heart to some elderly judge, everything would go right again."[3] It doesn't "go right again." His bewilderment keeps him calm throughout a trial, though his insides churn. Convicted, he is exiled to Tobolsk.

Chekhov on the other hand was eating well and would have enjoyed being exiled to Petersburg. He was seemingly only socializing and writing. He made friends fast. He met a new lifelong friend Ivan Leont'ev (his pen name was Shcheglov) on December 9. Within fifteen minutes, Leont'ev recalled, "I was already conversing from the heart with Chekhov, just as if with someone I had known for ten years."[4] By the time they said goodbye that first night, "he was calling me 'Jean' and I was calling him 'Antoine.'"

A day or two later, and within a half-hour of meeting sixty-three-year-old Aleksei Pleshcheev, the famous poet "was fully taken captive," remembered Leont'ev, as "Chekhov quickly went into his customary philosophical-humorous mood. If someone had happened to glance in at Pleshcheev's room then, he would have thought that two close old friends were chatting."[5]

Chekhov showed Leont'ev "The Kiss" ("Potseluy") on December 13 before submitting it to *New Times*, where it was published December 15. The story concerns an officer in a brigade in the countryside. Leont'ev had been an artillery captain in the late 1870s, and Chekhov wanted to know if he had got the military details right. He had.

Unusually, the time-setting of the beginning of the story, May 20, does not correspond to the issue date of "The Kiss." Chekhov, perhaps, had had this one up his sleeve for a while or, possibly, he had freed himself of the obligation to write to the season. A reserve artillery brigade is out in the field near a remote village doing maneuvers one evening when the officers are invited by a servant to go have tea at the local estate. The officers grumble, because they had this experience the year before, being invited to an estate, but then having to spend all night listening to their host's "anecdotes of his glorious past."

But this landowner is different:

> The General shook hands with everyone, made his apologies, and smiled, but it was evident by his face that he was by no means so delighted as their last year's count, and that he had invited the officers simply because, in his opinion, it was a social obligation to do so. And the officers themselves, as they walked up the softly carpeted stairs, as they listened to him, felt that they had been invited to this house simply because it would have been awkward not to invite them; and at the sight of the footmen, who hastened to light the lamps in the entrance below and in the anteroom above, they began to feel as though they had brought uneasiness and discomfort into the house with them. In a house in which two sisters and their children, brothers, and neighbors were gathered together, probably on account of some family festivity, or event, how could the presence of nineteen unknown officers possibly be welcome?[6]

Another way that "The Kiss" is unusual is that Chekhov has decided to fill it with a lot of people. His principle for at least the last couple of years has been simplicity and limitations . . . two people, three, rarely more than four. Maybe *Ivanov* had changed his orientation about that. Or he was newly confident or eager to experiment: If Tolstoy and Dostoevsky and Gogol and Pushkin could fill their pages with crowds, why couldn't he?

> "Gentlemen, there are so many of you that it is impossible to introduce you all!" said the General in a loud voice, trying to sound very cheerful. "Make each other's acquaintance, gentlemen, without any ceremony!"
>
> The officers—some with very serious and even stern faces, others with forced smiles, and all feeling extremely awkward—somehow made their bows and sat down to tea.
>
> The most ill at ease of them all was Ryabovich—a little officer in spectacles, with sloping shoulders, and whiskers like a lynx's. While some of his

comrades assumed a serious expression, while others wore forced smiles, his
face, his lynx-like whiskers, and spectacles seemed to say: "I am the shyest,
most modest, and most undistinguished officer in the whole brigade!" [. . .]

In an another unusual move, Chekhov has held off any appearance or indication of
the story's hero, until now, about four pages in. And what an unlikely hero of what the
title promises to be a romantic story!

We observe the scene with the shy man's eyes and Chekhov's understanding:

Von Rabbek and his family skillfully drew the officers into the discussion,
and meanwhile kept a sharp lookout over their glasses and mouths, to see
whether all of them were drinking, whether all had enough sugar, why some
one was not eating cakes or not drinking brandy. And the longer Ryabovich
watched and listened, the more he was attracted by this insincere but splendidly disciplined family.

This is a story where nothing is going to happen, except by accident.

The piano struck up; the melancholy strains of a valse floated out of the wide
open windows, and every one, for some reason, remembered that it was spring,
a May evening. Everyone was conscious of the fragrance of roses, of lilac, and
of the young leaves of the poplar.

(Was it Chekhov's imagination that, having conjured the sounds of the piano, set off the
chain of thoughts that reminded him, too, that in the story it is May, not December?)

Dancing began. . . . Ryabovich stood near the door among those who were
not dancing and looked on. He had never once danced in his whole life, and
he had never once in his life put his arm around the waist of a respectable
woman. He was highly delighted that a man should in the sight of all take a
girl he did not know around the waist and offer her his shoulder to put her
hand on, but he could not imagine himself in the position of such a man.
There were times when he envied the boldness and swagger of his companions
and was inwardly wretched; the consciousness that he was timid, that he was
round-shouldered and uninteresting, that he had a long waist and lynx-like
whiskers, had deeply mortified him, but with years he had grown used to this

feeling, and now, looking at his comrades dancing or loudly talking, he no longer envied them, but only felt touched and mournful.

And now Chekhov has activated our suspicions about how the story could unfold.

When the host leads a couple of officers to the billiards room, Ryabovich tags along. He watches, grows bored, is ignored, and decides to go back and observe the dancing. He gets lost:

> [. . .] he found himself in a little dark room which he had not seen on his way to the billiard-room. After standing there a little while, he resolutely opened the first door that met his eyes and walked into an absolutely dark room. Straight in front could be seen the crack in the doorway through which there was a gleam of vivid light; from the other side of the door came the muffled sound of a melancholy mazurka. Here, too, as in the drawing room, the windows were wide open and there was a smell of poplars, lilac and roses. . . .

So many smells! Characters' perception of flower-scents is often in Chekhov associated with sex:

> Ryabovich stood still in hesitation. . . . At that moment, to his surprise, he heard hurried footsteps and the rustling of a dress, a breathless feminine voice whispered "At last!" And two soft, fragrant, unmistakably feminine arms were clasped about his neck; a warm cheek was pressed to his cheek, and simultaneously there was the sound of a kiss. But at once the bestower of the kiss uttered a faint shriek and skipped back from him, as it seemed to Ryabovich, with aversion. He, too, almost shrieked and rushed toward the gleam of light at the door. . . .

At first, having returned to the drawing room, he is embarrassed. And then, realizing no one is looking at him or thinking of him, Chekhov gives him the gift of fulfillment:

> [. . .] as he became convinced that people were dancing and talking as calmly as ever, he gave himself up entirely to the new sensation which he had never experienced before in his life. Something strange was happening to him. . . . His neck, around which soft, fragrant arms had so lately been clasped, seemed to him to be anointed with oil; on his left cheek near his moustache where the unknown had kissed him there was a faint chilly tingling sensation as from

peppermint drops, and the more he rubbed the place the more distinct was the chilly sensation; all over, from head to foot, he was full of a strange new feeling which grew stronger and stronger . . . . He wanted to dance, to talk, to run into the garden, to laugh aloud. . . . He quite forgot that he was round-shouldered and uninteresting, that he had lynx-like whiskers and an "undistinguished appearance" (that was how his appearance had been described by some ladies whose conversation he had accidentally overheard). When Von Rabbek's wife happened to pass by him, he gave her such a broad and friendly smile that she stood still and looked at him inquiringly.

"I like your house immensely!" he said, setting his spectacles straight.

The General's wife smiled and said that the house had belonged to her father; then she asked whether his parents were living, whether he had long been in the army, why he was so thin, and so on. . . . After receiving answers to her questions, she went on, and after his conversation with her his smiles were more friendly than ever, and he thought he was surrounded by splendid people. . . .

Are we in a Pushkin story? Or in a Tolstoy novel?

Ryabovich is sensible and it takes him only a little while to solve the situational part of the mystery of the kiss. During the dinner he then tries but cannot figure which of the women it was who accidentally kissed him. The family bids the officers goodbye.

In bed in a hut that he shares with two other officers, Ryabovich wonders more who she is. But it's who *he* now is that matters:

> Ryabovich pulled the bed-clothes over his head, curled himself up in bed, and tried to gather together the floating images in his mind and to combine them into one whole. But nothing came of it. He soon fell asleep, and his last thought was that someone had caressed him and made him happy—that something extraordinary, foolish, but joyful and delightful, had come into his life. The thought did not leave him even in his sleep.

Everybody has an imagination. As the brigade sets out the next day, Chekhov shows us what Ryabovich can manage with his:

> When it was moving along the road by the granaries, Ryabovich looked at the house on the right. The blinds were down in all the windows. Evidently the household was still asleep. The one who had kissed Ryabovich the day before

was asleep, too. He tried to imagine her asleep. The wide-open windows of
the bedroom, the green branches peeping in, the morning freshness, the scent
of the poplars, lilac, and roses, the bed, a chair, and on it the skirts that had
rustled the day before, the little slippers, the little watch on the table—all this
he pictured to himself clearly and distinctly, but the features of the face, the
sweet sleepy smile, just what was characteristic and important, slipped through
his imagination like quicksilver through the fingers.

He is uninterested in and bored by what he actually sees around him as the brigade
slowly moves on. He has seen it all before. But he has never paid attention to his imagination like this, apparently:

At first when the brigade was setting off on the march he tried to persuade
himself that the incident of the kiss could only be interesting as a mysterious
little adventure, that it was in reality trivial, and to think of it seriously, to say
the least of it, was stupid; but now he bade farewell to logic and gave himself
up to dreams. . . . At one moment he imagined himself in Von Rabbek's
drawing room beside a girl who was like the young lady in lilac and the fair
girl in black; then he would close his eyes and see himself with another, entirely
unknown girl, whose features were very vague. In his imagination he talked,
caressed her, leaned on her shoulder, pictured war, separation, then meeting
again, supper with his wife, children. . . .

What is imagination? Is it simply making pleasing pictures? Why is it hard to maintain
it and fix it as precisely as a fiction writer can?

"Brakes on!" the word of command rang out every time they went downhill.
    He, too, shouted "Brakes on!" and was afraid this shout would disturb his
reverie and bring him back to reality. . . .

But now that Ryabovich has started this pleasing exercise of his imagination, it's hard
to stop! As Chekhov knows:

As they passed by some landowner's estate Ryabovich looked over the fence
into the garden. A long avenue, straight as a ruler, strewn with yellow sand
and bordered with young birch-trees, met his eyes. . . . With the eagerness

of a man given up to dreaming, he pictured to himself little feminine feet tripping along yellow sand, and quite unexpectedly had a clear vision in his imagination of the girl who had kissed him and whom he had succeeded in picturing to himself the evening before at supper. This image remained in his brain and did not desert him again.

And the gift of imagination, is it also a mixed blessing?

"All I am dreaming about now which seems to me so impossible and unearthly is really quite an ordinary thing," thought Ryabovich, looking at the clouds of dust racing after the general's carriage. "It's all very ordinary, and everyone goes through it. . . . That general, for instance, has once been in love; now he is married and has children. Captain Vahter, too, is married and beloved, though the nape of his neck is very red and ugly and he has no waist. . . . Salmanov is coarse and very Tatar, but he has had a love affair that has ended in marriage. . . . I am the same as every one else, and I, too, shall have the same experience as every one else, sooner or later. . . ."

And the thought that he was an ordinary person, and that his life was ordinary, delighted him and gave him courage. He pictured her and his happiness as he pleased, and put no rein on his imagination.

And the difference between what we have in our imagination and what we can describe to others—that's the challenge and disappointment of art, the disappointment for Chekhov in what he had intended in *Ivanov* and what many others saw. That evening . . .

[. . .] Ryabovich, whose head was confused from dreaming all day long, drank and said nothing. After three glasses he got a little drunk, felt weak, and had an irresistible desire to impart his new sensations to his comrades.

"A strange thing happened to me at those Von Rabbeks'," he began, trying to put an indifferent and ironical tone into his voice. "You know I went into the billiard-room. . . ."

He began describing very minutely the incident of the kiss, and a moment later relapsed into silence. . . . In the course of that moment he had told everything, and it surprised him dreadfully to find how short a time it took him to tell it. He had imagined that he could have been telling the story of the kiss till next morning. Listening to him, Lobytko, who was a great liar and consequently believed no one, looked at him sceptically and laughed. Merzlyakov twitched his eyebrows and, without removing his eyes from the *Vyestnik Evropi*, said:

"That's an odd thing! How strange! . . . throws herself on a man's neck, without addressing him by name. . . . She must be some sort of hysterical neurotic."

No, no, no. The story is all spoiled in front of those other men. Ryabovich, possessed by and possessing imagination, feels the disappointment of an artist.[7] But he restores it, privately, to himself:

> In the evenings when his comrades began talking of love and women, he would listen, and draw up closer; and he wore the expression of a soldier when he hears the description of a battle in which he has taken part. And on the evenings when the officers, out on the spree with the setter—Lobytko— at their head, made Don Juan excursions to the "suburb," and Ryabovich took part in such excursions, he always was sad, felt profoundly guilty, and inwardly begged *her* forgiveness. . . .

Three months later he returns with part of the brigade to the area. He anticipates going back into the dark room in the house and something happening.

> The "inner voice," which so often deceives lovers, whispered to him for some reason that he would be sure to see her . . . and he was tortured by the questions, Whether she had forgotten the kiss? If the worst came to the worst, he thought, even if he did not meet her, it would be a pleasure to him merely to go through the dark room and recall the past. . . .

He anticipates another invitation from the family. But it doesn't come and he goes for a walk:

> And everything on the near side of the river was just as it had been in May: the path, the bushes, the willows overhanging the water . . . but there was no sound of the brave nightingale, and no scent of poplar and fresh grass.

Which way will the story go? When did Chekhov decide with Ryabovich that believing in one's imagination was folly?

Now that he expected nothing, the incident of the kiss, his impatience, his vague hopes and disappointment, presented themselves in a clear light. It no longer seemed to him strange that he had not seen the General's messenger, and that he would never see the girl who had accidentally kissed him instead of some one else; on the contrary, it would have been strange if he had seen her. . . .

The water was running, he knew not where or why, just as it did in May. In May it had flowed into the great river, from the great river into the sea; then it had risen in vapor, turned into rain, and perhaps the very same water was running now before Ryabovich's eyes again. . . . What for? Why?

And the whole world, the whole of life, seemed to Ryabovich an unintelligible, aimless jest. . . . And turning his eyes from the water and looking at the sky, he remembered again how fate in the person of an unknown woman had by chance caressed him, he remembered his summer dreams and fancies, and his life struck him as extraordinarily meagre, poverty-stricken, and colorless. . . .

When he went back to his hut he did not find one of his comrades. The orderly informed him that they had all gone to "General von Rabbek's, who had sent a messenger on horseback to invite them. . . ."

For an instant there was a flash of joy in Ryabovich's heart, but he quenched it at once, got into bed, and in his wrath with his fate, as though to spite it, did not go to the General's.

I never did like that ending.

───※───

Chekhov had a goodbye meal with Shcheglov, Bilibin, and Leykin on December 15 before leaving on the 8:30 P.M. train for Moscow.[8]

From Moscow, within the next few days, he wrote to Shcheglov:

Dear Captain! I sit here at my table and work, I see before my eyes hearth and home, but my thoughts are still in Peter.

First of all, thank you for becoming acquainted with me. Beyond that thanks for the geniality and for the books. All's good and sweet with you: books and nerves and conversation and even the tragic laugh, which I now at home parody, but not successfully.

I send you two photo-cards: one to keep for yourself, the other give to the boyar Aleksei.

I await a photo and letter from you.

As this letter in all probability after my death will be published in a collection of my letters, I ask you to stick in some puns and sayings.[9]

Shcheglov refrained and left the humor as is to Chekhov.

———⁂———

"Boys" ("Mal'chiki," December 21) may have been written while he was still in Petersburg. Or maybe he wrote it immediately after his seventeen days away and he was back at his familiar desk; on his return on December 16 he would have been greeted by his anxious and happy family. "Boys" is after all a winter holiday story about a schoolboy who within days of his return wants to leave again:

"Volodya's come!" someone shouted in the yard.

"Master Volodya's here!" bawled Natalya the cook, running into the dining-room. "Oh, my goodness!"

The whole Korolyov family, who had been expecting their Volodya from hour to hour, rushed to the windows. At the front door stood a wide sledge, with three white horses in a cloud of steam. The sledge was empty, for Volodya was already in the hall, untying his hood with red and chilly fingers. His school overcoat, his cap, his snowboots, and the hair on his temples were all white with frost, and his whole figure from head to foot diffused such a pleasant, fresh smell of the snow that the very sight of him made one want to shiver and say "brrr!"[10]

Volodya's big surprise is that he has brought home with him for the holidays a classmate, his friend Lentilov. Everyone is delighted, except, it seems, the boys (Chekhov does not specify their age):

"Well, Christmas will soon be here," the father said in a pleasant sing-song voice, rolling a cigarette of dark reddish tobacco. "It doesn't seem long since the summer, when mamma was crying at your going . . . and here you are back again. . . . Time flies, my boy. Before you have time to cry out, old age is upon you. Mr. Lentilov, take some more, please help yourself! We don't stand on ceremony!"

Volodya's three younger sisters "noticed that Volodya, who had always been so merry and talkative, also said very little, did not smile at all, and hardly seemed to be glad to be home."

He and his "morose" friend have ambitions: to maraud their way to California.

On his former holidays Volodya, too, had taken part in the preparations for the Christmas tree, or had been running in the yard to look at the snow mountain that the watchman and the shepherd were building. But this time Volodya and Lentilov took no notice whatever of the colored paper, and did not once go into the stable. They sat in the window and began whispering to one another; then they opened an atlas and looked carefully at a map.

"First to Perm . . ." Lentilov said, in an undertone, "from there to Tiumen, then Tomsk . . . then . . . then . . . Kamchatka. There the Samoyedes take one over Bering's Straits in boats . . . . And then we are in America. . . . There are lots of furry animals there. . . ."

"And California?" asked Volodya.

"California is lower down. . . . We've only to get to America and California is not far off. . . . And one can get a living by hunting and plunder."

Volodya's sisters are in awe and curious:

At night, when the boys had gone to bed, the girls crept to their bedroom door, and listened to what they were saying. Ah, what they discovered! The boys were planning to run away to America to dig for gold: they had everything ready for the journey, a pistol, two knives, biscuits, a burning glass to serve instead of matches, a compass, and four rubles in cash. They learned that the boys would have to walk some thousands of miles, and would have to fight tigers and savages on the road: then they would get gold and ivory, slay their enemies, become pirates, drink gin, and finally marry beautiful maidens, and make a plantation.

The boys interrupted each other in their excitement. Throughout the conversation, Lentilov called himself "Montehomo, the Hawk's Claw," and Volodya was "my pale-face brother!"

Despite tearful misgivings by Volodya, who after all sort of likes being home and feels sorry for how his mother will feel, the boys set out on Christmas Eve day. When their disappearance is noticed, the family is frantic; a search party goes out. The boys spend the night in the train station, and the police find them on Christmas Day and bring them home.

As it was published in 1887, however, Chekhov concluded the story without the boys actually leaving the house.[11] Volodya is so wrought up that his sisters, overhearing his tears, begin bawling themselves and thus awaken the mother, to whom they spill the beans.[12]

Chekhov was glad to be home for Christmas, but he was growing up, longing to see the world, just as the boys are. Chekhov never made it to California or even America. But he did occasionally make plans to do so.

"Kashtanka" ("Kashtanka," December 25) is about a little red dog (*kashtan* means "chestnut") who, separated from her owner, is taken in by a "mysterious stranger" who has his own menagerie: a cat, a goose, and a pig. The stranger eventually trains Kashtanka, having dubbed her "Auntie," to participate in his circus act. At the circus, her former owner's son recognizes her, and she eagerly rejoins the boy and his father.

The story's original ironical title was "In Learned Society," a phrase that does not occur in the story; Chekhov was annoyed when Suvorin referred to it as "Kashtanka" in its run-up to book publication. Chekhov understood that the multipart story, about 5,000 words divided into four chapters, would make an attractive book for children. In its original form, "In Learned Society" was not designated as a children's story, but for the book he was pleased to modify it to make it more so. Several years later, having written another "children's" tale, "Whitebrow," he commented in a letter: "I lack the ability to write for children; I write for them once every ten years. I don't like what is known as children's literature; I don't recognize its validity. Children should be given only what is suitable for adults as well. . . . It is better and more to the point to learn to choose the correct medicine and to prescribe the correct dosage than to try to dream up some special medicine just because the patient is a child."[13]

It took four years for Suvorin to start moving on the book, however, as he doubted it would have much of a sale. The usually savvy publisher was quite wonderfully wrong; it was immediately popular in 1892 (Suvorin's own children gawked with amazement at Chekhov when he visited their home; this was the man who had created such a wonder, and they had named their own pets after the story's animals), and "Kashtanka" is still popular now. There are several editions in Russian in print. There are two full-length

Russian-language cartoons of it as well as a good live-action Soviet-era feature available on YouTube. When I taught "Kashtanka" this past semester to my Brooklyn community college students, a young woman who had grown up in Haiti told me she had read the story already and that it was her little sister's favorite. (She was referring to the out-of-print picture book, translated and slightly adapted by Ronald Meyer, and gorgeously illustrated by Gennady Spirin.)

Between its publication in *New Times* and the book's publication, Chekhov divided the four chapters into seven and added a completely new episode that increased the length by twenty percent. As regards phrasing (or "dosage" as he put it in his metaphor about children's literature), he changed the original's only very slightly. In a scene wherein Kashtanka's new owner, the clown, is rehearsing the goose to pull a string attached to a pistol, he goads the bird, "Now imagine: You have a passionately beloved wife. You return home from the club and find a friend with her."[14] Chekhov changed that situation to this: "Now imagine that you are a jeweler and you sell gold and diamonds. Imagine now that you go into your shop and find thieves in it." It is the book's only substantial rephrasing.

The greatest and most mysterious thing that happened to "In Learned Society" when it became "Kashtanka" is Chekhov's addition of a new episode, one of the most eerie and affecting scenes in all of his many volumes of creative work: the death of the goose Ivan Ivanych. In the original, the goose is disabled by having been stepped on by a horse during one evening's performance. He does not die, but his injury leads to the clown substituting Kashtanka (now "Auntie") to take the goose's place at the performance, which then brings the dog into the coincidental view of her former owner. In the revised version, Ivan Ivanych's death is slow and painful, and the animals react with apprehension:

When the master left and carried the light out with him, the darkness started again. It was frightening to Auntie. The goose was not crying out, but she again began to feel that in the darkness there was a stranger standing there. Most terrible of all was that it was impossible to bite this stranger, as he was invisible and formless. For some reason she thought that tonight there had to be something very bad coming for sure. Fyodor Timofeyich was also very disturbed. Auntie heard how he fussed on his mattress, yawned, and shook his head.

Somewhere outside there was a knocking at a gate, and the pig grunted in the shed. Auntie began to whine, stretched out her front paws and laid her head on them. In the knocking of the gate, in the grunting of the pig, who for some reason was not sleeping, in the darkness and quiet, she felt something as miserable and frightening as Ivan Ivanych's cry. Everything was upset and anxious, but why? Who was this stranger that couldn't be seen?

In 1887 Chekhov still wasn't expressing his apprehensions of that deathly "stranger" to his friends or family. By 1892, Kashtanka's and his own fears became more and more conscious.

I discovered the answer or an answer to something my students had asked about: If Kashtanka was kicked, cursed, and harshly pranked by the joiner Luka Aleksandrych and his son Fedyushka, and was then happy in her new environment with the clown, why does she go back to them?

I didn't have a good answer for my students or myself except that she's a dog, and all of us know humans who willingly, if resignedly, go back into abusive relationships and jobs. As I crawled back and forth over the story to translate it for a dual-language edition, I finally gleaned the depth of the pleasure of Kashtanka's life at the joiner's: "She remembered Luka Aleksandrych, his son Fedyushka, the comfortable little spot under the workbench . . . She remembered that in the long winter evenings when the joiner was planing or reading the newspaper aloud, Fedyushka usually played with her . . ." I also realized that Kashtanka's new life of fame and applause at the circus has not actually been fun; she is overwhelmed by the trumpeting of the elephant, the shock of the light, the roar of the crowd, and is unnerved by the music.

Fame for Chekhov was, perhaps, not all that pleasurable, either.

—⁓—

"A Lady's Story" ("Rasskaz Gospojhi N. N.," December 25) is an oddity. Told in the first person by a "lady," it is, for one thing, not a Christmas story. It begins:

> Nine years ago Pyotr Sergeyich, the deputy prosecutor, and I were riding
> toward evening in hay-making time to fetch the letters from the station.[15]

She remembers that on their storm-threatened ride to her estate, Pyotr declared his love for her. She lived with her father and brother.

> When I went to bed I lighted a candle and threw my window wide open, and
> an undefined feeling took possession of my soul. I remembered that I was free

and healthy, that I had rank and wealth, that I was beloved; above all, that I had rank and wealth, rank and wealth, my God! how nice that was! . . . Then, huddling up in bed at a touch of cold which reached me from the garden with the dew, I tried to discover whether I loved Pyotr Sergeyich or not, . . . and fell asleep unable to reach any conclusion.

Her reminiscing voice, from the very first phrase, is off-putting. She sounds like an actor reciting lines:

And what happened afterward? Why—nothing. [. . .] I had rank and wealth, while he was poor, and he was not even a nobleman, but only the son of a deacon and a deputy public prosecutor; we both of us—I through my youth and he for some unknown reason—thought of that wall as very high and thick [. . .]

We don't know Pyotr, who worked for her now deceased father, but on the basis of her reminiscences, I believe he has dodged a bullet:

I thought of the past, and all at once my shoulders began quivering, my head dropped, and I began weeping bitterly. I felt unbearably sorry for myself and for this man, and passionately longed for what had passed away and what life refused us now. And now I did not think about rank and wealth.

I broke into loud sobs, pressing my temples, and muttered:

"My God! My God! My life is wasted!"

She uses the phrase "rank and wealth" (*znatna i bogata*) five times in the story. Perhaps someone of "rank and wealth" spoke this very phrase and it stuck in Chekhov's craw.

———

Anton wrote Alexander a Christmas-day letter with the usual greetings and jokes. And could Alexander pick up his latest payment?: "I don't have any money."[16] He asked him to also buy for Anna some cookies from a Polish shop near Nevsky Prospect ("with my money"). He followed up two days later with a line-count on his stories for the *Petersburg Gazette* and the total fee. "Add it to the *New Times* fee and send it to me. [. . .] The family and I need to eat." The Soviet editors say that this last phrase parodied Chekhov's father.[17]

On December 27, Chekhov wrote a New Year's greeting to Leykin that contained apologies and excuses: "I am guilty before you up to my throat and sincerely recognize that. I gave you a promise, there were topics, but I couldn't write them. Up to Christmas I didn't sit down to write as I thought you didn't especially need my stories. I remembered that in the editorial office at my promise to send you Christmas stories, you answered me, in front of Bilibin, somewhat inconclusively and indeterminately. Receiving your letter during the holidays, I sat down to write and wrote something so nonsensical that I was ashamed to send it. You write that it's all the same to you what the story is, but I don't share this view. [. . .] In any case, this time don't be angry and put yourself in my situation. [. . .] In my immobility with which I work for you, for the Creator's sake, don't look for bad intent, don't think that I'm shirking *Fragments*. No, no! *Fragments* is my christening font and you are my godfather."[18]

He was absolutely shirking *Fragments*, though he and his "godfather" remained for years in occasional and friendly contact.

He had completed three stories for *New Times* this month, the last, "A Story without a Title," was published on New Year's Day, 1888. He wrote it, apparently, after his return from Petersburg. Had he been saving the idea of it since his trip to Holy Mountains? Or was it inspired by a joke he had heard or told? When Lazarev was visiting at Christmastime, Chekhov read "A Story without a Title" aloud to him and Ivan Chekhov.

It begins soberly, seemingly a historical Christian religious tale. If we had been listening outside the door, we might have wondered whose work it was:

> In the fifth century, just as now, the sun rose every morning and every eve-
> ning retired to rest. In the morning, when the first rays kissed the dew, the
> earth revived, the air was filled with the sounds of rapture and hope; while
> in the evening the same earth subsided into silence and plunged into gloomy
> darkness. One day was like another, one night like another. From time to
> time a storm-cloud raced up and there was the angry rumble of thunder, or
> a negligent star fell out of the sky, or a pale monk ran to tell the brotherhood
> that not far from the monastery he had seen a tiger—and that was all, and
> then each day was like the next.

The Father Superior of these monks is an organ master and a marvelously moving sermonist:

If he were moved to anger or abandoned himself to intense joy, or began speaking of something terrible or grand, then a passionate inspiration took possession of him, tears came into his flashing eyes, his face flushed, and his voice thundered, and as the monks listened to him they felt that their souls were spell-bound by his inspiration; at such marvelous, splendid moments his power over them was boundless, and if he had bidden his elders fling themselves into the sea, they would all, every one of them, have hastened to carry out his wishes.

The only such person Chekhov would have known about, or felt the similar affect of, was Tolstoy:

His music, his voice, his poetry in which he glorified God, the heavens and the earth, were a continual source of joy to the monks. It sometimes happened that through the monotony of their lives they grew weary of the trees, the flowers, the spring, the autumn, their ears were tired of the sound of the sea, and the song of the birds seemed tedious to them, but the talents of their Father Superior were as necessary to them as their daily bread.

The monks are in heavenly dull Eden:

Dozens of years passed by, and every day was like every other day, every night was like every other night. Except the birds and the wild beasts, not one soul appeared near the monastery. The nearest human habitation was far away, and to reach it from the monastery, or to reach the monastery from it, meant a journey of over seventy miles across the desert. Only men who despised life, who had renounced it, and who came to the monastery as to the grave, ventured to cross the desert.

A visitor arrives. He scolds them for isolating themselves from the hellish town. Why aren't they there in the town trying to save lost souls?

The Father Superior . . . yes, this is now sounding like a long joke . . . is awakened by the visitor's message and decides to go and do God's work. He is gone three months and when he returns he is so shaken he can't even speak to his anxious monks. After a week of silence he addresses them, furiously denouncing the vice and sin he has witnessed:

The old man, growing more and more incensed and weeping with wrath, went on to describe what he had seen. On a table in the midst of the revelers, he said, stood a sinful, half-naked woman. It was hard to imagine or to find in nature anything more lovely and fascinating. This reptile, young, long-haired, dark-skinned, with black eyes and full lips, shameless and insolent, showed her snow-white teeth and smiled as though to say: "Look how shameless, how beautiful I am." Silk and brocade fell in lovely folds from her shoulders, but her beauty would not hide itself under her clothes, but eagerly thrust itself through the folds, like the young grass through the ground in spring. The shameless woman drank wine, sang songs, and abandoned herself to anyone who wanted her.

Then the old man, wrathfully brandishing his arms, described the horse-races, the bull-fights, the theaters, the artists' studios where they painted naked women or molded them of clay. He spoke with inspiration, with sonorous beauty, as though he were playing on unseen chords, while the monks, petrified, greedily drank in his words and gasped with rapture. . . .

Even if we clever listeners can guess now how the story ends, there is, as in all elaborate comic stories, pleasure in having our expectations fulfilled.

There is no dialogue. Did Chekhov read it with a special voice or voices? Did he pause when Lazarev and Ivan, his brother, laughed? Or did he, as he usually preferred, read it deadpan? It would have taken him about fifteen minutes to read it all the way through. The story concludes: "After describing all the charms of the devil, the beauty of evil, and the fascinating grace of the dreadful female form, the old man cursed the devil, turned and shut himself up in his cell. . . . When he came out of his cell in the morning there was not a monk left in the monastery; they had all fled to the town." As Lazarev recounts the evening's reading, it seems as if Chekhov immediately had his youngest brother Mikhail run the manuscript to the station to send it on the overnight train to *New Times*.

The Chekhov family liked parties. There are no details, however, about how he and his parents and siblings celebrated New Year's Eve, 1887.

Conclusion

—◠◠◠—

> Chekhov: "Do you know for how many years I shall
> be read? Seven."
> "Why seven?" I asked.
> "Seven and a half, then."
>
> —Conversation with a fellow writer[1]

I n the years 1886 and 1887, in full command of his literary powers, Chekhov had written more short stories in total than he would in the rest of his productive life. But by 1888 he was no longer amazed or enlivened by his literary activity and success. The giddiness had worn off. "Before, I wrote the way a bird sings," he told Grigoriy Petrov. "*I sit down and write. I don't think about how or about what.* It went all by itself. I could write whenever it pleased me. Writing a sketch, a story, a skit, it didn't cost me any trouble. Like a little lamb or colt let loose into the open, I hopped, cavorted, kicked, wagged my tail, shook my head funnily. It was fun to me and from the outside it must have appeared very funny. I myself sometimes take up the old stories, read them and laugh. I think, 'I wrote like that.'"[2]

Though he became a celebrity in these two years, there was no fashion in Russia for interviewing popular authors. An interviewer's challenge would have been to get Chekhov to discuss his stories or his private life. Even with friends and admirers he avoided talking or writing about himself:

> One time a visitor rushed up to Chekhov and said, "Oh, my dear Chekhov, what artistic pleasure your last story gave us."
>
> But Chekhov immediately interrupted, "Tell me, where do you buy your herring? I will tell you where I get mine. At A's; he has fat, delicate ones."

Whenever someone talked to Chekhov about his works, he started talking about herring. He did not like to talk about his writings.[3]

How embarrassing this book would be to him. For one thing, I have tried to show how closely connected his own experiences are to his stories, which he adamantly (but disingenuously) denied; for another, I have tried to convey the "artistic pleasure" so many of his stories continue to give us. However rigorous he was about the "objectivity" of his writing, he suffered self-consciousness about its achievement being discussed in front of him.

In 1901, Chekhov and Tolstoy became neighboring invalids in Crimea. Maxim Gorky, the new great young Russian writer of the time, was visiting them. He recalled an awkward discussion:

> Tolstoy especially admired one of Chekhov's short stories. He said, "This is like a fine lace, the embroidery of words. You know, in the old days there was a type of lace made only by young maidens, who wove all their dreams of happiness into its design." Tolstoy spoke with tears in his eyes and with great emotion in his voice.
>
> Chekhov had a fever that day. He sat next to us, his face covered with red spots, his head bent to one side; he was wiping his glasses. He was quiet for a long time, and then he muttered, embarrassed, "This story was published with quite a few typos in it."[4]

Chekhov preserved his modesty and deflected praise from even the greatest writer in the world.

Pressed by an editor-friend for an account of his life in 1892, Chekhov feinted, joked and gave up:

> You want my biography? Here it is. I was born in Taganrog in 1860. I finished my course at the Taganrog Grammar School in 1879. In 1884 I took my medical degree at Moscow University. In 1888 I was awarded the Pushkin Prize. In 1890 I made a journey to Sakhalin across Siberia, returning by sea. In 1890 I made a tour in Europe, where I drank splendid wine and ate oysters. In 1892 I was at a birthday party where I had a spree with V. A. Tikhonov [It was Tikhonov who had asked for this autobiographical sketch]. I began to write in 1879 in *The Dragonfly*. My books of collected stories are: "Motley Stories," "In the Twilight," "Stories," "Gloomy People," and a long story "The

Duel." I have sinned also in the drama line, but with moderation. I have been translated into all the languages, except the foreign. In fact, I have been translated into German. I am approved of also by the Czechs and Serbians, nor are the French shy of intimacy. The mysteries of love I conceived when I was thirteen. With my colleagues, medical as well as literary, I am on the best terms. Am a bachelor. Should like to have a pension. I practice medicine, to such a degree even that sometimes in the summer I hold postmortems, though I have not done so for two or three years. Among writers I prefer Tolstoy . . .

But all this is nonsense. Write what you please. If you haven't enough facts, make up with lyricism.[5]

In conclusion, without any lyricism, after 1887, Chekhov slowed down a lot, immediately. It was like a double-time job he had had, and then he or his body decided that in 1888 he wouldn't or couldn't or needn't go so fast. His imagination never flagged, his commitment to the art of writing continuously evolved, but the delight of immediate and regular creation had had its time. He finished "The Steppe" in January and then he wrote seven more stories for *New Times*—and that was it for 1888. His brother Nikolay died the next year. Meanwhile, his stories became longer, usually, and his very long stories—what anybody but 19th-century Russians would call novels—extended the boundaries of fiction: full yet loose, intense but seemingly leisurely narratives. In 1890 Chekhov traveled all the way across Russia to conduct a health survey of all the prisoners and inhabitants of the Pacific coast island of Sakhalin. He came back and wrote a sociological study of that penal colony and more stories, but not a lot, most of them sterling, and eventually those comparatively dull plays. His tuberculosis was making him sicker and sicker and he spent more months of each year in the south of Russia and occasionally in Italy. He spent three years editing his collected works, fell in love with the actor Olga Knipper, and married her. He got sicker and sicker until the inevitable happened. He died in a German hospital with no grieving loved ones except his wife beside him—as he preferred. As noted in 1887's "The Schoolmaster," about the inadvertent funeral service for a fatally ill teacher, Chekhov revealed his own horror of being pitied: "at once on all the faces, in all the motionless eyes bent upon him, he read not the sympathy, not the commiseration which he could not endure, but something else, something soft, tender, but at the same time intensely sinister, like a terrible truth, something which in one instant turned him cold all over and filled his soul with unutterable despair."

I wouldn't want to embarrass or torture Chekhov with eulogies. The best model for praising him is in "Easter Eve," where the narrator imagines the monk Ieronim listening to his late friend's hymns: "I could fancy Ieronim standing meekly somewhere by the wall, bending forward and hungrily drinking in the beauty of the holy phrase. All this that glided by the ears of the people standing by me he would have eagerly drunk in with his delicately sensitive soul, and would have been spell-bound to ecstasy, to holding his breath, and there would not have been a man happier than he in all the church." Chekhov's work from these two years has left me feeling that when I am in the midst of reading particular stories there has not been a person happier than I. He has given me the illusion of standing (or sitting) shoulder to shoulder with him while we watch, with his quiet incisive commentary, the fears, joys, disappointments, and ecstasies of us everyday humans.

Appendix

—⁓—

All the stories in 1886–87 in chronological order with their translated and Russian titles.
A Chronological List of Chekhov's Work in 1886–1887

The unbracketed first title is that given by Constance Garnett in one of her 13 volumes of translations unless noted [not in CG]; the bracketed subsequent *differing* titles are those by the listed translator. If the titles are nearly identical, I do not list the other translators. Sources: David Magarshack, *Chekhov: A Life*; the Collected Works (30-volume Soviet Edition); Wikipedia ("Anton Chekhov Bibliography"); Prospero's Isle ("The complete (530) stories of Anton Chekhov: synopses, comments and ratings").	DATE OF ORIGINAL PUBLICATION	RUSSIAN TITLE IN THE SOVIET COLLECTED WORKS EDITION
The Maskers [no translation]	1 Jan 1886	Ряженые
New Year's Great Martyrs [not in CG] [Pimenoff, *Small Fry and Other Short Stories*]	4 Jan 1886	Новогодние Великомученики
Champagne: Thoughts from a New Year's Hangover [no translation]	4 Jan 1886	Шампанское (Мысли с новогоднего похмелья)
Visiting Cards [no translation]	4 Jan 1886	Визитные Карточки
Letters [no translation]	4 Jan 1886	Письма
Art	6 Jan 1886	Художество
A Night in the Cemetery [not in CG] [Sekirin, *A Night in the Cemetery and Other Stories of Crime and Suspense*]	8 Jan 1886	Ночь на Кладбище

A Blunder [Foiled! (Pitcher, *Chuckle with Chekhov*)]	11 Jan 1886	Неудача
The Contest [no translation]	11 Jan 1886	Конкурс
Tips for Husbands [not in CG] {This story was refused publication by the censor; it was not published in Russian until 30 Oct 1927 as "Boa Constrictor and Rabbit."} [See FitzLyon and Zinovieff, *The Woman in the Case and Other Stories*.]	[censored 11 Jan 1886]	К Сведению Мужей
His First Appearance [not in CG] [FitzLyon and Zinovieff, *The Woman in the Case and Other Stories*.]	13 Jan 1886	Первый Дебют
On the Telephone [not in CG] [Pitcher, *Chekhov: The Comic Stories*]	19 Jan 1886	У Телефона
Children [Kids (Pitcher, *Early Stories*)]	20 Jan 1886	Детвора
The Biggest City [no translation]	25 Jan 1886	Самый большой город
The Discovery [no translation]	25 Jan 1886	Открытие
Misery [Anguish, Pevear and Volokhonsky, *Fifty-two Stories*]	27 Jan 1886	Тоска
An Upheaval [A Commotion, Pevear and Volokhonsky, *Fifty-two Stories*]	3 Feb 1886	Переполох
Conversation of a Drunken Man with a Sober Devil [not in CG] [Sekirin, *A Night in the Cemetery and Other Stories of Crime and Suspense*]	8 Feb 1886	Беседа пьяного с трезвым чертом
An Actor's End	10 Feb 1886	Актерская гибель
The Requiem	15 Feb 1886	Панихида
The Stupid Frenchman [not in CG] [Lydia Razran-Stone, *Chtenia*: 2010]	15 Feb 1886	Глупый француз
Bliny [not in CG] [translators Robert Greenall and Mikhail Ivanov, *Russian Life Magazine*, Apr 1996]	19 Feb 1886	Блины
Anyuta	22 Feb 1886	Анюта
On Mortality: A Carnival Tale [not in CG] [Constantine, *The Undiscovered Chekhov*]	22 Feb 1886	О бренности
The Big Wig [no translation]	1 Mar 1886	Персона
Ivan Matveyich	3 Mar 1886	Иван Матвеич
The Witch	8 Mar 1886	Ведьма
Poison [no translation]	8 Mar 1886	Отрава
A Story Without an End	10 Mar 1886	Рассказ без конца
A Joke [The Little Joke, Pitcher, *Early Stories*]	12 Mar 1886	Шуточка
Agafya	15 Mar 1886	Агафья

My Conversation with the Postmaster [no translation]	15 Mar 1886	Мой разговор с почтмейстаром
Hydrophobia (The Wolf) [not in CG] [Yarmolinsky, *The Unknown Chekhov*]	17 Mar 1886	Волк
In Paris! [no translation]	22 Mar 1886	В Париж!
Spring [not in CG] [Pevear, *Fifty-two Stories*]	24 Mar 1886	Весной
A Nightmare	29 Mar 1886	Кошмар
The Rook [not in CG] [translator unnamed, *The Works of Anton Chekhov* (1929)]	29 Mar 1886	Грач
A Lot of Paper [no translation]	29 Mar 1886	Много Бумаги
On the River [not in CG] [Chamot, *Anton Chekhov: Short Stories*]	31 Mar 1886	На реке
Grisha [not in CG] [Fell, *Stories of Russian Life*]	5 Apr 1886	Гриша
Love	7 Apr 1886	Любовь
Easter Eve	13 Apr 1886	Святою ночью
Ladies	19 Apr 1886	Дамы
Strong Impressions	21 Apr 1886	Сильные ощущения
About Women [no translation]	26 Apr 1886	О Женщинах
A Fairy Tale [no translation]	3 May 1886	Сказка: Посвящ.<ается> балбесу, хвастающему своим сотрудничеством в газетах
A Gentleman Friend [An Acquaintance, Koteliansky, *The Bet and Other Stories*]	3 May 1886	Знакомый мужчина
A Happy Man	5 May 1886	Счастливчик
The Privy Councillor	6 May 1886	Тайный советник
A Literary Table of Ranks [no translation]	10 May 1886	Литературная табель о рангах
A Day in the Country	19 May 1886	День за городом
In a Pension [no translation]	24 May 1886	В пансионе
At a Summer Villa	25 May 1886	На даче
Nothing to Do: A Dacha Story [no translation]	26 May 1886	От нечего делать
Tedium Vitae [not in CG] [Chamot, *Anton Chekhov: Short Stories*]	31 May 1886	Скука жизни
Romance with Double-Bass [not in CG] [Pitcher, *Early Stories*]	7 June 1886	Роман с контрабасом

List of People Having the Right to Travel Free on the Russian Railroad [no translation]	7 June 1886	Список лиц, имеющих право на бесплатный проезд по русским железным дорогам
Panic Fears	16 June 1886	Страхи
The Chemist's Wife	21 June 1886	Аптекарша
Not Wanted	23 June 1886	Лишние люди
A Serious Step [not in CG] [Constantine, *The Undiscovered Chekhov*]	28 June 1886	Серьёзный шаг
The Chorus Girl	5 July 1886	Хористка
A Glossary of Terms for Young Ladies [not in CG] [Constantine, *The Undiscovered Chekhov*]	12 July 1886	Словотолкователь для «барышень»
The Schoolmaster	12 July 1886	Учитель
A Troublesome Visitor	14 July 1886	Беспокойный гость
A Rare Bird [no translation]	19 July 1886	Rara Avis
Other People's Misfortune [not in CG] [Yarmolinsky, *The Unknown Chekhov*]	28 July 1886	Чужая беда
Women Make Trouble [not in CG] [Yarmolinsky, *The Unknown Chekhov*]	4 Aug 1886	Ты и вы
The Husband	9 Aug 1886	Муж
A Misfortune [A Calamity, Yarmolinsky, *The Portable Chekhov*]	16 Aug 1886	Несчастье
A Pink Stocking	16 Aug 1886	Розовый чулок
Martyrs	18 Aug 1886	Страдальцы
The First-class Passenger	23 Aug 1886	Пассажир 1-го класса
Talent	6 Sept 1886	Талант
The Dependents	8 Sept 1886	Нахлебники
The Jeune Premier	13 Sept 1886	Первый любовник
In the Dark	15 Sept 1886	В потемках
A Trivial Incident	20 Sept 1886	Пустой случай
A Shining Character: The Story of an "Idealist" [no translation]	25 Sept 1886	Светлая личность: Рассказ «идеалиста»
Drama [no translation]	25 Sept 1886	Драма
A Tripping Tongue	27 Sept 1886	Длинный язык

A Trifle from Life	29 Sept 1886	Житейская мелочь
Difficult People	7 Oct 1886	Тяжелые люди
Oh, My Teeth! [no translation]	9 Oct 1886	Ах, зубы!
In the Court	11 Oct 1886	В суде
Revenge [not in CG] [Pitcher, *Early Stories*]	11 Oct 1886	Месть
Whining: A Letter from Far Away [no translation]	12 Oct 1886	Нытьё: Письмо издалека
Statistics [no translation]	18 Oct 1886	Статистика
The Proposal: A Story for Young Ladies [no translation]	23 Oct 1886	Предложение: Рассказ для девиц
A Peculiar Man	25 Oct 1886	Необыкновенный
My Domostroy [no translation]	26 Oct 1886	Мой Домострой
Mire	29 Oct 1886	Тина
The Lodger [not in CG] [Yarmolinsky, *The Unknown Chekhov*]	1 Nov 1886	Жилец
A Bad Night: Sketches [not in CG] [Sekirin, *A Night in the Cemetery and Other Stories of Crime and Suspense*]	3 Nov 1886	Недобрая ночь: Наброски
Kalkhas (Calchas) [no translation] [adapted by Chekhov into the one-act monologue "The Swan Song," Fell, *Plays by Anton Tchekoff*]	10 Nov 1886	Калхас
Dreams [Daydreams, Yarmolinsky, *The Portable Chekhov*]	15 Nov 1886	Мечты
Hush!	15 Nov 1886	Тссс!
At the Mill [not in CG] [Yarmolinsky, *The Portable Chekhov*]	17 Nov 1886	На мельнице
Excellent People	22 Nov 1886	Хорошие люди
An Incident	24 Nov 1886	Событие
Dramaturge [no translation]	27 Nov 1886	Драматург
The Orator	29 Nov 1886	Оратор
The Disaster [no translation]	1 Dec 1886	Беда
Assignment [not in CG] [Sekirin, *A Night in the Cemetery and Other Stories of Crime and Suspense*]	8 Dec 1886	Заказ
A Work of Art [The Objet d'Art, Pitcher, *Early Stories*]	13 Dec 1886	Произведение искусства
The Anniversary [no translation]	15 Dec 1886	Юбилей
Who Was to Blame?	20 Dec 1886	Кто виноват?
On the Road	25 Dec 1886	На пути
Vanka	25 Dec 1886	Ванька

The Person: A Bit of Philosophy [no translation]	27 Dec 1886	Человек: Немножко философии
Who Was She? [not in CG] [Goldberg and Schnittkind, *Nine Humorous Tales by Anton Chekhov*]	27 Dec 1886	То была она!
1887	1887	1887
New Year's Torture [no translation]	4 Jan 1887	Новогодняя пытка
Champagne (A Wayfarer's Story)	5 Jan 1887	Шампанское (рассказ проходимца)
Frost	12 Jan 1887	Мороз
The Beggar	19 Jan 1887	Нищий
Enemies	20 Jan 1887	Враги
The Good German [not in CG] [Constantine, *The Undiscovered Chekhov*]	24 Jan 1887	Добрый немец
Darkness	26 Jan 1887	Темнота
Polinka	2 Feb 1887	Полинька
Drunk	9 Feb 1887	Пьяные
An Inadvertence	21 Feb 1887	Неосторожность
Verotchka	21 Feb 1887	Верочка
Shrove Tuesday	23 Feb 1887	Накануне поста
A Defenseless Creature	28 Feb 1887	Беззащитное существо
A Bad Business	2 Mar 1887	Недоброе дело
Home	7 Mar 1887	Дома
The Lottery Ticket	9 Mar 1887	Выигрышный билет
Too Early!	16 Mar 1887	Рано!
An Encounter [not in CG] [Yarmolinsky, *The Portable Chekhov*]	18 Mar 1887	Встреча
Typhus	23 Mar 1887	Тиф
Everyday Troubles	28 Mar 1887	Житейские Невзгоды
In Passion Week	30 Mar 1887	На страстной неделе
A Mystery	11 Apr 1887	Тайна
The Cossack	13 Apr 1887	Казак
The Letter	18 Apr 1887	Письмо
Boa Constrictor and Rabbit [not in CG] [Yarmolinsky, *The Unknown Chekhov*]	20 Apr 1887	Удав и кролик

Spring: The Monologue of a Cat [no translation]	25 Apr 1887	Весной
The Critic [no translation]	27 Apr 1887	Критик
An Adventure	4 May 1887	Происшествие
The Examining Magistrate	11 May 1887	Следователь
Aborigines	18 May 1887	Обыватели
Volodya	1 June 1887	Володя
Happiness	6 June 1887	Счастье
Bad Weather	8 June 1887	Ненастье
A Play	13 June 1887	Драма
One of Many	15 June 1887	Один из Многих
First Aid [not in CG] [Constantine, *The Undiscovered Chekhov*]	22 June 1887	Скорая помощь
An Unpleasant Story	29 June 1887	Неприятная История
A Transgression	4 July 1887	Беззаконие
From the Diary of a Violent-tempered Man [Notes from the Journal of a Quick-Tempered Man, Pitcher, *Early Stories*]	5 July 1887	Из записок вспыльчивого человека
Uprooted	14 July 1887	Перекати-поле
A Father	20 July 1887	Отец
A Happy Ending	25 July 1887	Хороший конец
In the Coach-house	3 Aug 1887	В сарае
The Malefactors [no translation]	8 Aug 1887	Злоумышленики
Before the Eclipse [no translation]	9 Aug 1887	Перед затмением
Zinochka	10 Aug 1887	Зиночка
The Doctor	17 Aug 1887	Доктор
The Siren [not in CG] [Yarmolinsky, *The Portable Chekhov*]	24 Aug 1887	Сирена
The Pipe [The Reed-Pipe, Pitcher, *Early Stories*; The Shepherd's Pipe, Pevear and Volokhonsky, *Fifty-Two Stories*]	29 Aug 1887	Свирель
An Avenger	12 Sept 1887	Мститель
The Post	14 Sept 1887	Почта
The Wedding [no translation]	21 Sept 1887	Свадба
The Runaway	28 Sept 1887	Беглец
A Problem	19 Oct 1887	Задача
Intrigues [not in CG] [Constantine, *The Undiscovered Chekhov*]	24 Oct 1887	Интриги
The Old House	29 Oct 1887	Старый дом
The Cattle-Dealers	31 Oct 1887	Холодная кровь

Expensive Lessons	9 Nov 1887	Дорогие уроки
The Lion and the Sun	5 Dec 1887	Лев и Солнце
In Trouble [Misfortune, Constantine, *The Undiscovered Chekhov*]	7 Dec 1887	Беда
The Kiss	15 Dec 1887	Поцелуй
Boys	21 Dec 1887	Мальчики
Kashtanka	25 Dec 1887	Каштанка
A Lady's Story	25 Dec 1887	Рассказ госпожи NN
A Story Without a Title	1 Jan 1888	Без заглавия

Bibliography

—◦◦◦—

Chekhov, A. P. *Polnoe Sobranie Sochineniy i Pisem* [*Collected Works and Letters*]. 30 volumes
  [Works in 18 volumes]. Moscow: Izdatel'stvo "Nauka," 1976.
See also Chehov.Lit.Ru.

Stories and Plays

Listed by translator or editor

Birkett, G. A. and Gleb Struve. *Anton Chekhov: Selected Short Stories*. Oxford: Clarendon Press,
  1959.
Blaisdell, Bob. *The Lady with the Dog and Other Love Stories*. Garden City, New York: Dover
  Publications, 2021.
Brodskaya, Marina. *Five Plays*. Stanford, Calif.: Stanford University Press, 2011.
Chamot, Alfred Edward. *Anton Chekhov: Short Stories*. London: Commodore Press, 1941.
  [https://archive.org/stream/in.ernet.dli.2015.123706/2015.123706.Anton-Chekhov_djvu.txt].
Constantine, Peter. *The Undiscovered Chekhov: Fifty-One New Stories*. London: Duckbacks, 2002.
Cook-Horujy, Kathleen. *Anton Chekhov: Complete Works in 5 Volumes*. Vol. 2: Stories 1886–
  1887. Moscow: Raduga Publishers, 1988.
Fell, Marian. *Ivanoff: A Play*. New York: Charles Scribner's Sons, 1912.
Fell, Marian. *Stories of Russian Life*. New York: Charles Scribner's Sons, 1914.
Fen, Elisaveta. *Plays: Anton Chekhov*. Harmondsworth, England: Penguin, 1974.
FitzLyon, April, and Kyril Zinovieff. *The Woman in the Case and Other Stories*. London: John
  Calder, 1913.
Garnett, Constance. *Tales of Chekhov*. 13 volumes. 1929.
Goldberg, Isaac, and Henry T. Schnittkind. *Nine Humorous Tales by Anton Chekhov*. Boston:
  The Stratford Co., 1918.
Gorodetzky, Nadeja. *Shest' Rasskazov: Six Stories*. London: Bradda Books, 1963.
Jonson, Will, compiler, from Constance Garnett's translations. *Short Stories 1886 (The Complete
  Short Stories of Anton Chekhov)*. CreateSpace, 2013.
Jonson, Will, compiler, from Constance Garnett's translations. *Short Stories 1887 (The Complete
  Short Stories of Anton Chekhov)*. CreateSpace, 2013.

Kiernan, Brendan, Lydia Razran Stone, and Paul Richardson. *Chtenia: Readings from Russia: Chekhov Bilingual*. Vol. 3, No. 4. Russian Information Services, 2010.

Miles, Patrick, and Harvey Pitcher. *Anton Chekhov: Early Stories*. Oxford, UK: Oxford University Press, 1999.

Sekirin, Peter. *A Night in the Cemetery and Other Stories of Crime and Suspense*. New York: Pegasus Books, 2009.

Yarmolinsky, Avrahm. *The Portable Chekhov*. New York: Penguin, 1981.

Yarmolinsky, Avrahm. *The Unknown Chekhov: Stories and Other Writings of Anton Chekhov Hitherto Unpublished*. New York: The Noonday Press, 1958.

Letters

Chekhov, A. P. *Polnoe Sobranie Sochineniy i Pisem* [*Collected Works and Letters*]. 30 volumes [Letters in 12 volumes]. Moscow: Izdatel'stvo "Nauka," 1976.

Chekhova, M. P. *Pis'ma k bratu A. P. Chekhovu* [*Letters to Her Brother A.P. Chekhov*]. Moscow, 1954.

Perepiska A. P. Chekhova i Al. P. Chekhova [*Correspondence between A. P. Chekhov and Al. P. Chekhov*]. Vol. 1. Zhudozhestcennaya Literatura: Moscow, 1984. http://az.lib.ru/c/chehow _aleksandr_pawlowich/text_0050.shtml.

See also Chehov.Lit.Ru.

Listed by translator

Bartlett, Rosamund. *Anton Chekhov: A Life in Letters*. New York: Penguin, 2004.

Friedland, Louis S. *Letters on the Short Story, the Drama, and Other Literary Topics*. 1924. New York: Dover Publications, 1966.

Garnett, Constance. *Letters of Anton Chekhov to His Family and Friends*. London: Chatto and Windus, 1920.

Heim, Michael Henry, with Simon Karlinsky. *Anton Chekhov's Life and Thought: Selected Letters and Commentary*. Berkeley: University of California Press, 1975.

Koteliansky, S. S., and Philip Tomlinson. *The Life and Letters of Anton Tchekhov*. New York: Arno Press, 1977.

Lederer, Sidonie K. *The Selected Letters of Anton Chekhov*. Edited with an introduction by Lillian Hellman. New York: McGraw-Hill, 1965.

McKee, Sharon. *Anton Chekhov and His Times*. Moscow: Progress Publishers, 1990.

McVay, Gordon. *Chekhov: A Life in Letters*. London: The Folio Society, 1994.

Yarmolinsky, Avrahm. *Letters of Anton Chekhov*. New York: Viking Press. 1973.

Biographical

Balabanovich, Evgeniy Zenovich. *Dom A. P. Chekhova v Moskve* [*Chekhov's Home in Moscow*]. Moscow: Rabochiy, 1958.

Bartlett, Rosamund. *Chekhov: Scenes from a Life*. London: The Free Press, 2004.

Berdnikov, Georgii. *A. P. Chekhov*. Rostov-on-the-Don, Russia: Phoenix, 1997.

Bichkov, Yuriy. *Lychshiy iz Lyudey: Melikovskie Gody Chekhova, 1892–1899* [*The Best of People: The Melikhovo Years of Chekhov*]. Moscow: Gelios ARV, 2004.

Bunin, Ivan. *About Chekhov: The Unfinished Symphony*. Edited and translated from the Russian by Thomas Gaiton Marullo. Evanston, Ill.: Northwestern University Press, 2007.

Callow, Philip. *Chekhov: The Hidden Ground*. Chicago: Ivan R. Dee, 1998.

Carter, Richard. "Anton P. Chekhov, MD (1860–1904): Dual Medical and Literary Careers." *Annals of Thoracic Surgery*. The Society of Thoracic Surgeons. 1996; 61:1557–63.

Chekhov, Mikhail. *Anton Chekhov: A Brother's Memoir*. Translated by Eugene Alper. New York: Palgrave Macmillan, 2010.

Coope, John. *Doctor Chekhov: A Study in Literature and Medicine*. Chale, UK: Cross Publishing, 1997.

Davis, John P. *Russia in the Time of Cholera: Disease Under Romanovs and Soviets*. London, New York: I.B. Tauris, 2018.

Finke, Michael C. *Freedom from Violence and Lies: Anton Chekhov's Life and Writings*. London: Reaktion, 2021.

Finke, Michael C. *Seeing Chekhov: Life and Art*. Ithaca: Cornell University Press, 2005.

Frieden, Nancy Mandelker. *Russian Physicians in an Era of Reform and Revolution, 1856–1905*. Princeton, N.J.: Princeton University Press, 1981. https://muse-jhu-edu.i.ezproxy.nypl.org /chapter/1290918/pdf.

Goldenweizer, A. B. *Talks with Tolstoy*. Translated by S. S. Koteliansky and Virginia Woolf. New York: Horizon Press, 1969.

Gorky, Maxim, and Alexander Kuprin and I. A. Bunin. *Reminiscences of Anton Chekhov*. Translated by S. S. Koteliansky and Leonard Woolf. New York: B. W. Huebsch, 1921.

Gregory, Serge. *Antosha and Levitasha: The Shared Lives of Anton Chekhov and Isaac Levitan*. DeKalb: Northern Illinois University Press, 2015.

Gromova, L. D., and N. I. Gitovich. *Letopis' Zhizni i tvorchestva A. P. Chekhova*. Tom Perviy. 1860–1888. [*Chronicle of the Life and Work of A. P. Chekhov. Volume 1.*] Moscow: Nasledie, 2000.

Heim, Michael Henry. "Translating Chekhov's Plays: A Collaboration between Translator, Director, and Actors." In *Chekhov the Immigrant: Translating a Cultural Icon*. Michael C. Finke and Julie de Sherbinin, eds. Bloomington, Ind.: Slavica Publishers, 2007.

Hingley, Ronald. *A Life of Chekhov*. Oxford, UK: Oxford University Press, 1989.

Izmaylov, A. A. "Antosha Chekhonte." *Chekhov*. Moscow: 1916. http://chehov-lit.ru/chehov/bio /izmajlov-chehov/izmajlov-chehov-2-10.htm.

Kataev, Vladimir B. *A. P. Chekhov Entsiklopediya* [*A. P. Chekhov Encyclopedia*]. Prosveshchenie: Moscow, 2011.

Kataev, Vladimir. *If Only We Could Know! An Interpretation of Chekhov*. Translated by Harvey Pitcher. Chicago: Ivan R. Dee, 2002.

Khvatov, A. I., and I. E. Grudina, eds. *A. P. Chekhov: Materialy Literaturnogo Muzeya Pushkinskogo Doma* [*A. P. Chekhov: Materials of the Pushkin House Literature Museum*]. Nauka: Leningrad, 1982.

Kostin, A. L. *A. P. Chekhov v Vospominaniyakh Sovremennikov* [*A. P. Chekhov in Contemporaries' Reminiscences*]. Moscow: Gelios, 2004.

Koteliansky, S. S. *Anton Tchekhov: Literary and Theatrical Reminiscences.* Translated and edited by S. S. Koteliansky. New York: G.H. Doran, 1927.

Kuzicheva, Alevtina. *Chekhov: Zhizn' "Otdel'nogo Cheloveka"* [*Chekhov: The Life "of a Remarkable Person"*]. Moscow: Molodaya Gvardiya, 2012.

Laffitte, Sophie. *Chekhov, 1860–1904.* Translated by Moura Budberg and Gordon Latta. New York: Charles Scribner's Sons, 1973.

Livak, Leonid. "The Jewish Persona in the European Imagination: A Case of Russian Literature." 2010. DOI: 10.11126/Stanford/9780804770552.001.0001.

Llewellyn Smith, Virginia. *Anton Chekhov and the Lady with the Dog.* London: Oxford University Press, 1973.

Magarshack, David. *Chekhov: A Life.* New York: Grove Press, 1952.

Malcolm, Janet. *Reading Chekhov: A Critical Journey.* New York: Random House, 2001.

Mudrick, Marvin. "Chekhov." In *The Man in the Machine.* New York: Horizon Press, 1977.

Podorol'skiy, Aleksandr Nikolaevich. *Chekhov i Khudozhniki* [Chekhov and Artists]. Moscow: Sam Poligrafist, 2013.

Pritchett, V. S. *Chekhov: A Spirit Set Free.* New York: Random House, 1988.

Prokof'eva, E. M., ed. *A. P. Chekhov v Portretakh, Illyustratsiyakh, Dokumentakh* [*A. P. Chekhov in Portraits, Illustrations, Documents*]. Leningrad, 1957. 102.

Pursglove, Michael. *D. V. Grigorovich: The Man Who Discovered Chekhov.* Aldershot, UK: Avebury, 1987.

Rayfield, Donald. *Anton Chekhov: A Life.* New York: HarperCollins, 1997.

Rayfield, Donald. *Anton Chekhov: A Life.* second edition. London: Garnett Press, 2021.

Rayfield, Donald. "Chekhov's Stories and the Plays." In *The Cambridge Companion to Chekhov.* Edited by Vera Gottlieb and Paul Allain. Cambridge, UK: Cambridge University Press, 2000.

Rubina, Dina. "Preface: Chekhov's Blotter." In *Chekhov's Letters: Biography, Context, Poetics.* Edited by Carol Apollonio and Radislav Lapushin. Lanham, MD: Lexington Books, 2018.

Sanders, Edward. *Chekhov.* Santa Rosa, Calif.: Black Sparrow Press, 1995.

Sekirin, Peter, ed. and trans. *Memories of Chekhov: Accounts of the Writer from His Family, Friends and Contemporaries.* Jefferson, N.C.: McFarland & Co, 2011.

Shalyugin, Gennadiy. *"Zhit' v provintsii, u morya": A. P. Chekhov v Krim.* [*"Living in the Province by the Sea": A. P. Chekhov in the Crimea].* Simferopol': Tavriya, 2006.

Shimon, Gitit. "Old Age as a Reflection to Everyday Life: A Deliberation on Two Stories by Anton Chekhov," Things Chekhov Never Told O. Henry. http://www.chekhov-ohenry .com/old-age-as-a-reflection-to-everydays-life-a-deliberation-on-two-stories-by-anton -chekhov/?lang=en.

Simmons, Ernest J. *Chekhov: A Biography.* Boston: Atlantic Monthly Press, 1962.

Smetanko, Lyudmila. *The Photo Album: Taganrog, Chekhov's Motherland 150 Years Later.* 2010. Anniversary Edition, Southern Federal University. The Taganrog 150th anniversary of his birth album.[6]

Speirs, Logan. *Tolstoy and Chekhov.* Cambridge, UK: Cambridge University Press, 1971.

Struve, Gleb. "On Chekhov's Craftsmanship: The Anatomy of a Story." *Slavic Review.* Vol. 20,
    No. 3. October 1961.

Suvorin, Aleksei Sergeevich. *Dnevnik Alekseia Sergeevicha Suvorina [Diary of Aleksei Sergeevich
    Suvorin].* Edited by Donald Rayfield, Nataliia Roskina, and O. E. Makarova. London:
    Garnett Press, 1999.

Tchaikovsky Research. https://en.tchaikovsky-research.net/pages/Anton_Chekhov.

Tolstoy, Helena. "From Susanna to Sarra: Chekhov in 1886–1887." *Slavic Review.* Vol. 50. No. 3
    (Fall 1991). 590–600.

Ural'skiy, Mark. *Chekhov i Evrei (Chekhov and the Jews).* St. Petersburg: Aleteyya, 2020.

Varentsova, I., and G. Shcheboleva. *Anton Chekhov: Dokumenty, Fotografii [Documents,
    Photographs].* Moscow: Sovetskaya Rossiya, 1984.

See also Chehov.Lit.Ru.

Acknowledgments

—∿—

I thank my wife, Suzanne Carbotte, for listening, on our daily COVID-relief walks, to my excited "discoveries," which for the most part were rediscoveries of just how exciting and interesting Chekhov's stories are and how much they show about the amazing person he was. I could not have kept researching and writing without her patience and interest. I am most grateful to my mentor Max Schott, who read pieces and parts and sections at various times and finally the whole thing and continually offered unreasonably kind encouragement. Kia Penso, the best reader I know, helped me figure out what I was trying to do and in the final draft made many useful corrections and suggestions. Caroline Allen, John Wilson, Ross Robins, Howard Kaplan, and Matthew Flamm read drafts of sections and provided me with helpful criticism and queries. I enjoyed discussing Chekhov with my children, Max and Odette Blaisdell. I learned a lot from discussing Chekhov with my friends Jack Wolkenfeld, Elizabeth Gold, Michael Denner, Sandy Frazier, Jed Shahar, Enid Stubin, Lea Fridman, and Malik Atdadzhanov. Erin Stoodley provided help with formatting the penultimate draft. At Pegasus, Jessica Case again and again helped me understand what I was trying to show about Chekhov in his miraculous years of work. I am grateful to Drew Wesley Wheeler, Pegasus's copy editor, who neatened many phrases and caught many errors; I also need to thank Victoria Flickering for her detection and correction of numerous mistakes and inconsistencies in spelling and style. The stray mistakes and various excesses that have slipped through are all mine. I thank Maria Fernandez for her lovely design of the pages and Meghan Jusczak for publicizing and promoting the book. My editor at the *Los Angeles Review of Books*, Boris Dralyuk, who is also the finest translator from Russian that I know, pointed me toward the renowned Russian Chekhov critic Vladimir Kataev. In 2021, Fiona Hallowell and Janet Kopito at Dover Publications kindly guided my selection of Chekhov's love stories to publication. Paul Richardson at *Russian Life* has for years generously given me pages to indulge in my admiration of Chekhov and has helped make my attempts at translating Chekhov's prose more readable. I thank April Austin at the *Christian Science Monitor* for allowing me to put in my two cents about Chekhov translations, and to all the other editors over the decades who have allowed me to review books about Chekhov and write about his life. Finally, I owe this book to all of the previous biographers of Chekhov. Donald Rayfield and Rosamund Bartlett, today's deans of research and writing about Chekhov, politely responded to my email queries.

Endnotes

~~~

Introduction

1　Chapter 1 A New Order of Things. Translated by Louis S. Friedland. *Letters on the Short Story, the Drama, and Other Literary Topics.* 219. [To Leont'ev (Shcheglov), February 22, 1888.]

2　Translated by Rosamund Bartlett. *Anton Chekhov: A Life in Letters.* 194. [To Suvorin, October 17, 1889.]

3　This is how Vladimir B. Kataev, the editor of the Russian-language *A. P. Chekhov Entsiklopediya* (Moscow: Prosveshchenie, 2011. 14), and the editors of the *Collected Works* count them. More numbers from Kataev: "more than 130 pieces" in 1883, "more than 100" in 1884, "more than 130" in 1885, and only 12 (eight of them short stories) in 1888.

4　I use, for the most part, the standard transliteration of Russian names, most prominently among them Lev (rather than Leo) Tolstoy.

5　Quoted by Gleb Struve in "On Chekhov's Craftsmanship" (472) from Yu. Sobolev's *Chekhov* (Moscow, 1930).

6　Magarshack. *Chekhov: A Life.* 333. [To Maxim Gorky, November 16, 1898.]

7　For free and downloadable translations by Constance Garnett of Chekhov's stories, see the splendid "201 Stories by Anton Chekhov": https://www.ibiblio.org/eldritch/ac/jr/ or other Internet sites. The other translators of out-of-copyright or Internet-accessible stories are listed in the bibliography, page 407. Except for several in Garnett's last volume, *Love and Other Stories*, almost all of the 201 stories she translated were the ones that Chekhov selected for his *Collected Works* in 1899–1901. Chekhov was choosier than most of his readers would have been, and this means that part of my project has been reading in Russian all the pieces from these years that he chose *not* to include in the *Collected Works*. Eventually I discovered that many of the stories I thought I was discovering on my own in Russian had already been translated, just not by Garnett.

8　This site, Chehov-lit.ru, has the complete *Collected Works* and supplementary materials. I am grateful to the original Soviet editors of the *Collected Works* and to the unnamed coordinators of this 21st century Russian site who made those volumes and supplements accessible.

9　L. D. Gromova and N. I. Gitovich. *Letopis' Zhizni i Tvorchestva A. P. Chekhova* [*Chronicle of the Life and Works of A. P. Chekhov*]. Volume 1, 1860–1888. Moscow: Nasledie, 2000. Hereafter, this work will be noted as *Letopis'*.

10　"The worse the rows, the more the family longed for Anton, the one member of the family never to shout, hit out or weep." Rayfield. *Chekhov: A Life* (2021). 78.

11　Chekhov's grandfather, Egor Chekhov, bought his and his family's freedom from the aristocratic grandfather of Tolstoy's late-in-life closest friend, Vladimir Chertkov. (See Rayfield's *Chekhov: A Life.* [2021]. 2, 471.)

12　Mikhail Chekhov. *Anton Chekhov: A Brother's Memoir.* 7–8.

13　Quoted in Koteliansky, *Anton Tchekhov: Literary and Theatrical Reminiscences.* xxiv.

14　In *Memories of Chekhov: Accounts of the Writer from His Family, Friends and Contemporaries.* 16.

15　Rayfield. *Anton Chekhov: A Life* (1997). 25.

16 The biographies agree that Chekhov and Nikolay contracted tuberculosis in 1884: "The first discharge from the lungs had occurred in 1884," writes Dr. John Coope. "He had been attending the Moscow District Court as a part-time reporter. . . . Suddenly he was aware that blood was pouring into his mouth, and it seemed to be coming from his right lung every time he coughed. It continued on and off for four days. He did not seek further advice but he must have realized at once that such a symptom could have a very serious significance. There was known tuberculosis in his family." Dr. Coope explains: "He tried to talk himself into ignoring the signs of disease that he would immediately have recognized in a patient." (John Coope. *Doctor Chekhov: A Study in Literature and Medicine.* 133–134.)

17 "After I finished high school, my brother paid for me to take Ladies' Teachers Education Courses, a kind of teaching program. [. . .] After completing the Teachers Courses, I got a job as a history and geography teacher at a private school in Moscow." Maria Chekhova, "My Memories." In *Memories of Chekhov: Accounts of the Writer from His Family, Friends and Contemporaries.* 19.

18 Hingley. *A Life of Chekhov.* 30.

19 Ibid., 29.

20 Alexander Chekhov. In *Memories of Chekhov: Accounts of the Writer from His Family, Friends and Contemporaries.* 12.

21 Mikhail Chekhov. *Anton Chekhov: A Brother's Memoir.* 180.

22 Simmons. *Chekhov: A Biography.* 200.

23 Translated by Sidonie K. Lederer, *The Selected Letters of Anton Chekhov.* 243. [May 11, 1899.]

24 I mention the transliterated Cyrillic title of each story, as the translated titles widely vary. This particular story, "Отрава," was not translated by Constance Garnett, so I have translated the excerpt.

25 A. P. Chekhov. *Polnoe Sobranie Sochineniy i Pisem* [*Collected Works and Letters*]. Works, Vol. 5. Moscow: Izdatel'stvo "Nauka." 1976. 9. Hereafter, his creative works (stories and plays) from the thirty-volume Soviet edition will be noted as *Works.*

26 A. P. Chekhov. *Polnoe Sobranie Sochineniy i Pisem* (*Collected Works and Letters*). Vol. 1. Moscow. 1974. 209–210. [To Nikolay Leykin, March 4, 1886.] Hereafter, his letters, which comprise twelve volumes of the thirty-volume Soviet edition (the letters are labeled Volumes 1–12; the creative works are labeled Volumes 1–18), will be noted as *Pis'ma.*

27 Leykin replied, "'Poison' really turned out bad, but all the same it's being published in No. 10. I don't even understand why it's called 'Poison.'" Leykin later told Chekhov he had taken out "the recollection of the advocate," and because there's no surviving manuscript, there's no sign of which passage that was. Despite Leykin's harping at it (and if it truly was bad, Leykin would have squashed it), when Chekhov was sorting through all of his stories thirteen years later for his *Collected Works,* he had forgotten its existence or where it had been published until a bibliographer found it and brought it to his attention. Having reread it, Chekhov wrote across the top: "It doesn't go in the *Collected Works.*"

28 Translated by Heim and Karlinsky. *Anton Chekhov's Life and Thought: Selected Letters and Commentary.* 55.

29 Compared to English and Americans, the Russians are prudish about publishing details about their classic authors' sex lives. In the relatively open, pre-Putin days of the 1990s, the British scholar Donald Rayfield was able to delve into previously inaccessible Chekhov materials in Russian libraries. His biography has been translated into Russian and is frequently cited by Russian scholars.

30 John Richardson. *A Life of Picasso: The Early Years, 1881–1906.* New York: Random House, 1991. 3.

31 Alexander Kuprin recorded Evgenia Chekhova's words. See *Reminiscences of Anton Chekhov by Maxim Gorky, Alexander Kuprin, and I. A. Bunin.* Translated by S. S. Koteliansky and Leonard Woolf.

32 Translated by Heim and Karlinsky. *Anton Chekhov's Life and Thought: Selected Letters and Commentary.* 85. [To Aleksei Suvorin, January 7, 1889.]

33 The single-most important book in writing this biography beyond the *Collected Works* edition of Chekhov's works and letters is the *Letopis' Zhizni i tvorchestva A. P. Chekhova* (*Chronicle of the Life and Work of A. P. Chekhov*), edited by L. D. Gromova and N. I. Gitovich (2000).

January 1886

1 Translated by Heim and Karlinsky. *Anton Chekhov's Life and Thought: Selected Letters and Commentary*. 300. [To Rimma Vashchuk, March 28, 1897.]

2 Magarshack. *Chekhov: A Life*. 91.

3 How old was she, then? Unknown. Her brother, the artist Aleksandr Stepanovich Yanov, a friend of Chekhov's brother Nikolay, was born in 1857. *Pis'ma*. Vol. 1. 572.

4 Translated by Heim and Karlinsky. *Anton Chekhov's Life and Thought: Selected Letters and Commentary*. 65. See also: "In agony, the dying sister grabbed Anton's hand just before she passed away. Her cold handshake instilled such feelings of helplessness and guilt in Anton that he contemplated abandoning medicine altogether." (Mikhail Chekhov. *Anton Chekhov: A Brother's Memoir*. Translated by Eugene Alper. New York: Palgrave Macmillan, 2010.)

5 In *Seeing Chekhov: Life and Art*, Michael C. Finke makes much of Chekhov's habit of facing the camera.

6 Simmons. *Chekhov: A Biography*. 113. At the age of nineteen, departing from Taganrog, on his official "ticket of leave" for study in Moscow, his height was listed as 6′1″ and his characteristics as "dark auburn hair and eyebrows, black eyes, moderate nose, mouth and chin, long unmarked face, special marks: scar on forehead under hairline." (Rayfield. *Anton Chekhov: A Life*. 1997. 69.)

7 Translated by Heim and Karlinsky, *Anton Chekhov's Life and Thought: Selected Letters and Commentary*. 367. [To Grigory Rossolimo, October 11, 1899.]

8 *Works*. Vol. 4. 276–278.

9 *Letopis'*. 216. [January 1, 1886.]

10 *Pis'ma*. Vol. 1. 174.

11 *Works*. Vol. 4. 279–281.

12 (Gemorroy Dioskorovich Lodkin.)

13 Translation by Constance Garnett.

14 Magarshack. *Chekhov: A Life*. 76. [To Leykin, June 25, 1884.]

15 Hingley. *A Life of Chekhov*. 56.

16 Magarshack. *Chekhov: A Life*. 131. [To Ezhov, October 27, 1887.]

17 Translated by Rosamund Bartlett. *Chekhov: A Life in Letters*. This and the subsequent quotations from the letter to Alexander come from pages 48–51.

18 *Pis'ma*. Vol. 1. 569.

19 Rosamund Bartlett, whose excellent translation I am quoting here, uses *"Newspaper"* for *Gazette*. Since the original Russian title of the newspaper is *Gazette* ("*Gazeta*"), and I refer to it as the *Petersburg Gazette* throughout, I have rendered her *Newspaper* as *Gazette* here and beyond.

20 *Pis'ma*. Vol. 1. Moscow: 1974. 402–403.

21 Translated by S. S. Koteliansky and Philip Tomlinson. *The Life and Letters of Anton Tchekhov*. 55. [To Alexander Chekhov, April 1883.]

22 Magarshack. *Chekhov: A Life*. 10.

23 Published on the *Russian Life* blog for Chekhov's 162nd birthday (January 29, 2022). When I translated it I didn't realize that Constance Garnett had already translated "The Fiasco" perfectly well as "The Blunder." (My blunder.)

24 There is a lively, seven-and-a-half-minute video version of "Neudacha" (Russian) starring Anna Tambova available on YouTube (youtube.com/watch?v=elK1f4mXSdk) that carries what I think Chekhov would think is an appropriate tone and energy, a full-blast farce with an impressive soundtrack ("La donne è mobile" from *Rigoletto*). The director switches up the buffoonery so that it's the father rather than the mother who botches the blessing by grabbing instead of the ikon a still-life of a watermelon. There are other changes, but the basic situation, parents hoping to trap a suitor into a legal engagement, remains.

25 Translation by Peter Sekirin.

26   Chekhov rewrote "Tips for Husbands" as "Boa Constrictor and Rabbit" in the spring of 1887.

27   An illustration by Nikolay Chekhov.

28   *Pis'ma*. Vol. 1. 405. Rosamund Bartlett explains: "Tatyana's Day, on January 12, marked the date of
       the foundation of Moscow University in 1755 and the commencement of the winter vacation. It was
       celebrated by students, faculty and alumni with much revelry, a tradition revived in 2004." (*Anton
       Chekhov: A Life in Letters*. 79.)

29   Rayfield. *Anton Chekhov: A Life* (1997). 123.

30   *Pis'ma*. Vol. 1. 181. [To Rozanov, January 14, 1886.]

31   This story, translated by Kathleen Cook-Horujy, can be found in *Anton Chekhov: Complete Works
       in 5 Volumes*. Vol. 2: Stories 1886–1887. Moscow: Raduga Publishers. 1988. "Complete," however,
       is a misrepresentation in the series' title. There are many stories gone missing, particularly the ones
       sympathetic to religious feelings.

32   Mikhail Chekhov. *Anton Chekhov: A Brother's Memoir*. 95–96.

33   Rayfield. *Chekhov: A Life* (2021). 9, 685.

34   *Pis'ma*. Vol. 1. 182. [To Dyukovskiy, January 16, 1886.]

35   Ibid., 183–185. [To Bilibin, January 18, 1886.]

36   Magarshack. *Chekhov: A Life*. 100. [To Bilibin, January 18, 1886.]

37   Rayfield. *Anton Chekhov: A Life* (1997). 123 [To Leykin, January 19, 1886.]

38   *Works*. Vol. 4. 511.

39   *Pis'ma*. Vol. 1. 185. [January 19, 1886.]

40   Translation by Constance Garnett.

41   *Works*. Vol. 4. 321–324.

42   Ibid., 325.

43   Translation by Constance Garnett.

44   *Works*. Vol. 4. 544.

45   Ibid., 543.

46   Ibid., 543–544.

47   *Pis'ma*. Vol. 1. 188. [To Leykin, January 28, 1886.]

48 Levitan proposed to Maria Chekhova at Babkino; Levitan never married. (See Laffitte. *Chekhov, 1860–1904*. 100.)

49 *Pis'ma*. 187. [To Leykin, January 28, 1886.]

50 *Letopis'*. 223. [End of January 1886.]

51 Translated by Heim and Karlinsky. *Anton Chekhov's Life and Thought: Selected Letters and Commentary*. 56. [To Aleksei Suvorin, February 21, 1886.]

February 1886

1 Translated by Louis S. Friedland. *Letters on the Short Story, the Drama, and Other Literary Topics*. 97–98. [To Avilova, April 29, 1892.]

2 Translated by Heim and Karlinsky. *Anton Chekhov's Life and Thought: Selected Letters and Commentary*. 46. [To Viktor Bilibin, February 1, 1886.]

3 Hingley. *A Life of Chekhov*. 72–73.

4 *Pis'ma*. Vol. 1. 192–194. [To Alexander Chekhov, February 3, 1886.]

5 Translation by Peter Sekirin, *A Night in the Cemetery and Other Stories of Crime and Suspense*. 148–150.

6 *Letopis'*. 226. [By February 14, 1886.]

7 *Pis'ma*. 195–197. [To Bilibin, February 14, 1886.]

8 Translated by Heim and Karlinsky. *Anton Chekhov's Life and Thought: Selected Letters and Commentary*. 47. [To Bilibin, February 1, 1886.]

9 Chekhov was nervous, suggests Rosamund Bartlett, about the notoriety of *New Times'* right-wing news slant: "whatever its politics, *New Times* was considerably more prestigious as a place to publish than *The St. Petersburg Newspaper [Gazette]*. And it provided him with a greater creative freedom than he had enjoyed elsewhere. [. . .] But he also felt uneasy about contributing to a publication that was held in derision by the liberal intelligentsia, and immediately began to worry that he would be barred from publishing in literary journals as a result." (Bartlett, *Chekhov: Scenes from a Life*, 144.)

10 Translated by Constance Garnett.

11 The only English translation, by Lydia Razran Stone, is excellent, published in *Chtenia*. (Vol. 3, No. 4, 2010.)

12 *Works*. Vol. 4. 364.

13 *Pis'ma*. 200–201. [To Leykin, February 20, 1886.]

14 *Letopis'*. 228. [Around February 18, 1886.]

15 Laffitte. *Chekhov, 1860–1904*. 89.

16 Chekhov's behavior and social activities were forever "liberal" and progressive, and yet he always sought independence from any political movement. He preferred to be free to write and act as he liked. *New Times*, for all its autocratic propaganda, granted him that. The biographer Michael C. Finke observes: "Chekhov's political sentiments clearly leaned left, but they were also largely private. He addressed suffering, injustice, and governmental brutishness with a clinical eye for what he might actually do to help rather than an ideological perspective that told him what he should write and say. He did his part to create change through private philanthropy and unrecompensed medical practice, but he avoided public statements, propagandistic art, and membership in any party." (Finke, *Freedom from Violence and Lies: Anton Chekhov's Life and Writings*. 141–142.)

17 Translated by Louis S. Friedland. *Letters on the Short Story, the Drama, and Other Literary Topics*. 38. [To Suvorin, February 21, 1886.]

18 Translated by Heim and Karlinsky. *Anton Chekhov's Life and Thought: Selected Letters and Commentary*. 56. [To Suvorin, February 21, 1886.]

19 *Pis'ma*. Vol. 1. 202.

20 Translation by Constance Garnett.

21 Translation by Constance Garnett.

22 *Letopis'*, 229–230. [February 23–24, 1886.]

March 1886

1   To Suvorin (the second letter of August 18, 1891), quoted in Richard Carter, "Anton P. Chekhov, MD (1860–1904): Dual Medical and Literary Careers." 1557.

2   *Pis'ma*. Vol. 1. 203–206. [To Bilibin, dated February 28, 1886, written March 1.]

3   *Works*. Vol. 4. 365–368.

4   Mikhail Chekhov. *Anton Chekhov: A Brother's Memoir*. 57.

5   *Letopis'*. 233. [March 5, 1886.] Also, as recounted by Magarshack: "at the beginning of March he received a summons from another shopkeeper from whom Alexander and Nikolay had taken goods (presumably drinks) on credit in his name." (Magarshack. *Chekhov: A Life*. 101–102.)

6   Magarshack. *Chekhov: A Life*. 101–102. [To Leykin, March 8, 1886.]

7   Bartlett. *Anton Chekhov: A Life in Letters*. 74.

8   Magarshack. *Chekhov: A Life*. 107.

9   Mikhail Chekhov. *Anton Chekhov: A Brother's Memoir*. 14–15.

10   Simmons. *Chekhov: A Biography*. 46.

11   Translated by Heim and Karlinsky. *Anton Chekhov's Life and Thought: Selected Letters and Commentary*. 49.

12   Coope. *Doctor Chekhov: A Study in Literature and Medicine*. 107.

13   As Garnett skipped over the last sentence of the paragraph, I quote there from Heim and Karlinsky, 50.

14   These two sentences are translated by Heim and Karlinsky (as Garnett skipped over one phrase and fractured the one after that).

15   Heim and Karlinsky's translation of the rest of this point follows here, as Garnett skipped over it.

16   A Soviet edition deletion here, as well as a walk-over by Garnett.

17   Garnett translates "good breeding" as *culture*.

18   *Pis'ma*. Vol. 1. 211. [To Leykin, March 8, 1886.]

19   Translated by Constance Garnett.

20

21   Logan Speirs, discussing the ideas expressed by Chekhov's characters, observes: "An argument is impressive only if the person who uses it is." (*Tolstoy and Chekhov*. 160.)

22   Mikhail Chekhov: "Levitan occasionally suffered from depression. During these bouts, he would either take his shotgun and leave home for a week or two or sit at home, silent and sullen and all alone." (*Anton Chekhov: A Brother's Memoir*. 111.)

23   *Pis'ma*. Vol. 1. [To Leykin, January 12, 1886.]

24   Translated by Louis S. Friedland. *Letters on the Short Story, the Drama, and Other Literary Topics*. 58–59. [To Aleksei Suvorin, May 30, 1888.]

25   *Pis'ma*. Vol. 1. 212–214. [To Bilibin, March 11, 1886.]

26   Or as translated by Rayfield: "As a columnist you are like a lover to whom a woman says 'You take me too tenderly . . . You must be rougher!' (By the way, women are just like chickens, they like to be hit at that particular moment.)" Rayfield. *Chekhov: A Life* (2021). 142.

27   To repeat: Chekhov's frequent use of pauseful, slowing ellipses are often ignored by translators, but I'm going to use all of them. Chekhov had frequent chances in various editions to take them out if he didn't after all want them, but he left them in.

28   *Works*. Vol. 5. 490.

29   Two other translations of that sentence: "Oh, the emotions that play across that dear face" [Miles and Pitcher]; "Oh, the play of feeling on that sweet face!" [Garnett]; theirs are better (clearer), but, in my defense, Chekhov does not use the word "feeling" or "emotions."

30   *Works*. Vol. 5. 36.

31   Translated by Avrahm Yarmolinsky as "Hydrophobia" in *The Unknown Chekhov*. 99.

32   Laffitte. *Chekhov, 1860–1904*. 83.

33   Simmons. *Chekhov: A Biography*. 95–97.

34   Pursglove. *D. V. Grigorovich: The Man Who Discovered Chekhov*. 96.

35   There should be a semicolon between "the snowstorm" and "the night," as there is no snow in summery "Agafya"; Grigorovich might be referring to the snowstorm in "The Witch."

36   Magarshack. *Chekhov: A Life*. 271. [To Suvorin, n.d., 1891.] Grigorovich's remark stuck with Chekhov, who refuted it at least once more: "In my opinion, this express-train writing is not at all a drawback, as Grigorovich thinks, but a peculiarity of talent. One village wench will thrash around like a sturgeon for two days before she gives birth; for another, to give birth is like running into a lavatory." [To Suvorin, November 28, 1893.] (Simmons. *Chekhov: A Biography*. 298.)

37   Rayfield. *Chekhov: A Life* (2021). 153.

38   Translated by Constance Garnett.

39   See *Letters*. Vol. 1. 217.

40   Rayfield translates it this way: "I shall free myself of hack work, but it will take time." (Rayfield. *Chekhov: A Life* [2021]. 154.)

41   See his letter of January 18, 1887. (*Pis'ma*. Vol. 2. 17.)

42   Koteliansky and Tomlinson note that Chekhov had this inscribed photograph ("From an old writer to a young talent") on the wall of his Yalta house at the time of his death (*The Life and Letters of Anton Tchekhov*. 75). The inscription itself is quoted from *Letopis'*, 241. [April 2, 1886.]

43   *Works*. Vol. 5. 75.

44   Translation by Constance Garnett.

45   Translation by Constance Garnett.

46   Coope. *Doctor Chekhov: A Study in Literature and Medicine*. 138.

April 1886

1   Translated by S. S. Koteliansky and Philip Tomlinson. *The Life and Letters of Anton Tchekhov*. 75. [To Alexander Chekhov, April 6, 1886.]

2   *Letopis'*. 241. [April 2, 1886.]

3   *Pis'ma*. Vol. 1. 226. [To Bilibin, April 4, 1886.]

4   Richard Carter. "Anton P. Chekhov, MD (1860–1904): Dual Medical and Literary Careers." 1559.

5   Coope. *Doctor Chekhov: A Study in Literature and Medicine*. 136–137. [To Suvorin, November 13, 1891.]

6   Coope. *Doctor Chekhov: A Study in Literature and Medicine*. 137. Michael C. Finke usefully adds Dr. Robert Coles' similar and exasperated point on this matter: "Look, he was a doctor and he had an illness that is not silent and secret. I know as a physician what tuberculosis is. I treated some tuberculous patients many years ago in medical school, and you know when you have tuberculosis. You cough up blood. You feel chest pain. There is an illness there—we're not talking about something spreading like cancer cells for a long time that aren't even known. This is a tangible, physical, concrete, palpable phenomenon of the body that Chekhov knew; he knew it as a physician, and he also knew it because at that time tuberculosis was a major prevalent illness. Of course he knew it. He knew that he was dying. He knew he was dying as a human being knows." (Finke. *Freedom from Violence and Lies: Anton Chekhov's Life and Writings*. 133.)

7   Coope. *Doctor Chekhov: A Study in Literature and Medicine*. 138. [Quoted from Suvorin's diary, c. April 1897.]

8   Translated by Marian Fell.

9   Translated by S. S. Koteliansky and Philip Tomlinson. *The Life and Letters of Anton Tchekhov*. 73–76. [To Alexander Chekhov, April 6, 1886.]

10   Translated by Constance Garnett.

11   *Pis'ma*. Vol. 1. 233–234.

12   "Being a doctor was Chekhov's unalloyed gift to the poor and to friends and family," writes Dr. Coope. (Coope. *Doctor Chekhov: A Study in Literature and Medicine*. 28.)

13   Translated by Bartlett. *Anton Chekhov: A Life in Letters*. 65.

14   Mikhail Chekhov. *Anton Chekhov: A Brother's Memoir*. 23.

15   Rayfield. *Anton Chekhov: A Life* (1997). 13.

16   Laffitte. *Chekhov: 1860–1904*. 24. [To Suvorin, February 6, 1889.]

17   *Pis'ma*. Vol. 1. 235. [To Leykin, April 13, 1886.]

18   Magarshack. *Chekhov: A Life*. 101–102. [To Leykin, April 13, 1886.]

19   *Letopis'*. 245. [April 13, 1886.]

20   *Pis'ma*. Vol. 1. 238. [To Leykin, April 19, 1886.]

21   Mikhail Chekhov. *Anton Chekhov: A Brother's Memoir*. 154.

22   Translated by Heim and Karlinsky. *Anton Chekhov's Life and Thought: Selected Letters and Commentary*. 40.

23   Mikhail Chekhov. *Anton Chekhov: A Brother's Memoir*. 153.

24   Magarshack. *Chekhov: A Life*. 64. [To Leykin, January 1883.]

25   Ibid., 66. [To Leykin, April 24, 1885 and April 18, 1885.]

26   Hingley. *A Life of Chekhov*. 58.

27   Magarshack. *Chekhov: A Life*. 67. [From Leykin to Chekhov, May 19, 1885.]

28   Ibid., 68. [To Suvorin, November 3, 1888.]

29   Translated by Constance Garnett.

30   Bartlett. *Anton Chekhov: A Life in Letters*. 149.

31   Rayfield. *Chekhov: A Life* (2021). 102.

32   Chekhov would repeat this line in an August 1887 letter to his brother Alexander.

33   *Pis'ma*. Vol. 1. 238–239. [To Mikhail Chekhov, April 25, 1886.]

34   Ibid., 241. [To Maria Chekhova, May 6, 1886.]

35   Unpublished *as yet*. Editorial director Rosamund Bartlett's complete edition of the previously untranslated earliest stories is in the hands of a publisher as of May 2022. (Personal communication.)

May 1886

1   Translation by Marina Brodskaya. *Five Plays*. 85.

2   *Letopis'*. 248. [May 3, 1886.]

3   Ibid., [May 6, 1886.]

4   Translated by Constance Garnett.

5   *Letters*, Vol. 1. 241–242. [To Alexander Chekhov, May 10, 1886.]

6   Simmons. *Chekhov: A Biography*. 129.

7   *Works*. Vol. 5. 632.

8   *Letopis'*. 249. [May 11 or 12, 1886.]

9   Magarshack. *Chekhov: A Life*. 85. [To Leykin, April 28, 1885.]

10   *Pis'ma*. Vol. 1. 243. [To Leykin, May 24, 1886.]

11   In Cyrillic: А.П. Чехов—"На даче." YouTube. https://www.youtube.com/watch?v=9YcqKHUpRN4&t=94s.

12   Titled "Out of Sheer Boredom" and translated by April FitzLyon and Kyril Zinovieff. 107.

13   Translated by FitzLyon and Zinovieff. 111. "'Nature herself,' Mikhail writes, describing Chekhov's life at Babkino, 'provided Chekhov with innumerable subjects and purely Babkino stories emerged from his pen. The moon-lit garden in 'Verochka' with the wisps of mist floating through it is the Babkino garden. . . . 'The Witch' was suggested by the lonely church and its caretaker's lodge near the highway in the big Babkino forest. In almost all his stories of that period, some traces of the Babkino landscape

or some figure from Babkino itself or from the neighboring villages can be detected." (Magarshack. *Chekhov: A Life*. 87–88.)

14   The translators FitzLyon and Zinovieff entitled the story "Taedium Vitae" in *The Woman in the Case and Other Stories*. London: John Calder, 1913. 149–162. (The translators spell the estate name as *Jenino*. Otherwise I have left their words as they are.)

15   There's a reproduction of the handwritten manuscript in the Russian edition with Chekhov's note on it. *Works*. Vol. 5. 167.

16   The only discussion in English that I have found about it is Gitit Shimon's excellent "Old Age as a Reflection to Everyday Life: A Deliberation on Two Stories by Anton Chekhov," on her website: Things Chekhov Never Told O. Henry. http://www.chekhov-ohenry.com/old-age-as-a-reflection-to -everydays-life-a-deliberation-on-two-stories-by-anton-chekhov/?lang=en.

June 1886

1   Quoted in Gleb Struve. "On Chekhov's Craftsmanship." (Boris Pasternak. *Dr. Zhivago*. New York: Pantheon, 1958. 285.)

2   *Letopis'*. 252. [June 1 or 2, 1886.]

3   *Pis'ma*. Vol. 1. 248. [Letter to Leykin from Nikolay Chekhov, not earlier than June 5, 1886.]

4   "I write under the most abominable conditions. In front of me sits my nonliterary work drumming away at my conscience. The child of a visiting relative is screaming in the next room. Nearby my father is reading aloud to my mother from 'The Sealed Angel' [Leskov] and someone has wound up the musical box and I can hear strains of *La Belle Helene*. It makes me want to flee into the country. You can hardly imagine more difficult conditions for a writer. My bed is taken by a visiting relative who comes along now to ask my medical advice. 'My daughter must have colic to make her scream like that.' I have the misfortune of being a medical student and everyone thinks they can come and have a little chat about medicine. And when they are tired of medicine they want to talk about literature." Coope. *Doctor Chekhov: A Study in Literature and Medicine*. 24–25. [To Leykin, August 1883.]

5   Translated by Louis S. Friedland. *Letters on the Short Story, the Drama, and Other Literary Topics*. 283. [To Ivan Leont'ev (Shcheglov), March 22, 1890.]

6   Quoted in *Chekhov i Evrei* (Chekhov and the Jews) by Mark Ural'skiy. 307–308.

7   Translated by Constance Garnett.

8   Magarshack. *Chekhov: A Life*. 1952. 88.

9   Translated by Constance Garnett.

10   Translated by Constance Garnett.

11   Translated by Peter Constantine.

12   *Pis'ma*. Vol. 1. 249–251. [To Leykin, June 24, 1886.]

13   Ural'skiy. *Chekhov i Evrei*. n.p.

14   According to the Soviet editors of the *Collected Works*, Kiseleva was born "about 1859" (*Pis'ma*. Vol. 1. 544). According to Rosamund Bartlett, Kiseleva was born in 1859 (*A Life in Letters*, lvi). Donald Rayfield (2021), having little patience for Kiseleva, calls her a "prude" (115) and accepts her birth-year as 1847. Ernest Simmons, who also never met her, says, "She was a beautiful, vivacious, strong-minded woman" (83). In *Chekhov. Dokumenty. Fotografii*. (Moscow: Sovetskaya Rossiya, 1984), her birth year is given as "about 1850." The photo that Vladimir Kataev uses of Maria Kiseleva in the *A. P. Chekhov Entsiklopediya* (383) is labeled in *A. P. Chekhov v Portretakh, Illyustratsiyakh, Dokumentakh* as Sasha Kiseleva, Maria's daughter, in the 1890s. (*A. P. Chekhov v Portretakh, Illyustratsiyakh, Dokumentakh*. Edited by E. M. Prokof'eva. Leningrad. 1957. 102.) Kataev's Chekhov encyclopedia sets her birth in 1847, in accordance with the "Russian Writers" reference series (Gitovich, *Russkie Pisateli, 1800–1917*). There are thirty-five known letters from Chekhov to her; thirty-one from her to him. . . . Tchaikovsky wrote her a letter, *in verse*!, in 1876 [http://en.tchaikovsky-research.net/pages/Letter_460]. She was the

only child from her father's first marriage. Her mother died. Her father remarried in 1866. . . . Mikhail Chekhov says Kiseleva's stepmother was jealous of her beauty. So, 1847 makes sense.

July 1886

1   Sergei Yakovlev, "Memories of A. P. Chekhov," in *Memories of Chekhov: Accounts of the Writer from His Family, Friends and Contemporaries*. 22.
2   Translated by Constance Garnett.
3   Kenneth Branagh's reading and performance of the story (translation by Garnett) is superb. Read/hear *In the Ravine and Other Stories* (CD). Then compare, if you will, two Russian-language very short film versions of the story. The first one is as dreary as could be, with nothing of Chekhov's spirit. The second, bawdy, loud, over-the-top, would have pleased him.
    1. https://www.youtube.com/watch?v=8hN1tX3J6Sg&t=631s
    2. https://www.youtube.com/watch?v=G9EbtcYGD2k
4   *Letopis'*. 257. [July 5, 1886.]
5   Ibid., 257. [July 8, 1886.]
6   Translated by Constance Garnett.
7   Finke. *Freedom from Violence and Lies: Anton Chekhov's Life and Writings*. 193.
8   Translated by Constance Garnett.
9   Translated by Avrahm Yarmolinsky.
10 *Pis'ma*. Vol. 1. 254–255. [To Leykin, July 30, 1886.]

August 1886

1   *Letters on the Short Story, the Drama, and Other Literary Topics*, 65. [To Lidia Avilova, October 6, 1897.]
2   Translated by Constance Garnett.
3   Cited by Armin Arnold in "D. H. Lawrence, the Russians, and Giovanni Verga," *Comparative Literature Studies*, Vol. 2, No. 3 (1965). Letter to Rhys Davies in *Collected Letters II*. 1109.
4   Translated by Thomas Marullo. *About Chekhov: The Unfinished Symphony* by Ivan Bunin. xxx. [To Suvorin, July 24, 1891.]
5   Translated by Constance Garnett.
6   I made a few minor emendations to Garnett's translation in a new edition of Chekhov's love stories, *The Lady with the Dog and Other Love Stories* (Dover, 2021), and I repeat one here: I changed Garnett's "making love to" to "wooing" to prevent misunderstandings by my fellow 21st-century Americans.
7   Finke, in *Freedom from Violence and Lies: Anton Chekhov's Life and Writings*: "Rayfield's 1997 biography of Chekhov, where every ambiguous remark in letters to or from Chekhov is interpreted as evidence of a liaison." 214.
8   Hingley. *A Life of Chekhov*. 11.
9   Mikhail Chekhov. *Anton Chekhov: A Brother's Memoir*. 39.
10 *Pis'ma*. Vol. 1. 256–257. [To Leykin, August 20, 1886.]
11 Translated by Constance Garnett.
12 *Letopis'*. 261. [August 28–30, 1886.]
13 Ibid. [August 25, 1886.]
14 Translated by Constance Garnett.

Part 3: At Home with Family and Fame

1   *Pis'ma*. Vol.1. 255. [Letter to Leykin, July 30, 1886.]
2   Magarshack. *Chekhov: A Life*. 107.

3   Here is one remark, from Yuriy Sobolev's "Tchekhov's Creative Method," though I have been unable
     to date the letter: "'It is pleasanter to read than to write,' he wrote to Suvorin. 'I think that if I could
     live another forty years and read, read, read, and learn to write with talent, that is, concisely—at the
     end of the forty years I would fire on you all from so huge a canon that the heavens would shake. But
     now I am but a Lilliputian, like the rest.'" (In Koteliansky's *Anton Tchekhov: Literary and Theatrical
     Reminiscences*. 23.)

4   Simmons. *Chekhov: A Biography*. 108.

5   Magarshack. *Chekhov: A Life*. 107.

6   Mikhail Chekhov. *Anton Chekhov: A Brother's Memoir*. 150.

7   Ibid.

September 1886

1   Personal correspondence. March 19, 2021.

2   Translation by Constance Garnett.

3   *Works*. Vol. 5. 312.

4   Translation by Constance Garnett.

5   *Pis'ma*. Vol. 1. 259–260. [To Leykin, September 20, 1886.]

6   *Letopis'*. 264. [September 27, 1886.]

7   *Pis'ma*. Vol. 1. 265–266. [To Leykin, September 30, 1886.]

8   Tatiana Shchepkina-Kupernik, "Young Years": "He was constantly teasing me, but all of it was
     in a very friendly way, and he always made me laugh. I knew that Anton Pavlovich only teased
     people whom he liked." In *Memories of Chekhov: Accounts of the Writer from His Family, Friends and
     Contemporaries*. 67.

9   *Pis'ma*. Vol. 1. 260–262. [To Kiseleva, September 21, 1886.]

10   Translation by Constance Garnett. *Letters of Anton Chekhov to His Family and Friends*. 48. [To
     Kiseleva, September 21, 1886.]

11   *Pis'ma*. Vol. 1. 260–262.

12   Translated by Constance Garnett.

13   *Pis'ma*. Vol. 1. 260–262.

14   Translated by Heim and Karlinsky. *Anton Chekhov's Life and Thought: Selected Letters and Commentary*. 206.

15   There are thirty-five known letters from Chekhov to Kiseleva, and thirty-one from her to him. *Pis'ma*.
     Vol. 1. 544.

16   Translated by Rosamund Bartlett. *Anton Chekhov: A Life in Letters*. 71–73.

17   *Pis'ma*. Vol. 1. 264.

18   *Letopis'*. 265. [October 1, 1886.]

October 1886

1   Translated by Louis S. Friedland. *Letters on the Short Story, the Drama, and Other Literary Topics*. [To
     Leont'ev (Shcheglov), January 22, 1888.]

2   Translated by Heim and Karlinsky. *Anton Chekhov's Life and Thought: Selected Letters and
     Commentary*. 206. [To Shavrova, September 16, 1891.]

3   Translated by Constance Garnett.

4   Rayfield. *Chekhov: A Life* (2021). 328.

5   *Pis'ma*. Vol. 2. 98. [To Georgy Chekhov, June 23,1887.]

6   Magarshack. *Chekhov: A Life*. 15. [To Alexander Chekhov, January 2, 1889.]

7   In *A. P. Chekhov: Entsiklopediya*. Edited by V. B. Kataev. 196.

8   *Works*. Vol. 5. 573.

9   Ibid., 340.

10   Translated by Constance Garnett.

11   A pood is a Russian farming unit of weight of approximately thirty-six pounds.

12   *Works*. Vol. 5. 353.

13   Translated by Constance Garnett.

14   *Pis'ma*. 456.

15   Ibid., 266. [To Leykin, October 7, 1886.]

16   *Letopis'*. 267. [October 12–13, 1886.]

17   *Pis'ma*. 267. [To Schechtel, October 19, 1886.]

18   Chekhov uses the unusual word *khapanniy* (хапанный).

19   *Pis'ma*. Vol. 1. 269–271. [Letter to Kiseleva, Oct. 29, 1886.]

20   *Works*. Vol. 5. 691.

21   Translated by Heim and Karlinsky. *Anton Chekhov's Life and Thought: Selected Letters and Commentary*. 51.

22   As Constance Garnett renders her name.

23   Translated by Constance Garnett.

24   I thank Donald Rayfield for providing me with the link.

25   *Pis'ma*. 271.

26   Rayfield. *Anton Chekhov: A Life* (1997). 125.

27   *Chekhov i Evrei* (*Chekhov and the Jews*) by Mark Ural'skiy. In "From Susanna to Sarra: Chekhov in 1886–1887," Helena Tolstoy writes most groundedly and most thoroughly about Efros and Chekhov, and she makes the same kind of disappointed observations I have been inclined to make. His relationship with her over the year is the only time I see Chekhov where he seems like any young man prone to defensiveness and self-justification and pettiness. He was smitten but got cold feet about her. He could have married her. She was well off (but not rich, says Rayfield), she was attractive—but he called her names and teased her and wrote other people about her as if he didn't *really* like her. The stories that seem to reveal his feelings and experiences about her are "The Witch," "The Joke," and indeed "Mire." Helena Tolstoy calls him out about the differences between Susanna of "Mire" and Efros, that such differences were his disingenuous way to plausibly deny it was about her—but everyone who knew her and him recognized her in the descriptions of her looks and scent and wiriness. Helena Tolstoy explains how he tried to make up for his rudeness and meanness to Efros. She is convincing.

　　　See also Leonid Livak: "Chekhov's correspondence attests to the consistent function of 'the Jews' in his imagination as a negative marker for a wide range of phenomena. This function exists quite independently from the writer's own experience of dealing with individuals of Jewish origin and is most probably conditioned by the unselfconscious Judeophobia of the Christian milieu in Chekhov's native Taganrog." (*The Jewish Persona in the European Imagination: A Case of Russian Literature*. 23.)

28   *Letopis'*. 269. [October 29, 1886.]

29   *Pis'ma*. Vol. 1. 272. [To Leykin, October 31 or November 1, 1886.]

November 1886

1   Translated by S. S. Koteliansky and Philip Tomlinson. *The Life and Letters of Anton Tchekhov*. 273. [To Menshikov, January 28, 1900.]

2   *Works*. Vol. 5. 388.

3   *Pis'ma*. Vol. 2. [To Leykin, November 6, 1886.]

4   Translated by Constance Garnett.

5   Translated by A. E. Chamot. 139–142.

6   Translated by Constance Garnett.

7   *Works*. 589. In "Tchekhov's Creative Method," Yuriy Sobolev recounts: "'Good God!' his friends used to say indignantly, 'his manuscripts should be taken away from him. Otherwise he will reduce his stories only to this: that they were young, fell in love, then married and were unhappy.'" In Koteliansky, *Reminiscences*. 21–22.

8   *Letopis'*. 271. [November 21, 1886.]

9   Translated by Constance Garnett.

10 Translated by Constance Garnett.

11 Mikhail Chekhov. *Anton Chekhov: A Brother's Memoir*. 154.

12 *Pis'ma*. 278. [To Kiseleva, December 13, 1886.]

December 1886

1   Nina Drozdova, "Memories of Chekhov." In *Memories of Chekhov: Accounts of the Writer from His Family, Friends and Contemporaries*. 63.

2   *Works*. Vol. 5. 439.

3   *Letopis'*. 273. [December 5, 1886.]

4   Translated by Constance Garnett.

5   Alexander Kuprin recorded this in *Reminiscences of Anton Chekhov*. 94.

6   Zakhar Pichugin. In *Memories of Chekhov: Accounts of the Writer from His Family, Friends and Contemporaries*. 27–28.

7   "Excellent People." Translated by Constance Garnett.

8   Hingley. *A Life of Chekhov*. 204.

9   A. B. Goldenweizer. *Talks with Tolstoy*. 96.

10 *Works*. Vol. 5. 440–446.

11 Peter Sekirin, in *A Night in the Cemetery and Other Stories of Crime and Suspense*. 158.

12 Mikhail Chekhov. *Anton Chekhov: A Brother's Memoir*. 107.

13 Magarshack. *Chekhov: A Life*. 108.

14 Hingley. *A Life of Chekhov*. 204.

15 *Letopis'*. 274. [December 11, 1886.]

16 *Pis'ma*. Vol. 1. 277–278. [To Kiseleva, December 13, 1886.]

17 Ibid., 281. [To Suvorin, December 21, 1886.]

18 *Letopis'*. 277. [December 26, 1886.]

19 *Pis'ma*. 282. [To Leykin, December 24, 1886.]

20 Translated by Constance Garnett.

21 Translated by Constance Garnett.

22 Isaac Goldberg and Henry T. Schnittkind's translation of "To Byla Ona!" is from 1918.

January 1887

1   Dina Rubina. "Preface: Chekhov's Blotter." In *Chekhov's Letters: Biography, Context, Poetics*. 241.

2   *Letopis'*. 233. [March 6–7,1886.]

3   Ibid., 280. [January 1, 1887.]

4   *Pis'ma*. Vol. 2. 345.

5   Magarshack. *Chekhov: A Life*. 107–108.

6   According to Mark Ural'skiy, there are thirty-eight letters in existence from Chekhov to Ezhov; there are 114 from Ezhov to Chekhov. There are thirty-three letters from Chekhov to Lazarev; there are sixty-one from Lazarev to Chekhov. (*Chekhov i Evrei*, 572, 577.)

7   *Letopis'*. 280–281. [January 1, 1887.]

8   *Works*. Vol. 6. 7–11.

9   Translated by Constance Garnett.

10   *Letopis'*. 284. [January 11, 1887.]

11   Magarshack. *Chekhov: A Life*. 69.

12   *Pis'ma*. Vol. 2. 8–9. [To Leykin, January 12, 1887.]

13   Ibid., 347. The rest of the letter is translated by Heim and Karlinsky in *Anton Chekhov's Life and Thought: Selected Letters and Commentary*. 64–65.

14   Translated by S. S. Koteliansky and Philip Tomlinson. *The Life and Letters of Anton Tchekhov*. 82. The majority of the rest of the letter is translated by Constance Garnett, except where noted.

15   Garnett deletes "wing-porch [for lodge] or the main-house terrace in the presence of Ma-Pa [Maria Pavlovna Chekhova], the Counterfeiter and Levitan sort of flavor to it." (Translated by Heim and Karlinsky. *Anton Chekhov's Life and Thought: Selected Letters and Commentary*. 61.)

16   Garnett deletes this: "even though Olga Andreyevna [Golokhvastova] thinks she has settled it." (Translated by Heim and Karlinsky. *Anton Chekhov's Life and Thought: Selected Letters and Commentary*. 61.)

17   Garnett's footnote: Bobo is P. D. Boborykin.

18   Translated by Louis S. Friedland. *Letters on the Short Story, the Drama, and Other Literary Topics*. 64. [To Aleksei Suvorin, April 1, 1890.]

19   See p. 331 of Vol. 5 in *Collected Works* for the title page of *Rasskazi* ("Stories"), 1888. The collection includes "Mire" and Chekhov has scrawled a message to Kiseleva on it.

20   This paragraph is translated by Heim and Karlinsky. (*Anton Chekhov's Life and Thought: Selected Letters and Commentary*. 63.)

21   "Kalkhas," retitled as "Swansong."

22   Translated by Constance Garnett.

23   *Letopis'*. 285–286. [January 14 and 16, 1887.]

24   *Letters of Anton Chekhov*. Translated by Yarmolinsky. 44. [January 17, 1887.]

25   "Pavel's phrase 'shall perish without the law' became a family saying." Rayfield. *Chekhov: A Life* (2021). 119.

26   *Letopis'*. 288. [January 23, 1887.]

27   Translated by Constance Garnett.

28   Translated by S. S. Koteliansky and Philip Tomlinson. *The Life and Letters of Anton Tchekhov*. 86. [To Mitrofan Chekhov, January 18, 1887.]

29   *Pis'ma*. Vol. 2. 19. [January 18, 1887.]

30   *Letopis'*. 288. [January 1, January 24, 1887.]

31   Translated by Constance Garnett.

32   I'll run that sentence now through an online Russian dictionary: "On the bed, near the window, lay a boy with open eyes and a surprised expression on his face." Fine, but it has to be "the boy" rather than "a boy," because we all know who that boy is.

33   *Works*. Vol. 6. 629–630.

34   Coope. *Doctor Chekhov: A Study in Literature and Medicine*. 123.

35   Fyodor Dostoevsky. *Crime and Punishment*. Translated by, who else, Constance Garnett.

36   Translated by Peter Constantine. 157.

37   *Pis'ma*. Vol. 2. 20. [Letter to Leykin, January 26, 1887.]

38   Ibid., 22. [Letter to Alexander Chekhov, January 26, 1887.]

39   *Letopis'*. 289. [January 29, 1887.]

40   *Pis'ma*. Vol. 2. 24. [Letter to Alexander Chekhov, January 31, 1887.]

February 1887

1   Oliver Sacks. In *The River of Consciousness*. New York: Alfred A. Knopf, 2017. 147.

2   *Pis'ma*. Vol. 2. 25. [Letter to Alexander Chekhov, early February 1887.]

3   Translated by Constance Garnett.

4   Translated by Constance Garnett.

5   *Pis'ma*. Vol. 2. 27–28. [To Suvorin, February 10, 1887.]

6   *Letopis'*. 291. [February 6, 1887.]

7   Gleb Struve. "On Chekhov's Craftsmanship." 467.

8   In the draft of the letter, Chekhov deleted and rephrased various sentences, including this one, perhaps for being too obsequious: "Oh, I'm sorry I'm a bad critic and can't express my impressions in all their completeness." (*Pis'ma*. Vol. 2. 360–361.) See also the facsimile of the first manuscript page (*Pis'ma*, Vol. 2, 29).

9   Translation by Constance Garnett.

10 This point (1), I translated. Garnett overlooked it.

11 Magarshack. *Chekhov: A Life*. 170. [To Aleksei Suvorin, January 6, 1889.]

12 Ibid., 98.

13 Gleb Struve. "On Chekhov's Craftsmanship." 470.

14 *Letopis'*. 297–298. [March 10, 1887.]

15 *Pis'ma*. Vol. 2. 362.

16 Translated by Constance Garnett.

17 *Pis'ma*. Vol. 2. 35. [To Leykin, February 25, 1887.]

18 *Letopis'*. 295. [February 28, 1887.]

19 Ibid. [February 27, 1887.]

20 Translated by Heim and Karlinsky. *Anton Chekhov's Life and Thought: Selected Letters and Commentary*. 40.

21 *Memories of Chekhov: Accounts of the Writer from His Family, Friends and Contemporaries*. 117.

22 *Letopis'*. 296. [February 1887.]

March 1887

1   Translated by Heim and Karlinsky. *Anton Chekhov's Life and Thought: Selected Letters and Commentary*. 206. [To Shavrova, September 16, 1891.]

2   Translated by Constance Garnett.

3   *Letopis'*. 296. [March 2, 1887.]

4   Translated by Constance Garnett.

5   I believe it was in a friendly effort to downplay his astounding productivity that Chekhov told Korolenko, "'Would you like to know how I write my short stories? Here, observe.' He glanced at my writing desk and picked up the first object that he saw. It was an ashtray. Placing it on the desk right in front of me, he said, 'If you wish, by tomorrow, I will write a short story. Its title will be "An Ashtray."'" *Memories of Chekhov: Accounts of the Writer from His Family, Friends and Contemporaries*. 39.

6   Letters. Vol. 2. 33.

7   Translated by Constance Garnett.

8   Translated by Bartlett. *Anton Chekhov: A Life in Letters*. 87.

9   *Pis'ma*. Vol. 2. 36–37.

10 Rayfield. *Chekhov: A Life* (2021). 174.

11 Yarmolinsky. *Letters of Anton Chekhov*. 45. [To Schechtel, March 11–14, 1886.]

12 Eventually I found an English translation of "An Encounter" in Yarmolinsky's *The Portable Chekhov*. Why did Chekhov leave it out of his Collected Works? In the Russian there's an epigraph, which isn't in Yarmolinsky's translation, by a poet named Maximov: "Why do his eyes shine, why has he small ears, a short and almost round head, like a savage predatory animal?"

13 Translated by S. S. Koteliansky and Philip Tomlinson. *Life and Letters of Anton Tchekhov*. 99. [To Shcheglov, January 1, 1888.] Also, Alexander Kuprin describes the study at Chekhov's house in Yalta: "The room smells of very fine scents of which A. Pavlovich was very fond." (*Reminiscences of Anton Chekhov*. 43.)

14 *Letopis'*. 303. [April 3, 1887.]

15   "While Anton's cull disposed of his weaker humorous stories, and his revisions cut the purple passages
      from many stories, very often he reacted to some fine work with a distaste that is unaccountable,
      unless the work that he rejected had some private unhappy associations," writes Donald Rayfield in
      Anton Chekhov: A Life (1997). 488.

16   *Pis'ma*. Vol. 2. 38. [To the Chekhov family, March 13, 1887.]

17   *Pis'ma*. Vol. 2. 39–40. [To Kiseleva, March 17, 1887.]

18   The *Letopis'* repeats Chekhov's mention of sixteen but *names* seventeen stories. *Letopis'*. 299. [March 18, 1887.]

19   *Pis'ma*. Vol. 2. 41–42. [To Suvorin, March 18, 1887.]

20   Ibid., 368–369.

21   Ibid., 39–40. [To Kiseleva, March 17, 1887.]

22   Translated by Heim and Karlinsky. *Anton Chekhov's Life and Thought: Selected Letters and Commentary*.
      269–270. [To Shavrova, February 28, 1895.]

23   My translation was published in *Russian Life* on April 23, 2020, with editor Paul Richardson's helpful
      corrections.

24   *Pis'ma*. Vol. 2. 46.

25   Ibid., 47.

26   Ibid., 372.

27   Ibid.

28   "Zhiteyskie Nevzrody" has never been translated into English, as far as I can find.

29   *Works*. Vol. 6. 140.

30   Translated by Constance Garnett.

31   *Letopis'*. 301. [March 29–30, 1887.]

32   *Pis'ma*. Vol. 2. 53, 373. [To Leykin, April 30, 1887.]

Part 5: To the South and Back

1   Translated by Constance Garnett.

2   Translated by Sidonie K. Lederer. *The Selected Letters of Anton Chekhov*. 30. [To the Chekhov family,
     April 7–19, 1887.]

April 1887

1   Translated by Sidonie K. Lederer. *The Selected Letters of Anton Chekhov*. 25. [To the Chekhov family,
     April 7–19, 1887.]

2   *Pis'ma*. Vol. 2. 53.

3   Translated by Constance Garnett.

4   The last four sentences are translated by Sidonie K. Lederer. *The Selected Letters of Anton Chekhov*. 31.

5   *Letopis'*. 303. [April 3, 1887.]

6   Translated by Yarmolinsky. *Letters of Anton Chekhov*. 46. [April 7, 1887 to Leykin.]

7   *Letopis'*. 305. [April 7, 1887.]

8   Translated by Constance Garnett.

9   Translated by Constance Garnett.

10   *Pis'ma*. Vol. 2. 68. [To the Chekhov family, April 14–19, 1887.]

11   Ibid., 70. [To Leykin, April 17, 1887.]

12   Alexander Serebrov-Tikhonov, "About Chekhov": "'What a wonderful sport, fishing!' Chekhov told
     me while baiting his hook. 'It is a sort of quiet insanity. You are happy with life, you are happy with
     yourself, and you are not a danger to anyone. And the most marvelous thing is that life is good.'" In
     Memories of Chekhov: Accounts of the Writer from His Family, Friends and Contemporaries. 95.

13   *Pis'ma*. Vol. 2. 71. [To Alexander Chekhov, April 20, 1887.]

14   Translated by Avrahm Yarmolinsky. *The Unknown Chekhov*. 131.

15 *Letopis'*. 307. [April 23, 1887.]

16 Translated by Constance Garnett. [To the Chekhov family, April 25, 1887.]

17 Translated by Sidonie K. Lederer. *The Selected Letters of Anton Chekhov*. 36–37.

18 Donald Rayfield supplies the Soviet-censored word "pee." (*Chekhov: A Life* (2021). 177.)

19 *Works*. Vol. 2. 146–147.

20 *Letopis'*. 309. [April 29, 1887.]

21 Translated by Constance Garnett.

May 1887

1 Translated by Heim and Karlinsky. *Anton Chekhov's Life and Thought: Selected Letters and Commentary*. 261. [To Suvorin, March 27, 1894.]

2 *Letopis'*. 310. [May 5, 1887.]

3 Translated by Constance Garnett.

4 *Pis'ma*. Vol. 2. 98. [To Georgy Chekhov, June 23, 1887.] See also *Letopis'*, 310. [May 5, 1887.]

5 Translated by Constance Garnett. [To the Chekhov family, May 11, 1887.]

6 Translated by Constance Garnett.

7 Donald Rayfield. *Chekhov: A Life* (2021). 146.

8 M. P. Chekhova. *Pis'ma k bratu A. P. Chekhovu*. 18–19. [From Maria Chekhova to Chekhov, May 8, 1887.] Chekhova's own notes on this letter: "Anton Pavlovich was at this time on a trip to Taganrog and sent us from the road a letter-diary, with his humorous descriptions of his impressions of Taganrog life, which he now saw by a more idiosyncratic way than when we ourselves lived there." (This is the only surviving letter from Maria to her brother in these two years.)

9 "After the high demands that Maupassant placed on his art, it would be difficult to write anything after him, but one must work just the same," Chekhov told Ivan Bunin. "We Russians must be particularly bold in our work. There are big dogs and little dogs, but little dogs must not fret over the existence of the big ones. Everyone is obligated to howl in the voice that the Lord God has given him." Bunin introduces this quotation by saying Chekhov "often said." (*About Chekhov: The Unfinished Symphony*. 20.)

10 Coope. *Doctor Chekhov: A Study in Literature and Medicine*. 21

11 *Pis'ma*. Vol. 2. 84. [To Leykin, May 14, 1887.]

12 Magarshack. *Chekhov: A Life*. 114. [To the Chekhov family, April 7, 1887.]

13 Translated by Bartlett. *Anton Chekhov: A Life in Letters*. 108. [To Leykin, May 22, 1887.]

14 *Pis'ma*. Vol. 2. 87–88. [To Leykin, May 22, 1887.]

June 1887

1 Eugene Vodolazkin, *Solovyov and Larionov*. Translated by Lisa C. Hayden. London: Oneworld, 2018. 184–185.

2 *Dnevnik Alekseia Sergeevicha Suvorina* [*Diary of Aleksei Sergeevich Suvorin*]. 72. [May 2, 1887.]

3 Ibid., 559–560.

4 Ibid., 560.

5 *Works*. Vol. 6. 536.

6 *Pis'ma*. Vol. 2. 91. [To Leykin, June 4, 1887.]

7 Rayfield. *Anton Chekhov: A Life* (2021). 182.

8 Translated by Constance Garnett.

9 *Pis'ma*. Vol. 2. 390.

10 Translated by Constance Garnett.

11 *Pis'ma*. Vol. 2. 94. [To Leykin, June 9, 1887.]

12 Sergei Semenov: "When the first volume of the *Complete Works of Chekhov* was published by Marx, [Tolstoy] read and reread it. He enjoyed the Chekhovian humor, and came to call Chekhov one of the best humor writers. 'Drama' was Tolstoy's favorite story from this collection. He recommended it to

others, and sincerely laughed every time he read it." (In *Memories of Chekhov: Accounts of the Writer from His Family, Friends and Contemporaries*. 83.)

13 Translated by Constance Garnett.

14 Translated by Constance Garnett.

15 *Works*. Vol. 6. 230–235.

16 *Pis'ma*. Vol. 2. 98. [To Georgy Chekhov, June 23, 1887.]

17 Dina Rubina, "Preface: Chekhov's Blotter." In *Chekhov's Letters: Biography, Context, Poetics*. 239–240.

18 The only translation into English is by Peter Constantine in *The Undiscovered Chekhov*.

19 *Pis'ma*. Vol. 2. 100. [To Lazarev, June 27 or 28, 1887.]

20 *Works*. Vol. 6. 242.

21 *Memories of Chekhov: Accounts of the Writer from His Family, Friends and Contemporaries*. 86.

July 1887

1 To Elena Shavrova, June 20, 1891. Translated by Louis S. Friedland. *Letters on the Short Story, the Drama, and Other Literary Topics*. 77–78.

2 In *Memories of Chekhov: Accounts of the Writer from His Family, Friends and Contemporaries*. 47.

3 Translated by Constance Garnett.

4 Translated by Constance Garnett.

5 *Pis'ma*. Vol. 2. 101.

6 Magarshack. *Chekhov: A Life*. 342 [To Olga Knipper, July 8, 1899.]

7 *Pis'ma*. Vol. 2. 393.

8 *Letopis'*. 318. [July 15, 1887.]

9 Ibid., 364. Dated "1887–1888."

10 Ibid., 318–319. [July 15, 1887.]

11 *Pis'ma*. Vol. 2. 102–103. [To Leykin, July 17, 1887.]

12 Ibid., 393.

13 *Letopis'*. 319. [July 22, 1887.]

14 Translated by Constance Garnett.

15 *Pis'ma*. Vol. 2. 394.

August 1887

1 Alexander Kuprin. *Reminiscences of Anton Chekhov*. 79–80.

2 Alexander Chekhov. *Perepiska*. [September 5, 1887.]

3 *Pis'ma*. Vol. 2. 103. [To Lazarev, early August 1887.]

4 Chekhov would have read a discussion of this custom in Nikolay Leskov's *The Enchanted Wanderer* (1873).

5 *Pis'ma*. Vol. 2. 104 [To Alexander Chekhov, early August 1887.]

6 *Pis'ma*. 107. [To Leykin, August 11, 1887.]

7 *Works*. Vol. 6. 287.

8 Ibid., 290–292.

9 Translated by Constance Garnett.

10 This is a happier echo of Agafya's fearful approach toward her deceived husband: "At one time she moved in zigzags, then she moved her feet up and down without going forward, bending her knees and stretching out her hands, then she staggered back."

11 *Pis'ma*. Vol. 2. 106–108. [To Leykin, August 11, 1887.]

12 Ibid., 109–110. [To Schechtel, August 12, 1887.]

13 Magarshack. *Chekhov: A Life*. 117. [Letter to Schechtel, August 12, 1887.]

14 *Pis'ma*. Vol. 2. 109. [To Alexander Chekhov, August 12, 1887.]

15 Translated by Constance Garnett. For an eerily similar experience of hallucinations brought on by a brain tumor, see "A Passage to India" by Oliver Sacks in *The Man Who Mistook His Wife for a Hat*.

16 *Pis'ma*. Vol. 2. 111–112.

17 *Letopis'*. 323. [August 20, 1887.]

18 Translated by Yarmolinsky, *The Portable Chekhov*. 90–97.

19 Translated by Constance Garnett.

20 *Letopis'*. 324–325. ["Summer."]

September 1887

1 Magarshack. *Chekhov: A Life*. 383. [To Olga Knipper, April 20, 1904.]

2 *Pis'ma*. [September 2, 1887 to Leykin.]

3 *Perepiska A. P. Chekhova i Al. P. Chekhova [Correspondence between A. P. Chekhov and Al. P. Chekhov]*. Vol. 1. Moscow: Zhudozhestcennaya Literatura, 1984. http://az.lib.ru/c/chehow_aleksandr_pawlowich /text_0050.shtml.

4 Magarshack. *Chekhov: A Life*. 118. [Alexander Chekhov to Anton Chekhov, September 5, 1887.]

5 *Pis'ma*. Vol. 2. 403.

6 Magarshack. *Chekhov: A Life*. 118. [To Leykin, September 11, 1887.]

7 *Letopis'*. 329. [September 12, 1887.]

8 *Pis'ma*. Vol. 2. 118–120.

9 Translated by Constance Garnett.

10 Simmons. *Chekhov: A Biography*. 114. [To Suvorin, June 9, 1889.]

11 *Pis'ma*. 120–121. [To Alexander Chekhov, September 25, 1887.]

12 *Pis'ma*. 406.

13 *Letopis'*. 332. [September 26 or 27, 1887.]

14 *Pis'ma*. 122–123. [To Trefolev, September 30, 1887.]

15 *Letopis'*. 333–334. [September—first half of October 1887.]

Part 6: *Ivanov* & Others

1 Translated by Heim and Karlinsky. *Anton Chekhov's Life and Thought: Selected Letters and Commentary*. 81–82. [To Suvorin, December 30, 1888.]

October 1887

1 *Pis'ma*. Vol. 2. 125. [To Ezhov, October 5, 1887.]

2 Ibid., 410.

3 Rayfield. *Chekhov: A Life* (2021). 185.

4 I am using an out-of-copyright accessible version translated by Marian Fell for quoting and reference. *Ivanoff: A Play*. https://gutenberg.org/cache/epub/1755/pg1755-images.html.

5 Donald Rayfield has an answer and sees this differently from the way I do: "The play's sympathy for the Jewish victim is a counterblast to the anti-Semitic letters Chekhov was receiving from Suvorin's son Aleksei Alekseievich, who saw Jews in Russia as 'five million barrels of dynamite under the Kremlin,' as a sexual and financial threat to the nation. If such stories as 'The Slough' ('Mire') contributed to that view of the Jew, then *Ivanov* was an act of contrition, for the Jew is seen as victim, not oppressor." (Rayfield, "Chekhov's Stories and Plays," in *The Cambridge Companion to Chekhov*, 204–205.)

6 Translated by Heim and Karlinsky. *Anton Chekhov's Life and Thought: Selected Letters and Commentary*. 76. [To Suvorin, December 30, 1888.]

7 Translated by Heim and Karlinsky. *Anton Chekhov's Life and Thought: Selected Letters and Commentary*. 84. [To Suvorin, January 7, 1889.]

8   *Pis'ma*. Vol. 2. 126–127. [To Alexander Chekhov, October 6 or 7, 1887.]

9   Translated by S. S. Koteliansky and Philip Tomlinson. *The Life and Letters of Anton Tchekhov*. 90–91. [To Alexander Chekhov, October 10 (or 12), 1887.]

10   *Pis'ma*. Vol. 2. 414. Chekhov wrote to Suvorin about this work on June 9, 1888: "I think it is still a little too soon to discuss the date of publication of my magnificent novel. I mean, it is too soon to promise anything. When it is finished I shall send it to you to read and we shall then decide what is to be done." After he wrote to his friend A. N. Pleshcheev on June 26, 1888, he never mentioned it again: "I go on writing my novel slowly, but I am crossing out more than I write." The manuscript of it was never found. (Magarshack. *Chekhov: A Life*. 122.)

11   Translated by Koteliansky and Tomlinson. *The Life and Letters of Anton Tchekhov*. 89. [To Korolenko, October 17, 1887.]

12   Tolstoy had read *Walden* in English and greatly admired Thoreau; he recommended its translated publication to Suvorin.

13   *Pis'ma*. 131. [To Georgy Chekhov, October 17, 1887.]

14   Ibid., 132–133. [To Leykin, October 19, 1887.]

15   Translated by Koteliansky and Tomlinson. *The Life and Letters of Anton Tchekhov*. 91–92. [To Alexander Chekhov, October 21, 1887.]

16   *Letopis'*. 342. [October 23, 1887.]

17   *Pis'ma*. Vol. 2. 137. [To Alexander Chekhov, October 24, 1887.]

18   Translated by Peter Constantine. 171–178.

19   Magarshack. *Chekhov: A Life*. 118.

20   *Pis'ma*. Vol. 2. 140. [This is the first of two October 29, 1887, letters to Alexander Chekhov.]

21   Ibid., 139–140. [To Ezhov, October 27, 1887.]

22   *Letopis'*. 345. [End of October.]

23   *Pis'ma*. Vol. 2. 426.

24   Ibid., 141. [To Alexander Chekhov, second of two letters on October 29, 1887.]

25   Translated by Constance Garnett.

26   *Letopis'*. 346. [November 3, 1887.]

27   Rayfield. *Anton Chekhov: A Life* (1997). 488.

28   *Letopis'*. 345. [End of October to November 19, 1887.]

29   Alexandra Glama-Mesherskaya, in *Memories of Chekhov: Accounts of the Writer from His Family, Friends and Contemporaries*. 112–113.

November 1887

1   Yuriy Sobolev. "Tchekhov's Creative Method." In Koteliansky, *Reminiscences*. 21.

2   *Letopis'*. 346. [November 2, 1887.]

3   *Pis'ma*. Vol. 2. 140. [To Alexander Chekhov, first of two letters of October 29, 1887.]

4   Ibid., 142–143. [To Leykin, November 4, 1887.]

5   *Letopis'*. 346. [November 4, 1887.]

6   Virginia Llewellyn Smith. *Anton Chekhov and the Lady with the Dog*. 92–93.

7   Translated by Constance Garnett.

8   *Pis'ma*. Vol. 2. 146. [To Aleksei Kiselev, November 10, 1887.]

9   Ibid., 150. [To the Society of Russian Playwrights and Opera Composers, November 16, 1887.]

10   Translated by Heim and Karlinsky. *Anton Chekhov's Life and Thought: Selected Letters and Commentary*. 70–71. [To Leykin, November 15, 1887.]

11   Translated by Constance Garnett.

12   *Letopis'*. 351. [November 21, 1887.]

13   Translated by Heim and Karlinsky. *Anton Chekhov's Life and Thought: Selected Letters and Commentary.* 73–75. [To Alexander Chekhov, November 24, 1887.]

14   *Pis'ma.* Vol. 2. 155–156. [To Lazarev, November 26, 1887.]

December 1887

1   Translated by Heim and Karlinsky. *Anton Chekhov's Life and Thought: Selected Letters and Commentary.* 376. [To Leontyev (Shcheglov), February 2, 1900.]

2   Translated by Constance Garnett.

3   Translated by Constance Garnett.

4   *Letopis'.* 357. [December 9, 1887.]

5   Ibid., 357–358. [December 10 or 11, 1887.]

6   Translated by Constance Garnett.

7   Janet Malcolm observes: "What poor Ryabovich fails to communicate to his comrades in his amateur's innocence Chekhov succeeds in communicating to us with his professional's guile." (*Reading Chekhov: A Critical Journey.* 44–45.)

8   *Pis'ma.* Vol. 2. 161. [To Barantsevich, December 15, 1887.]

9   Ibid. [To Shcheglov, between December 16 and 20, 1887.]

10   Translated by Constance Garnett.

11   *Works.* Vol. 6. 600–601.

12   An Internet edition of the story adds a note to Garnett's translation suggesting that the boys are ten; the eldest sister is eleven, however, and their awe of and respect for the boys suggests more strongly to me that all the girls are younger and that the brother is the family's firstborn, thus a prince, perhaps thirteen years old. In the original publication the oldest sister is twelve.

13   Translated by Heim and Karlinsky. *Anton Chekhov's Life and Thought: Selected Letters and Commentary.* 372. [To Rossolimo, January 21, 1900.]

14   *Works.* Vol. 6. 601.

15   Translated by Constance Garnett.

16   *Pis'ma.* Vol. 2. 162.

17   Ibid., 438.

18   Ibid., 164.

Conclusion

1   Ivan Bunin in *Reminiscences of Anton Chekhov by Maxim Gorky, Alexander Kuprin, and I. A. Bunin.* 108.

2   A. A. Izmaylov. "Antosha Chekhonte."

3   Ivan Bunin told this to Galina Kuznetzova on May 25, 1925. (*About Chekhov: The Unfinished Symphony.* xviii.)

4   Maxim Gorky. In *Memories of Chekhov: Accounts of the Writer from His Family, Friends and Contemporaries.* 79.

5   Translated by S. S. Koteliansky and Philip Tomlinson. *The Life and Letters of Anton Tchekhov.* 203–204. [To Vladimir Tikhonov, February 22, 1892.]

6   This title is difficult to track down. I went here: NYPL Research Libraries: 33433 10989 2541. ReCAP 13-25282.

Index